PREPARING COMPANY AC(

2016–17

Small and Micros

PREPARING COMPANY ACCOUNTS
2016–17

Small and Micros

Julia Penny and Andy Holton

SWAT UK Ltd

Twenty-fourth Edition

 Wolters Kluwer

© 2016 Wolters Kluwer (UK) Ltd

Wolters Kluwer (UK) Limited
145 London Road
Kingston upon Thames
KT2 6SR
Tel: 0844 561 8166
Fax: 0208 547 2638
E-mail: cch@wolterskluwer.com
www.cch.co.uk

© Financial Reporting Council (FRC). Financial Reporting Council material is adapted and reproduced with the kind permission of the Financial Reporting Council. All rights reserved. For further information, please visit www.frc.org.uk or call +44 (0)20 7492 2300.

ISBN   978-1-78540-257-9

British Library Cataloguing-in-Publication Data

A catalogue record for this book is available from the British Library.

Typeset by Innodata Inc., India.
Printed by Gutenberg Press Ltd, Malta.

Preface

Preparing Company Accounts: Small and Micros is the 24th edition of the book. For over 30 years, it has focused on what has come to be known as the 'small companies regime' – the statutory accounting requirements for the 'small' company.

GAAP (generally accepted accounting practice) has developed considerably over this period. The FRSSE (*Financial Reporting Standard for Smaller Entities*), originally introduced in November 1997, will, for accounting periods commencing on or after 1 January 2016, be replaced by FRS 102 (*The Financial Reporting Standard Applicable in the UK and the Republic of Ireland*). To cater for their more limited legal requirements, section 1A of the 2015 version of that standard sets out the presentation and disclosure requirements applicable to small entities. At the time of writing, in early 2016, the measures in section 1A are not generally applicable to limited liability partnerships, as the legislation underlying the requirements has not yet been updated. This book therefore deals with the position for companies and other entities not restricted by the Companies Act or other regulatory requirements.

For a number of years now, the availability of audit exemption for small companies has been a welcome relief in terms of compliance costs. The government confirmed in January 2016 that the audit exemption limit would rise to the same as the small company accounting limits for accounting periods commencing on or after 1 January 2016.

The recent past has seen the introduction into UK GAAP of the concept of the 'micro' or the 'micro-entity' and the evolution of accounting for smaller companies and their deregulation continues apace. Although the underlying legislation has changed little in the past two years, the accounting requirements will change for accounting periods commencing on or after 1 January 2016, when micro-entities will be required to use FRS 105 (*The Financial Reporting Standard applicable to the Micro-entities Regime*), a new standard based on FRS 102 but with significant simplifications.

As a result, the reporting requirements for a small company can be complicated and the exemptions and opportunities (or the rules to take advantage of them) can be easy to miss or misinterpret.

The main objective of this book remains the same as it has always been; a companion rather than a comprehensive technical treatise – a quick and, we hope, relatively straightforward guide, simplifying where possible, concentrating on basic principles, providing appropriate tools and illustrating changes and opportunities.

In itself, implementation of the CA 2006 was a major landmark. However, the dawn of this new era of company legislation is now followed by the end of another – UK GAAP in the form many of us have grown up with. The issue of the new UK Financial Reporting Standard (FRS 102 *The Financial Reporting Standard applicable in the UK and Republic of Ireland*) has seen the end of SSAPs, FRSs and UITFs. If they have not done so already, companies must now plan for the implications of whichever is their applicable part of the new financial reporting framework which FRS 100 *Application of financial reporting requirements* makes mandatory for small companies from 1 January 2016.

For the first time in many years, the team at Buzzacott LLP are no longer the authors and it is with many thanks for the sterling work in previous years that the SWAT UK team now undertake the updating of this volume.

Julia Penny and Andy Holton

February 2016

Contents

Contents

Scope of Preparing Company Accounts: Small and Micros 2016–17

This volume covers the requirements for small and micro-entities applying the relevant provisions in FRS 102, section 1A or FRS 105 as relevant and including the legislative requirements in the *Companies Act* 2006 and specifically SI 2008/409 as updated by SI 2015/980.
In particular the volume covers:

- small company accounts using FRS 102 (2015), section 1A presentation options;
- abridged small company accounts using FRS 102 (2015), section 1A and the option to abridge;
- micro-entity accounts using FRS 105 (2015); and
- filing requirements for the above.

Note that small companies are not required to use FRS 102, section 1A. They may instead use the full presentation and disclosure requirements of FRS 102. However, this volume assumes small entities will wish to use the small regime within section 1A. If small entities wish to use the full presentation and disclosure requirements of FRS 102, reference should be made to CCH *Preparing FRS 102 Accounts*.

Summary of dates

Periods commencing	Micro	Small	Non-small
Before 1 January 2015	FRSSE (2008) micro sections	FRSSE (2008)	Old UK GAAP
From 1 January 2015 if not early adopting new regime	FRSSE (2015) micro sections	FRSSE (2015)	FRS 102
From 1 January 2015 if taking optional early adoption	FRS 105	FRS 102 with section 1A or full FRS 102	N/A
From 1 January 2016	FRS 105	FRS 102 with section 1A or full FRS 102	FRS 102

Part I   General

Chapter 1 Introduction

1.1 Purpose of the book

1.1.1 Accounts of small companies and micro-entities

This book is principally concerned with the accounts of small companies (as defined by CA 2006) and micro-entities (a subset of small companies) preparing accounts under new UK GAAP. No references are made to the requirements of previous legislation or standards within this edition.

For accounting periods beginning on or after 1 January 2016, a company is treated as micro or small (or medium-sized) if it does not exceed more than one of the following criteria, for two consecutive years:

	Micro	Small	Medium-sized
Turnover	£632,000	£10.2m	£36m
Balance sheet total	£316,000	£5.1m	£18m
Average number of employees (on a monthly basis)	10	50	250

Chapter 5 sets out the qualifying criteria in detail and should be referred to when considering the limits.

Certain categories of company, regardless of size, are not entitled to any exemptions. These are:

- public companies;
- members of 'ineligible' (basically, publicly traded or regulated) groups;
- companies carrying on an insurance market activity; and
- companies that are authorised insurance companies, banking companies, e-money issuers, MiFID investment firms or UCITS management companies.

Under the new regime brought into legislation primarily in the *Companies, Partnerships and Groups (Accounts and Reports) Regulations* 2015 (SI 2015/980), small companies have a choice of preparing either full or abridged accounts for their members and for filing. As abridged accounts contain less information, though they are still required to give a true and fair view, 100% of members must agree each year to having abridged accounts.

Abbreviated accounts, solely for filing, no longer exist under the regime, although the same exemptions from filing the profit and loss and directors' report still exist as discussed in more detail in **Chapter 6**.

Audit exemption limits have increased from the old 'small company limits' to the new limits set out above for accounting purposes. This move was confirmed by the Government in January 2016 and takes effect for accounting periods beginning on or after 1 January 2016. Note that although the new limits shown above can be applied for accounting purposes optionally from 1 January 2015, this option is not available for audit purposes. An audit continues to be required for 2015 if the old thresholds for small companies are exceeded.

The book endeavours to simplify the somewhat complex requirements for small company accounts. While not purporting to give comprehensive coverage of all accounting provisions, the aim of the book is to explain many of the company accounting requirements that affect small companies and the exemptions (both accounting and audit) that are available to them. The book concentrates on those matters of practical relevance as far as accounts are concerned. In essence, it aims to resolve the following issues.

What sort of statutory accounts are required? The Act, together with the regulations under the *Small Companies and Groups (Accounts and Directors' Report) Regulations* 2008 (SI 2008/409) set out the requirements for small company accounts. These were both amended by the *Companies, Partnerships and Groups (Accounts and Reports) Regulations* 2015 (SI 2015/980), for accounting periods commencing on or after 1 January 2016, or optionally from 1 January 2015. Earlier amendments were also made by the *Small Companies (Micro-Entities' Accounts) Regulations* 2013 (SI 2013/3008) for periods ended on or after 30 September 2013.

FRS 102 accounts for small entities using section 1A. The FRSSE is no longer available for accounting periods beginning on or after 1 January 2016 and instead, small companies that are not able or choosing to take advantage of the micro regime must prepare their accounts using FRS 102. If they wish, there are reduced presentation and disclosure requirements contained in section 1A to the 2015 version of FRS 102.

Abridged accounts. Small companies are no longer permitted to prepare separate abbreviated accounts for filing purposes. However, there is provision for them to prepare abridged accounts. These accounts still follow FRS 102 measurement and recognition requirements, but they have further reductions in presentation and disclosure requirements compared to the main body of section 1A of FRS 102. Abridged accounts are still required to present a true and fair view and require members' agreement.

Micro-entities. Certain small companies may be able to take advantage of additional reduced disclosure requirements and other exemptions if they qualify as a 'micro-entity'. The new requirements for these are contained in FRS 105. This is based upon FRS 102 but with much simplified requirements for recognition, measurement, disclosure and presentation. Such accounts are deemed to give a true and fair view.

Is an audit required or necessary? The audit exemption limit was raised to that of the new small company limits for periods commencing on or after 1 January 2016. Many companies, while qualifying as 'audit exempt', nevertheless need to consider whether a Companies Act audit or alternatively some other form of assurance or accountants' report is appropriate.

International accounting standards. The smaller company currently has the choice of adopting international accounting standards, being full IAS accounts and in some circumstances it will also qualify to apply FRS 101, which allows recognition and measurement based on international accounting standards with some changes for UK law and many disclosure exemptions.

What needs to be filed? With the advent of web-filing, the options for filing companies' accounts with the Registrar of Companies have added complexity. **Chapter 16** looks at these requirements in more depth.

The book is written from the perspective of the small company and focuses on matters currently relevant to small companies preparing accounts under current UK GAAP. It provides the following:

- a summary of statutory company accounts provisions in general – to put 'small companies' and 'micro-entities' in context;
- an explanation of the company accounts provisions for micro and small companies – for both full statutory and abridged accounts and any reduced requirements for filing;
- an explanation of the audit exemptions available to certain small companies;
- guidelines and definitions – for accounting presentation, disclosure and terminology; and
- illustrative examples and checklists – including statutory accounts of a 'small company' and a 'micro-entity'.

Consolidated accounts and accounting for consolidations and group situations are generally not dealt with in detail, although the basic statutory provisions affecting small group accounts and group audit exemptions are inevitably covered.

1.1.2 Small companies in the 'small companies regime'

Legislation, of both domestic and European origin, has resulted in a measure of standardisation for company accounts, the codification of accounting rules and principles and, to some extent, the simplification of disclosure. Increasingly, the accounts provisions of company law have been supplemented by guidance in the form of Financial Reporting Standards issued by the Financial Reporting Council (FRC).

UK company law, nevertheless, has remained comprehensive and complex. Preparers of accounts have to contend with a significant level of legislation and regulation.

With the aim of reducing the administrative burden on smaller companies, over the years the whole process of accounts production for the small company has gradually been simplified, the result being that:

- small company accounts are less detailed than those of larger companies;
- a subset of the smallest companies, known as 'micro-entities', can prepare a very simplified set of accounts;
- abridged accounts provide further reduction in disclosures for small companies;
- filing exemptions allow small and micro companies to keep more information off the public record;
- there is statutory recognition of a dedicated regime for small companies dealt with in both legislation and FRS 102, section 1A; and
- audit exemption affords the opportunity for many smaller companies to avoid the cost and effort involved in what is sometimes regarded as a 'statutory burden'.

1.2 Legislation – Accounting regime under the Companies Act 2006

The *Companies Act* 2006 (CA 2006) is the primary source of regulation for small companies. When it came into force, it consolidated virtually all existing companies legislation and introduced many reforms.

Company law was rewritten and represented in an attempt to make it easier to understand and more flexible – especially for smaller companies.

Since 2006, several changes have been made that aimed to relax the requirement for smaller companies to have an audit.

In 2013, an additional subcategory of 'small companies', known as 'micro-entities' was introduced, by the *Small Companies (Micro-Entities' Accounts) Regulations* 2013 (SI 2013/3008), again with the aim being to reduce the administrative burdens on small companies.

In 2015, major changes were made to the requirements for small companies, following implementation of the latest EU accounting directive. The *Companies, Partnerships and Groups (Accounts and Reports) Regulations* 2015 (SI 2015/980) amended the existing small company regulations and introduced a reduced set of presentation and disclosure requirements for small companies.

Reference should always be made to the actual legislation itself in order to ensure adherence to current and up-to-date legislation. The *Small Companies and Groups (Accounts and Directors' Report) Regulations* 2008 (SI 2008/409) as amended by the *Companies, Partnerships and Groups (Accounts and Reports) Regulations* 2015 (SI 2015/980) are reproduced in full in **Appendix B** and all UK legislation is available on the website www.legislation.gov.uk.

This book covers the legislation in force and guidance issued for accounting periods commencing on or after 1 January 2016. The regulations and requirements can also be adopted early at the directors' option for accounting purposes only for accounting periods from 1 January 2015. The book reflects legislative changes up until 28 February 2016.

1.3   The death of the FRSSE

For accounting periods commencing on or after 1 January 2016, the FRSSE has been withdrawn. Instead, new UK GAAP in the form of FRS 102 with section 1A for small companies or FRS 105 for micro-entities contain the required accounting regimes.

1.4   New UK GAAP

The FRC has now published five standards under the new UK GAAP regime as follows:

- FRS 100 *Application of Financial Reporting Requirements (2015)*;
- FRS 101 *Reduced disclosure framework – Disclosure exemptions from EU-adopted IFRS for qualifying entities (2015)*;
- FRS 102 *The Financial Reporting Standard applicable in the UK and Republic of Ireland (2015)*;
- FRS 103 *Insurance Contracts*;
- FRS 104 *Interim Financial Reporting*; and
- FRS 105 *The Financial Reporting Standard applicable to the Micro-entities Regime*.

This volume does not deal with FRS 101, 103 or 104, but they are included above for the sake of context and completeness.

The implementation date of the revised framework differs for small and non-small entities.

Non-small (i.e. medium/large) entities were required to adopt FRS 102 (unless opting for IFRS or FRS 101) for accounting periods commencing on or after 1 January 2015. Reduced disclosures for qualifying entities are also available under FRS 102.

Small companies are required to adopt FRS 102, with the optional section 1A dealing with reduced disclosure and presentation requirements, for accounting periods commencing on or after 1 January 2016. (The new legislation is also available to adopt early together with the new standards. This is discussed in later chapters.)

Micro-entities qualifying for and wishing to adopt the micro regime must use FRS 105 for accounting periods commencing on or after 1 January 2016. Previously, the rules for micros were contained within the FRSSE. FRS 105 may be adopted early. If a micro entity is part of a group preparing consolidated accounts it is not permitted to use the micro-regime.

The new framework replaces all previous Financial Reporting Standards, Statements of Standard Accounting Practice and Urgent Issues Task Force Abstracts.

FRS 100 introduced a reduced disclosure framework for the financial reporting by certain qualifying entities (FRS 101 for those companies applying EU-adopted IFRS and within FRS 102 for those companies applying that standard).

A summary comparison of the key accounting treatments of FRSSE 2015, FRS 102 for small entities and FRS 105 is given in **Table 8.1**, which demonstrates that there are a number of situations in which changes in accounting treatment will be necessary. Entities moving from their old UK GAAP accounting framework to a new UK GAAP one are required to follow the rules within the relevant standards for transition. In essence the transition process involves establishing what the figures in the accounts would have been for the current and comparative period, under the relevant new UK GAAP standard subject to certain exemptions and exceptions. A prior year adjustment for this transition is then made to adjust the relevant balance sheets and profit and loss account. The CCH volume *The Transition Guide* provides more detailed information on the transition to FRS 102.

Table 1.1						

Table 1.1 New Financial Reporting Framework as set out in FRS 100 for periods commencing on or after 1 January 2016 (or optionally from 1 January 2015).

	IFRS	Reduced disclosures (FRS 101)	FRS 102	FRS 102 with Section 1A	Reduced disclosures (FRS 102)	FRS 105
Micro-entities						
Group	Optional	Not available	Optional	Optional	Not Available	Not available
Individual entity	Optional	Optional	Optional	Optional[1]	Available	Optional[2,3]
Small unlisted entities (not micro)						
Group consolidated	Optional	Not available	Optional	Optional	Not available	Not available
Parent or subsidiary	Optional	Optional	Optional	Optional	Available	Not available
Individual entity	Optional	Not available	Optional	Optional	Not available	Not available
Large or medium-sized unlisted entities						
Group consolidated	Optional	Not available	Optional	Not available	Not available	Not available
Parent or subsidiary[4]	Optional	Available	Optional	Not available	Available	Not available
Individual entity	Optional	Not available	Optional	Not available	Not available	Not available
Listed entities						
Group consolidated	Required	Not available	Not available	Not available	Not available	Not available
Parent or subsidiary[4]	Optional	Available	Optional	Not available	Available	Not available
Individual entity	Optional	Not available	Optional	Not available	Not available	Not available

[1] At the time of writing, the LLP legislation has not been updated, so making the use of section 1A impracticable as it is not compatible with the current LLP Regulations.

[2] If a micro-entity is part of consolidated accounts, it is not permitted to use the micro-regime.

[3] At the time of writing, LLPs are not included in the micro-entity regime. However, legislation is expected to be enacted in the summer of 2016 allowing LLPs to also use the micro-entity regime. Otherwise, it is currently limited to companies.

[4] A qualifying entity is a member of a group that prepares publicly available financial statements, which are intended to give a true and fair view, in which that member is consolidated.

* Note that optional indicates the regime is available for the entity, but one of the regimes listed must be adopted. So, for example, a small entity can adopt either IFRS, FRS 102 in full or FRS 102 with section 1A, hence all are listed as optional. It cannot however, continue using the FRSSE.

Chapter 2   Companies Act 2006

2.1   Annual accounts under Companies Act 2006

2.1.1   *Basic approach*

The *Companies Act* 2006 (CA 2006) received Royal Assent on 8 November 2006. Since then, it has been amended by the changes contained in subsequently approved regulations which are referred to below. Of particular relevance to this volume is the update in the *Companies, Partnerships and Groups (Accounts and Reports) Regulations* 2015 (SI 2015/980), which significantly changed the requirements in respect of small companies, as well as making a number of other amendments.

Working on the 'think small first' approach, company law is presented on a basis that clearly recognises categories of company or group (CA 2006, s. 380). Different provisions apply to different kinds of company; the main distinctions are between:

- companies qualifying as micro-entities (CA 2006, s. 384A);
- companies excluded from being treated as micro-entities (CA 2006, s. 384B);
- companies and parent companies subject to the 'small companies regime' (CA 2006, s. 381 and 383);
- companies excluded from the 'small companies regime' (CA 2006, s. 384); and
- quoted and unquoted companies (CA 2006, s. 385).

In addition to the main distinctions above, there are some changes in the nature of an ineligible group. Prior to SI 2015/980, the presence of a public company within the group made the whole group ineligible for the small companies regime. Now, however, only a plc which is a traded company within the group makes the whole group ineligible, although the untraded plc itself remains ineligible. This allows an additional flexibility for small companies where there is a 'vanity' plc within the group, which does not actually trade on a market. More information is given in sections **5.1** and **5.2**.

Provisions applying to companies subject to the small companies regime appear in the legislation before the provisions applying to other companies (CA 2006, s. 380(4)).

The small companies regime (which includes micro-entities as a subset of small companies) applies for a financial year in relation to which the company:

- qualifies as small (CA 2006, s. 382–383); and
- is not excluded from the regime (CA 2006, s. 384).

The small companies regime was further divided with the changes made to CA 2006 by the *Small Companies (Micro-Entities' Accounts) Regulations* 2013 (SI 2013/3008). The introduction of the concept of the 'micro-entity' provided even more simplicity for the preparers of the accounts of the smallest companies. SI 2015/980 further updated the micro-entity regime, although little of substance changed at that point. Although, as yet, not many companies have adopted the micro-entity regime, with the requirement for small companies to otherwise adopt FRS 102 from 2016, there may be many more micro-entities deciding that the simplified regime in FRS 105 suits their circumstances better than FRS 102.

2.1.2 Implementation

The changes introduced in the *Companies, Partnerships and Groups (Accounts and Reports) Regulations* 2015 (SI 2015/980) generally come into effect for accounting periods beginning on or after 1 January 2016. However, directors could choose to adopt the changes for accounting periods beginning on or after 1 January 2015, though an accounting standards regime commensurate with the legislation needs to be selected. This means, for example, that a company adopting the provisions of SI 2015/980 in 2015 would have to apply FRS 102 (or another new UK GAAP standard) rather than the FRSSE. This volume does not specifically deal with the accounting for periods prior to 1 January 2016, although users will find it helpful if early adopting the changes.

2.1.3 Small companies accounts regime

The Act presents the 'small companies regime' within:

- Pt. 15 (s. 380–474) – 'Accounts and reports'; and
- Pt. 16 (s. 475–539) – 'Audit' (where relevant for the smaller company).

Preparing small company accounts is governed by reference to:

- CA 2006, Pt. 15 (relevant sections) (the 'primary legislation'); and
- regulations made under Statutory Instruments for small companies ('secondary legislation'), covering the form and content of accounts and directors' report – the *Small Companies and Groups (Accounts and Directors' Report) Regulations* 2008 (SI 2008/409).

All of the above are as amended by other legislation, such as the *Small Companies (Micro-Entities' Accounts) Regulations* 2013 (SI 2013/3008), the *Companies Act 2006 (Strategic Report and Directors' Report) Regulations* 2013 (SI 2013/1070) and the *Companies, Partnerships and Groups (Accounts and Reports) Regulations* 2015 (SI 2015/980).

2.1.4 Micro-entities

The 'micro-entity' was conceived in February 2012, when the European Council passed a set of limited exemptions for such entities from the requirements of the Fourth and Seventh Directives with the aim of reducing the administrative burden of complying with the full requirements for small companies. These exemptions arrived in UK law by way of the *Small Companies (Micro-Entities' Accounts) Regulations* 2013 (SI 2013/3008) which came into effect on 1 December 2013. These regulations made amendments to CA 2006 and SI 2008/409 and thus introduced the micro-entity into UK company law. It should be noted that although the legislation refers to a micro-entity regime, at this time it only applies to companies. This means that other entities using the general provisions of the Companies Act are not permitted to use the micro-entity regime. One exception to this, expected to be legislated for in the summer of 2016, is to allow limited liability partnerships (LLPs) to use the micro-entity regime, possibly retrospectively from as early as 2015.

2.1.5 SI 2008/409

The *Small Companies and Groups (Accounts and Directors' Report) Regulations* 2008 (SI 2008/409) specify the form and content of the accounts and directors' report of companies subject to the small companies regime under CA 2006, Pt. 15. CA 2006, s. 381 defines what is meant by 'small companies regime'. The full text of SI 2008/409 as amended (in particular by SI 2015/980) is contained in **Appendix B**.

2.2 Contents of annual accounts and reports

Table 2.1 below compares the contents of the annual reports of micro-entities, small companies, medium-sized and large companies (public or private), following company law reform (see also Table 1.1):

Table 2.1   Contents of annual reports

Annual reports – Companies Act 2006

	Micro-entity regime	Small Companies (excl. micro-entities)	Medium Companies	Large Companies
Primary Financial Statements				
Form and content determined by:				
• Statutory regulation	✓	✓	✓	✓
• IFRS	✓ (optional)	✓ (optional)	✓ (optional)	✓ (optional)
• FRS 102	✓ (optional)	✓ (optional)	✓ (optional)	✓ (optional)
• FRS 102 with section 1A	✓ (optional)	✓ (optional)	×	×
• FRS 105	✓ (optional)	×	×	×
Abridged accounts – statutory	×	✓ (optional)	×	×
Group accounts	×	✓ (optional)	✓	✓
Directors' report	×	✓	✓	✓
Strategic report	×	×	✓	✓

2.3 Contents of annual accounts and reports of micro-entities

Chapter 7 provides detail of the exemptions available to preparers of the accounts of a small company which meets the definition of a micro-entity and adopts that regime.

2.4 Auditing and audit reports

Audit is covered in CA 2006, Pt. 16, which contains provisions concerning, for example, the requirement for audited accounts, the appointment of auditors, the auditor's report, the duties and rights of auditors, and removal, resignation, etc. of auditors.

The audit report must include an introduction identifying the annual accounts and the financial reporting framework under which they are prepared, together with a description of the scope of the audit identifying the auditing standards adopted. It will be especially important this year to ensure that the accounting regime is specified accurately, for example, FRS 102 with the presentation and disclosure exemptions in section 1A.

In essence, under CA 2006, s. 495, the auditor is required to report his opinion on four elements.

- *True and fair view* – whether the annual accounts show a 'true and fair view' (having regard to the directors' statutory duty under CA 2006, s. 393(1)).
- *Relevant reporting framework* – whether the accounts have been prepared in accordance with the relevant financial reporting framework.

- ***Appropriate legislation*** – whether the accounts have been prepared in accordance with CA 2006 (Pt. 15) or IAS (IAS Regulation, art. 4), if applicable.
- ***Form of report or emphasis*** – whether the report is 'unqualified or qualified' or contains reference to any emphasis of matters without qualifying the report.
- ***Narrative reports*** – whether the directors' report/strategic report, where relevant, are prepared in accordance with applicable legal requirements and are inconsistent or misleading (s. 496).

The auditor's report must state the name of the auditor and be signed and dated. Where the auditor is a firm, the report must be signed by the 'senior statutory auditor' in his own name, for and on behalf of the auditor (CA 2006, s. 504). This only applies to the set of the accounts provided to the members of the company. A signature is not required on the set of accounts delivered to Companies House. However, if the auditor wishes to physically sign the accounts for Companies House, they can be signed in the name of the firm rather than the individual.

The form of report by auditors to be adopted with respect to Companies Act accounts is determined by CA 2006 and auditing standards. Following the adoption of International Standards on Auditing (ISAs), auditors' reports on accounts are required to follow, inter alia, ISA (UK and Ireland) 700 (Revised) *The Auditor's Report on Financial Statements*. The audit report is commented on within **Chapter 15** – see **Example 15.1**.

Chapter 3 General accounting provisions

3.1 Introduction

This chapter summarises the accounting provisions of the CA 2006 which relate to: the prescriptive formats of accounts; the content of accounts; and the principles and rules for determining amounts to be included in the accounts.

Annual accounts may be prepared:

- as 'Companies Act individual accounts' (CA 2006, s. 396) or 'Companies Act group accounts' (CA 2006, s. 404); or
- in accordance with international accounting standards ('IAS individual accounts' or 'IAS group accounts') (CA 2006, s. 395(1)).

Unless otherwise indicated, this chapter summarises and comments upon the accounts provisions of the CA 2006 insofar as they relate to Companies Act individual accounts, that is, as prepared in accordance with the requirements of the CA 2006. This excludes the provisions within FRS 101 for the IFRS-based Companies Act individual accounts, which are outside the scope of this volume.

3.2 Accounts

Accounts must be prepared for members for all companies, irrespective of size (except some dormant companies – see **9.7**).

Chapter 6 provides more detailed guidance on the company accounts provisions of CA 2006 as they affect the accounts of companies under the 'small companies regime' and **Chapter 7** provides guidance on the disclosure exemptions available and measurement restrictions applicable in the accounts of a company which is being treated as a 'micro-entity'. **Chapter 8** considers the additional impact on the accounts of small companies of FRS 102 and section 1A of that standard. **Chapter 9** considers the simplifications and other requirements relevant to micro-entities as a result of adopting FRS 105.

The requirements for filing small company accounts have changed with the implementation of SI 2015/980. There is now no provision to permit filing of abbreviated accounts (which are a different set of accounts to those prepared for members). However, there is an abridged accounts regime for small companies (but not micros or medium-sized entities) which permits certain information to be aggregated or not disclosed. These accounts are used both for members and filing so must still give a true and fair view. Details of the requirements for abridged accounts are contained in **Chapter 11**.

The filing exemptions for small companies, allowing the profit and loss and directors' report not to be filed are still essentially as they were before SI 2015/980 and can be found in CA 2006, s. 444. A summary of the requirements for filing is given in Table 6.6 and explanatory notes on what need not be filed are included in the example accounts in **Chapter 14**. The effect of the rules is that regardless of which type of accounts a small company prepares for its members the same filing exemptions apply. This means that a 'filleted' version of the accounts, without the profit and loss or directors' report may be filed by small companies.

Micro-entities are only required to file the balance sheet, together with its related notes, with Companies House.

Matters relating to small groups of companies are covered in **Chapter 12**.

Depending on certain criteria, small companies may be exempt from the requirement for audit. Certain subsidiaries and dormant companies may also take advantage of audit exemption (see **Chapter 13**).

s. 394   Company accounts are produced from the company's underlying financial records ('adequate accounting records') as explained at **3.10** (CA 2006, s. 386–389 'Accounting Records').

Table 3.1 summarises the requirements which directors must follow in respect of a company's 'individual accounts' which are set out in CA 2006, s. 396.

Table 3.1   Individual accounts (CA 2006, s. 396)

For each financial year, the directors must prepare individual accounts comprising:

- a balance sheet; and
- a profit and loss account;

showing a true and fair view of:

- the state of affairs at the year end; and
- the profit or loss for the financial year;

complying with:

- the provisions of the *Small Companies and Groups (Accounts and Directors' Report) Regulations* 2008 (SI 2008/409) as amended (as to form, content and notes);

containing:

- any additional information (or departure from requirement) necessary to show a true and fair view. (In the case of the accounts of a micro-entity, the micro-entity minimum accounting items (see **Chapter 7**) included in the company's accounts for the year are presumed to give the true and fair view.)

3.3   'True and fair' concept

3.3.1   True and fair view

The concept of a true and fair view lies at the heart of financial reporting in the UK. This requirement was recently reconfirmed by the FRC in its June 2014 document '*True and Fair*'; the true and fair requirement remains of fundamental importance in both UK GAAP and IFRS.

s. 393   The directors of a company must not approve accounts unless they are satisfied that they give a true and fair view of the company's assets, liabilities, financial position and profit or loss. As mentioned above though, micro-entity accounts complying with the form and content set out in the law are presumed to give a true and fair view.

Other than for micro-entities, the requirement for full or abridged accounts to show a 'true and fair' view applies irrespective of whether or not the accounts are subject to audit. Any decision concerning the method of accounting or means of disclosing information must take this overriding requirement into account.

The basic accounting principle is that annual accounts should show a 'true and fair' view, a term that has never been defined in statute or case law.

In essence, accounts are deemed to present a 'true and fair' view if they:

- comply with any relevant legislation or regulatory requirements;
- comply with accounting standards and generally accepted accounting practice (GAAP);
- provide an unbiased (fair and reasonable) presentation;
- are compiled with sufficient accuracy within the bounds of materiality; and
- faithfully represent the underlying commercial activity (the concept of 'substance over legal form').

There is continued debate over the concept of true and fair, but, as mentioned above, the FRC reaffirmed in its June 2014 document entitled *True and Fair* the primacy of true and fair and the fact that the application of legal and accounting requirements, together with the judgement of the preparer or auditor, are necessary in ensuring a true and fair view is provided.

An added area of uncertainty created with new UK GAAP and in particular the more limited presentation and disclosure requirements of FRS 102, section 1A for small companies, is what extra disclosures might be required to give a true and fair view. Further information can be found on this aspect within **Chapter 6**.

As noted above, micro-entity accounts are presumed to give a true and fair view, although there may be rare cases where ethical considerations come to bear, when the accountant believes such accounts to be misleading. This is discussed further in **Chapter 7**. Other than for micro-entities, companies that prepare Companies Act accounts in accordance with UK accounting standards are subject to the overriding requirement of CA 2006 (and regulations made under it) that accounts give a 'true and fair' view, which, in all but highly exceptional cases, requires compliance with UK accounting standards.

UK tax legislation requires that the profits of a trade, profession or vocation be computed in accordance with generally accepted accounting practice on an accounting basis which gives a true and fair view, subject to any adjustment required by tax law in computing those profits.

Accounts are required to give a 'true and fair' view of the state of affairs of the company (and consolidated undertakings (if applicable)) as at the end of the financial year and of the profit or loss of the company (and consolidated undertakings (if applicable) so far as concerns members of the parent company) for the financial year.

Where compliance with the provisions of CA 2006 as to the matters to be included in 'annual accounts' ('individual accounts' or 'group accounts') or the notes would not be sufficient to give a true and fair view, the necessary additional information must be given in the accounts or in a note to them.

3.3.2 True and fair override

If, in special circumstances, such compliance with the legal requirements is inconsistent with the requirement to show a 'true and fair' view, the directors must depart from the relevant provision of CA 2006 to the extent necessary to show a 'true and' fair view (the true and fair 'override' principle).

A departure from an accounting standard must be justified and explained in a note to the accounts.

Although this would normally only arise in exceptional circumstances, one relatively common example of this is the non-depreciation of fixed asset investment properties.

3.3.3 Application to IAS accounts

Companies adopting international accounting and financial reporting standards (IFRS) are required to prepare accounts that are 'fairly presented'. Although in essence this may constitute a 'true and fair' view, unlike UK Accounting Standards, IFRS are explicitly part of the law rather than deriving from it.

The requirement for accounts to give a 'true and fair view' is also embodied within European Accounting Directives. In the case of IAS accounts, there is a requirement under international accounting standards that such accounts must achieve a 'fair presentation'.

Both UK GAAP and IFRS accounts must give a true and fair view and if necessary extra disclosures or changes in presentation and accounting should be adopted to achieve this. Again, further guidance on this can be found in the FRC *True and Fair* 2014 document.

3.4   Format of accounts

The form and content of accounts is governed by regulations made under CA 2006.

The form and content of Companies Act individual accounts is determined in accordance with:

- the *Small Companies and Groups (Accounts and Directors' Report) Regulations* 2008 (SI 2008/409) for small companies; and
- the *Large and Medium-sized Companies and Groups (Accounts and Reports) Regulations* 2008 (SI 2008/410) for medium-sized companies and large companies.

The *Small Companies and Groups (Accounts and Directors' Report) Regulations* 2008 (SI 2008/409) is set out in full in **Appendix B** and is discussed in greater detail in **Chapter 6**. The version of these regulations to be used is the version applicable from 1 January 2016, incorporating the extensive amendments of SI 2015/980.

Schedules within SI 2008/409 and SI 2008/410 prescribe the required formats from which companies may choose for Companies Act individual and group accounts. Formats which are most commonly used are illustrated in **Chapter 6** for small companies and in **Chapter 7** for micro-entities.

Once a format has been adopted, the company must use the same format for subsequent years unless, in the directors' opinion, there are special reasons for changing; these must be disclosed in the year of change. For accounting periods commencing on or after 1 January 2016 small companies are required to move to FRS 102, if not adopting the micro-regime should they be eligible. This means that there could be a significant change in presentation for some companies and whilst the requirements of FRS 102, section 1A for small companies do not include transitional disclosure notes, some explanation of the changes will be required by this provision.

SI 2008/409,
Sch. 1.2

Every balance sheet and profit and loss account must show the items listed in the adopted format if they apply either in the financial year or the preceding year. Note that for abridged accounts more limited line items are required, as discussed in **Chapter 11**.

Sch. 1.1

Adopting a particular format is not as restricting as it may seem, as there are a variety of options, for example, including abridged accounts:

Sch. 1.3

Sch. 1.10(2)

- departure from the format is allowed if it is made to ensure a true and fair view (see above);
- certain headings (which the Schedules identify by the use of Arabic numbers) may be combined (provided combination is disclosed);

Sch. 1.4
Sch. 1.1A(1)
and (2)

- further aggregation of items is permitted when preparing abridged accounts;
- immaterial items may be disregarded;
- information can be given in greater detail than prescribed and items not listed in a format may be included, if directors so wish; and
- certain information may be given in notes instead of on the face of the accounts (the order of the notes should reflect the order of items in the primary statements where relevant).

Sch. 1.42

Where there is no amount to be shown for a format item for the financial year, a heading or sub-heading corresponding to the item must not be included, unless an amount can be shown for the item in question for the immediately preceding financial year under the relevant format heading or sub-heading.

Sch. 1.5

For every balance sheet or profit and loss account item, the corresponding amount for the immediately preceding financial year must also be shown. Where that corresponding preceding year amount is not comparable, the prior year amount may be adjusted, but particulars of the non-comparability and of any adjustment must be disclosed in a note to the accounts.

Sch. 1.7

Every profit and loss account must show the amount of a company's profit or loss before taxation (see **Chapter 6** at **6.5**). (Note that prior to SI 2015/980, the requirement was to show the profit or loss on ordinary activities before taxation, but with the removal of extraordinary items from the legislation it is no longer required to specify 'on ordinary activities'.)

Sch. 1.6

3.5 Accounting principles

Company accounts are required to be prepared in accordance with the principles set out in:

- SI 2008/409, Sch. 1 – small companies;
- SI 2008/409, Sch. 6 – small groups;
- SI 2008/410, Sch. 1 – medium-sized (and large) companies; and
- SI 2008/410, Sch. 6 – medium-sized (and large) groups.

The requirements for medium-sized companies and groups are outside the scope of this book, but are covered in the Wolters Kluwer sister volume *Preparing FRS 102 Accounts*.

These principles are the fundamental accounting concepts that underlie accounts and are also incorporated within accounting standards generally.

The basic statutory accounting principles in SI 2008/409 are as follows.

(1) *Going concern* – The company or reporting entity is presumed to be carrying on business as a going concern.
(2) *Consistency* – Accounting policies must be applied consistently within the same accounts and from one financial year to the next.
(3) *Prudence* – The amount of any item must be determined on a prudent basis and in particular:
    (a) only profits realised at the balance sheet date must be included in the profit and loss account; and
    (b) all liabilities having arisen in respect of the financial year (or preceding financial years) must be taken into account (including those liabilities becoming apparent up to the date of approval of the accounts (in accordance with CA 2006, s. 414)).
(4) *Accruals* – All income and charges relating to the financial year to which the accounts relate must be taken into account, without regard to the date of receipt or payment. *Sch. 1.14*
(5) *Individual determination* – In determining the aggregate amount of any item, the amount of each individual asset or liability that is taken into account must be determined separately. *Sch. 1.15*
(6) *Netting* – Amounts in respect of items representing assets or income must not be set off against amounts in respect of items representing liabilities or expenditure (as the case may be), or vice versa. *Sch. 1.8*
(7) *Substance of transactions* – In determining how amounts are presented within the accounts, regard should be had to the substance of the reported transaction or arrangement in accordance with GAAP. *Sch. 1.9*

References to Sch. 1 are to Schedule 1 of SI 2008/409.

If it appears to the company's directors that there are special reasons for departing from any of the accounting principles in preparing the company's accounts in respect of any financial year, they may do so. Particulars of the departure, the reasons for it and its effect must be given in a note to the accounts.

For fixed assets, stocks, investments and goodwill, rules regarding valuation, accounting and disclosure are laid down in the Regulations.

Sch. 1.16–29

Sch. 1.30–35

Historical cost principles are stated as the normal method of accounting but alternative bases (e.g. revaluation and current cost) are allowed provided that details and related historical cost figures are disclosed.

3.5.1   Realised profits

Sch. 1.13(a)

Only 'realised' profits can be included in the profit and loss account.

s. 853(4)–(5)

In determining for accounting purposes 'realised profits' (and 'realised losses'), such profits or losses mean profits or losses of the company that fall to be treated as realised in accordance with principles generally accepted at the time when the accounts are prepared, unless CA 2006 specifies some other treatment.

Sch. 1.36–41

Financial instruments, including derivatives, may be included under CA 2006 at fair value.

Despite the apparent requirement above to include only realised profits in the profit and loss account you will see in **Chapters 6** and **8** that FRS 102 requires certain items based on fair value, such as the gain or loss on an investment property, to be recognised in profit or loss, notwithstanding that the gain is not realised. This is because Sch. 1.40(2) overrides para. 13 in requiring certain specific fair value movements to be recognised in profit or loss subject to certain exceptions as explained below:

> '40(2) Notwithstanding paragraph 13 in this Part of this Schedule, and subject to sub-paragraphs (3) and (4), a change in the value of the financial instrument or of the investment property or living animal or plant must be included in the profit and loss account.'

(See also paragraph A4.27 of FRS 102 for explanation.)

Under the micro-entity regulations, a micro-entity is not permitted to use the alternative accounting rules or indeed include any items at a valuation in its accounts. This and other principles introduced by the micro-entity regulations are discussed in **Chapter 7** and **9**.

The ICAEW technical guidance on distributable profits (Tech 02/10), which has relevance when considering whether an item is realised or not, is currently in the process of being updated to take account of certain requirements in FRS 102. Although there is no underlying change in the law on distributable profits, the advent of FRS 102 creates opportunities for confusion to arise in establishing what is or is not realised. It is expected that new finalised guidance will be available in the summer of 2016.

3.6   Notes to accounts – disclosures

Sch. 1.42–63

For small companies, Sch. 1 of the *Small Companies and Groups (Accounts and Directors' Report) Regulations* 2008 (SI 2008/409) sets out the now more limited information required to be disclosed in the notes to a small company's accounts, following the changes arising from SI 2015/980, covering the following headings:

Sch. 1.44 ● disclosure of accounting policies;
Sch. 1.48 ● fixed assets;
Sch. 1.51 and 1.54 ● assets and liabilities valued at fair value and related information;
Sch. 1.55 ● details of indebtedness (including payments by instalments and nature of security);
Sch. 1.57 ● guarantees and other financial commitments;
Sch. 1.61 ● miscellaneous matters, including exceptional and preceding year items;
Sch. 1.64 ● post balance sheet events;
Sch. 1.65 ● parent undertaking information;
Sch. 1.66 ● related party transactions if not concluded under normal market conditions.

Schedule 1 of SI 2008/409 is included in **Appendix B**.

The contents of the accounts of small companies taking advantage of the reduced disclosures available to micro-entities are discussed separately in **Chapter 7**.

3.7 Narrative reports included with the accounts

3.7.1 Directors' report – contents and requirements

The directors of a company must prepare a directors' report for each financial year of the company (unless they are a micro-entity). *s. 415*

Where the company is a parent company, and the directors of the company prepare group accounts, the directors' report must be a consolidated report (a 'group directors' report') covering all the undertakings included in the consolidation. A group directors' report may, where appropriate, give greater emphasis to matters that are significant to the undertakings included in the consolidation, taken as a whole.

Small companies, however, are permitted to prepare a directors' report that is much reduced in content, omitting much of the information otherwise required to be included in the directors' report of a medium-sized or large company.

Companies which meet the definition of 'small' which are otherwise not able to take advantage of exemptions available to 'small companies' because they are part of an ineligible group (defined in **5.1**) are still entitled to the small companies exemption in respect of their directors' report (and strategic report). *s. 415A(1)(b)*

Additionally, such a company need not file its directors' report with the Registrar of Companies

s. 446(5)(aa) and s. 444A91

The directors' report of a small company is covered in **Chapter 6** at **6.7**.

3.7.2 Strategic report

The *Companies Act 2006 (Strategic Report and Directors' Report) Regulations* 2013 (SI 2013/1970), which came into force on 1 October 2013, introduced a requirement for directors to prepare a Strategic Report for each financial year. However, this is not a requirement for companies which are entitled to the small companies exemption.

3.8 Group accounts

A parent company (other than a small parent company which has 'subsidiary undertakings') is required (with certain exceptions) to prepare group accounts in the form of consolidated accounts of the company and its subsidiary undertakings. Consolidation is not restricted to subsidiaries which are companies.

Group accounts (when prepared) are required to comply with the provisions of CA 2006 as to the form and content of consolidated accounts and additional information to be given. Regulations under CA 2006 provided by SI 2008/409, Sch. 6 require the following accounting for consolidations:

- elimination of group transactions;
- provisions for acquisition and merger accounting;
- treatment and disclosure of non-controlling interests (previously called 'minority interests');

- joint ventures and associated undertakings;
- deferred tax balances;
- related party transactions; and
- preparation 'as if' the group were a single company.

s. 405(2)–(3)   A subsidiary may be excluded from consolidation on the grounds of immateriality and *must* be excluded in the following circumstances:

- severe long-term restrictions; or
- temporary control – holding with a view to subsequent resale.

The exemptions available for small groups are explained in **Chapter 12**.

Exemptions from the requirement to prepare consolidated accounts otherwise available for groups generally are under:

- CA 2006, s. 400 (company included in EEA accounts of larger group);
- CA 2006, s. 401 (company included in non-EEA accounts of larger group); and
- CA 2006, s. 402 (company none of whose subsidiary undertakings need be included in the consolidation).

3.9   Audit reports

Full (for instance following FRS 102, or FRS 102 with section 1A), abridged or micro-entity accounts together with an audit, if appropriate, are required for members for all companies (see **6.2**).

s. 475   Audit exemption, for accounting periods commencing on or after 1 January 2016, is available for companies qualifying as small under the new limits for turnover of £10.2m, a balance sheet total of £5.1m and 50 employees, together with the other qualifying criteria (see **Chapter 13**).

s. 496   Where an audit is performed, the auditor must state whether, in his opinion, based on the work undertaken in the course of the audit the information given in the strategic report (if any) and the directors' report is consistent with those accounts. He must also state whether any such strategic report and directors' report have been prepared in accordance with applicable legal requirements. Additionally, if in the light of the knowledge and understanding of the company and its environment obtained in the course of the audit, any material misstatements have been identified in the directors' or strategic report a statement regarding this must be made by the auditor in his report.

The requirements to state explicitly whether the reports are in accordance with the legal requirements and contain any misstatements based on the auditor's knowledge and understanding of the company are new in 2016, the previous s. 496 only requiring mention of the consistency with the accounts.

3.10   Adequate accounting records

Companies are required to keep 'adequate accounting records' in accordance with CA 2006, s. 386. Company accounts are produced from these underlying financial records.

CA 2006, s. 386 is summarised in **Table 3.2**.

Table 3.2   Adequate accounting records

A company is required to keep accounting records ('adequate accounting records') which are sufficient to show and explain the company's transactions. The accounting records must:

- disclose with reasonable accuracy, *at any time*, the financial position of the company *at that time*;
- enable the directors to ensure that any accounts required to be prepared comply with the requirements of CA 2006 (and, where applicable, of Article 4 of the IAS Regulation*);
- contain entries from day to day of all receipts and expenditure (with sufficient identifying detail); and
- contain a record of company assets and liabilities.

If the company deals in goods, the accounting records must also contain statements of:

- stock held at the year end;
- stocktaking (records and procedures) underlying the year end stock; and
- all goods sold and purchased (except for retail sales), in sufficient detail to identify the goods and the buyers and sellers.

A parent company must ensure that any subsidiary undertaking keeps such accounting records as ensure compliance with CA 2006 or IAS.

(Directors should be constantly aware of the company's financial position and progress. The exact nature and extent of the accounting systems and management information needed to exercise adequate control will depend on the nature, complexity and extent of the company's business.)

Adequate control over records and transactions involves monitoring:

- cash;
- debtors and creditors;
- stock and work in progress;
- capital expenditure;
- contractual arrangements; and
- plans and budgets.

* Article 4 of the IAS Regulation relates to the consolidated accounts of publicly traded companies and explains the requirement for the preparation of the consolidated accounts in accordance with International Accounting Standards.

Accounting records are required by CA 2006, s. 388(4) to be preserved for:

- three years (private company); or
- six years (public company),

from the date on which they are made; although, having regard to other legislation, it is generally considered that documents should be kept for at least six years (and 12 years in the event of contracts under seal).

A practical point that arises with the implementation of FRS 102 is the manner in which the directors keep a record of the distributable profits of the entity. Under old UK GAAP, for most entities, the profit and loss reserves would provide a sufficiently accurate record of distributable profit, thus providing the directors with enough information to meet their statutory requirements. Under FRS 102, there is likely to be a significant difference between profit and loss reserves and distributable profits for a wide variety of companies. The directors will need therefore to either keep a separate reserve on the face of the balance sheet distinguising distributable and non-distributable reserves, or maintain a memorandum of such a figure, if it differs from the profit and loss reserves. Readers may wish to refer to the FRC's lab project report (November 2015) on the disclosure of dividends and distributable profits.

3.11   Approval and signature of accounts

The directors' report, statutory accounts and the auditor's report all require appropriate approval and signature.

s. 414

A company's annual accounts must be approved by the board of directors and signed on behalf of the board by a director of the company. The signature must be on the company's individual balance sheet and the name of the signatory must be stated.

s. 419(1)

The directors' report must also be approved by the board of directors and signed on their behalf by a director *or* the secretary of the company; the name of the signatory must be similarly stated. On occasions when the secretary signs the directors' report this is generally 'by order of the board'.

s. 503

The auditor's report must state the name of the auditor and be signed and dated. Where the auditor is an individual, the report must be signed by him or her. Where the auditor is a firm, the report delivered to the members must be signed by the senior statutory auditor in his or her own name, for and on behalf of the firm of auditors.

If the accounts are prepared in accordance with the small companies regime, the balance sheet must contain, in a prominent position above the signature:

(a)   in the case of individual accounts prepared in accordance with the micro-entity provisions, a statement to that effect; or

(b)   in the case of accounts not prepared as mentioned in paragraph (a), a statement to the effect that the accounts have been prepared in accordance with the provisions applicable to companies subject to the small companies regime (see **6.8**).

s. 414(3), 419(2)

3.12   Publication of statutory and non-statutory accounts

s. 434

If a company publishes any of its statutory accounts, they must be accompanied by the auditor's report on those accounts (unless the company is exempt from audit and the directors have taken advantage of that exemption). A company that prepares statutory group accounts for a financial year must not publish its statutory individual accounts for that year without also publishing with them its statutory group accounts.

s. 435(1)

If a company publishes non-statutory accounts, it must publish with them a statement indicating:

- that they are not the company's statutory accounts;
- whether statutory accounts dealing with any financial year with which the non-statutory accounts purport to deal have been delivered to the Registrar of Companies; and
- whether an auditor's report has been made on the company's statutory accounts for any such financial year, and if so whether the report:
  (a) was qualified or unqualified, or included a reference to any matters to which the auditor drew attention by way of emphasis without qualifying the report; or
  (b) contained a statement under CA 2006, s. 498(2) (accounting records or returns inadequate or accounts or directors' remuneration report (where applicable) not agreeing with records and returns), or CA 2006, s. 498(3) (failure to obtain necessary information and explanations).

s. 435(2)

A company must not publish with any non-statutory accounts the auditor's report, (i.e. the full audit report) on the company's statutory accounts.

s. 435(3)

'Non-statutory accounts' are accounts or other published financial information that are not the company's statutory accounts (e.g. simplified accounting information such as an account in any form purporting to be a balance sheet or profit and loss account relating to the financial year of a company or group).

Chapter 4   Accounts and accounting standards

4.1   Basic contents of financial statements

Accounting information is normally presented in the form of a structured set of financial statements comprising:

- primary statements; and
- the notes to the financial statements, including the accounting policies.

Together these will form the 'true and fair view accounts' (as the term is used in this book).

4.2   Primary statements

The new UK GAAP regime for small companies requires that small companies adopt FRS 102 (unless eligible and choosing to adopt FRS 105) for accounting periods commencing on or after 1 January 2016. However, rather than adopt the full presentation and disclosure requirements of FRS 102 small companies are able, if they wish, to take advantage of section 1A of the standard.

Section 1A sets out simplified and more limited presentation and disclosure requirements. It should be noted, however, that there are no simplications for small companies in the recognition and measurement of items in their accounts. All such rules in FRS 102 need to be followed by small and larger entities alike.

Micro-entities also have limited presentation and disclosure requirements, but in addition, as set out in **Chapter 7** and **9**, they have simplified recognition and measurement rules. A summary of the differences in accounting treatment requirements between FRSSE 2015, FRS 102 and FRS 105 is given in **Table 8.1**.

The formats of the primary statements, as they apply to small and micro companies, are determined as in **Table 4.1**.

Table 4.1	Formats of the primary statements for small companies preparing Companies Act accounts				
Primary Statement	Required for non-small entity	Required for small entity	Encouraged for small entity	Required for micro-entity	Format determined by:
Income Statement (IS or profit or loss)	✓	✓	N/A	✓	CA 2006 SI 2008/409/ FRS 102 3.17 and section 5/FRS 102 1A.9 /FRS 105
Statement of Other Comprehensive Income (OCI)	✓	✗	✓	✗	FRS 102 3.17 and section 5/FRS 102 1A.9

Table 4.1	Formats of the primary statements for small companies preparing Companies Act accounts (cont'd)				
Primary Statement	Required for non-small entity	Required for small entity	Encouraged for small entity	Required for micro-entity	Format determined by:
Single Statement of Comprehensive Income (SOCI)	Optional, instead of above two statements	x	x	x	FRS 102 3.17 and section 5
Statement of Changes in Equity (SOCE)	✓	x	✓	x	FRS 102 3.17 and section 6/FRS 102 1A.9
Statement of income and retained earnings (SOIRE)	Optional in certain circumstances*	x	✓ where relevant**	x	FRS 102 3.17 and section 6/FRS 102 1A.9
Statement of Financial Position (SOFP or Balance Sheet)	✓	✓	N/A	✓	CA 2006 SI 2008/409/ FRS 102 3.17 and section 4/FRS 102 1A.9 /FRS 105
Statement of Cash Flows	x	x	x	x	FRS 102 3.17 and section 7

*A statement of income and retained earnings is available where the only changes to reserves are dividends and/or a prior year adjustment (PYA). In this situation, the SOIRE can be used in place of an income statement and statement of changes in equity.

** Where a small entity has just dividends and a PYA it is encouraged to provide a SOIRE, or if further changes to equity a full SOCE FRS 102.1A9.

4.3 Income statement and statement of other comprehensive income

FRS 102 uses the phrase income statement, rather than profit or loss account, but it is still permissible to call it the profit and loss account if desired. There is an option within the standard to provide a single statement with both profit and loss items and items of other comprehensive income. However, it is also permissible to provide a two statement approach similar to the old UK GAAP style, with an income statement (IS) and then a statement of other comprehensive income (OCI). As the latter is not required, but only encouraged (where relevant) for a small company, it is likely that in practice, just an income statement (profit and loss account) will be provided.

A statement of other comprehensive income (or the relevant section of the statement of comprehensive income) includes those items, being gains or losses, that are recognised in the period, but which do not pass through the profit and loss account/income statement. Gains, such as a revaluation surplus on an item of property, plant and equipment (PPE) are recognised in the statement of other comprehensive income.

As mentioned above, small companies applying FRS 102, section 1A are not required to show a statement of other comprehensive income, although it is encouraged (FRS 102, section 1A.9). However, the preparer needs to remember that the financial statements are still required to give a true and fair view, so if the omission of the statement impacts this, then it will, in fact, be needed.

4.4   Statement of cash flows

FRS 102 requires, with some exceptions, non-small entities producing true and fair view accounts to include a statement of cash flows (also known as a cash flow statement) within the accounts drawn up in accordance with the FRS.

An exemption is available from preparing a statement of cash flows under FRS 102 for a 'qualifying entity', which is defined as 'a member of a group where the parent of that group prepares publicly available consolidated financial statements which are intended to give a true and fair view (of the assets, liabilities, financial position and profit or loss) and that member is included in the consolidation'. However, this exemption is not quite the same as the old UK GAAP exemption, as any of the reduced disclosure options available to qualifying entities require that the shareholders have been notified in writing and do not object to the use of the disclosure exemptions (FRS 102.1.11).

Companies which are eligible to adopt the small companies regime as set out in CA 2006, our focus here, are not required to provide a cash flow statement.

4.5   Accounting standards

4.5.1   True and fair view

CA 2006, s. 393 requires that directors of a company must not approve accounts unless they are satisfied that they give a true and fair view of the assets, liabilities, financial position and profit or loss:

- of the company (in the case of the company's individual accounts); and
- of the undertakings included in the consolidation as a whole, so far as concerns members of the company (in the case of the company's group accounts).

s. 393(1)

For a company that is subject to audit, the auditor of the company, in carrying out his functions in relation to the company's annual accounts under CA 2006, must have regard to the directors' statutory duty in this respect.

s. 393(2)

For a small company, applying the more limited requirements in FRS 102, section 1A, note that it is still necessary to comply with s. 393 and ensure that the accounts give a true and fair view. The FRC has set out, in FRS 102, section 1AD, a number of encouraged disclosures which in its view may be necessary to give a true and fair view. In summary those items are:

(a)   a statement of compliance with the FRS;
(b)   a statement that the entity is a public benefit entity (PBE) if applicable;
(c)   disclosures relating to going concern;
(d)   dividends declared and paid or payable; and
(e)   details of transition on first time adoption.

FRS 102.1AD

In reality though, it will be necessary for the preparers of accounts to consider any additional disclosures or primary statements that might be required in order to give a true and fair view. This is likely to require more judgment than the equivalent requirement under the FRSSE, as that standard was specifically designed to ensure that in the vast majority of cases the disclosure would be sufficient to provide a true and fair view. Section 1A of FRS 102 has been written based on EU legislation that prohibits any extra disclosures from being required by governments or standard setters. Note, however, that an entity can always choose to give extra disclosures or, as described above, be required to give extra disclosures to meet the true and fair obligation in s. 393.

For an entity which qualifies as a micro-entity, s. 393(1A) specifically requires directors to disregard any requirement to provide information in addition to that required by the micro-entity regime. The effect of this is that micro-entity accounts, if drawn up in a manner compliant with that regime, are presumed to give a true and fair view.

The term 'true and fair view' has never been defined precisely in statute or case law, although eminent authority has been given over the years in the form of legal opinion. There is likely to be further debate as the new regime for small companies is adopted, as to what a true and fair view for a small company means. In practice, as before these changes, the preparer or auditor of accounts should consider whether the view that users are obtaining is true and fair using their judgment. For example, if there were going concern issues not disclosed, it seems almost certain that the accounts will not give a true and fair view.

4.5.2 Accounting standards

s. 464

Accounting standards are defined as 'such standards as are, in accordance with their terms, relevant to the company's circumstances and to the accounts'.

For the purposes of CA 2006, Pt. 15 (Accounts and Reports), the term 'Accounting Standards' means financial reporting standards issued by such body or bodies as may be prescribed by regulations or the Secretary of State.

The FRC is the prescribed standard setting body for the purposes of CA 2006, s. 464.

Accounting standards do not need to be applied to items judged to be immaterial.

In preparing accounts giving a true and fair view, a company should therefore follow any applicable accounting standard unless there are good reasons for not doing so.

Accounting standards comprise:

● Financial Reporting Standards (being the new regime as set out in **1.4**); and
● International Financial Reporting Standards (IFRSs including IASs and IFRIC interpretations) (for IAS accounts only).

The *Companies Act* 2006 requires individual accounts, other than those prepared by small or medium-sized companies (as defined by the Act), to include a specific disclosure stating whether they have been prepared in accordance with applicable accounting standards and to give particulars of any material departure from those standards and the reasons for it. All companies, including small and medium-sized companies, must disclose and explain any departure from accounting standards necessary to provide a true and fair view (see **3.3**).

4.5.3 Generally accepted accounting practice (GAAP)

There is no precise technical or legal definition of 'GAAP' in the UK. 'Generally accepted' means a practice that is accepted by accountants generally as being permissible in the particular circumstances of a business – the practice may not necessarily be the 'best' or 'only' accounting method available. GAAP may therefore be regarded as encompassing:

● accounting principles contained in 'Accounting Standards';
● Companies Acts and listing rules of quoted companies;
● industry-specific accounting treatments, including SORPs; and
● any other acceptable accounting treatment, including treatments for which there is currently no adopted Accounting Standard.

4.6 Application of accounting standards to smaller companies

Although the *principles* of accounting (in terms of accounting methods and treatment, measurement criteria and estimation techniques) should apply equally to *all* companies, it is frequently recognised that the burden of complying with accounting standards falls proportionately more heavily upon the smaller company.

The UK has differential regimes for small companies, in terms of presentation and disclosure only, contained in FRS 102. It also has a regime for micro-entities, which simplifies both the accounting treatment and the disclosure for those eligible and adopting FRS 105.

Unlike large companies, a small company is not required by the Companies Act to make a statement in its individual accounts as to whether they have been prepared in accordance with applicable accounting standards and to give particulars of and reasons for any material departure from those standards (although if a true and fair override is applied, details of this must be disclosed – see **3.3**). However, this exemption relates only to disclosure – it does not diminish in any way the obligation of a small company to adopt and comply with appropriate accounting standards and prepare accounts which give a true and fair view.

4.7 International Accounting Standards

4.7.1 Introduction of IAS

The EU requirement to adopt international accounting standards (IAS) has been in place since 2005. Recent years have seen a continuing programme aiming at convergence (that is, harmonisation) of domestic UK, international and US financial reporting on the basis of globally accepted accounting standards.

Despite the fact that changes from 2005 onwards (in the UK) have impacted primarily on the consolidated accounts of quoted (that is, publicly traded) groups of companies, there has been an inevitability about the cascading effect of international harmonisation. The introduction of the new standards (see **1.4**) means that UK GAAP is now firmly based on international standards for smaller entities. This harmonisation has been achieved through the UK standard setters basing FRS 102 and FRS 105 on the *International Financial Reporting Standard for Small and Medium Sized Entities*, or the IFRS for SMEs. Whilst changes have been made to adapt the new standards to both UK and Irish law and accounting practice, UK GAAP is now more aligned with international standards than ever before.

4.7.2 IAS accounts and the option to choose

The *Companies Act* 2006 states that a company's individual accounts may be prepared either in accordance with UK GAAP (i.e. the accounting regulations specified by the Secretary of State as defined in s. 395(1)), which are referred to in the Act as 'Companies Act individual accounts' (s. 396), or in accordance with international accounting standards (s. 397) which the Act refers to as 'IAS individual accounts', subject to certain provisions.

s. 395(1)

The adoption of IAS in the UK is broadly illustrated in **Table 4.2**.

Table 4.2   The adoption of IAS accounts by UK companies

	IAS accounts	CA 2006 accounts
Publicly traded companies (trading on an EU-regulated market) consolidated accounts	Required	Not permitted
ISDX listed	Permitted	Permitted
AIM listed companies consolidated accounts	Required (by AIM rules)	Not permitted
Non-publicly traded companies or individual accounts of traded companies, including small and micro-entities	Permitted	Required (unless IAS accounts adopted)
Incorporated charities	Not permitted	Required

As part of the adoption of the new financial reporting framework set out in FRS 100, the Companies Act was amended by the *Companies and Limited Liability Partnerships (Accounts and Audit Exemptions and Change of Accounting Framework) Regulations* 2012 (SI 2012/2301) such that for financial years ended on or after 1 October 2012, the directors of a company that has voluntarily converted to IAS accounts in previous periods may choose to revert back to preparing Companies Act (UK GAAP) accounts (provided they have not changed to Companies Act accounts in the period of five years preceding the first day of that financial year). Prior to this revision, reverting to Companies Act accounts was only allowed under special circumstances.

This relaxation of the rules was partly to allow companies to move to FRS 101, the IFRS-based reduced disclosure framework, in their subsidiary and individual parent company accounts. Technically, FRS 101 accounts are still Companies Act accounts, as they do not fully comply with IFRS, but the measurement and recognition of items is in line with IFRS. This gives an opportunity to streamline accounts production in listed groups, allowing both fewer adjustments to obtain the consolidated figures, but also reduced disclosures in the individual accounts.

FRS 101 *The Reduced Disclosure Framework* is outside the scope of this book, but is included in the Wolters Kluwer products *Model Accounts* and the CCH *Interactive Companies Accounts Disclosure Checklist*, and covered by the new volume *Preparing FRS 101 Accounts.*

All companies within a group must consistently adopt the same accounting framework (that is, IAS or Companies Act accounts). Upon adopting IAS accounts, a company will still need to apply a variety of provisions of CA 2006 where the scope is beyond IAS (for example, disclosures of staff or directors' remuneration, or contents of the directors' report).

Small companies (as defined) should be alert to various factors if considering a move to full IAS accounts:

- no equivalent exemptions as afforded by CA 2006 are available under IAS;
- the determinants to define a 'small company' are different within IAS formats; and
- exemptions concerning audit exemption, the directors' report, strategic report and group accounts continue to be available.

4.8   Future changes for small company reporting

Now that new UK GAAP is in place it is expected that a relatively stable platform will exist for the next three years. The FRC has undertaken, in general, to conduct triennial reviews of FRSs 102, 103 and 105 and update as required only after each such review.

Before we reach this stable platform though a further change was made in March 2016 (following FRED 62), to amend the fair value hierarchy for pension schemes and financial institutions. There is also a proposal to make amendments to FRS 103 Insurance Contracts, in FRED 64, to take account of legislative changes in Solvency II. FRS 103 applies to any insurance contracts issued by an entity, so although unlikely to affect most small entities it could be relevant (and is more likely to be an issue for LLPs committing to payments for retired members).

FRS 101 will be updated more frequently, due to the changing nature of IFRS, and at the time of writing FRED 63 proposes changes regarding the introduction of IFRS 15 *Revenue from Contracts with Customers.*

Part II   Smaller companies

Chapter 5   Qualifying as a small or micro company

5.1   The 'small companies regime'

As set out in **2.1.1**, CA 2006 provides for different provisions to apply in certain respects to different kinds of company. As far as the smaller (and unquoted) company is concerned, the main distinction is between:

- companies subject to the 'small companies regime'; and   *s. 381*
- all other companies (companies that are not subject to that regime).   *s. 380(3)*

The concept of 'micro-entities' as a sub-classification of small companies was introduced in 2013. In order for a company to qualify as a micro-entity, it must first qualify as a small company.   *s. 384A*

The small companies' regime applies to a company for a financial year in relation to which the company:

- qualifies as small; and   *s. 382–383*
- is not excluded from the regime.   *s. 384*

The small companies regime cannot apply to the following companies: *s. 384(1)*

(a)   public companies;
(b)   authorised insurance companies, banking companies, e-money issuers, MiFID investment firms or UCITS management companies;
(c)   companies carrying on insurance market activity[1]; or
(d)   members of an ineligible group.

Such companies are therefore excluded from the small companies regime.

A group[2] is ineligible if any one or more of its members is: *s. 384(2)*

(a)   a traded company[3];
(b)   a body corporate (other than a company) whose shares are admitted to trading on a regulated market in an EEA State;
(c)   a person (other than a small company) who has permission under the *Financial Services and Markets Act* 2000, Pt. 4 to carry on a regulated activity;
(d)   an e-money issuer;
(e)   a small company that is an authorised insurance company, a banking company, a MiFID investment firm or a UCITS management company; or
(f)   a person who carries on insurance market activity[1].

[1] *As defined by the Financial Services and Markets Act 2000, s. 316(3), 'insurance market activity' means a regulated activity relating to contracts of insurance written at Lloyd's.*

[2] *A group is defined in CA 2006, s. 474 as 'a parent undertaking and its subsidiary undertakings', as defined in CA 2006, s. 1162. A company is generally a subsidiary if more than 50% of its voting shares are held by another (parent) company.*

[3] *Note that this used to be a public company until the implementation of SI 2015/980.*

5.2   Qualifying conditions – 'micro', 'small' and 'medium-sized' companies

Three classifications of companies – 'micro', 'small' and 'medium-sized'[4] – are entitled to certain special provisions with regard to the contents of the statutory accounts and for filing with the Registrar of Companies. This publication deals with the provisions available for small and micro companies.

CA 2006, s. 382(3), 384A and 465(3) set out the conditions to be met by a company to qualify as 'micro', 'small' or 'medium-sized' as appropriate.

As set out in **1.1**, under CA 2006, a company is treated as micro, small or medium-sized if it does not exceed more than one of the following criteria for two consecutive years:

	Micro *s. 384A*	Small *s. 382(3)*	Medium-sized *s. 465(3)*
Turnover	£632,000	£10.2m	£36m
Balance sheet total	£316,000	£5.1m	£18m
Average number of employees (on a monthly basis)	10	50	250

Note that the limits above for small and medium-sized entities increased for accounting periods commencing on or after 1 January 2016, or, at the directors' discretion, from 1 January 2015 for accounting (not audit) purposes only.

*s. 382(4),
384A(5) and
465(4)*

Turnover figures should be proportionately adjusted where the financial 'year' is not 12 months.

*s. 382(5),
384A(6) and
465(5)*

'Balance sheet total' means the aggregate of the amounts shown as assets in the company's balance sheet (i.e. gross assets before deduction of liabilities, accruals and provisions; that is, the aggregate of headings A to D in Format 1 or the 'Assets' headings in Format 2).

The average number of employees is determined by establishing the number of persons employed under contracts of employment by the company each month and calculating an average. This is therefore *not* a measurement of 'full time equivalent' employees.

As a general rule, for a company to qualify as micro, small or medium-sized, the criteria must be met for the current (Y1) and previous year (Y0). If the criteria are not met for the following year (Y2), a company may still continue to be treated as micro, small or medium-sized, as appropriate, for that following year (Y2) if it met the criteria and qualified as micro, small or medium-sized in the previous year (Y1). However, if the criteria are not met in the year after that (Y3), then the company must file accounts according to its size for Y3. Growing companies can therefore continue to be treated as micro, small or medium-sized in the first year that they fail to meet the qualifying criteria.

*s. 384(3)
s. 382*

If the company is in its first year and if the criteria are met for that first year, the company will qualify as micro, small or medium-sized for that year.

s. 382(1)

Appendix C contains a decision chart to help determine the availability of different types of accounts for different types of entity.

[4] The exemptions for medium-sized companies are now extremely limited, as no abbreviated accounts or filing exemptions exist.

5.3 Small company size criteria examples

In order to demonstrate the 'drop in-drop out' rules, where a company must fail to meet the size criteria for two years in a row before moving up to being a medium-sized company, it is helpful to set out an example to illustrate the way this works.

The below example is a company incorporated on 1 January 20X2. This company is not in a group and is not ineligible in any other way (see **5.1** above).

For each period, the '"size" this period' line in the table below applies the size criteria just to the period in question, and applies the test to establish if the company meets two out of the three limits in that period alone.

The last line in the table, 'Qualify as small?', applies the 'drop in-drop out' rule, where criteria are not met for the following year (Y2), a company may still continue to be treated as small for that following year. The table is based on the limits applicable from 1 January 2016 and the years are notional, solely to illustrate how the drop-in, drop-out works.

	Limits	31 December 20X2	31 December 20X3	31 December 20X4	31 December 20X5	30 June 20X6 (6 months)
Turnover	£10.2m	£7m	£11m	£10m	£15m	£6m
Balance sheet total	£5.1m	£5m	£6m	£6m	£6m	£5m
Employees	50	40	45	49	55	55
'Size' *this period*		Small	Medium	Small	Medium	Medium
Qualify as small?		Yes	Yes	Yes	Yes	No

In the example above, for the year ended 31 December 20X4, the company qualified as small in the previous year (bottom row of 20X3). In 20X4, it is 'small-sized' as only one of the three criteria (penultimate row) has been breached. It did not breach the medium criteria for two years in a row. Therefore, it continues to qualify as small.

For the period ended 30 June 20X6, the company fails the turnover limit as this has been pro-rated for the shorter period to £5.1m for six months. Remember that it is only the turnover limit that gets pro-rated, as the other limits are at a point in time or are an average.

In the current year there has been a change of limits and so the calculation varies slightly, although the same principles as above apply. The requirement now is to retrospectively consider whether an entity meets the requirements, based on the new limits, for two years running. SI 2015/980, reg. 2(4) provided for these transitional rules to require the retrospective calculation of 'size' to be based on the new limits. The effect of this is that if a company meets the new small limits in 2015 (if early adopting) it doesn't just fail to be treated as a small company due to the fact that the limits were lower in the previous year. The example below demonstrates this point where although the company would originally not have been small in 2014, using the new limits it is small and so the 2015 accounts can be prepared as 'small' accounts:

Year ended 31 December	New limits s. 382(3)	2013	2014	2015	2016 (expected)
Turnover	£10.2m	£11m	£10m	£11m	£11m
Balance Sheet Total	£5.1m	£6m	£5m	£5m	£5m
Employees	50	55	55	49	48
'Size' this period		Medium	Small	Small	Small
Qualify as small?		No	No	Small (if early adopting new regulations and FRS 102)	Small

33

If, in fact, the company was not small based on size that period in 2014, but was still small in 2015 and 2016, it would not be able to use the exemptions for small companies until 2016.

5.4   Micro-entities

The micro-entities regime was introduced in 2013 by the *Small Companies (Micro-Entities' Accounts) Regulations* 2013 (SI 2013/3008).

In order for a company to qualify as a micro-entity, the company must first qualify as small (and not be excluded from the small companies regime).

After the 'small' test, a company is excluded from the micro-entities regime if it is:

- an investment undertaking (as defined in art. 2(14) of Directive 2013/34/EU of 26 June 2013 on the annual financial statements, etc. of certain types of undertakings);
- a financial holding undertaking (as defined in art. 2(15) of that Directive);
- a credit institution (as defined in art. 4 of Directive 2006/48/EC of the European Parliament and of the Council of 14 June 2006 relating to the taking up and pursuit of the business of credit institutions, other than one referred to in art. 2 of that Directive);
- an insurance undertaking (as defined in art. 2(1) of Council Directive 91/674/EEC of 19 December 1991 on the annual accounts of insurance undertakings); or
- a charity.

There are further restrictions on the application of the micro-entities regime to group companies as set out in **5.5** below.

The micro-entities regime applies only to companies and not currently to limited liability partnerships or other types of entity. It is expected that legislation will be issued in the summer of 2016 to allow LLPs to make use of the micro-entities regime if they meet the criteria. It is possible for entities with no statutory accounts requirements, such as sole traders, to use the micro-entity provisions and FRS 105 if they wish.

5.5   Parent companies and small groups

CA 2006, s. 383(2)–(7) and 466(2)–(7) set out the conditions to be met by a group for the parent company to qualify as 'small' or 'medium-sized' as appropriate.

s. 383(1)   A parent company qualifies as a small company in relation to a financial year only if the group headed by it qualifies as a small group.

s. 383(1) et seq.   The size classification of a parent company is determined firstly by considering whether the parent itself qualifies as small per s. 382. That section requires additional consideration of s. 383 if the company is a parent company. This has the effect that a parent only qualifies as small if the group (parent company and subsidiary undertakings) headed by it also qualifies as small (see **Chapter 12**).

Micro-entity provisions do not apply to group companies if:

s. 384A(8)   - the company is a parent company and the group headed by the company does not qualify as a small group;
s. 384B(2)   - the company is a parent company which prepares group accounts for that year; or
s. 384(B)   - the company is not a parent company but its accounts are included in consolidated group accounts for that year.

Chapter 6   Contents of small company accounts

6.1   Introduction

The reporting environment for small companies has changed significantly with the advent of both new UK GAAP and the introduction of the *Companies, Partnerships and Groups (Accounts and Reports) Regulations* 2015 (SI 2015/980). The latter implemented the requirements of the latest EU Accounting Directive, which took what is referred to as a 'maximum harmonisation' approach. This means that the directive prohibits member states from adding to the disclosure or presentation requirements for small entities, above what is required in the Directive.

The result of this is that there are relatively limited disclosures requirements for small entities, centred around a list of 13 notes included in the Directive. Importantly however, even though the member states are prohibited from requiring small entities to disclose specific extra items, the accounts must still give a true and fair view. This means it is up to the directors and the preparers of the accounts to ensure that not only the list of required disclosures are provided, but that the accounts also give a true and fair view (see **3.3** for more details).

For accounting periods commencing on or after 1 January 2016, small companies that are not able, or not choosing, to take advantage of FRS 105 *The Financial Reporting Standard applicable to the Micro-entities Regime* or IFRS, must adopt FRS 102 *The Financial Reporting Standard applicable in the UK and Republic of Ireland (2015)*. They can choose, within that standard, to apply the more limited presentation and disclosure requirements in section 1A. This volume assumes that the small company wishes to take advantage of section 1A. If the entity adopts FRS 102 in full, then readers should refer to the sister volume, *Preparing FRS 102 Company Accounts 2015–16* for further guidance.

This chapter summarises the company accounts provisions of CA 2006 as they affect companies under the 'small companies regime', together with the presentation and disclosure requirements of FRS 102, section 1A. CA 2006 lays down provisions relating to:

- prescriptive formats of accounts;
- the content of accounts; and
- principles and rules for determining amounts included in the accounts.

This chapter discusses 'Companies Act individual accounts' prepared in accordance with CA 2006, s. 396, including the new provision to 'adapt' the formats to be more IFRS-like in style and terminology. **Chapter 8** goes on to consider the additional impact on the accounts of small companies of FRS 102 *The Financial Reporting Standard applicable in the UK and Republic of Ireland (2015)*

The contents of the accounts of small companies eligible and choosing to take advantage of the micro-entity exemptions are covered in **Chapter 7**, together with explanation of FRS 105 in **Chapter 9**.

'Abbreviated accounts' (modified statutory accounts for filing purposes) no longer exist, post the implementation of SI 2015/980. However, filing exemptions still exist for small companies, as discussed in **6.7**. In addition, there is an option to prepare abridged accounts which are dealt with in **Chapter 11**.

6.1.1   Summary of the changes

There have been numerous changes as a result of SI 2015/980 and the advent of FRS 102 with section 1A for small companies, which have in general been mentioned where significant in the following analysis and in **Table 8.5**. However, it is useful to consider some of the key changes in summary, to provide a sense of the differences.

Item of disclosure	Description	Reference
Abbreviated accounts no longer available	Separate accounts for filing in the form of abbreviated accounts are no longer available.	Former s. 444(3)
Abridged accounts for members introduced	Abridged accounts (see **Chapter 11**) are available as an alternative to full accounts.	Sch. 1.1A
Filing exemptions	Exemptions from filing the profit and loss and directors' report are still available for whichever type of accounts prepared (full, abridged, micro).	s. 444
Related undertaking disclosures – alternative compliance	For accounts approved prior to 1 July 2015 it was possible to provide only information about key undertakings in the company's annual accounts where the length of the disclosure would otherwise be excessive and to provide the detailed information annexed to the annual return. It is now mandatory to provide all the information regarding related undertakings within the annual accounts. The disclosures themselves are discussed in **12.5**.	s. 410(2)
Turnover split	Split of turnover in geographical areas no longer required.	Sch. 1.60
Staff costs	Staff cost note no longer required for small entities.	s. 411(5)
Employee numbers	This is now required to be given for small companies.	s. 411(1)
Ordinary activities	The requirement to describe profit/loss, etc. as on ordinary activities has been repealed, due to the deletion from the Act of mention of extraordinary items.	Sch. 1, Section B formats
Related party disclosure	Disclosure only required for a limited list of related parties and only then if not concluded under normal market conditions.	Sch. 1.66
Emoluments	The provision in the FRSSE to allow emoluments that are employment earnings to be ignored for related party transaction purposes are no longer available, though as stated above many emoluments will not need to be disclosed.	FRSSE 2015 15.7
Details of share capital	Details of alloted shares and information about redeemable shares is no longer required.	Sch. 1.46 and 47
Dormant companies acting as agent	Disclosure no longer required.	Sch. 1.63
Reserves and dividends	Disclosure no longer required.	Sch. 1.43
Investments, biological assets, investment property	Disclosure of listed investments and other market value information no longer required (though note in effect this is partly replaced by the disclosures for fair value movements as shares and investment property will have to be measured at fair value).	Sch. 1.50, 52, and 53
Change in audit report regarding narrative information	A more detailed opinion is required regarding whether narrative reports are prepared in accordance with applicable legislation, are inconsistent or otherwise misleading based on the work that the auditor has done.	s. 496

6.2 Accounts – provisions for small companies

For each financial year accounts must be prepared for all companies, irrespective of size.

s. 394, etc.

The accounts of a 'small' company, however, are often less detailed with reduced statutory disclosure requirements compared to larger companies.

By virtue of the provisions applicable for companies subject to the small companies regime set out in CA 2006, a small company is therefore entitled to prepare:

- annual accounts for members – a profit and loss account with a balance sheet and reduced disclosure requirements for the notes to the accounts and the directors' report (as determined by SI 2008/409), with the option to file just the balance sheet and notes; or
- abridged accounts for its members, again with the option of filing just the balance sheet and notes with the Registrar of Companies – under CA 2006, s. 444.

Company accounts prepared in accordance with the provisions of CA 2006, s. 396 and requirements within the Regulations contained in SI 2008/409, Sch. 1, as amended by SI 2015/980, together with the requirements of FRS 102, section 1A are referred to as 'small company accounts' in this book. The *Companies Act* 2006, s. 396 and SI 2008/409 together determine the minimum disclosure required in a small company's annual accounts. However, a small company does not have to take advantage of all the exemptions and modifications permitted if it does not wish to do so. Note that this is despite the EU taking a maximum harmonisation approach as discussed above. Though a small company cannot be required to include more information in its accounts and reports, it is able to provide additional disclosure if it so wishes or not take up the exemptions available for small companies.

For example, SI 2008/409 provides that Companies Act individual accounts 'are treated as having complied with any provision of Schedule 1 to these Regulations [i.e. the *Small Companies Accounts Regulations* (SI 2008/409)] if they comply instead with the corresponding provision of Schedule 1 to the Large and Medium-Sized Companies and Groups (Accounts and Reports) Regulations 2008 [SI 2008/410]'.

SI 2008/409, reg. 3(3)

Similarly, Companies Act group accounts are treated as having complied with any provision of Pt. 1 to Sch. 6 of SI 2008/409 ('Form and content of Companies Act group accounts') if they comply instead with the corresponding provision of SI 2008/410, Sch. 6.

SI 2008/409, reg. 8(2)

The provisions applicable to small companies apply not only to the individual accounts of such companies but also to the group accounts where a small company produces them. If at the end of a financial year a company subject to the small companies regime is a parent company, the directors, as well as preparing individual accounts for the year, have the option to prepare group accounts for the year, if they so wish.

s. 399

6.3 Format of small company accounts

6.3.1 SI 2008/409

Under the small companies regime of CA 2006, the form and content of:

- Companies Act individual accounts for small companies;
- Companies Act group accounts for small companies; and
- abridged or adapted balance sheets/profit and loss accounts,

are determined in accordance with the *Small Companies and Groups (Accounts and Directors' Report) Regulations* 2008 (SI 2008/409).

The regulations in SI 2008/409 prescribe the required formats for Companies Act individual accounts from which small companies may choose. Formats which are most commonly used are illustrated later in this chapter.

Sch. 1.2(1)

Once a format has been adopted, the company must use the same format for subsequent years unless, in the directors' opinion, there are special reasons for changing; these must be disclosed in the year of change.

Sch. 1B(1) and (2)

SI 2015/980 introduced further flexibility into the format of accounts with the addition of adapted balance sheets and/or profit and loss accounts to the possible formats in Sch. 1B(1) and (2). These sections are designed to allow both new, FRS 102 terminology in place of the standard Companies Act terminology and also an IFRS style of presentation. This latter point is unlikely to be of particular relevance to a company using FRS 102, as users are more likely to be familiar with the Companies Act formats. However, it is possible that an IFRS style may be desirable, for instance because the users of the accounts are likely to be more familiar with that layout.

6.3.2   Form and content of accounts prepared by small companies required by company law

The form and content of individual accounts prepared by small companies are determined in accordance with regulations provided by the *Small Companies and Groups (Accounts and Directors' Report) Regulations* 2008 (SI 2008/409) and in particular Sch. 1.

Schedule 1 to SI 2008/409 (Companies Act individual accounts), as most noticeably amended by SI 2015/980, is structured as set out in **Table 6.1**.

Table 6.1   Schedule 1 Companies Act individual accounts – SI 2008/409 'The Small Companies and Groups (Accounts and Directors' Report) Regulations 2008'

Part 1   *General rules and formats*

Section A	General rules
Section B	Required formats for accounts of companies other than micro-entities

- Balance sheet Formats 1 and 2 and notes thereon
- Profit and loss account Formats 1 and 2 and notes thereon (note that formats 3 and 4 were deleted by SI 2015/980)

Section C	Required formats for the accounts of micro-entities

- Balance sheet Formats 1 and 2
- Profit and loss Format

Part 2   *Accounting principles and rules*

Section A	Accounting principles
Section B	Historical cost accounting rules

- Fixed assets
- Depreciation and diminution in value
- Intangible assets
- Current assets
- Miscellaneous and supplementary provisions (*including determination of purchase price and production cost, and equity method*)

Table 6.1   Schedule 1 Companies Act individual accounts (cont'd)

Section C   Alternative accounting rules

- Alternative accounting rules
- Application of the depreciation rules
- Additional information to be provided in case of departure from historical cost account rules
- Revaluation reserve

Section D   Fair value accounting

- Inclusion of financial instruments at fair value
- Determination of fair value
- Hedged items
- Other assets that may be included at fair value
- Accounting for changes in value
- The fair value reserve

Part 3   *Notes to the accounts*

- Disclosure of accounting policies
- Information supplementing the balance sheet (*fixed assets, fair values, revalued fixed assets, indebtedness, and guarantees and other financial commitments*)
- Miscellaneous matters (including prior year items in the profit and loss account, exceptional items, post balance sheet events, parent undertaking information, related party transactions)

Schedule 1 is reproduced in full in **Appendix B**.

6.3.3   The statutory formats

The accounts formats from which a small company may choose are given in SI 2008/409, Sch. 1 (Pt. 1, Section B – 'The required formats for accounts').

There is a choice of:

- *two* profit and loss account formats (see **6.5**); and
- *two* balance sheet formats (see **6.4**).

The two remaining profit and loss account formats and one of the balance sheet formats are in the 'vertical' styling in which most accounts are prepared. The two previously available 'horizontal' styles of profit and loss account (Formats 3 and 4) are no longer available. They were rarely used and SI 2015/980 omitted them from the regulations. The horizontal style balance sheet (Format 2) though not generally used, is still available.

6.3.4   Accounting principles

Small company accounts are prepared in accordance with the principles set out in SI 2008/409, Sch. 1 (Pt. 2, Section A). These principles are the fundamental accounting concepts that underlie accounts and are also incorporated within UK GAAP generally. As we have moved into the era of new UK GAAP, this generally means the application of FRS 102, albeit with the disclosure and presentation simplifications available in section 1A. Note though, that notwithstanding Sch. 1.13 requiring only realised profits or losses to be included in the profit and loss account, Sch. 1.40(2) requires that movements in the value of a financial instrument, investment property or living plant or animal must be included in the profit and loss account. This ensures congruence with the requirements or options available in FRS 102.

Sch. 1.10–15

Accounting principles including more detail on realised profits are explained further in **3.5** (**Chapter 3**).

6.4   Small company balance sheet

The formats of balance sheet set out in SI 2008/409, Sch. 1 (Pt. 1, Section B) from which a small company must choose for its annual (individual) accounts are set out in **Table 6.2**.

Table 6.2 illustrates the differences between the two balance sheet formats available.

Table 6.2   Small company balance sheets – the two formats compared

The items shown as boxed in Format 1 need not be disclosed in Format 2. For illustrative purposes, the Arabic number sub-headings (which are common to both formats) are not reproduced in this table but are set out in **Table 6.3**.

Format 1	Format 2
	ASSETS
A Called up share capital not paid	A Called up share capital not paid
B Fixed assets	B Fixed assets

I Intangible assets
   II Tangible assets
   III Investments
	I Intangible assets
	   II Tangible assets
	   III Investments

C Current assets	C Current assets

I Stocks
   II Debtors
   III Investments
   IV Cash at bank and in hand
	I Stocks
	   II Debtors
	   III Investments
	   IV Cash at bank and in hand

D Prepayments and accrued income	D Prepayments and accrued income
E Creditors: amounts falling due within one year	– – – – – – – – – – – – – – – – – – – –
F Net current assets (liabilities) G Total assets less current liabilities	CAPITAL, RESERVES AND LIABILITIES

H   Creditors: amounts falling due after more than
   one year
	A Capital and reserves
	   I Called up share capital
	   II Share premium account
	   III Revaluation reserve
	   IV Other reserves
	   V Profit and loss account

I Provisions for liabilities J Accruals and deferred income	B Provisions for liabilities
– – – – – – – – – – – – – – – – – – – –	
K Capital and reserves	C Creditors:

I Called up share capital
   II Share premium account
   III Revaluation reserve
   IV Other reserves
   V Profit and loss account
	Amounts falling due within one year and after one year must be shown separately for each of these items and for the aggregate of all of these items.

	D Accruals and deferred income

The dotted line above in Format 1 illustrates the usual 'break-point' in the balance sheet, although in practice the balance sheet total could be 'struck' after item G. Format 2 would usually have a total struck after assets and after Capital, reserves and liabilities.

Table 6.3 Small company balance sheets – Arabic number sub-headings

B I INTANGIBLE ASSETS

1 Goodwill
2 Other intangible assets

B II TANGIBLE ASSETS

1 Land and buildings
2 Plant and machinery, etc.

B III INVESTMENTS

1 Shares in group undertakings and participating interests
2 Loans to group undertakings and undertakings in which the company has a participating interest
3 Other investments other than loans
4 Other investments

C I STOCKS

1 Stocks
2 Payments on account

C II DEBTORS

1 Trade debtors
2 Amounts owed by group undertakings and undertakings in which the company has a participating interest
3 Other debtors

C III INVESTMENTS

1 Shares in group undertakings
2 Other investments[1]

E CREDITORS: AMOUNTS FALLING DUE WITHIN ONE YEAR

1 Bank loans and overdrafts
2 Trade creditors
3 Amounts owed to group undertakings and undertakings in which the company has a participating interest
4 Other creditors

H CREDITORS: AMOUNTS FALLING DUE AFTER MORE THAN ONE YEAR

1 Bank loans and overdrafts
2 Trade creditors
3 Amounts owed to group undertakings and undertakings in which the company has a participating interest
4 Other creditors

[1] *For group balance sheets, the format headings are as set out in* SI 2008/409, Sch. 6 *(Part I paragraph 1(2) – see Note 1 to Table 6.4).* The balance sheet format of a small company which adopts balance sheet Format 1 would be as set out in **Table 6.4**.

For group balance sheets the format headings are as set out in SI 2008/409, Sch. 6, see note 1 to Table 6.4.

Table 6.4   Small company balance sheet (Format 1)

CALLED UP SHARE CAPITAL NOT PAID

FIXED ASSETS
Intangible assets
Goodwill
Other intangible assets

Tangible assets
Land and buildings
Plant and machinery, etc.

Investments   (*Note 1*)
Shares in group undertakings and participating interests
Loans to group undertakings and undertakings in which the company
has a participating interest
Other investments other than loans
Other investments

CURRENT ASSETS
Stocks
Stocks
Payments on account

Debtors   (*Note 2*)
Trade debtors
Amounts owed by group undertakings and undertakings in which the company has a participating interest
Other debtors

Investments
Shares in group undertakings
Other investments

Cash at bank and in hand

PREPAYMENTS AND ACCRUED INCOME

CREDITORS: amounts falling due within one year

Bank loans and overdrafts
Trade creditors
Amounts owed to group undertakings and undertakings in which the
company has a participating interest
Other creditors   (*Note 3*)

NET CURRENT ASSETS (LIABILITIES)

TOTAL ASSETS LESS CURRENT LIABILITIES

CREDITORS: amounts falling due after more than one year

Bank loans and overdrafts
Trade creditors
Amounts owed to group undertakings and undertakings in which the
company has a participating interest
Other creditors

Table 6.4   *Small company balance sheet (Format 1) (cont'd)*

PROVISIONS FOR LIABILITIES

ACCRUALS AND DEFERRED INCOME   *(Note 4)*

CAPITAL AND RESERVES
Called up share capital
Share premium account
Revaluation reserve
Other reserves
Profit and loss account

Note 1   *Where a small company prepares small group accounts, in a consolidated balance sheet the format for 'Investments' is:*
   1.   *shares in group undertakings;*
   2.   *interests in associated undertakings;*
   3.   *other participating interests;*
   4.   *loans to group undertakings and undertakings in which a participating interest is held;*
   5.   *other investments other than loans; and*
   6.   *others.*   **SI 2008/409, Sch. 6.1(2)**

Note 2   A small company must disclose the aggregate total of 'debtors falling due after more than one year' but such disclosure (if the amount is not material) may be in the notes to the accounts rather than in the balance sheet.

Note 3   The amount of any creditors in respect of taxation and social security and convertible loans should be shown separately.

   Payments received on account must be included in so far as they are not shown as deductions from stock.

Note 4   Accruals and deferred income may also be shown under 'other creditors'.

6.5   Small company profit and loss account

The choice of profit and loss account formats for a small company, as set out in SI 2008/409, Sch. 1 (Pt. 1, Section B), is illustrated in **Table 6.5**.

In practice, care needs to be taken in the choice of format and presentation of the profit and loss account. **Table 6.5** presents a comparison of the two formats (Formats 1 and 2) showing the differences in presentation and disclosure. It is particularly relevant to note:

- *gross profit or loss* is specifically disclosed only in Format 1; and
- *depreciation* may require allocation over various cost headings in Format 1 but needs only to be shown as one item in a Format 2 profit and loss account.

The amount of a company's 'profit or loss before taxation' must be included on every profit and loss account. This item is not specified in the formats, but is required by SI 2008/409, Sch. 1.6. Note the change in terminology from previously, where there was a requirement to state the profit or loss on ordinary activities before taxation. SI 2015/980 removed the words 'on ordinary activities'.

All formats require similar items and items in the profit and loss account formats (being represented by Arabic numbers) could be combined and given in the notes to the accounts, provided the profit and loss account contains a summarised linking figure.

For small companies choosing to take advantage of the more limited filing requirements with the Registrar of Companies (which omit a profit and loss account), the choice of profit and loss account format in their accounts may be of less consequence.

Table 6.5   Small company profit and loss account formats (SI 2008/409, Sch. 1 (Part I Section B))

Items boxed show the differences in disclosure required by the formats.

Expenses classified by function

Format 1

1   Turnover

| 2   Cost of sales |
| 3   Gross profit or loss |
| 4   Distribution costs |
| 5   Administrative expenses |

6   Other operating income

(In Format 1, staff costs must be allocated over items 2, 4 and 5. Staff costs disclosure in the notes is not applicable for small companies (CA 2006, s .411).)

(In Format 1, depreciation must be allocated over items 2, 4 and 5 (Sch. 1, Pt. I, s. B, note 11) and disclosed separately in Notes (Sch. 1.19).)

7   Income from shares in group undertakings
8   Income from participating interests
9   Income from other fixed asset investments
10   Other interest receivable and similar income
11   Amounts written off investments
12   Interest payable and similar expenses

12A   Profit or loss before taxation (Sch. 1.6)

13   Tax on profit or loss
14   Profit or loss after taxation
15   omitted (note 1)
16   omitted (note 1)
17   omitted (note 1)
18   omitted (note 1)
19   Other taxes not shown under the above items
20   Profit or loss for the financial year

Expenses classified by type

Format 2

1   Turnover

| 2   Change in stocks of finished goods and work in progress |
| 3   Own work capitalised |

4   Other operating income

| 5   (a) Raw materials and consumables |
| (b) Other external charges |

6   Staff costs:
     (a) Wages and salaries
     (b) Social security costs
     (c) Other pension costs

7   (a) Depreciation and other amounts written off tangible and intangible fixed assets

| (b) Amounts written off current assets, to the extent that they exceed write-offs which are normal in the undertaking concerned |
| 8   Other operating expenses |

9   Income from shares in group undertakings
10   Income from participating interests
11   Income from other fixed asset investments
12   Other interest receivable and similar income
13   Amounts written off investments
14   Interest payable and similar expenses

14A   Profit or loss before taxation (Sch. 1.6)

15   Tax on profit or loss
16   Profit or loss after taxation
17   omitted (note 1)
18   omitted (note 1)
19   omitted (note 1)
20   omitted (note 1)
21   Other taxes not shown under the above items
22   Profit or loss for the financial year

Note 1 – Items in the formats relating to extraordinary items were removed with the implementation of SI 2015/980.

Where a small company prepares group accounts, the items in **Table 6.5** headed 'Income from participating interests' in the above formats (item 8 (Format 1) and item 10 (Format 2)) become two items:

- Income from interests in associated undertakings; and
- Income from other participating interests.

SI 2008/409, Sch. 6.1(3)

6.6 Notes to the accounts – small company

A small company must set out in the notes (if not given in the company's accounts) the following information specified in SI 2008/409, Sch. 1, Pt. 3 – Notes to the accounts, paragraphs 42–63. The notes must be presented in the order in which, where relevant, the items to which they relate are presented in the balance sheet and in the profit and loss account (Sch. 1.42(2) inserted by SI 2015/980).

Sch. 1.42

Disclosure of accounting policies

- The accounting policies adopted by the company in determining the amounts to be included in respect of items shown in the balance sheet and in determining profit or loss of the company must be stated (including such policies with respect to the depreciation and diminution in value of assets).

Sch. 1.44

Information supplementing the balance sheet:

- *Fixed assets*
  Additions, disposals, revaluations, depreciation and other movements for each category of fixed assets.

Sch. 1.48–49

- *Information about fair value of assets and liabilities*
  Assumptions and techniques used; fair value and transfers to/from profit or loss or reserves for each category of financial instruments; terms and details of each class of derivatives. A fair value table of any movements in the fair value reserve must also be given.

Sch. 1.51

- *Information about revalued fixed assets*
  Movements in the revaluation reserve, an explanation of the tax treatment of items therein and the carrying amount that would have been recognised if the assets had not been revalued.

Sch. 1.54

- *Details of indebtedness*
  Creditors payable or repayable in more than five years; indication of nature and form of any security.

Sch. 1.55

- *Guarantees and other financial commitments*
  The total amount of any financial commitments, guarantees and contingencies not included in the balance sheet; An indication of the nature of any related valuable security; Separate disclosure of any commitments concerning pensions and amounts in respect of other group undertakings or undertakings in which the company has a participating interest.

Sch. 1.57

Other Information

- *Miscellaneous*
  Effect of prior year items included in current profit or loss; exceptional transactions.

Sch. 1.61

- *Post balance sheet events*
  The nature and effect of material events arising after the balance sheet date that are not reflected in the profit and loss or balance sheet.

Sch. 1.64

Sch. 1.65

- *Parent undertaking information*
  The name of the parent which draws up group accounts, the address of the registered office or principal place of business if unincorporated.

Sch. 1.66

- *Related party transactions*
  Particulars of transactions which have not been concluded under normal market terms with owners holding a participating interest, companies in which the company itself has a participating interest and the company's directors.

  (Note that SI 2015/980 amended the requirements deleting a number of disclosures, so this list of items is more limited than in previous years.)

s. 411(1)

- *Employee numbers*
  Section 411(1) of the Companies Act now requires the notes to a company's annual accounts to disclose the average number of persons employed by the company in the financial year. For small companies no split is required between the category of employees as it is for larger companies. As for other similar requirements, the number of employees is calculated using a monthly average and includes all those with a contract of service for the relevant month. Note, this is therefore not a full time equivalent number, but an actual number of people.

- *Directors' benefits – advances, credit and guarantees*
  CA 2006, s. 413 provides for the disclosure of advances and credits granted by a company to its directors, and guarantees of any kind entered into by a company on behalf of its directors (see **6.10**).

SI 2008/489, reg. 4

- *Disclosure of auditors' remuneration*
  A note to the annual accounts of a small or medium-sized company must disclose the auditor's remuneration, including any benefits-in-kind (see **6.12**).

CA 2006, s. 538 and SI 2008/489, reg. 8

(Note that this requirement is expected to be repealed when draft legislation for SI 2008/489 becomes final, which should be in the summer of 2016.)

- *Liability limitation agreements*
  A company (subject to audit) which has entered into a liability limitation agreement limiting an auditor's liability must disclose in the notes: the principal terms of the agreement; and the date of the resolution approving the agreement (or its principal terms) or, in the case of a private company, the date of the resolution waiving the need for such approval.

6.7   Filing obligations and narrative reports for a small company

CA 2006 requires that a company's annual accounts for the shareholders should be accompanied by a directors' report and a strategic report. It also sets out various exemptions, both from preparation and filing of certain documents as discussed below.

6.7.1   Entitlement to exemptions

A company is entitled to the small companies exemption in relation to the directors' report and strategic report for a financial year if:

- it is entitled to prepare accounts for the year in accordance with the small companies regime; or

s. 415A

- it would be so entitled but for being or having been a member of an ineligible group.

This latter exemption allows a company which is a member of an ineligible group, and which as a result cannot be treated as small for the purposes of preparing its financial statements, to nonetheless take advantage of the exemptions in connection with the directors' and strategic report.

The exemption enables a small company:

- not to provide a strategic report (and as a result, not disclose the principal activity);
- not to provide a statement of the amount recommended by way of dividend (under s. 416(3)); and
- to take advantage of certain filing exemptions set out in s. 444–446 as set out below.

S. 444 sets out the filing obligations for a company subject to the small companies regime. Such companies:

(a) must file a balance sheet;
(b) may also file:

    (i) a copy of the company's profit and loss account (and a copy of the auditor's report unless exempt from audit and the directors have taken advantage of the exemption); and   *s. 444(2)*

    (ii) a copy of the directors' report for that year.

Where the balance sheet or profit and loss account is abridged the directors must also deliver to the registrar a statement by the company that all the members of the company have consented to the abridgement.   *s. 444(2A)*

Where the company does not deliver a copy of the directors' report, or profit and loss account, the copy of the balance sheet must contain in a prominent position a statement that the company's annual accounts and reports have been delivered in accordance with the provisions applicable to companies subject to the small companies regime.   *s. 444(5)*

Additionally, where no copy of the profit and loss is delivered to the registrar the balance sheet must disclose that fact and unless exempt from audit and taking advantage of that exemption, the notes to the balance sheet must set out certain information regarding the audit report.   *s. 444(5A)*

The information in respect of the audit report required is as follows (but is not needed for those preparing micro-entity accounts s. 444(5C)):   *s. 444(5B)*

(a) state whether the audit report was qualified or unqualified;
(b) where qualified disclose the basis of qualification, including any statement regarding adequate account records, accounts not agreeing with the records, (s. 498(2)) and if the auditor fails to obtain all the information and explanations required (s. 498(3));
(c) where the report was unqualified include a reference to any emphasis of matter issues; and
(d) state the name of the auditor, including the name of the senior statutory auditor (unless exempt due to s. 506).

The sections above, though altered in detailed wording by SI 2015/980, largely have the same effect as before. That is to allow the small company to only file its balance sheet and notes thereto, albeit that certain extra disclosures are needed to alert readers of the accounts to the fact that exemptions have been taken, for example. **Table 6.6** below summarises these extra statements.

Small company directors' report – contents

Micro-entities are not required to prepare a director's report.   *s. 415(1A)*

Small companies, not eligible or choosing to use the micro-entity regime, are only required to provide the following information in their directors' report:

- names of directors during the year;   *s. 416*
- political donations (to a party, organisation or election candidate) and expenditure (exceeding £2,000); (see **Appendix B** for full disclosure requirements)   *Sch. 5.2*
- employment of disabled persons (where average weekly employees exceed 250);   *Sch. 5.5*
- qualifying third party indemnity provision; and   *s. 236*
- certain information relating to the directors' responsibilities where an audit is performed (see **Table 6.6**).

(The previously required disclosures regarding purchase of own shares and charitable donations were repealed by SI 2013/1970.)

For a company entitled to small companies' exemptions in relation to the directors' report and strategic report (CA 2006, s. 415A) to take advantage of the exemptions, the directors' report must contain a statement to that effect under s. 419(2). This statement is explained in **6.8**.

s. 418   Unless a company is exempt for the financial year in question from the requirements of CA 2006, Pt. 16 as to audit of accounts (and the directors take advantage of that exemption), the directors' report must contain a statement as to disclosure of relevant audit information to auditors.

6.8   Directors' statements

A company which qualifies as a small company in relation to a financial year (other than a dormant company) and takes advantage of the provisions applicable to companies subject to the small companies regime with respect to the preparation of annual accounts and/or directors' report and strategic report must include statements in its accounts as described below.

s. 433   For small (unquoted) companies, every copy of any balance sheet and directors' report that is published by or on behalf of the company must state the name of the person who signed it on behalf of the board.

6.8.1   Directors' statement – small company accounts preparation: s. 414 and 419

A company's annual accounts must be approved by the board of directors and signed on behalf of the board by a director of the company. The signature must be on the company's balance sheet.

s. 414   If the accounts are prepared in accordance with the provisions applicable to companies subject to the small companies regime, the balance sheet must contain a statement to that effect in a prominent position above the signature. If micro-entity accounts are prepared the statement should be to that effect (s. 414(3)(a)), otherwise it will state that the accounts have been prepared in accordance with the provisions applicable to companies subject to the small companies regime (s. 414(3)(b)).

s. 414   The balance sheet therefore must contain (in a 'prominent position' above the signature of a director required by s. 414(1)–(2)) a statement that the accounts have been prepared in accordance with the provisions applicable to companies subject to the small companies regime (or the micro-entity provisions as applicable) within CA 2006, Pt. 15. Whilst not required the directors could also disclose that the provisions of FRS 102, section 1A (FRS 105 for micro-entities) are being followed. See **Example 6.1** below.

Example 6.1

Section 414 Directors' statement – balance sheet

The financial statements, which have been prepared in accordance with the [special provisions relating to companies subject to the small companies regime] *or* [micro-entity provisions] within CA 2006, Pt. 15, were approved by the board of directors on [ ] and signed on its behalf.

---

s. 419(1)   The directors' report must be approved by the board of directors and signed on behalf of the board by a director or the secretary of the company.

s. 419(2)   If the report is prepared in accordance with the small companies regime, the directors' report must contain (in a 'prominent position' above the signature of a director or secretary required by s. 419(1)) a statement that the report has been prepared in accordance with the provisions applicable to companies subject to the small companies regime as set out within CA 2006, Pt. 15 relating to small companies.

Example 6.2

Section 419 Directors' statement – directors' report

Small companies regime

This report has been prepared in accordance with the special provisions relating to companies subject to the small companies regime within CA 2006, Pt. 15.

6.8.2 Directors' statement – small company audit exemption entitlement: Section 475

The audit exemption criteria for a small company are explained in **Chapter 13**. A small company eligible for audit exemption is required to provide a statutory statement in accordance with CA 2006, s. 475(2) to appear in the balance sheet above the director's signature of approval.

Example 6.3

Section 475 Directors' statement – entitlement to exemption from audit (Balance sheet)

For the financial year ended 31 December 2016, the company was entitled to exemption from audit under CA 2006, s. 477 relating to small companies and the members have not required the company to obtain an audit of its accounts for the year in question in accordance with s. 476*. The directors acknowledge their responsibilities for complying with the requirements of the *Companies Act* 2006 with respect to accounting records and the preparation of accounts.

---

* S. 477 relates to the exemption for small companies; if the company is dormant, replace s. 477 with s. 480, and if the company is claiming the subsidiary audit exemption, replace with s. 479A. See **Chapter 12.**

6.8.3 Directors' statement – directors' responsibilities

Where a small company is subject to audit, it is necessary (in order to accord with international standards on auditing) to prepare a more detailed statement appearing, generally, within the directors' report.

ISA (UK and Ireland) 700 (last revised in September 2014), *The independent auditor's report on financial statements*, requires the auditor's report to include a statement that those charged with governance are responsible for the preparation of the financial statements and a statement that the responsibility of the auditor is to audit and express an opinion on the financial statements in accordance with applicable legal requirements and International Standards on Auditing (UK and Ireland).

FRC Bulletin 2010/2, *Compendium of illustrative auditor's reports on United Kingdom private sector financial statements for periods ended on or after 15 December 2010 (revised)*, envisages a 'Directors' Responsibilities Statement' within the financial statements or accompanying information (for example, in the directors' report) to include an adequate statement of directors' responsibilities. Specific reference is made to this statement in the auditor's report.

Example 6.4 provides an example directors' responsibilities statement based on FRC Bulletin 2010/2 (Revised) (FRC Bulletin Appendix 17 Example 47).

An independent accountants' report on unaudited (audit-exempt) accounts, should, on the same basis, include a statement that the directors are responsible for the preparation of the accounts.

Example 6.4

Example Directors' Responsibilities Statement
Auditor's reports on financial statements in the United Kingdom

FRC Bulletin 2010/2 (Revised) Appendix 17 *Example 47*
Directors' responsibilities statement

The directors are responsible for preparing the Directors' Report and the financial statements in accordance with applicable law and regulations.

Company law requires the directors to prepare financial statements for each financial year. Under that law, the directors have elected to prepare the financial statements in accordance with United Kingdom Generally Accepted Accounting Practice (United Kingdom Accounting Standards and applicable law). Under company law the directors must not approve the financial statements unless they are satisfied that they give a true and fair view of the state of affairs of the company and of the profit or loss of the company for that period.

In preparing these financial statements, the directors are required to:

- select suitable accounting policies and then apply them consistently;
- make judgments and estimates that are reasonable and prudent;
- [state whether applicable UK Accounting Standards have been followed, subject to any material departures disclosed and explained in the financial statements *(not applicable for companies subject to the small companies regime and medium sized companies)*]; and
- prepare the financial statements on the going concern basis unless it is inappropriate to presume that the company will continue in business *[included where no separate statement on going concern is made by the directors]*.

The directors are responsible for keeping adequate accounting records that are sufficient to show and explain the company's transactions and disclose with reasonable accuracy at any time the financial position of the company and enable them to ensure that the financial statements comply with the *Companies Act* 2006. They are also responsible for safeguarding the assets of the company and hence for taking reasonable steps for the prevention and detection of fraud and other irregularities.

[Where the financial statements are published on the internet]

[The directors are responsible for the maintenance and integrity of the corporate and financial information included on the company's website. Legislation in the United Kingdom governing the preparation and dissemination of financial statements may differ from legislation in other jurisdictions.] [Author's note – not illustrated in FRC Bulletin 2010/2].

6.8.4   Directors' statement – disclosure of information to auditors

s. 418(2)   For audited companies, the directors' report must contain a statement as set out in **Example 6.5**.

Example 6.5

Directors' statement as to disclosure of information to auditors (Directors' report)

Statement of disclosure of information to auditors

The directors of the company who held office at the date of approval of this directors report confirm that:

- so far as they are aware, there is no relevant audit information needed by the company's auditors in connection with preparing their report, of which the company's auditors are unaware; and
- they have taken all the steps that they ought to have taken as a director in order to make themselves aware of any relevant audit information and to establish that the company's auditors are aware of that information.

In practice, the directors' statements provided in accordance with FRC Bulletin 2010/2 (Revised) **Appendix 17** and CA 2006, s. 418(2) (**Examples 6.4** and **6.5**) may be combined into one statement.

6.9   Small dormant companies

Dormant companies which are exempt from audit (as explained in **10.3 (Chapter 10)**) may file 'small company' accounts without an auditor's report, provided the balance sheet contains a statement by the directors in accordance with s. 475(2) (see Example accounts in **Chapter 13**).

Dormant subsidiaries are exempt from the obligation to file accounts if certain conditions are met.   *s. 448A*

Dormant subsidiary companies are exempt from the requirement to prepare and file accounts where certain conditions are met. See **10.7**.   *s. 394A*

6.10   Disclosure of directors' remuneration and benefits – small companies

SI 2008/409, Sch. 3 used to require disclosure of information about directors' remuneration. This Schedule was ommitted by SI 2015/980 with effect either for accounting periods commencing on or after 1 January 2015 if the directors so chose, or from 1 January 2016.

Directors' remuneration is a related party transaction, as defined by FRS 102, however for small entities following section 1A of that standard, disclosure of such transactions need only be made where they are not concluded under normal market conditions. This area is discussed in more detail within **Table 8.5**.   *FRS 102.1AC.35*

CA 2006, s. 413 provides for the disclosure of directors' benefits: advances, credit and guarantees.

In the case of a company that does not prepare group accounts, details of:

- advances and credits granted by the company to its directors; and
- guarantees of any kind entered into by the company on behalf of its directors,

must be shown in the notes to the company's individual accounts.   *s. 413(1)*

6.11   Summary of statements required

As you can see, the requirements relating to what can be prepared or filed by a small company and the additional statements needed are complex. The table below sets out a summary of the key requirements. (Note, the table does not deal with the additional statements regarding director's responsibilities and audit required by Bulletin 2010/2 and s. 418. These are dealt with, though, in **examples 6.4** and **6.5** above.)

Table 6.6   Summary of preparation and filing requirements

	Prepare	Extra statements required re preparation exemptions	ref.	File	Extra statements required re filing exemptions/*notes*	ref.
Small companies unabridged (not micro-entities)			s. 414(3)(b)			
Strategic report (note 1)	✗		s. 414A(1)	✗		
Directors' report (note 1)	✓	Statement required above the director's or secretary's signature: **The company has taken advantage of the small companies' exemptions in preparing the directors' report in Part 15 of the *Companies Act* 2006.** Example 6.2	s. 419(2)	✗		
Balance sheet	✓	The balance sheet must contain, in a prominent position above the signature a statement to the effect: **The financial statements have been prepared in accordance with the special provisions relating to companies subject to the small companies regime within CA 2006, Pt. 15.** Example 6.1	s. 396(1)(a), s. 414(3)(b)	✓	*Those notes not specific to the profit and loss will need to be filed with the balance sheet*	s. 444(1)
		Where the company has taken advantage of **audit exemption under s. 477 a statement is required to that effect and that the members have not required an audit under s. 476 and the directors' acknowledge their responsibility for the accounts.** Example 6.3	s. 475			

Table 6.6	*Summary of preparation and filing requirements (cont'd)*					
	Prepare	**Extra statements required re preparation exemptions**	**ref.**	**File**	**Extra statements required re filing exemptions/***notes*	**ref.**
Profit or loss account	✓		s. 396(1)(b)	✗	If P/L *is* filed a copy of any audit report must also be filed	s. 444(1) s. 444(2)
					If P/L or Directors' report *not* filed the B/S must contain a statement in a prominent position that the company's annual accounts and reports have been **delivered in accordance with the provisions applicable to companies subject to the small companies regime**	s. 444(5)
					If P/L *not* filed the copy of the B/S must **disclose that fact** and unless exemption from audit taken the notes to the B/S must **include information about audit report**, including any qualification or emphasis of matter and the name and firm of the senior statutory auditor … see **6.7.1**.	s. 444(5A) and s.444(5B)
Abridged						
Abridged profit or loss	optional			✗	Where the P/L or B/S is abridged a statement by the company that all the members of the company have **consented to the abridgment** must also be filed.	s. 444(2A)

Table 6.6 *Summary of preparation and filing requirements (cont'd)*						
	Prepare	Extra statements required re preparation exemptions	ref.	File	Extra statements required re filing exemptions/*notes*	ref.
Abridged balance sheet	optional	The balance sheet must contain, in a prominent position above the signature a statement to the effect: **The financial statements have been prepared in accordance with the special provisions relating to companies subject to the small companies regime within CA 2006, Pt. 15.** Example 6.1	s. 414(3)	✓	Where the P/L or B/S is abridged a statement by the company that all the members of the company have **consented to the abridgment** must also be filed.	s. 444(2A)
		Where the company has taken advantage of audit exemption under **s. 477 a statement is required to that effect and that the members have not required an audit under s. 476 and the directors' acknowledge their responsibility for the accounts.** Example 6.3	s. 475			
					Abridged accounts also require all the statements listed above for small companies unabridged where filing exemptions under s. 444 taken.	s. 444
Micro-entities						
Strategic report	✗		s. 414A(1)	✗		
Directors' report	✗		s. 415(1A)	✗		
Balance sheet and notes	✓	The balance sheet must contain, in a prominent position above the signature of the directors, a statement that **the financial statements are prepared in accordance with the micro-entity provisions of the *Companies Act* 2006.** Example 7.1	s. 396(1)(a) s. 414(3)	✓	If P/L or Directors' report **not** filed the B/S must contain a statement in a prominent position that the company's annual accounts and reports have been **delivered in accordance with the provisions applicable to companies subject to the small companies regime.** See 6.7.1	s. 444(1) s. 444(5)

	Prepare	Extra statements required re preparation exemptions	ref.	File	Extra statements required re filing exemptions/*notes*	ref.
Table 6.6 **Summary of preparation and filing requirements (cont'd)**						
		Where the company has taken advantage of audit exemption under s. 477 **a statement is required to that effect and that the members have not required an audit under s. 476 and the directors' acknowledge their responsibility for the accounts. Example 7.3**	s. 475			
Profit or loss account	✓		s. 396(1)(b)	✗	No statement regarding any audit report need be made in micro-entity accounts.	s. 444(1) s. 444(5C)
Abridged accounts (note 2)	✗		Sch 1.1A	N/A		
Notes						
1	Exemption also available if company otherwise small, but for being part of ineligible group					
2	Abridged accounts are only available in respect of the formats in SI 2008/409, Sch. 1, Section B which are the formats for small companies. Section C contains the forms for micro entities and therefore no abridgement is possible. There is no abridgement of the directors' report.					

6.12 Disclosure of auditor's remuneration – small audited companies

Requirements for the disclosure of auditors' remuneration in respect of small and medium-sized companies are provided by the *Companies (Disclosure of Auditor Remuneration and Liability Limitation Agreements) Regulations* 2008 (SI 2008/489), as amended by the *Companies (Disclosure of Auditor Remuneration and Liability Limitation Agreements) (Amendment) Regulations* 2011 (SI 2011/2198).

Remuneration receivable by a small company's auditor for auditing the accounts must be disclosed in a note to the annual accounts. Remuneration includes benefits in kind and the nature and estimated money-value of those benefits must also be disclosed. (Note however, that this requirement is expected to be repealed in June 2016 when the EU audit directive is implemented in the UK legislation.)

reg. 4(1)–(2)

Where more than one person has been appointed as a company's auditor in respect of any financial period, separate disclosure is required in respect of the remuneration of each such person.

SI 2008/489, reg. 4(1)–(3)

A small eligible parent company preparing audited group accounts must disclose consolidated auditor's remuneration information on the basis of SI 2008/489, reg. 6, in which case the parent company's individual accounts need not disclose auditor's remuneration.

SI 2008/489, reg. 6

Chapter 7   Contents of micro-entity accounts

7.1   Introduction

This chapter summarises the micro-entities accounts provisions of CA 2006 as they affect companies under the 'micro-entities regime'. Details of the criteria for companies to qualify under the regime are dealt with in **5.4**. Note that the regime currently only applies to companies, is not available for charities and is not available to LLPs until expected legislation is passed (due in summer 2016).

The *Small Companies (Micro-Entities' Accounts) Regulations* 2013 (the micro-entities regulations) modified CA 2006, Pt. 15 and 16 and the *Small Companies and Groups (Accounts and Directors' Report) Regulations* 2008 (SI 2008/409) for financial years ended on or after 30 September 2013. There were some further amendments as a result of SI 2015/980, although these are of minor importance to micro-entities.

7.2   Accounts – provisions for micro-entities

The accounts of a company qualifying as a 'micro-entity' (see **Chapter 5**) have significantly reduced statutory disclosure requirements compared even to 'small' companies.

A micro-entity can also take advantage of reduced requirements with respect to filing with the Registrar of Companies, using the same part of the Companies Act applying to small companies s. 444, which permit only the balance sheet and notes to be filed (see **Table 6.6**).

Company accounts prepared in accordance with the micro-entities regime are referred to as 'micro-entity accounts' in this book. These always refer to the individual accounts of the entity; note that entities preparing group accounts cannot apply the micro-entities regime to their individual financial statements. (See **Chapter 5** for more details.)

A micro-entity does not have to take advantage of all the exemptions and modifications permitted if it does not wish to do so.

Consideration must be given to other users of the financial statements (such as banks) before an entity opts to prepare accounts under this regime. As the disclosure requirements are minimal, these users may require additional information to be prepared.

In addition, if the micro-entity plans to voluntarily have an audit, careful consideration should be made of the fact that this regime is not a 'fair presentation framework' as defined by ISAs and consequently it is not possible to merely state in the audit report that the accounts are true and fair based on their deemed true and fair status in law. A draft amendment to ISA 210 (UK and Ireland) identifies the risk of any audit report being misleading and the steps required to deal with this. In practice, it may be safer and more appropriate to adopt a different framework for reporting if an audit is required.

7.3   Format of micro-entity accounts

The form and content of individual accounts prepared by micro-entities are determined in accordance with regulations provided by the *Small Companies and Groups (Accounts and Directors' Report) Regulations* 2008 (SI 2008/409).

7.3.1   The statutory formats

The accounts formats from which a micro-entity may choose are given in SI 2008/409, Sch. 1 (Pt. 1, Section C).

There is a choice of two balance sheet formats and there are no choices with respect to profit and loss account format.

Balance sheet

In its annual accounts, a micro-entity must adopt one of the formats of balance sheet set out in SI 2008/409, Sch. 1 (Pt. 1, Section C). The formats are also illustrated in **Table 7.1**.

Profit and loss account

The profit and loss account format for a micro-entity is set out in SI 2008/409, Sch. 1 (Pt. 1, Section C). The format is also illustrated in **Table 7.2**.

Accounting principles

The general accounting principles of the small company regulations must be applied by micro-entities unless they are specifically amended by the micro-entities regulations. See **7.9** for details of differences.

Accounting principles are explained further in **3.5** (**Chapter 3**).

Micro-entity accounts, properly prepared, are deemed by law to give a true and fair view. However, as discussed above this is not considered a fair presentation framework from an auditing standards point of view, it is instead a compliance framework.

7.4   Micro-entity balance sheet

The formats of balance sheet from which a micro-entity must choose for its annual accounts are set out in SI 2008/409, Sch. 1 (Pt. 1, Section C) and are reproduced in **Table 7.1**.

Table 7.1 Micro-entity balance sheets	
Format 1	Format 2
A Called up share capital not paid B Fixed assets C Current assets D Prepayments and accrued income E Creditors: amounts falling due within one year F Net current assets (liabilities) G Total assets less current liabilities H Creditors: amounts falling due after more than one year I Provisions for liabilities J Accruals and deferred income K Capital and reserves	ASSETS A Called up share capital not paid B Fixed assets C Current assets D Prepayments and accrued income --- CAPITAL RESERVES AND LIABILITIES A Capital and reserves B Provisions C Creditors (aggregate amounts falling due within one year and after one year must be shown separately) D Accruals and deferred income

7.5   Micro-entity profit and loss account

The format of the profit and loss account which a micro-entity must prepare is set out in SI 2008/409, Sch. 1 (Pt. 1, Section C) and is reproduced in **Table 7.2**.

Table 7.2   *Micro-entity profit and loss account format*

A   Turnover
B   Other income
C   Cost of raw materials and consumables
D   Staff costs
E   Depreciation and other amounts written off assets
F   Other charges
G   Tax
H   Profit or loss

Note that the above headings cannot be changed (unlike items with Arabic numbers in the small company accounts format set out in **Table 6.5**).

Sch. 1.1(3)

7.6   Footnotes to the balance sheet – micro-entities

No notes to the accounts are required under the micro-entities regime; however, there are some limited additional items that must appear at the foot of the balance sheet. These are disclosures relating to the following more detail in respect of which is provided in **9.2.4**:

- Directors' benefits – advances, credit and guarantees
  CA 2006, s. 413 provides for the disclosure of advances and credits granted by a company to its directors, and guarantees of any kind entered into by a company on behalf of its directors (see **6.10**).

  s. 413
  reg. 5A
- Guarantees and other financial commitments
  Particulars of charges on assets, contingent liabilities, capital commitments not provided for, pension commitments and other financial commitments.

  Sch. 1.57
- Information about the company including:
  - the part of the UK in which the company is registered;
  - its registered number;
  - its registered office address;
  - whether it is a public or private company and whether it is limited by shares or guarantee; and
  - where appropriate the fact that it is being wound up.

  s. 396(A1)

FRS 105 additionally requires information about the identification of the company including:

- the name of the company and any change in its name since the preceding reporting period;
- the date of the end of the reporting period and the period covered by the financial statements;
- the presentation currency; and
- the level of rounding, if any, used in the financial statements.

FRS 105.3.13

7.7   Directors' report of a micro-entity

A micro-entity is now exempt from the requirement to prepare a directors' report, following the implementation of SI 2015/980.

s. 415(1A)

7.8   Directors' statements

A company which qualifies as a micro-entity in relation to a financial year (other than a dormant company) and takes advantage of the provisions applicable to companies subject to the micro-entities regime with respect to the preparation of annual accounts must include statements in its accounts, on the balance sheet, confirming preparation in accordance with the micro-entities regime.

s. 414(3)

For small (unquoted) companies, every copy of any balance sheet (and if prepared, the directors' report and strategic report) that is published by or on behalf of the company must state the name of the person who signed it on behalf of the board. **Table 6.6** provides a summary of directors' statements.

s. 433

s. 414   ### 7.8.1   *Directors' statement – micro-entity accounts preparation:*

A company's annual accounts must be approved by the board of directors and signed on behalf of the board by a director of the company. The signature must be on the company's balance sheet.

If the accounts are prepared in accordance with the provisions applicable to companies subject to the micro-entities regime, the balance sheet must contain (in a 'prominent position' above the signature of a director required by s. 414(3)) a statement to that effect. See **Example 7.1** below and also **Table 6.6**.

Example 7.1

Section 414 Directors' statement – balance sheet

The accounts are prepared in accordance with the micro-entity provisions of the *Companies Act* 2006.

7.8.2   *Directors' statement – small company audit exemption entitlement: section 475*

A micro-entity eligible for the small companies' audit exemption is required to provide a statutory statement in accordance with CA 2006, s. 475(2) to appear in the balance sheet above the director's signature of approval, as set out in **Example 7.3** below.

Example 7.3

Section 475 Directors' statement – entitlement to exemption from audit (Balance sheet)

For the financial year ended 31 December 2016 the company was entitled to exemption from audit under CA 2006, s. 477 relating to small companies and the members have not required the company to obtain an audit of its accounts for the year in question in accordance with s. 476. The directors acknowledge their responsibilities for complying with the requirements of CA 2006 with respect to accounting records and the preparation of accounts.

7.8.3   *Directors' statement – directors' responsibilities*

Where a micro-entity is subject to audit, it is necessary (in order to accord with International Standards on Auditing) to prepare a more detailed statement appearing, generally, within the directors' report.

The ISA (UK and Ireland) 700 (revised in June 2013), *The independent auditor's report on financial statements*, requires the auditor's report to include a statement that those charged with governance are responsible for the preparation of the financial statements and a statement that the responsibility of the auditor is to audit and express an opinion on the financial statements in accordance with applicable legal requirements and International Standards on Auditing (UK and Ireland).

APB Bulletin 2010/2, *Compendium of illustrative auditor's reports on United Kingdom private sector financial statements for periods ended on or after 15 December 2010 (revised)* (last updated April 2014), envisages a 'Directors' Responsibilities Statement' within the financial statements or accompanying information (for example, in the directors' report) to include an adequate statement of directors' responsibilities. Specific reference is made to this statement in the auditor's report.

See **Chapter 6**, **Example 6.4**.

As mentioned above in **7.2**, there are draft changes to ISA 210 to deal with the fact that the micro-entity regime is not a fair presentation regime as defined in the ISAs and that further steps may be needed to avoid the auditor's report being misunderstood. It is also expected that there will be amendments to ISA 700 in the summer of 2016.

An independent accountants' report on unaudited (audit-exempt) accounts, should, on the same basis, include a statement that the directors are responsible for the preparation of the accounts.

7.8.4   Directors' statement – disclosure of information to auditors

For audited companies, the directors' report must contain a statement that so far as each of the directors, at the time the report is approved, is aware: *s. 418(2)*

- there is no relevant audit information of which the company's auditor is unaware; and
- the directors have taken all steps that they each ought to have taken to make themselves aware of any relevant audit information and to establish that the company's auditor is aware of that information.

See **Chapter 6 Example 6.5**.

7.9   Differences in accounting treatment between small companies and micro-entities

7.9.1   General accounting principles

The general accounting principles of the small company regulations must be applied by micro-entities unless they are specifically amended by the micro-entities regulations.

Also, if a micro-entity chooses to disclose information additional to the minimum requirements, it shall have regard to the provisions of the relevant accounting standard, including the disclosure requirements.

7.9.2   FRS 105 requirements for micro-entities

FRS 105 *The Financial Reporting Standard applicable to the Micro-entities Regime* was issued by the FRC in 2015 and contains the requirements for micro-entities for accounting periods commencing on or after 1 January 2016, but with early adoption available. FRS 105 is based on FRS 102, but with significant simplifications. The requirements of the standard are looked at in more detail in **Chapter 9**. The micro-entity regulations state that fair value accounting as set out in SI 2008/409 cannot be applied in micro-entity accounts and therefore micro-entities applying the micro-entities regime are not able to revalue any fixed assets or current assets. As a result, any previous revaluations would need to be reversed if advantage is to be taken of the micro-entities regime.

As investment properties are not to be revalued, the micro-entities regime may significantly simplify the accounting burden for investment property companies. Even with significant balance sheet totals before evaluation of size, if their turnover is no more than £632,000, they have fewer than ten employees and otherwise meet the micro-entity criteria, the need for annual revaluations of investment property will cease.

7.9.3   Transitional requirements

Section 28 of FRS 105 sets out transitional arrangements to be applied for the first period of adoption of the standard. In outline, the section requires items to be remeasured and represented on the basis of the new requirements in FRS 105. However, there are a number of transitional exceptions and exemptions which either mandatorily, in the case of the former, or optionally, in the case of the latter, mean that retrospective accounting is not done or is limited in some way. This is discussed further in **9.2.6**.

Chapter 8   Essentials of FRS 102 for small entities

8.1   Essentials of FRS 102 for small entities

Small entities have, in the past, made use of the FRSSE, *The Financial Reporting Standard for Smaller Entities*. This was a cut down version of full UK GAAP both in terms of presentation and disclosure and the recognition and measurement of items. It also combined the Companies Act requirements for small entities with the accounting standard to create a 'one-stop shop'.

As set out in **Chapter 1**, the FRSSE has now been withdrawn and small entities must use FRS 102. One very important point to note is the fact that the recognition and measurement requirements within FRS 102 apply equally to all entities applying the standard, whether small or not. There are no simplifications in terms of accounting treatment for small companies (unless they are micro-entities adopting the micro-entity regime, as dealt with in **Chapter 9**).

Set out below is a table summarising the key areas of difference between the FRSSE, FRS 102 and the micro-entities regime. Note that there are many other more minor differences as well and a full understanding of FRS 102 is required to prepare a set of small company accounts correctly. This volume's role is to focus on the presentation and disclosures required for companies. If you need further guidance discussing in depth, the full requirements of FRS 102 and how they should be implemented refer to CCH Online and Navigate GAAP as well as other Wolters Kluwer volumes, such as Applying New UK GAAP and the Deloitte GAAP series.

Table 8.1   Summary of key measurement similarities and differences between FRSSE, FRS 102 and FRS 105

FRSSE (2015)	FRS 102 for small entities	FRS 105 for micros
Fixed assets can be at cost or value	Fixed assets can be at cost or value	No revaluations permitted
Development expenditure may be capitalised or written off	Development expenditure may be capitalised or written off	Development expenditure <u>must</u> be written off as incurred
Borrowing costs may be capitalised	Borrowing costs may be capitalised	Borrowing costs <u>must</u> be written off as incurred
Only cash settled share-based payments are recognised	Full recognition of cash or equity settled share-based payments	No requirement to account for equity settled share-based payments prior to the issue of the shares
Grants received must be recognised on the accruals basis	Grants received can be recognised on the accruals or performance basis (charities must use the performance basis)	Grants received <u>must</u> be recognised on the accruals basis.
Goodwill and intangibles shall not be revalued	Intangibles may be measured using the cost or valuation model. Goodwill shall not be revalued	Revaluation of goodwill and intangibles is not permitted

---

Table 8.1   Summary of key measurement similarities and differences between FRSSE, FRS 102 and FRS 105 (cont'd)

FRSSE (2015)	FRS 102 for small entities	FRS 105 for micros
Purchased goodwill is amortised over its useful life with a maximum life of five years (FRSSE 2015) if there is no reliable estimate	Purchased goodwill is amortised over its useful life with a maximum life of ten years where there is no reliable estimate	Purchased goodwill is amortised over its useful life with a maximum life of ten years where there is no reliable estimate
An entity may prepare consolidated accounts using the principles in full UK GAAP	An entity may prepare consolidated accounts using section 9 of FRS 102	An entity is not permitted to prepare consolidated accounts
Intangibles acquired as part of an acquisition are separately recognised only if they are separable	Intangibles acquired as part of a business combination are recognised separately if identifiable (either separable or arising from legal or contractual rights)	If a micro-entity effects a trade and assets acquisition then it applies section 19 of FRS 102 except it does not separately recognise intangible assets, deferred tax or share-based payments
Contracted rate for foreign currency transactions may be used instead of spot rate	Transactions must be translated at the spot rate and any derivative contract for foreign currency held at fair value through profit and loss unless hedge accounting rules used	A contracted rate/forward rate for a foreign currency must be used to translate the transaction
Derivatives are recognised at cost (which is often zero)	Derivative contracts are recognised at fair value through profit and loss (or using the hedge accounting rules)	Derivative contracts are recognised at cost (which is often zero)
Debt/equity distinction required as per old UK GAAP	Debt/equity distinction similar to old UK GAAP	Simplified debt/equity distinction rules
No requirement to impute interest where loan is at below market rate and not repayable on demand	Requirement to impute interest where loan is at other than at market rate and not repayable on demand	No requirement to impute interest where loan is at below market rate and not repayable on demand
Investments in ordinary or preference shares would be measured at cost less impairment, with an option to measure at current cost	Investments in equity instruments must be measured at fair value, where a reliable value is available	Investments in ordinary or preference shares are measured at cost less impairment
Deferred tax is recognised using timing difference method	Deferred tax is recognised using timing difference 'plus' approach, meaning there is deferred tax on valuations	No deferred tax is recognised
Defined benefit pension schemes' net liability or asset should be recognised in the balance sheet (assets at fair value and liabilities at actuarial valuation)	Defined benefit pension schemes' net liability should be recognised as the difference between the present value of its obligations and the fair value of the assets. Various other differences in accounting also exist	Contributions for the year for defined benefit schemes should be recognised together with any liability for agreed deficit funding

Table 8.1   Summary of key measurement similarities and differences between FRSSE, FRS 102 and FRS 105 (cont'd)

FRSSE (2015)	FRS 102 for small entities	FRS 105 for micros
Related party transactions need disclosing (including names for FRSSE 2008, but not FRSSE 2015)	There is a limited list of related parties and only disclosure of transactions not concluded under normal market conditions is required	No related party transaction disclosure is required
No specific rules on agriculture and biological assets	Option for agriculture businesses to have biological assets stated at fair value with changes to profit and loss	Biological assets are measured at the lower of cost and estimated selling price less costs to complete and sell (i.e. NRV)

8.1.1   The structure of FRS 102

FRS 102 *The Financial Reporting Standard applicable in the UK and Republic of Ireland (2015)* is similar to the FRSSE, in that it is a single document, divided into sections which deal with different topics. In total, there are 35 sections as shown in the table below. In particular note that it is section 1A which deals with the presentation and disclosure requirements for small entities and that defined terms are shown in the standard in bold with the definitions in the Glossary, Appendix 1 to the full standard.

Table 8.2   Structure of FRS 102

Section 1   *Scope* 1.1–1.15

Section 1A   *Small Entities* 1a.1–1a.22

Section 2   *Concepts and Pervasive Principles* 2.1–2.52

Section 3   *Financial Statement Presentation* 3.1–3.25

Section 4   *Statement of Financial Position* 4.1–4.14

Section 5   *Statement of Comprehensive Income and Income Statement* 5.1–5.11

Section 6   *Statement of Changes in Equity and Statement of Income and Retained Earnings* 6.1–6.5

Section 7   *Statement of Cash Flows* 7.1–7.21

Section 8   *Notes to the Financial Statements* 8.1–8.7

Section 9   *Consolidated and Separate Financial Statements* 9.1–9.38

Section 10   *Accounting Policies, Estimates and Errors* 10.1–* 10.23

Section 11   *Basic Financial Instruments* 11.1–11.48c

Section 12   *Other Financial Instruments Issues* 12.1–12.29a

Section 13   *Inventories* 13.1–13.22

Section 14   *Investments in Associates* 14.1–14.15a

Section 15   *Investments in Joint Ventures* 15.1–15.21a

Section 16   *Investment Property* 16.1–16.11

Section 17   *Property, Plant and Equipment* 17.1–17.32a

Section 18   *Intangible Assets other than Goodwill* 18.1–18.29a

Section 19   *Business Combinations and Goodwill* 19.1–19.33

Section 20   *Leases* 20.1–20.35

Section 21   *Provisions and Contingencies* 21.1–21.17a

Section 22   *Liabilities and Equity* 22.1–22.19

Table 8.2   Structure of FRS 102 (cont'd)

Section 23	*Revenue 23.1–23.32*
Section 24	*Government Grants 24.1–24.7*
Section 25	*Borrowing Costs 25.1–25.3a*
Section 26	*Share-based Payment 26.1–26.23*
Section 27	*Impairment of Assets 27.1–27.33a*
Section 28	*Employee Benefits 28.1–28.44*
Section 29	*Income Tax 29.1–29.27*
Section 30	*Foreign Currency Translation 30.1–30.27*
Section 31	*Hyperinflation 31.1–31.15*
Section 32	*Events after the End of the Reporting Period 32.1–* 32.11*
Section 33	*Related Party Disclosures 33.1–33.14*
Section 34	*Specialised Activities 34.1–pbe34.97*
Section 35	*Transition to this FRS 35.1–35.15*
Approval by the FRC	
Appendix I:	Glossary
Appendix II:	Significant differences between FRS 102 and the IFRS for SMEs
Appendix III:	Table of equivalence for UK Companies Act terminology
Appendix IV:	Note on legal requirements a4.1–a4.3
Appendix V:	Previous consultations a5.2–a5.3
Appendix VI:	Republic of Ireland (RoI) legal references

8.1.2   Small companies – true and fair view

As set out in **Chapter 3**, there is an overriding requirement for UK Companies Act accounts (including small company accounts) to give a true and fair view. Therefore, even if the disclosures listed in section 1A and any other Companies Act disclosures are given, further information might still be necessary in order to give a true and fair view.

This point is perhaps now particularly important, as there are very limited disclosure requirements for small companies in the law. In addition, the FRC was unable, due to legal restrictions, to add to the legal disclosure requirements. This means it is more likely than with FRSSE compliant accounts that small company accounts compliant with the individual rules within FRS 102 will need extra disclosures.

To aid the preparer of accounts, the FRC has indicated particular areas where extra disclosures are encouraged. A number of these are in Appendix AD1 in section 1A, but others are scattered throughout section 1A. We will look at these points as we go through the chapter. Remember though, that for a particular entity's accounts there might be other disclosures or presentation changes required in order to give a true and fair view.

Reaching a judgment on any extra disclosures required may in practice be fraught with uncertainty. As discussed in **3.3.1**, the FRC Document True and Fair View provides some guidance on the issue, but as true and fair as a concept develops it may be necessary to update your thinking based on current understanding at the time of preparing the accounts.

8.2 FRS 102, section 1A requirements

8.2.1 Scope

Section 1A sets out the information that must be presented and disclosed in the financial statements of a small entity that chooses to apply the small entity regime. Unless a requirement of the rest of FRS 102 is specifically excluded in section 1A it applies to a small entity.

If a small entity wishes, it can adopt FRS 101 (if eligible), IFRS or full FRS 102 instead of the section 1A variant.

The requirements of this section apply to all small entities, even if they do not report under the Companies Act. If this is the case the entity complies with as much of the Act and small company regulations as it can to the extent permitted by its statutory framework.

Note that whilst there is no mention of it in FRS 102 small charities will not in practice be able to make use of section 1A as Bulletin 1 to the Charity SORP requires all charities to follow the FRS 102 SORP. The disclosure requirements in this generally exceed those in section 1A. Those wishing to prepare charity accounts should refer to CCH Preparing Charity Accounts. Additionally, the legislation for LLPs that would align the Regulations with section 1A is not expected to be implemented until the summer of 2016.

8.2.2 A complete set of financial statements of a small entity

Section 1A sets out the paragraphs of FRS 102 which a small entity is not required to comply with, all of which relate to presentation and/or disclosure. To aid use of FRS 102 by small entities the FRC has added asterisks against disclosure requirements in individual sections which still apply to small entities. For instance paragraph 3.24a requires disclosure of the legal form of the entity, its country of incorporation and the address of its registered office or principal place of business, if different, for all entities.

Those paragraphs which small entities are exempt from when applying section 1A and a brief description of their content are set out in the table below:

Table 8.3	**Exemptions from FRS 102 paragraphs for small entities (102.1A.7 and 102.1A.17)**
Paragraph	**Summary of content**
3.3	Explicit and unreserved statement of compliance with FRS 102
PBE 3.3A	Explicit and unreserved statement that entity is a PBE if applying those PBE paragraphs
3.9	Going concern disclosures
3.17	List of complete set of financial statements, including statement of comprehensive income; statement of financial position; statement of changes in equity; statement of cash flows; notes, etc.
3.18	If the only changes to equity are prior year adjustments and dividends, can use Statement of Income and Retained Earnings
3.19	If no items of other comprehensive income (OCI) may present only income statement or label bottom line profit or loss
3.24(b)	A description of the nature of the entity's operations and principal activities, unless in business review or similar
Section 4	Statement of Financial Position
Section 5	Statement of Comprehensive Income and Income Statement
Section 6	Statement of Changes in Equity and Statement of Income and Retained Earnings
Section 7	Statement of Cash Flows
Sections 8–35 disclosure requirements only (102.1A.17)	All remaining sections of the standard – a small entity is required to apply these sections, except for the paragraphs dealing with disclosures, though these should be considered in terms of giving a true and fair view

A complete set of financial statements for a small entity therefore comprises:

- a statement of financial position in accordance with 1A.14;
- an income statement in accordance with 1A.14; and
- notes in accordance with 1A.16–1A.20.

FRS 102.1A9

A small entity is also encouraged to include a statement of comprehensive income where it has such items to report and either a statement of income and retained earnings or a statement of changes in equity where it has transactions with equity holders to report. Neither of these latter two statements are required by law though, unlike the items listed above.

In addition to the statements the following disclosures are required by FRS 102 paragraph 3.23 where there is no exemption for small entities (emphasis added by author):

'**3.23** An entity shall clearly **identify each of the financial statements** and the **notes** and distinguish them from other information in the same document. In addition, an entity shall **display the following information prominently**, and repeat it when necessary for an understanding of the information presented:

(a) the **name** of the reporting entity and any change in its name since the end of the preceding reporting period;

(b) whether the financial statements cover the **individual entity or a group** of entities;

(c) the **date** of the end of the reporting period and the period covered by the financial statements;

(d) the **presentation currency**, as defined in Section 30 *Foreign Currency Translation*; and

(e) the **level of rounding**, if any, used in presenting amounts in the financial statements.'

8.2.3   Comparatives

As might be expected, a small entity is still required to present comparative information, unless FRS 102 specifically excludes this (e.g. for fixed asset notes, the reconciliation for both small and larger entities does not have to be repeated for the previous period).

8.2.4   Alternative titles

A small entity may use titles for the financial statements other than those used in the FRS as long as they are not misleading. So for example, the term balance sheet can be used instead of statement of financial position, or profit and loss account instead of income statement.

8.2.5   Formats

The income statement and statement of financial position must be presented in accordance with the requirements set out in either Part 1 (General Rules and Formats of Schedule 1) to the Small Company Regulations or Part 1 (General Rules and Formats of the Schedule) to the Small LLP Regulations. Note however, that as at the time of writing the new legislation to reflect the equivalent requirements of SI 2015/980 for LLPs has not yet been enacted, though is likely to be in the summer of 2016. This means that LLPs cannot, in effect, use section 1A of FRS 102, or the micro regime until the new Regulations are issued. (This volume does not deal in any detail with the requirements for LLPs, which also require the application of the LLP SORP. CCH's *Preparing LLP Accounts* will cover this in due course.)

Guidance on application of the formats is set out in FRS 102 Appendix B and is also dealt with in **Chapter 6**.

8.2.6 Notes

Information, as always, is only required to be disclosed if material.

As a minimum, a small entity has to provide all of the disclosures set out in section 1A Appendix C (i.e. FRS 102 1AC). Items which are also highlighted in other sections as being applicable to a small entity are marked with an asterisk in this section too.

In addition, a small entity is encouraged to make the disclosures in Appendix D (i.e. FRS 102 1AD).

8.2.7 Consolidated financial statements

If a small entity chooses to prepare consolidated financial statements it needs to apply section 9 *Consolidated and Separate Financial Statements* and is encouraged to provide the disclosures in 9.23. Otherwise, it follows section 1A as far as practicable and includes the disclosures required by Sch. 6 of the Small Company Regulations (SI 2008/409).

Sch. 6

8.3   Appendices A and B to section 1A – commentary

Appendix A and B are integral to the standard and set out requirements in respect of:

- adapted accounts; and
- abridged accounts.

8.3.1   Abridged Accounts

The requirements for abridged accounts are contained in the Small Company Regulations, Sch. 1.1A(1). They are discussed in more detail in **Chapter 11**, but note that they are not the same as the old abbreviated accounts, which have now been abolished.

Abridged accounts show more limited disclosure, for example commencing the income statement with gross profit rather than turnover and providing less detail on fixed assets. They do, however, still need to give a true and fair view as these are the accounts that shareholders receive, as well as the ones used for filing. In order to take advantage of the option to prepare abridged accounts 100% of the members must consent for the year in question and that consent must be confirmed in a statement to the registrar (it is expected that its inclusion within the notes to the balance sheet will be sufficient to meet this requirement).

8.3.2   Adapted Accounts

SI 2015/980 brought with it the concept of adapted accounts. These serve two basic purposes, first, to allow a more IFRS style of presentation (particularly important for FRS 101 accounts, but not especially relevant for FRS 102 accounts). Second, to allow the use of the newer, IFRS style terminology in FRS 102 as an option. So for example, whilst the Companies Act formats refer to Tangible Fixed Assets, FRS 102 calls them Property, Plant and Equipment. The effect of the option to adapt accounts essentially allows either new or old terminology to be used as long as it makes sense.

If a small company chooses to adapt its balance sheet then it must as a minimum present the following items distinguishing those that are current and non-current:

FRS 102.1AA.3

Table 8.4   Adapted balance sheet list

(a) property, plant and equipment;
(b) investment property carried at fair value through profit or loss;
(c) intangible assets;
(d) financial assets (excluding amounts shown under (e), (f), (j) and (k));
(e) investments in associates;
(f) investments in jointly controlled entities;
(g) biological assets carried at cost less accumulated depreciation and impairment;
(h) biological assets carried at fair value through profit or loss;
(i) inventories;
(j) trade and other receivables;
(k) cash and cash equivalents;
(l) trade and other payables;
(m) provisions;
(n) financial liabilities (excluding amounts shown under (l) and (m));
(o) liabilities and assets for current tax;
(p) deferred tax liabilities and deferred tax assets (classified as non-current);
(q) non-controlling interest, presented within equity separately from the equity attributable to the owners of the parent; and
(r) equity attributable to the owners of the parent.

FRS 102.1AA.4

Certain subclassifications of the above items are also required:

(a) property, plant and equipment in classifications appropriate to the small entity;
(b) goodwill and other intangible assets;
(c) investments, showing separately shares and loans;
(d) trade and other receivables, showing separately amounts due from related parties and amounts due from other parties;
(e) trade and other payables, showing separately amounts payable to trade suppliers and amounts payable to related parties; and
(f) classes of equity, such as called up share capital, share premium, retained earnings, revaluation reserve, fair value reserve and other reserves.

FRS 102. 1AB.3

A small entity choosing to adapt its profit and loss account formats must, as a minimum, include the following items:

(a) revenue;
(b) finance costs;
(c) share of the profit or loss of investments in associates (see section 14 *Investments in Associates*) and jointly controlled entities (see section 15 *Investments in Joint Ventures*) accounted for using the equity method;
(d) profit or loss before taxation;
(e) tax expense excluding tax allocated to other comprehensive income or equity; and
(f) profit or loss.

There is some flexibility in 1AA.5 and 1AB.4 to include additional line items or amend the descriptions and ordering where necessary to properly explain the financial position or performance, providing it is at least equivalent.

8.4   Required disclosures – Section 1A Appendix C

Section C deals with the notes required for small entities. These notes must be presented in the order in which, where relevant, the items to which they relate are presented in the statement of financial position or income statement. Whilst usually this would be the order used in any case, it does limit the ability to group similar items together, for instance financial instruments, which might

Sch. 1.42(2)

fall across a number of different headings in the accounts.

Set out in the table below is a precis of the disclosure requirements for companies adopting section 1A of FRS 102 as permitted for small entities.

Table 8.5   Required notes for small entity FRS 102 section 1A Appendix C

Accounting policies

Accounting policies

Sch. 1.44 and 102.1AC.3

Development costs capitalised, the reason, amortisation period and details if not treated as realised loss.

Sch. 1. 21(2), s. 844 and 102.1AC.4 and 5

Period over which intangible assets are being written off when their useful life cannot be reliabliy estimated.

Sch. 1.22(4) and 102. 1AC.6

Prior year adjustments and changes in policies or presentation

Details of any changes in presentation of a small entity's accounts, including the reason for the change.

Sch. 1.2(2) and 102.1AC.7

Any particulars of non-comparability in preceding year amounts that have been adjusted.

Sch. 1.7(2) and 102.1AC.8

> *This point might be applicable in a small company's first FRS 102 accounts. There are no specific requirements for transition disclosures for small entities (though they are encouraged in FRS 102.1AD.1), so if not given elsewhere information on changes in the accounts would be required. This might be in the form of a description of the item changed, the reason for the change and the amounts involved, for example.*

Where any amount relating to a preceding period is included in the income statement.

Sch. 1.61(1) and 102.1AC.9

> *This latter point refers to situations where an amount relating to a previous period is not dealt with by means of a prior year adjustment and so is recognised in the income statement. It seems at first glance that this is unlikely to occur very often as material changes in presentation or prior year errors are required by the standard to be dealt with as a prior year adjustment.*
>
> *However, an area where it might occur is in respect of taxation for example, or other changes in accounting estimates. If last year's current taxation figure has now changed, due to the finalisation of the tax return, any difference is recognised this year. The disclosure used to be taken account of in the required tax note under FRSSE 9.2 and would be required by FRS 102, paragraph 29.26 if the full standard were being followed. As neither of these is applicable, this general disclosure requirement will pick up such changes in estimates which result in material amounts relating to a preceding year impacting this year's income statement.*

True and fair override

Any true and fair override, including particulars of the override, the reason and its effect.

Sch. 1.10(2)

Notes supporting the balance sheet

Where an asset or liability relates to more than one item in the balance sheet, the relationship must be disclosed.

Sch. 1.9A and 102.AC.11

> *For example, a liability split into less and more than one year components needs a note to explain that they are part of the same item.*

Fixed assets

Details of fixed asset movements in the year (e.g. a fixed asset note, comparatives not required).

Sch. 1.48(1), 1.48(2) and 102.1AC.12

Details of depreciation/impairments in respect of fixed assets (usually as part of the fixed asset note, again comparatives not required).

Sch. 1.48(3) and 102.1AC.13

Table 8.5   Required notes for small entity FRS 102 section 1A Appendix C (cont'd)

Fixed assets measured at revalued amounts

Sch. 1.34(2)
102.1AC.14,
Sch 1.49 and
102.1AC.15

Details regarding fixed assets held at revalued amounts (excluding investment property and biological assets), including the basis of valuation, the year in which assets were valued and in the year of valuation the persons who valued them or the particulars of their qualifications for doing so and the basis used.

Sch. 1.34(4) and
102.1AC.16

The historic cost amount of any item measured at a revalued amount, i.e. its comparable cost and accumulated depreciation/impairments.

Sch. 1.54(2) and
102.1AC.17

A table of revaluation movements for all fixed assets measured at a revalued amount, showing movements in revaluation reserve, explanation of tax treatments and carrying amount in the balance sheet had they not been revalued.

> *Note that the above two items essentially require equivalent historic cost data for the cost; cumulative depreciation; and/or impairments and the net carrying value of revalued assets.*

Sch. 1.35(6) and
102.1AC.18

The treatment for taxation purposes of amounts debited or credited to the revaluation reserve.

Capitalisation of borrowing costs

Sch. 1.27(3) and
102.1AC.19

If borrowing costs are capitalised within the cost of an asset the amount of interest included is disclosed in a note.

Impairments

Sch. 1.19(3) and
102.1AC20

Any provision for impairment of fixed assets, including fixed asset investments must be disclosed separately.

Sch. 1.20(2) and
102.1AC.21

Any provision for impairment of fixed assets that are reversed because the reasons for them have ceased to apply must be disclosed.

Fair value measurement

Where financial instruments or other assets have been measured at fair value through profit and loss (FVTPL) disclosure is required of:
- significant assumptions underlying the valuation models and techniques;
- for each categoriy of financial instrument or other asset the fair value of the assets in that category and the change in value:

Sch. 1.51(2)(a),
(b) and 102.
1AC.22

  - included directly in the income statement;
  - credited/debited to the fair value reserve.

Sch. 1.51(2)(c)
and 102.1AC.23

Where financial instruments or other assets measured at FVTPL for each class of derivatives state the extent and nature of the instruments, including significant terms and conditions that may affect the amount, timing and certainty of future cash flows.

Sch. 1.51(3)
and 102.1AC.24

Where any amount is transferred to/from the fair value reserve provide a table of movements.

Sch. 1.41(2)
and 102.1AC.25

The treatment for taxation purposes of amounts credited or debited to the fair value reserve must be disclosed.

> *Accounting for financial instruments under FRS 102 is in many cases significantly more complex than under old UK GAAP. In particular all derivatives and a number of other financial instruments are required to be recognised at fair value through profit and loss (FVTPL). The Act sets out a basic rule that only realised profits can be included in the profit and loss, Sch. 1.13, but then Sch. 1.40 amends this with regard to financial instruments, investment property and biological assets.*
>
> *The upshot of this is that gains might be included in the profit or loss which are not realised, for instance gains on unlisted equity investments or investment properties perhaps, that cannot be easily sold. It therefore becomes important to record the level of distributable and non-distributable reserves. There is currently no required disclosure of these figures (unless needed to provide a true and fair view), but it may be easier to include a note within the accounts showing how much of the reserves are not distributable, in order not to lose track of the figure if recorded elsewhere.*

Table 8.5   Required notes for small entity FRS 102 section 1A Appendix C (cont'd)

Financial instruments measured at fair value

Financial instruments which under IAS may be included at fair value (e.g. investments in associates, subsidiaries or joint ventures) may be so included if the IAS disclosures are given.

Sch. 1.36(4) and 102.1AC.26

Indebtedness, guarantees and financial commitments

For the aggregate of all items shown under creditors state amounts:
- which are payable/repayable otherwise than by instalments and fall due in more than five years; and
- if due by instalments state any amount of instalment due in more than five years.

Sch. 1.55(1) and 102.1AC.27

State the amount of any creditors for which any security has been given indicating the nature and form of security.

Sch. 1.55(2) and 102.1AC.28

The total amount of any financial commitments, guarantees and contingencies that are not included in the balance sheet must be stated. Separate disclosure of pension commitments and amounts undertaken for group entities or those in which there is a participating interest is required.

Sch. 1.57(1), (3), (4) and 102.1AC.29

An indication of the nature and form of any valuable security given by the entity in respect of commitments, guarantees and contingencies as above.

Sch. 1.57(2) and 102.1AC.30

Disclosure of material off balance sheet arrangements, such as risk sharing debt-factoring, securitisation, take or pay and operating lease arrangements, etc. must be made.

s. 410A and 102.1AC.31

Notes supporting the income statement

Amount and nature of any items of income or expense of exceptional size or incidence.

Sch. 1.61(2) and 102.1AC.32

Average number of employees employed.

s. 411 and 102.1AC.33

> As these are described as income statement notes, it seems likely that they would not be required when filing, as the profit and loss and related notes, are not required to be filed. However, it is not clear exactly which notes are and are not required to be filed so it might be the case that further guidance is issued in the future. In the absence of such guidance, it may be safer to include this information in what is delivered to the Registrar.

Related party disclosures

Where the small entity is a subsidiary disclose, in respect of the smallest group for which consolidated accounts are prepared:
- the name of the parent;
- the address of the registered office; or
- if unincorporated its principal place of business.

Sch. 1.65 and 102.1AC.34

Particulars of material transactions with the small entity that have not been concluded under normal market conditions (though if preferred all such transactions, whether concluded under normal market conditions or not can be disclosed) with:
- owners holding a participating interest;
- companies in which the entity has a participating interest; and
- the small entity's directors (or members of its governing body).

Table 8.5   Required notes for small entity FRS 102 section 1A Appendix C (cont'd)

Particulars include:
(a) the amount of such transactions;
(b) the nature of the related party relationship; and
(c) other information about the transactions necessary for an understanding of the financial position of the small entity.

Information of a similar nature may be aggregated.

Sch. 1.66 and 102.1AC.35

Particulars of transactions between two or more members of the group, where any subsidiary is 100% held need not be given.

Applying the requirements in practise

This is a very important change from the previous requirements for disclosure of related party transactions for small entities. First, the list of related parties has been significantly reduced, so now, for instance, close family members of directors are not included unless they are related parties in their own right. This will mean that permanent file lists of related parties will need updating.

Second, only transactions not concluded under normal market conditions need to be disclosed, though the standard clarifies that if the entity prefers it can meet the disclosure requirements by including all transactions with related parties, whether or not concluded under normal market conditions.

Third, there is no specific mention of materiality to the individual who is the related party. Under old UK GAAP (though not FRSSE), materiality needed to be judged in terms of both the entity and the related party. However, there is no mention of this materiality to the individual in FRS 102. This doesn't necessarily mean that there is no relevance of the impact on the individual as of course materiality is always judged by its nature as well as magnitude. What it does mean though, is that consideration of materiality for related party transactions is essentially done in the same way as for other items in the financial statements, looking at qualitative and quantitative aspects.

The question arises, particularly in the case of directors' remuneration and dividends, as to whether such transactions are concluded under normal market conditions. The view of the author is that it is normal for small companies, often owned and run by the directors, to make decisions about remuneration based on factors such as how profitable a company is and the tax impact of the different methods of profit extraction.

In my view, most of the time it seems likely that such remuneration and dividend are therefore concluded under normal market conditions. However, there is scope for further guidance to be issued by the FRC or other authoritative bodies clarifying what is meant by normal market conditions or for different commentators to have a different view, or for this view to change over time.

For instance, if the legislation was intended to mean not at normal market rates for instance, a different answer on disclosure might well be reached. In the absence of further guidance a practical course of action would be to consider whether in your view there is anything that appears not to be concluded under normal market conditions and if so to ensure disclosure. The alternative is to disclose all such items as a catch-all, although arguably it would be necessary to state if a transaction was not concluded under normal market conditions as part of explaining the transaction.

Details of advances, credits and guarantees to directors must be disclosed. In respect of an advance or credit:
(a) its amount;
(b) an indication of the interest rate;
(c) its main conditions;
(d) any amounts repaid;
(e) any amounts written off; and
(f) any amounts waived.

Also required are the total amounts under (a), (d), (e) and (f).

Table 8.5   Required notes for small entity FRS 102 section 1A Appendix C (cont'd)

Details for a guarantee are:
(a) its main terms;
(b) the amount of the maximum liability that may be incurred by the entity; and
(c) any amount paid and any liability incurred by the entity for the purpose of fulfilling the guarantee (including any loss by reason of enforcement).

The totals of (b) and (c) must also be given.

s. 413 and 102.1AC.36

The requirements here have not changed from the previous ones, which presented some problems in terms of the way that s. 413 is drafted, as effectively it requires disclosure of each advance to a director. Where a current account is used with frequent changes in an overdrawn balance this can be problematic. A practical solution is to aggregate similar amounts, if not individually material. In many cases a template like the one below, together with separate disclosure of any individually material items, might enable the disclosure requirements to be met in a practical manner:

	£
Opening balance	*X*
Plus loans made in the period (advances)	*X*
Plus private expenditure in the period	*X*
Less undrawn remuneration	*(X)*
Less loan repayments in the period	*(X)*
Less dividends declared in the period	*(X)*
Closing balance	*X*

An article in May 2010 by the ICAEW Audit and Assurance faculty suggested a seven point approach to establish the disclosures needed:

(1) Create a chronological record of transactions between the company and the director to establish whether there were any 'advances' (i.e. whether the account was overdrawn at any time).

(2) Identify opening and closing debit balances and the maximum amounts outstanding (the account may be overdrawn on more than one occasion and be rectified in between times).

(3) Identify individually material advances in the overdrawn periods and list them separately (loans exceeding £10,000 in aggregate require prior approval by the members).

(4) Identify any other individually material advances (e.g. where the director used company money for personal purposes) and consider whether these need reporting separately.

(5) Aggregate the remaining advances.

(6) Identify amounts repaid by the director, listing material amounts individually and separately.

(7) Compile the note, adding details of interest, security, etc.

Other

The financial statements must state:
(a) the part of the UK in which the entity is registered;
(b) its registered number;
(c) whether it is public or private and whether limited by shares or guarantee;
(d) address of registered office; and
(e) if applicable the fact that it is being wound up.

s. 396 and 102.1AC.37

Where arabic numbers have been combined the individual amounts so combined (unless immaterial).

Sch. 1.4(3) and 102.1AC.38

Sch. 1.64 and
102.1AC.39

> **Table 8.5 Required notes for small entity FRS 102 1A Appendix C (cont'd)**
>
> The nature and financial effect of material post balance sheet events not reflected in the financial statements.
>
> **Entities subject to audit**
>
> Although not mentioned in FRS 102, the requirements for disclosure of auditors' remuneration where an audit is carried out for a small entity have not yet been repealed. A small company must therefore disclose the amount of remuneration, including any benefits in kind, paid to the company's auditor in respect of audit. SI 2008/489, reg. 4 In addition, details of any limitation of liability clause that the company has entered into with the auditor also needs to be disclosed.

SI 2008/489,
reg. 8

8.5 Encouraged disclosures – Section 1A Appendix D

This section sets out disclosures which a small entity is encouraged to provide where relevant:

(a) a statement of compliance with the FRS;
(b) a statement that it is a public benefit entity, if relevant;
(c) disclosures regarding going concern (see **8.6**);
(d) dividends declared and paid/payable in the period; and
(e) an explanation of transition as set out in FRS 102.35.13.

As mentioned before in **3.3**, small company accounts are still required to show a true and fair view. With the more limited disclosure requirements embodied in legislation and the standard itself, this means there is more likelihood of extra disclosures being required. Appendix D sets out some areas where the FRC particularly believe that disclosures which are not required might nonetheless be desirable or even necessary to give a true and fair view. A discussion of the relevance of each of these points follows.

8.5.1 A statement of compliance with FRS 102

A statement of compliance with FRS 102, whilst not required, seems a helpful piece of information to include, especially given the options for various versions of new UK GAAP.

8.5.2 A statement that the entity is a public benefit entity

As FRS 102 contains some differential accounting treatments for Public Benefit Entities (PBEs) the normal requirement for non-small entities is to disclose that the entity is in fact a PBE. Whilst small companies are not required to disclose this it might be helpful, especially if the alternative policies available to PBEs have been used.

8.5.3 Going concern

As mentioned above, the requirements in FRS 102, paragraph 3.9 to disclose material uncertainties related to events or conditions that cast significant doubt upon the entity's ability to continue as a going concern, is not applicable to small entities.

However, Appendix D encourages going concern disclosures to be made. So what should the preparer of accounts include? The basic answer is that 'it depends', but as a small entity's accounts still need to give a true and fair view, it is likely in practice that going concern disclosures **will** be necessary.

In October 2015, the FRC issued a draft document '*Guidance on the Going Concern Basis of Accounting and Reporting on Solvency and Liquidity Risk*'. The comment period only closed on 31 January 2016 so at the time of writing no final version of the guidance is available. However, the guidance encourages going concern disclosures to be made not only when an issue arises, but as a more normal part of reporting. Additionally, it encourages directors to think of both an assessment of going concern in the accountancy sense and of the viability of the business in terms of the entity's ability to continue in operational existence.

Even though these disclosures will not be required, as such, by a small entity applying section 1A of FRS 102, the guidance might, once finalised, provide useful information on what procedures for monitoring risks relating to going concern and viability a business should have and what disclosures might sensibly be needed.

8.5.4 Dividend disclosure

Whilst the FRC encourages this disclosure there are many small companies that would prefer not to provide this information. In some cases, it might be considered necessary to give a true and fair view, but there are likely to be many situations in which it is not considered essential. Whilst dividends will also fall to be treated as a related party transaction in many cases, disclosure of these is only required where the transaction has not been concluded under normal market conditions. Again, it seems likely that most dividends will not require disclosure, although see also the discussion about directors' remuneration in **Table 8.5** above.

8.5.5 Transition

Section 35 of FRS 102 deals with the adjustments required on transition to the new standard. The section sets out various exceptions (mandatory) and exemptions (optional) from the basic requirement to restate all figures for the current and comparative period using the new policies as required in FRS 102. The complexity of this exercise will depend on the particular transactions and balances that the entity has and also on the various accounting policy choices made. **Table 8.1** can be used as a rough guide to the areas where accounting policy changes are likely to be required and reference can be made to section 35 to see if there is a relevant exemption.

Although there is no requirement for small companies to provide specific disclosures on transition as listed in section 35, there is a requirement to give basic information about changes in accounting policies. Also, as there is a requirement for even small company accounts to give a true and fair view, consideration will be needed as to whether transition disclosures are necessary to acheive this. It is likely to be helpful for many small entities to provide at least a simple reconciliation of balance sheet figures as altered at the date of transition. The transition date is the beginning of the earliest comparative period presented in the accounts, so for a December year-end entity preparing its first FRS 102 accounts in 2016 the date of transition will be 1 January 2015.

Sch. 1.2(2) and 102.1AC.7

Disclosures might be set out for example as shown in the FRC Staff Education Note 13 (extract below), or a brief summary in narrative form, with key figures, of the changes could be given.

Reconciliation of equity			
		At 1 Jan 2014	At 31 Dec 2014
	Note	CU '000	CU '000
Capital and reserves (as previously stated)		2,678	2,807
Recognition of derivative financial instruments	(i)	(2)	1
Re-measurement of stock using spot exchange rate	(ii)	–	(1)
Short-term compensated absences	(iii)	(5)	(6)
Capital and reserves (as restated)		2,671	2,801

Reconciliation of profit or loss for the year

	Note	Year ended 31 Dec 2014
		CU '000
Profit for the year (as previously stated)		129
Recognition of derivative financial instruments	(i)	3
Re-measurement of stock using spot exchange rate	(ii)	(1)
Short-term compensated absences	(iii)	(1)
Profit for the year (as restated)		130

Financial instruments

(1) Entity F was not previously required to recognise derivative financial instruments on the balance sheet. Instead the effects of the derivative financial instruments were recognised in profit or loss when the instruments were settled. Derivative financial instruments are classified as 'other financial instruments' in FRS 102 and are recognised as a financial asset or a financial liability, at fair value, when an entity becomes party to the contractual provisions of the instrument. Consequently, financial assets of CU15,000 and financial liabilities of CU17,000 have been recognised in the opening balance sheet at 1 January 2014. Financial assets of CU18,000 and financial liabilities of CU17,000 have been recognised in the balance sheet as at 31 December 2014. Derivatives are measured to fair value with gains (losses) from changes in fair value recognised in profit or loss. The effect on profit for the year ended 31 December 2014 is an increase of CU3,000.

(2) The derivative financial instruments are foreign exchange forward contracts. In applying SSAP 20 *Foreign currency translation*, Entity F previously chose to translate purchases in foreign currencies at the rate of exchange specified in a matching forward contract. This is not permitted by FRS 102, which requires purchases to be translated using the spot exchange rate on the date of the transaction. FRS 102 does not provide an exemption from measuring stock bought in a foreign currency and paid for before the transition date in accordance with its required accounting policies, but the difference is not material and accordingly no adjustment has been made. Items purchased since the transition date have been remeasured based on spot exchange rate. Consequently, stock at 31 December 2014 has been reduced and cost of sales for the year end has been increased by CU1,000 and costs of CU2,000 have been reclassified as administrative expenses rather than cost of sales.

Short-term compensated absences

(1) Prior to applying FRS 102, Entity F did not make provision for holiday pay (i.e. holiday earned but not taken prior to the year-end). FRS 102 requires the cost of short-term compensated absences to be recognised when employees render the service that increases their entitlement. Consequently an additional accrual of CU5,000 at 1 January 2014 has been made to reflect this. The additional provision at 31 December 2014 is CU6,000 and the effect on profit for the year ended 31 December 2014 is an additional expense of CU1,000.

8.6 Small company accounts and checklist

A checklist for small company accounts under section 1A (not abridged) is given in **Appendix E**.

Example accounts are shown in **Part III Chapter 14.2**.

Chapter 9   Essentials of FRS 105 for micro-entities

9.1   FRS 105 The Financial Reporting Standard applicable to the Micro-entities Regime

FRS 105 *The Financial Reporting Standard applicable to the Micro-entities Regime* sets out the requirements for entities (currently just companies) wishing to adopt the micro-entity regime. The standard was issued in July 2015 and is effective for accounting periods commencing on or after 1 January 2016, though early adoption is permitted.

Unlike FRS 102 for small entities, which contains only simplifications of presentation and disclosure and none of accounting treatments, FRS 105 is significantly simplified in all respects. A summary of the key differences between this standard, the (now withdrawn) FRSSE and FRS 102 is given in **Chapter 8 Table 8.1**. You will see from this that there may be considerable incentives for the very small, i.e. micro-entity, to adopt FRS 105 instead of FRS 102.

However, this standard is not always the best choice, even if an entity is eligible to use it, as its simplicity brings with it a number of limitations including the following:

- There are no policy choices, so for example, interest or development costs cannot be capitalised and deferrred tax cannot be recognised.
- There are no revaluations of any kind.
- The framework is not a fair presentation framework as defined by International Standards on Auditing (UK and Ireland) (ISAs) and therefore may not be particularly suitable for those entities wishing to have an audit.
- There is very limited information in the primary statements and virtually no information in the notes, which can make it difficult for a credit score to be allocated.

If these shortcomings are not relevant or important to the entity though, the standard provides a useful simple framework for accounting. It ignores many of the complexities introduced by FRS 102, such as the required recognition of derivatives and certain investments at fair value through profit and loss; imputed market rate interest where financing transactions exist and complications when dealing with foreign currency at the spot rate, rather than a forward or contracted rate.

FRS 105 is still based upon FRS 102 though, so users familiar with the main standard should find it relatively easy to get to grips with this new one.

9.1.1   The structure of FRS 105

Like FRS 102, FRS 105 is set out in sections, each dealing with a different topic. These sections are not quite the same as those in FRS 102 because some sections have been removed. The resulting sections and numbers are set out below in **Table 9.1**.

Table 9.1

Section 1   *Scope 1.1–1.4*
Section 2   *Concepts and Pervasive Principles 2.1–2.37*
Section 3   *Financial Statement Presentation 3.1–3.14*
Section 4   *Statement of Financial Position 4.1–4.4*
Section 5   *Income Statement 5.1–5.4*
Section 6   *Notes to the Financial Statements 6.1–6a.3*
Section 7   *Subsidiaries, Associates, Jointly Controlled Entities and Intermediate Payment Arrangements 7.1–7.8*
Section 8   *Accounting Policies, Estimates and Errors 8.1–8.17*
Section 9   *Financial Instruments 9.1–9.29*
Section 10   *Inventories 10.1–10.22*
Section 11   *Investments in Joint Ventures 11.1–11.9*
Section 12   *Property, Plant and Equipment and Investment Property 12.1–12.29*
Section 13   *Intangible Assets other than Goodwill 13.1–13.18*
Section 14   *Business Combinations and Goodwill 14.1–14.3*
Section 15   *Leases 15.1–15.33*
Section 16   *Provisions and Contingencies 16.1–16a.8*
Section 17   *Liabilities and Equity 17.1–17.15*
Section 18   *Revenue 18.1–18a.35*
Section 19   *Government Grants 19.1–19.10*
Section 20   *Borrowing Costs 20.1–20.2*
Section 21   *Share-based Payment 21.1–21.10*
Section 22   *Impairment of Assets 22.1–22.21*
Section 23   *Employee Benefits 23.1–23.22*
Section 24   *Income Tax 24.1–24.13*
Section 25   *Foreign Currency Translation 25.1–25.6*
Section 26   *Events after the End of the Reporting Period 26.1–26.10*
Section 27   *Specialised Activities 27.1–27.6*
Section 28   *Transition to this FRS 28.1–28.12*

Appendix I: Glossary
Appendix II: Table of equivalence for UK Companies Act terminology
Appendix III: Note on legal requirements a3.1–a3.6
Appendix IV: Republic of Ireland (RoI) legal references

9.1.2   Micro-entities: true and fair view

Unlike in a set of FRS 102 accounts for small entities, micro-entity accounts are presumed in law to give a true and fair view with only the specified presentation and disclosure requirements. There is generally no need to consider if any further disclosure is required.

The exception to this requirement is if the micro-entity accounts are actually misleading as a result of sticking solely to the legislative and FRS 105 requirements. If this is the case, the professional accountant has a duty to consider whether having their name associated with accounts that could be misleading might bring the profession into disrepute. The various professional bodies will have their own guidance on this, but the ICAEW Technical Release AAF 02/10 covers the issue for incorporated entities. Note that it is expected this release will be updated to include specific consideration of micro-entity accounts.

9.2   FRS 105 requirements

As already explained, the purpose of this volume is primarily to explain the presentation and disclosure issues related to small and micro-entity accounts. The detailed treatment of items from a recognition and measurement point of view is outside the scope of the book, but **Table 8.1** provides an overview of the differences between FRS 105, FRS 102 and FRSSE 2015. You will also find that FRS 105 itself is relatively straightforward to follow, especially if you are already familiar with FRS 102.

9.2.1 Scope

FRS 105 applies to the financial statements of a micro-entiy which, as explained above, are deemed to show a true and fair view. The FRS permits, but does not require, additional information to be included in a set of micro-entity accounts. If this is done, then reference should be made to section 1A of FRS 102 requirements in respect of the relevant item. Note that although additional information can be disclosed it is not possible to optionally change accounting policies from those listed in the standard. So for example, if a micro-entity wished to include deferred taxation in its accounts, it would need, instead, to apply FRS 102.

9.2.2 Concepts and pervasive principles

With the exception of the deemed true and fair view, the concepts and pervasive principles applying to micro-entity accounts are largely the same as apply to both old UK GAAP and FRS 102. So definitions of assets, liabilities, income, expenses and equity do not differ in their impact. However, as mentioned in **Chapter 8**, there is no option to revalue any asset so all measurement for assets is at cost/cost less impairment and amortisation as appropriate. Most liabilities are measured at the best estimate of the amount required to settle the liability. Other concepts included in FRS 105 will be familiar: going concern, the accruals concept, materiality, consistency of presentation and the provision of comparative information.

9.2.3 A complete set of financial statements

A complete set of micro-entity financial statements includes:

(a) a statement of financial position (balance sheet) with notes at the foot of the statement; and
(b) an income statement.   *s. 396(1)*

Companies Act individual accounts, including those of micro-entities, must state:

(a) the part of the United Kingdom in which the company is registered;
(b) the company's registered number;
(c) whether the company is a public or a private company and whether it is limited by shares or by guarantee;
(d) the address of the company's registered office; and
(e) where appropriate, the fact that the company is being wound-up.   *s. 396(A1)*

The entity should clearly identify each of the statements and the notes and in addition, prominently display:

(a) the name of the entity and any change of name since the last period;
(b) the date of period covered;
(c) the presentation currency; and
(d) the level of rounding.   *FRS 105.3.13*

Also, as set out in **Chapter 7 Example 7.1**, a statement is required that in accordance with s. 423(3) the financial statements are prepared in accordance with the micro-entity provisions. This statement is included on the statement of financial position in a prominent position above the signature.

The requirements for the format of the profit and loss and balance sheet are as set out in **7.4** and **7.5**.

9.2.4 Notes

A micro-entity set of accounts does not contain full notes as such, rather it just has a few footnotes to the balance sheet. These include:

(a) advances, credit and guarantees granted to directors as required by s. 413; and   *Sch. 1.5A and*
(b) financial commitments, guarantees and contingencies.   *Sch 1.57*

The detail of these legal requirements is set out for ease of use, within the Appendix to section 6 of FRS 105 itself. The requirements though, are the same as the equivalent requirement for small entities. In summary, disclosures are needed of:

Details of advances, credits and guarantees to directors must be disclosed. In respect of an advance or credit:

(a) its amount;
(b) an indication of the interest rate;
(c) its main conditions;
(d) any amounts repaid;
(e) any amounts written off; and
(f) any amounts waived.

Also required are the total amounts under (a), (d), (e) and (f).

Details for a guarantee are:

(a) its main terms;
(b) the amount of the maximum liability that may be incurred by the entity; and
(c) any amount paid and any liability incurred by the entity for the purpose of fulfilling the guarantee (including any loss by reason of enforcement).

s. 413 and 105.6A.1 The totals of (b) and (c) must also be given. (See **8.4** for a discussion of the practical issues with compliance with s. 413.)

Sch. 1.57(1), (3), (4) and 105.6A.2 **The total amount of any financial commitments, guarantees and contingencies** that are not included in the balance sheet must be stated. Separate disclosure of pension commitments and amounts undertaken for group entities or those in which there is a participating interest is required.

Sch. 1.57(2) and 105.6A.3 **An indication of the nature and form of any valuable security** given by the entity in respect of commitments, guarantees and contingencies as above.

9.2.5 Consolidated financial statements

A micro-entity is excluded from using the micro-entity regime and FRS 105 if it chooses to prepare consolidated accounts, or is included in consolidated accounts.

9.2.6 Transition

FRS 105 requires adjustments to be made on transition to implement, where necessary, new policies that are compliant with the standard. Section 28 of FRS 105 sets out the accounting treatment required, which is in general to put through a prior year adjustment for any changes needed. There are however, a number of exemptions and exceptions on transition to help simplify the process, so reference should be made to the standard to check if these apply.

One of the major changes that might be necessary for many micro-entities on transition to FRS 105 is to remove the effect of any revaluations that have previously been made. As the regime does not permit any fair value figures to be used it is necessary to 'unwind' any past revaluations and revert to cost. Additionally, as there is no deferred tax permitted under the standard any such figure will need to be reversed out through profit and loss reserves. The summary of differences in treatment set out in **Table 8.1** can help in identifying other areas where a transition adjustment may be required.

FRS 105 does not require any special disclosures related to transition, but a company can optionally decide to include extra disclosures should it wish. If this is done, reference should be made to the disclosure requirements in FRS 102, section 35.

9.3 Micro-entity model accounts

Example accounts for a micro-entity can be found in **Part III Chapter 14.3**.

Chapter 10 Dormant companies

10.1 Introduction

For the purposes of the Companies Act, a company is 'dormant' during any period in which it has no significant accounting transaction ('significant accounting transaction' is explained below in **10.2**).

s. 1169(1)

Dormant companies (as defined) qualify automatically for exemption from audit provided 10% of the members do not request an audit, as explained in **10.3** below.

Example accounts are provided in **Chapter 14**.

Conditions for audit exemption are subject to:

- the requirement for a statement to be contained in the balance sheet (see **10.5**);
- the right of members to require audit (see **10.3**); and
- companies excluded from dormant companies exemption (see **10.4**).

Dormant subsidiary companies meeting certain requirements may be exempt from preparing and filing individual accounts (see **10.7**).

10.2 Definition of 'dormant company'

A dormant company is a company which (during any period) has no 'significant accounting transaction'.

A 'significant accounting transaction' means a transaction which is required by CA 2006, s. 386 to be entered in the company's accounting records, *other than* transactions:

- consisting of penalties or payments to the Registrar of Companies for:
  - change of name fee;
  - re-registration fee *(on the re-registration of a company's status, e.g. to public company)*;
  - penalty for failure to deliver accounts *(under s. 453)*;
  - annual return registration fee; or
- arising from the taking of shares in the company by a subscriber to the memorandum, on the formation of the company.

s. 1169(2)

10.3 Conditions for exemption from audit

A company is exempt from the requirements for audit of its accounts in respect of a financial year if:

- it has been dormant since its formation; or
- it has been dormant since the end of the previous financial year.

s. 480

Further, to be exempt the company must also:

- be entitled to prepare its individual accounts in accordance with the small companies regime (see s. 381–384), or would be so entitled but for having been a public company or a member of an ineligible group; and
- not be required to prepare group accounts for that year.

There are circumstances where small companies which are part of a group are not entitled to the audit exemption. However, where a company is both a subsidiary undertaking and dormant throughout the whole of the period or periods during the financial year when it is a group company, it is entitled to the audit exemption.

s. 479(3)

CA 2006, s. 476 states that members of a company that would otherwise be entitled to exemption from audit may require it to obtain an audit of its accounts for a financial year by giving notice under the section. The notice must be given by members representing not less than:

s. 476
- 10% in total of the nominal value of the company's issued share capital (or any class of it); or
- 10% in number of the members of the company (for a company not having a share capital).

The notice may not be given before the financial year to which it relates and must be given not later than one month before the end of that year.

A dormant company is not entitled to audit exemption unless its balance sheet contains a statement or statements under CA 2006, s. 475(2) as explained in **10.5** below.

A dormant company is not exempt from audit (and an audit of the accounts is, therefore, necessary) if there is a specific requirement in the company's articles of association to appoint auditors.

10.4   Companies excluded from dormant companies' exemption

A company is not entitled to the exemption from audit (conferred by CA 2006, s. 480) if:

(a)   it was at any time within the financial year one of the following:
    (i)   an authorised insurance company;
    (ii)   a banking company;
    (iii)   an e-money issuer;
    (iv)   a MiFID investment firm;

SI 2007/2932
    (v)   a UCITS management company; or
s. 481   (b)   the company carries on insurance market activity.

10.5   Directors' statements – entitlement to exemption

A dormant company is not entitled to audit exemption unless its balance sheet contains a statement or statements by the directors to the effect that:

s. 480(3)

s. 475(1)–(2)
- the company is entitled to exemption from audit by virtue of CA 2006, s. 480 (dormant companies);
- the members have not required the company to obtain an audit of its accounts for the year in question in accordance with CA 2006, s. 476; and

s. 475(3)
- the directors acknowledge their responsibilities for complying with the requirements of CA 2006 with respect to accounting records and the preparation of accounts.

s. 475(3)

The statements required to entitle audit exemption as above must appear on the balance sheet above the signature required to approve the accounts under CA 2006, s. 414.

s. 475(4)

10.6   Dormant company acting as agent

SI 2015/980 removed the requirement to disclose that a dormant company was acting as agent.

10.7 Dormant subsidiary company exemption from preparing or filing accounts

The *Companies and Limited Liability Partnerships (Accounts and Audit Exemptions and Change of Accounting Framework) Regulations* 2012 (SI 2012/2301) introduced CA 2006, s. 394A which provides that for accounting periods ended on or after 1 October 2012, a dormant subsidiary company is exempt from the requirement to prepare and file accounts if it fulfils the following conditions:

s. 394A

(a)   its parent undertaking is established under the law of an EEA state;

(b)   the company's shareholders unanimously agree to the exemption in respect of the financial year in question;

(c)   the parent gives a statutory guarantee of all the outstanding liabilities to which the subsidiary is subject at the end of the financial year in accordance with CA 2006, s. 394C;

(d)   the company is included in the consolidated accounts drawn up for that year or to an earlier date in that year by the parent undertaking, which must be prepared in accordance with Directive 2013/34/EU or International Accounting Standards;

(e)   the use of the exemption by the subsidiary must be disclosed in the notes in the consolidated accounts drawn up by the parent;

(f)   the following documents must be filed by the directors of the subsidiary at Companies House on or before the date that they were due to file the subsidiary's accounts:

   (i)   written notice of the agreement in (b);

   (ii)   a statement by the parent that it guarantees the subsidiary company under the particular section of the Act;

   s. 394A, 448A

   (iii)   a copy of the consolidated annual report and accounts referred to in (d) and the auditor's report on those accounts;

   s. 448A

(g)   the company is not traded as defined in s. 474 of the Companies Act;

(h)   it is not an authorised insurance company, a banking company, an e-Money issuer, a MiFID investment firm or a UCITS management company, or carries on insurance market activity; and

(i)   it is not a trade union or an employer's association.

s. 394B, 448B

An annual return will still be required to be filed at Companies House.

If a dormant company is not entitled to the exemption from preparing and delivering its accounts, then it could opt for abridged accounts, as explained in **Chapter 11**. As for all other companies, abbreviated accounts are not available for accounting periods commencing on or after 1 January 2016.

10.8 Dormant companies and transition to new UK GAAP

Dormant companies may elect to retain their accounting policies for reported assets, liabilities and equity at the date of transition to this FRS until there is any change to those balances or the company undertakes any new transaction.

FRS 102.35.10(m)

This means that the change to GAAP does not require any immediate action for dormant companies. Changes will only be needed where something else happens that requires action to be taken. This exemption is offered in FRS 102, section 35 but it does not have to be taken. If desired, the dormant company could transition to FRS 102 in the normal way.

10.9 Dormant company model accounts

Example accounts for a dormant company may be found in **Part III Chapter 14.4**.

Chapter 11   Abridged accounts

11.1   Introduction

The *Companies, Partnerships and Groups (Accounts and Reports) Regulations* 2015 (SI 2015/980) removed the concept of abbreviated accounts from the legislation, but introduced instead 'abridged accounts'.

It is important to note that abridged accounts are not a separate set of accounts for filing, in the way that abbreviated accounts were, but rather a replacement to the full accounts that members would otherwise receive.

This means that abridged accounts, despite having a number of exemptions from a disclosure and presentation point of view, are still required to give a true and fair view.

11.2   Requirements for abridged accounts

Schedule 1.1A(1) and (2) to SI 2008/409 set out the regulations with regard to abridged accounts. The main sections are set out below:

'**1A(1)** Where appropriate to the circumstances of a company's business, the company's directors may, with reference to one of the formats in Section B, draw up an abridged balance sheet showing only those items in that format preceded by letters and roman numerals, provided that:

(a) in the case of format 1, note (5) of the notes to the formats is complied with;

(b) in the case of format 2, notes (5) and (10) of those notes are complied with; and

(c) all of the members of the company have consented to the drawing up of the abridged balance sheet.

1A(2) Where appropriate to the circumstances of a company's business, the company's directors may, with reference to one of the formats in Section B, draw up an abridged profit and loss account, combining under one item called 'Gross profit or loss':

(a) items 1, 2, 3 and 6 in the case of format 1, and

(b) items 1 to 5 in the case of format 2

provided that, in either case, all of the members of the company have consented to the drawing up of the abridged profit and loss account.

1A(3) Such consent as is referred to in sub-paragraphs (1) and (2) may only be given as regards the preparation of, as appropriate, the balance sheet or profit and loss account in respect of the preceding financial year.

1A(4) Sub-paragraphs (1) and (2) do not apply in relation to the preparation of, as appropriate, a company's balance sheet or profit and loss account for a particular financial year if the company was a charity at any time within that year.'

11.2.1   Consent of members and statement to the registrar

Notice that consent of all of the members of the company, each year, will be necessary in order to be able to issue abridged accounts instead of a normal set of section 1A accounts. The consent is required after the year-end and before the accounts are approved. This means it will only be practicable where there are a limited number of shareholders all of whom are content with receiving more limited information.

Sch. 1, 1A(2) and (3)

In addition, the directors must also deliver to the registrar a statement that all the members of the company have consented to the abridgement.

s. 444(2A)

11.2.2   Charities

Sch. 1.1A(4)

As might be expected the provisions are not available to charities.

11.2.3   Micro-entity accounts

Abridged accounts are not available for micro-entity accounts, as the legislation allows the abridgment of the formats in Sch. 1, Section B. The formats for micro-entities are in Section C of the Schedule. In any case, as micro-entity accounts are very limited in their contents, they should not find themselves at a disadvantage in this respect.

Sch. 1.1A(1) and (2)

11.2.4   Dormant companies

If dormant companies are not able or do not choose to take advantage of the exemption from preparing and filing their annual accounts, they would be able to use the abridged accounts option, if otherwise following the small, rather than micro-entity, legislation and standards. Given the likely lack of information in the dormant accounts, this might be a somewhat irrelevant point.

11.3   Contents of abridged accounts

As explained above, the abridged balance sheet needs only to show items prefixed with letters and roman numerals, with no requirement to show further analysis of these figures in the notes. This would mean, for example, that investment property would not be shown separately, as it is just an item within tangible assets. The only proviso is that as these accounts are still required to give a true and fair view, if separate disclosure were needed to acheive this then more detail than shown below would be required. (See **14.2** for example accounts showing the reduced detail in abridged accounts.)

If we take the formats set out in Sch. 1, Section B and delete the items with Arabic numbers, we are left with the following requirements:

11.3.1   Balance sheet formats – Format 1

A.	Called up share capital not paid
B.	Fixed assets
	I Intangible assets
	II Tangible assets
	III Investments
C.	Current assets
	I Stocks
	II Debtors *(5)*
	III Investments
	IV Cash at bank and in hand

D. Prepayments and accrued income

E. Creditors: amounts falling due within one year

F. Net current assets (liabilities)

G. Total assets less current liabilities

H. Creditors: amounts falling due after more than one year

I. Provisions for liabilities

J. Accruals and deferred income

K. Capital and reserves

  I Called up share capital

  II Share premium account

  III Revaluation reserve

  IV Other reserves

  V Profit and loss account

Note (5) Debtors

(Formats 1 and 2, items C.II.1 to 3.)

The amount falling due after more than one year must be shown separately for each item included under debtors and, in the case of format 2, the aggregate amount falling due after more than one year must also be shown.

11.3.2 Balance sheet formats – Format 2

ASSETS

A. Called up share capital not paid

B. Fixed assets

  I Intangible assets

  II Tangible assets

C. Current assets

  I Stocks

  II Debtors *(5)*

  III Investments

  IV Cash at bank and in hand

D. Prepayments and accrued income

CAPITAL, RESERVES AND LIABILITIES

A. Capital and reserves

  I Called up share capital

  II Share premium account

  III Revaluation reserve

  IV Other reserves

  V Profit and loss account

B. Provisions for liabilities

C. Creditors *(10)*

D. Accruals and deferred income

---

(5) Debtors

(Formats 1 and 2, items C.II.1 to 3.)

The amount falling due after more than one year must be shown separately for each item included under debtors and, in the case of format 2, the aggregate amount falling due after more than one year must also be shown.

(10) Creditors

(Format 2, Liabilities items C.1 to 4.)

Amounts falling due within one year and after one year must be shown separately for each of these items and for the aggregate of all of these items.

Note that although the balance sheet looks quite normal, as many of the arabic numbered items would have been relegated to a note, the difference here is that no such notes are required. So, for example, fixed assets are merely split between tangible and intangible with no further breakdown of their nature in the notes. Example accounts are given in Part III to this volume, with the items not required to be shown for abridged accounts marked in greyed-out text boxes.

11.3.3   Profit and loss format 1

Profit and loss account formats – Format 1

3   Gross profit or loss*

4   Distribution costs

5   Administrative expenses

7   Income from shares in group undertakings

8   Income from participating interests

9   Income from other fixed asset investments

10   Other interest receivable and similar income

11   Amounts written off investments

12   Interest payable and similar expenses

13   Tax on profit or loss

14   Profit or loss after taxation

19   Other taxes not shown under the above items

20   Profit or loss for the financial year

* Combining 1 Turnover, 2 Cost of sales and 6 Other operating income

---

11.3.4   Profit and loss format 2

Profit and loss account formats – Format 2

Gross profit or loss**

6   Staff costs

    (a) wages and salaries

    (b) social security costs

    (c) other pension costs

7   (a) Depreciation and other amounts written off tangible and intangible fixed assets

    (b) Amounts written off current assets, to the extent that they exceed write-offs which are normal in the undertaking concerned

8   Other operating expenses

---

9   Income from shares in group undertakings

10   Income from participating interests

11   Income from other fixed asset investments

12   Other interest receivable and similar income

13   Amounts written off investments

14   Interest payable and similar expenses

15   Tax on profit or loss

16   Profit or loss after taxation

21   Other taxes not shown under the above items

22   Profit or loss for the financial year

** *Combining 1 Turnover, 2 Change in stocks of finished goods and in work in progress, 3 Own work capitalised, 4 Other operating income, 5 a) Raw materials and consumables and b) Other external charges*

Note (11) *Cost of sales: distribution costs: administrative expenses*

(Format 1, items 2, 4 and 5.)

These items must be stated after taking into account any necessary provisions for depreciation or diminution in value of assets.

Note (12) *Income from other fixed asset investments: other interest receivable and similar income*

(Format 1, items 9 and 10; Format 2, items 11 and 12.)

Income and interest derived from group undertakings must be shown separately from income and interest derived from other sources.

Note (13) *Interest payable and similar expenses*

(Format 1, item 12; Format 2, item 14.)

The amount payable to group undertakings must be shown separately.

As you can see, the main difference in the profit and loss account format is that the starting point can be at gross profit, instead of turnover. It should be borne in mind however, that in some cases it might be considered necessary to show turnover and cost of sales (or other constituents of gross profit) in order to give a true and fair view.

11.4   Filing requirements

There is no difference in the filing obligations for a small company preparing abridged accounts or unabridged accounts. The filing requirements are set out in **Chapter 6** and a summary of the requirements to file are included in **Table 6.6**.

In outline the profit and loss and directors' report do not need to be filed, but the balance sheet and notes must be filed. As mentioned in **11.2.1** above, a statement must be filed with the registrar confirming that approval for the preparation of abridged accounts has been received from all of the members.

11.5   Small company abridged accounts checklist

A checklist for abridged accounts is included in **Appendix G**.

The model accounts in **Part III Chapter 14** indicate the areas not required for abridged accounts.

Chapter 12   Small groups

12.1   Small companies – option to prepare group accounts

If at the end of a financial year a company subject to the small companies regime is a parent company, the directors, as well as preparing individual accounts for the year, *may* prepare group accounts for the year. On this basis, a small parent company (as defined) is not, therefore, required to prepare group accounts.

s. 398

All other parent companies (being companies that are ineligible or excluded from the small companies regime under CA 2006, s. 384) *must* prepare group accounts for the year *unless* the company is otherwise exempt from that requirement under exemptions set out in CA 2006, s. 399(3).

Notwithstanding the above, a small parent company may prepare group accounts for its own management accounting purposes and not submit them to the Registrar of Companies but file instead its own individual statutory accounts with appropriate disclosures.

12.1.1   Summary of changes

Many of the requirements for small companies in group situations are not radically changed by the new Regulations. However, the key features of difference can be summarised as follows.

Area of change	Description	Reference
New small company limits	Many more companies will be eligible for the exemptions	s. 383
Changes to ineligibility for small regime	The presence of a plc in the group no longer makes the whole group ineligible and therefore unable to make use of the regime. However, if there is a traded company in the group, this will make the whole group ineligible.	s. 383(2)
Exemption from requirement to prepare group accounts for a plc, which would otherwise qualify, but for being a plc	To align with the exemption above, a plc is able to take advantage of the exemption to prepare group accounts, even though usually this would not be permitted.	s. 399(2A)
Disclosure of location of related undertakings address changed	The requirements now ask for the address of the registered office of the related undertaking regardless of whether it is in or outside the UK. Previously, just the country of incorporation was required if outside the UK.	Sch. 6

12.2   Qualifying conditions – group accounts exemptions

CA 2006, s. 383(4) and 466(4) set out the conditions to be met by a group for the parent company to qualify as 'small'.

A parent company qualifies as a small company in relation to a financial year only if the group headed by it qualifies as a small group.

s. 383(1)

The size classification of a parent company is determined firstly by considering whether the parent itself qualifies as small per s. 382. That section requires additional consideration of s. 383 if the

s. 383(1)
et seq.

company is a parent company. This has the effect that a parent only qualifies as small if the group (parent company and subsidiary undertakings) headed by it also qualifies as small.

A group qualifies as small in relation to the parent company's first financial year if the qualifying conditions are met in that year. In subsequent years, a group qualifies as small if the qualifying conditions:

- are met in that year and the preceding financial year;
- are met in that year and the group qualified as small in relation to the preceding financial year; or

s. 383(2)–(3)
- were met in the preceding financial year and the group qualified as small in relation to that year.

A group meets the qualifying conditions (and is, therefore, exempt from producing group (consolidated) accounts if it is a small group) if it does not exceed more than one of the following criteria on one or other of the following two bases: These limits are applicable for accounting periods commencing on or after 1 January 2016, or at the directors' option from 1 January 2015.

s. 383(4)–(7)

Criteria	*(The bases may be mixed)*	
	Net Basis	*Gross basis*
Small group (CA 2006, s. 383(4))		
Turnover	£10.2m	£12.2m
Balance sheet total	£5.1m	£6.1m
Average number of employees (on a monthly basis)	50	50

It is important to note that the 'net' and 'gross' bases may be mixed in determining whether the criteria have been met. For example, if a group has a turnover of £12m (gross) and £11m (net), a balance sheet total of £6.3m (gross) and £4.8m (net) and 60 employees, on the size criteria the group would qualify as a small group. The gross figure of £11m for the turnover is less than the gross limit of £12.2m and the net figure of £4.8m for the balance sheet, is less than the net limit of £5.1m. Therefore, although it exceeds the employee number threshold, it meets each of the other two criteria.

The aggregate figures are ascertained by aggregating the relevant figures from individual statutory accounts (determined in accordance with CA 2006, s. 382) for each member of the group.

The alternative bases for turnover and balance sheet totals (as qualifying conditions for exemption) as defined in the Act are:

(1) **'net'** means after any set-offs and other adjustments made to eliminate group transactions:
   (a) in the case of Companies Act accounts, in accordance with regulations under s. 404;
   (b) in the case of IAS accounts, in accordance with international accounting standards; and
(2) **'gross'** means without those set-offs and other adjustments. A company may satisfy any relevant requirement on the basis of either the net or the gross figure.

s. 383(6)

Care should be taken when making the adjustments to reach the 'net' figure, that *all* consolidation adjustments are made. So for example, the cost of investment is taken out, but goodwill is added in.

CA 2006 under SI 2008/409, Sch. 6 consolidation adjustments include:

- elimination of intra-group transactions and assets and liabilities;
- elimination of intra-group unrealised profits or losses; and
- adjustments to effect uniform accounting policies within the group.

Sch. 6.6

Because the gross thresholds are higher than the individual thresholds, it is possible for a group containing a medium sized company to be a small group, for example in the following circumstances.

Holding Company Limited owns 100% of its subsidiary, Subsidiary Limited (assume circumstances do not change year on year):

	Holding Company Limited	**Subsidiary Limited**
Turnover	£0	£10.8m
Balance sheet total	£250,000	£5.5m
Average number of employees	0	40
Ineligible?	No	No

On its own, Subsidiary Limited is a medium sized company as it breaches two out of three of the size criteria for two years in a row (see **Chapter 5**). However, the group headed by Holding Company Limited is small, as Holding Company Ltd is itself small and the group headed by it is small as the total turnover and total assets are both below the gross thresholds (as are the employee numbers).

This means that the parent is exempt from the requirement to prepare group accounts and exempt from audit. However, its subsidiary, as a medium sized company, will still require an audit.

Note, however, that if the example were the other way around and Holding Company Ltd was medium sized, there would be no question of the group being small, as it is both the parent and the group that must meet the criteria for it to be considered a small group. This is because the legislation is s. 382 must first be applied and it is then subject to the additional rules in s. 383 if the company is a parent (see **12.3**).

See **Appendix D** for a flowchart explaining small and subsidiary company audit exemption.

12.3 Medium-sized companies – group accounts

To be considered a small group, the parent company within the group must be a small company. Therefore, even if the gross income and balance sheet totals of a group are below the small group thresholds, if the *parent* is a medium-sized company (being companies that are ineligible or excluded from the small companies regime under CA 2006, s. 384) group accounts must be prepared *unless* the company is otherwise exempt from that requirement under exemptions set out in CA 2006, s. 399(3).

Note that the requirements in s. 384(2) changed slightly with the implementation of SI 2015/980 so that a plc in the group no longer causes the group to be ineligible. Only if there is a traded company within the group is the whole group ineligible from the small company regime. This change is effective in terms of judging audit exemption only from 1 January 2016. It can be applied early in terms of determining whether group accounts are required.

SI 2015/980
s. 2(3)

A further exemption was added with SI 2015/980 so that a company is exempt from the requirement to prepare group accounts if it would be subject to the small company regime but for being a public company and it is not traded.

s. 399(2A)

The other exemptions available are under:

- CA 2006, s. 400 (company included in EEA accounts of larger group);
- CA 2006, s. 401 (company included in non-EEA accounts of larger group); and
- CA 2006, s. 402 (no subsidiary undertakings need to be included in the consolidation).

CA 2006, s. 400–402 contain a number of requirements which must be met before a medium-sized company can take advantage of the exemptions provided by these sections. These sections of CA 2006 should be referred to before a conclusion is reached as to whether a company may take these exemptions.

Note that these detailed requirements change as a result of SI 2015/980 so care should be taken to ensure reference to the correct version of the Act dependent upon the date of the financial statements and whether the changes are being adopted early (in 2015) as permitted. Appendix B1 sets out the legislation. Further information on medium-sized company accounts can be found in CCH *Preparing FRS 102 Accounts*.

12.4   Preparing small group accounts

12.4.1   Companies Act small group accounts

Where the directors of a parent company, which is subject to the small companies regime and has prepared Companies Act individual accounts, choose to prepare Companies Act group accounts under CA 2006, s. 398 (Option to prepare group accounts), those group accounts must comply with the following provisions:

- Companies Act group accounts must state, in respect of the parent:
    - the part of the UK in which the company is registered;
    - the company's registered number;
    - whether the company is a public or a prrivate company and whether it is limited by shares or guarantee;
    - the address of the registered office; and

s. 404(A1)
    - where appropriate the fact that the company is being wound up.

(This is a new requirement inserted by SI 2015/980. The same disclosures are required for individual company accounts, where group accounts are not prepared.)

- SI 2008/409, Sch. 6 (Part 1) – Form and content of Companies Act group accounts (consolidated balance sheet and consolidated profit and loss account, and additional information to be provided by way of notes to the accounts);
- SI 2008/409, Sch. 6 (Part 2) – Information must be given with respect to the undertakings that are the subsidiary undertakings of the parent company at the end of the financial year:

Sch. 6.22(2)
    - the name of each undertaking;
    - the address of the undertaking's registered office;

Sch. 6.22(3)
    - if unincorporated its principal place of business;

Sch. 6.22(4)
    - whether the subsidiary is included in the consolidation and if not the reasons; and
    - by which conditions in s. 1162(2) or (4) the subsidiary is an undertaking of the immediate parent (unless subsection (2) and the immediate parent holds the same proportion of shares

Sch. 6.33(5)
as it holds voting rights).

Sch. 6.27
The equivalent information needs to be given for joint ventures (Sch. 6.26) and associated undertakings.

Sch. 6.23
Information must be given about the shares held in subsidiary undertakings by the parent and the group, including the identity of each class and the nominal value of the shares held of that class.

Sch. 6.24
Information must be given about subsidiaries not included in the consolidation, including the aggregate capital and reserves at the end of the year and its profit for the year.

Sch. 6.25
Information about the shares of the company held by subsidiary undertakings is required.

Sch. 6.28–33
Information about other significant (20% or more) shareholdings held by the parent that are not associated undertakings or joint ventures is required.

Sch. 6.34
Information where the parent company or group is a member of a qualifying entity (such as a qualifying partnership, or unlimited company in certain situations).

If the parent is itself a subsidiary then it must provide information about the parent which heads:

- the largest group of undertakings for which group accounts are drawn up and of which the company is a member and the smallest such group;
- the name of the undertaking;
- country of incorporation if outside the UK;
- if unincorporated its principal place of business; or
- where accounts can be obtained.   *Sch. 6.35*

Identification of the ultimate parent is required.   *Sch. 6. 36*

Further detail regarding the above disclosure requirements is given in **12.5**.

Note that Sch. 3 – information about the directors' benefits: remuneration (companies or IAS accounts) was omitted from the Small Company Regulations by SI 2015/980.

The group accounts of a small company are treated as having complied with any provision of SI 2008/409, Sch. 6 (Part 1) (Form and content of Companies Act group accounts) if they comply instead with the corresponding (additional) provisions of SI 2008/410, Sch. 6 (Part 1) the *Large and Medium-Sized Companies and Groups (Accounts and Reports) Regulations* 2008.

12.4.2   Small groups and FRS 102

A small group voluntarily preparing group accounts may take advantage of the provisions and exemptions afforded by FRS 102, section 1A (see **8.5**) but must have regard to the legal requirements reflected in the standard and in CA 2006 under SI 2008/409, Sch. 6 (see **12.4.1** above).

Where group accounts are prepared, the balance sheet should contain in a prominent position, above the director's approval signature, a statement that they are prepared in accordance with the provisions applicable to companies subject to the small companies' regime (see **Chapter 6** at **6.8**).

12.4.3   Small group accounts – balance sheet format heading ('Investments')

Where small group accounts are prepared, Sch. 6 ('Group Accounts') of SI 2008/409 amends the balance sheet format headings for 'Investments'.   *SI 2008/409 Sch. 6.1(2)*

For item B.III in each of the balance sheet formats, the sub-headings of 'Investments' are modified as follows:

'B. III. Investments

(1)   Shares in group undertakings
(2)   Interests in associated undertakings
(3)   Other participating interests
(4)   Loans to group undertakings and undertakings in which a participating interest is held
(5)   Other investments other than loans
(6)   Others.'

12.5   'Related undertakings' disclosures

If group accounts are prepared, the disclosures required regarding related undertakings are given in SI 2008/409, Sch. 6, Pt. 2. As set out in the table below, 'related undertakings' may include parent, subsidiary and associated undertakings, joint ventures and other undertakings in which the company has an interest.

Note that SI 2015/980 amended most of the requirements regarding the location of the undertaking to disclose 'the address of the undertaking's registered office (whether in or outside the United Kingdom)'. This replaced the previous requirement to disclose the country of incorporation if outside the United Kingdom.

If group accounts are not prepared no disclosure is required of related undertakings information, as Sch. 2 to the Regulations was omitted by SI 2015/980.

The table below sets out the disclosures which are required in either case.

Definitions are in **Appendix A(6)**.

	Small group accounts prepared
	SI 2008/409, Sch. 6, Pt. 2
SUBSIDIARY UNDERTAKINGS If at the end of the financial year the company has subsidiary undertakings, the name of each subsidiary undertaking must be stated. The address of its registered office, or if it is unincorporated, the address of its principal place of business.	Sch. 6, Pt. 2, para. 22(1)–22(3)
It must also be stated whether the subsidiary undertaking is included in the consolidation and, if it is not, the reasons for excluding it from consolidation must be given.	Sch. 6, Pt. 2, para. 22(4)
It must be stated with respect to each subsidiary undertaking by virtue of which of the conditions specified in CA 2006, s. 1162(2) or (4) it is a subsidiary undertaking of its immediate parent undertaking. (This information need not be given if the relevant condition is that specified in CA 2006, s. 1162(2)(a) (holding of a majority of the voting rights) and the immediate parent undertaking holds the same proportion of the shares in the undertaking as it holds voting rights.)	Sch. 6, Pt. 2, para. 22(5)
HOLDINGS IN SUBSIDIARY UNDERTAKINGS With respect to the shares of a subsidiary undertaking held (a) by the parent company and (b) by the group, the identity of each class of shares and the proportion of the nominal value of the shares of that class held by the company and group respectively must be disclosed.	Sch. 6, Pt. 2, para. 23(1)–(2)
FINANCIAL INFORMATION ABOUT SUBSIDIARY UNDERTAKINGS The aggregate amount of capital and reserves as at the end of its relevant financial year** and the profit or loss for that year, must be disclosed in respect of each subsidiary undertaking (not included in the consolidated accounts). This information is not required: • if the company would (if it were not subject to the small companies regime) be exempt by virtue of CA 2006, s. 400 or s. 401 (parent company included in accounts of larger group) from the requirement to prepare group accounts;	Sch. 6, Pt. 2, para. 24(1)
• if the company's investment in the subsidiary undertaking is included in the company's accounts by way of the equity method of valuation;	Sch. 6, Pt. 2, para. 24(2)
• if the subsidiary undertaking is not required by any provision of CA 2006 to deliver a copy of its balance sheet for its relevant financial year and does not otherwise publish that balance sheet in the United Kingdom or elsewhere, and the company's holding is less than 50% of the nominal value of the shares in the undertaking; or	Sch. 6, Pt. 2, para. 24(2)

• if it is not material.	Sch. 6, Pt. 2, para. 24(3)
** **'relevant financial year'** of a subsidiary undertaking is that year if its financial year ends with that of the company and if not, its financial year ending last before the end of the company's financial year.	Sch. 6, Pt. 2, para. 24(4)
SHARES OF COMPANY HELD BY SUBSIDIARY UNDERTAKINGS (this information (Sch. 6.25) is not required to be filed. SI 2008/409 11(b)	
The number, description and amount of the shares in the company held by or on behalf of its subsidiary undertakings must be disclosed.	Sch. 6, Pt. 2, para. 25(1)
This information is not required if the subsidiary undertaking is concerned as personal representative or, subject as follows, as trustee. Unless the company, or any subsidiary undertaking of the company, is beneficially interested under the trust, otherwise than by way of security only for the purposes of a transaction entered into by it in the ordinary course of a business which includes the lending of money.	Sch. 6, Pt. 2, para. 25(2)–(3)
JOINT VENTURES The following information must be given in relation to joint ventures: • the name of the undertaking; • the address of the undertaking's registered office; • the factors on which joint management of the undertaking is based; and • the proportion of the capital of the undertaking held by undertakings included in the consolidation.	Sch. 6, Pt. 2, para. 26(1)
If the financial year end of the joint venture is not the same as the reporting company the financial year end of the joint venture prior to the reporting company's year end must be stated.	Sch. 6, Pt. 2, para. 26(2)
ASSOCIATED UNDERTAKINGS If an undertaking included in the consolidation has an interest in an associated undertaking the name of each associated undertaking must be stated. There must also be stated with respect to each associated undertaking the its registered office, or if it is unincorporated, the address of its principal place of business.	Sch. 6, Pt. 2, para. 27(1)–(3)
The identity of each class of shares held in the associated undertaking by the parent company and the group and the proportion of the nominal value of the shares of that class represented by those shares must be disclosed. The disclosure should show the parent company and group holdings separately.	Sch. 6, Pt. 2, para. 27(4)–(5)
SIGNIFICANT HOLDINGS IN UNDERTAKINGS OTHER THAN SUBSIDIARY UNDERTAKINGS If group accounts are prepared, the following information must be given where at the end of the financial year the company has a significant holding in an undertaking which is not a subsidiary undertaking, joint venture or associated undertaking of the company. OR If group accounts are not prepared, the following information must be given where at the end of the financial year the company has a significant holding in an undertaking which is not a subsidiary undertaking of the company.	Sch. 6, Pt. 2, para. 28(1)

(A holding is significant for this purpose if it amounts to 20% or more of the nominal value of any class of shares in the undertaking, or the amount of the holding (as stated or included in the company's accounts) exceeds 20% of the amount (as so stated) of the company's assets.)	Sch. 6, Pt. 2, para. 28(2)
• The name of the undertaking must be stated.	Sch. 6, Pt. 2, para. 29(1)
• There must also be stated the address of its registered office or if it is unincorporated, the address of its principal place of business.	Sch. 6, Pt. 2, para. 29(2)
• The identity of each class of shares and the proportion of the nominal value of the shares of that class held by the company in the undertaking must be disclosed.	Sch. 6, Pt. 2, para. 29(4)
• The aggregate amount of the capital and reserves of the undertaking as at the end of its relevant financial year, and its profit or loss for that year must also be disclosed. ***	Sch. 6, Pt. 2, para. 30(1)
*** This information is not required if: • the company would (if it were not subject to the small companies regime) be exempt by virtue of CA 2006. s. 400 or s. 401 (parent company included in accounts of larger group) from the requirement to prepare group accounts; and • the company's investment in all undertakings in which it has a significant holding is included in the company's accounts by way of the equity method of valuation; or • the subsidiary undertaking is not required by any provision of CA 2006 to deliver a copy of its balance sheet for its relevant financial year and does not otherwise publish that balance sheet in the United Kingdom or elsewhere, and the company's holding is less than 50% of the nominal value of the shares in the undertaking; or • it is not material.	 Sch. 6, Pt. 2, para. 30(2) Sch. 6, Pt. 2, para. 30(3)
Where group accounts are prepared, the following information must be given where at the end of the financial year the group has a significant holding in an undertaking which is not a subsidiary undertaking of the parent company, joint venture or associated undertaking of the company.	Sch. 6, Pt. 2, para. 31(1)
(A holding is significant for this purpose if it amounts to 20% or more of the nominal value of any class of shares in the undertaking, or the amount of the holding (as stated or included in the group accounts) exceeds 20% of the amount (as so stated) of the group's assets.)	Sch. 6, Pt. 2, para. 31(2)
• The name of the undertaking must be stated.	Sch. 6, Pt. 2, para. 32(1)
• There must also be stated with respect to each undertaking the address of its registered office or, if it is unincorporated, the address of its principal place of business.	Sch. 6, Pt. 2, para. 32(2)
• The identity of each class of shares and the proportion of the nominal value of the shares of that class held by the company in the undertaking must be disclosed.	Sch. 6, Pt. 2, para. 32(4)

• The aggregate amount of the capital and reserves of the undertaking as at the end of its relevant financial year, and its profit or loss for that year must also be disclosed. ***	Sch. 6, Pt. 2, para. 33(1)
*** This information is not required:	
• if the subsidiary undertaking is not required by any provision of CA 2006 to deliver a copy of its balance sheet for its relevant financial year and does not otherwise publish that balance sheet in the United Kingdom or elsewhere, and the company's holding is less than 50% of the nominal value of the shares in the undertaking; or	Sch. 6, Pt. 2, para. 33(2)
• if it is not material.	Sch. 6, Pt. 2, para. 33(3)
MEMBERSHIP OF CERTAIN UNDERTAKINGS	
The following information must be given where at the end of the financial year the reporting company (or group) is a member of a qualifying undertaking.	Sch. 6, Pt. 2, para. 34
'qualifying undertaking' means: (a) a qualifying partnership; or (b) an unlimited company each of whose members is: (i) a limited company; (ii) another unlimited company each of whose members is a limited company; (iii) a Scottish partnership which is not a limited partnership, each of whose members is a limited company; or (iv) a Scottish partnership which is a limited partnership, each of whose general partners is a limited company.	Sch. 6, Pt. 2, para. 34(6)
• The name and legal form of the undertaking, and	Sch. 6, Pt. 2, para. 34(2)
• The address of the undertaking's registered office (whether in or outside the United Kingdom) or, if it does not have such an office, its head office (whether in or outside the United Kingdom).	Sch. 6, Pt. 2, para. 34(4)
(This information is not required if it is not material.)	Sch. 6, Pt. 2, para. 34(7)
Where the undertaking is a qualifying partnership there must also be stated either that a copy of the latest accounts of the undertaking has been or is to be appended to the copy of the company's accounts sent to the Registrar of Companies under CA 2006 s. 444, or the name of at least one body corporate (which may be the company) in whose group accounts the undertaking has been or is to be dealt with on a consolidated basis.	Sch. 6, Pt. 2, para. 34(3)
(The name of at least one body corporate need not be given if the notes to the company's accounts disclose that advantage has been taken of the exemption conferred by regulation 7 of the *Partnerships (Accounts) Regulations 2008*.)	Sch. 6, Pt. 2, para. 34(5)
PARENT UNDERTAKING DRAWING UP ACCOUNTS FOR LARGER GROUP	Sch. 6, Pt. 2, para. 35
Where the parent company is itself a subsidiary undertaking, the following information must be given with respect to that parent undertaking of the company which heads: (a) the largest group of undertakings for which group accounts are drawn up and of which that company is a member; and (b) the smallest such group of undertakings.	Sch. 6, Pt. 2, para. 35(2)–(3)
The name of the parent undertaking, if incorporated outside the United Kingdom its country of incorporation, if unincorporated the address of its principal place of businss.	Sch. 6, Pt. 2, para. 35(1)

If copies of the group accounts referred to above are available to the public, there must also be stated the address from which copies of the accounts can be obtained.	Sch. 6, Pt. 2, para. 35(3)
IDENTIFICATION OF ULTIMATE PARENT COMPANY	Sch. 6, Pt. 2, para. 35(4)
If any company is regarded by the directors as being the reporting company's ultimate parent company. The name of that ultimate parent company must be disclosed.	Sch. 6, Pt. 2, para. 36(1)–(2)
If the ultimate parent company is incorporated outside the United Kingdom, the country in which it is incorporated must be stated (if known to the directors).	Sch. 6, Pt. 2, para. 36(3)

12.6   Group accounts filing

A small group is required to file at Companies House either:

- individual accounts of the parent company, if no group accounts are filed where the group qualifies as exempt; or
- consolidated (small or medium-sized company) accounts of the group.

12.7   Entitlement to group exemption – auditor's report

If the directors of the company:

(a)   have prepared accounts in accordance with the small companies regime; or

(b)   have taken advantage of small companies exemption from the requirement to prepare a strategic report or in preparing the directors' report, and in the auditor's opinion they were not entitled to do so, the auditor shall state that fact in his report.

s. 498(5)

12.8   Group companies – availability of small audit exemption

If a company is a member of a small group, then the company may be able to take advantage of the audit exemption for small companies. Furthermore, a new audit exemption was introduced for accounting periods ended on or after 1 October 2012 for subsidiary companies of any size meeting certain additional requirements.

Audit exemption, including the requirements of each type of exemption available to group companies, is covered in **Chapter 13**.

Part III   Example accounts and reports

Chapter 13   Determining company audit exemption

13.1   Introduction

The *Companies and Limited Liability Partnerships (Accounts and Audit Exemptions and Change of Accounting Framework) Regulations* 2012 (SI 2012/2301) amended CA 2006 to align small company audit thresholds with accounting thresholds. They also exempt certain subsidiary companies from audit. This revised legislation applied to accounting periods ended on or after 1 October 2012.

However, when the *Companies, Partnerships and Groups (Accounts and Reports) Regulations* 2015 (SI 2015/980) was implemented, the link with the small company thresholds was temporarily removed, in terms of the ability to early adopt the legal changes. This was because there was ongoing consultation on whether the audit thresholds should rise to the much increased new small company thresholds available for accounting purposes. So whilst the new limits of £10.2m turnover and £5.1m for the balance sheet total could be applied for accounting purposes for accounting periods commencing on or after 1 January 2015 if the directors so chose, none of the changes can be applied early for audit purposes. This means that the limits and other criteria for audit exemption, remain those in the old legislation for 2015.

In January 2016, the Government finally announced that it would, in fact, be raising the audit thresholds in line with the small company accounting thresholds. Thus, for accounting periods commencing on or after 1 January 2016, the audit limits and the accounting limits, together with the other criteria for small companies, are once again aligned. The rules set out in this chapter for audit purposes are based on the changes in SI 2015/980 and are therefore applicable for accounting periods commencing on or after 1 January 2016.

In addition to the size criteria under s. 477 for audit exemption, there are other routes to audit exemption available under CA 2006:

- small companies (s. 477);
- subsidiary companies (s. 479A);
- dormant companies (s. 480); and
- non-profit-making companies subject to public sector audit (s. 482) (special rules apply to these companies – details of these are outside the scope of this book).

The audit exemption available for small companies under s. 477 is not available if the company is part of a non-small group (see **Chapter 12**). There are also a number of other restrictions and requirements for each exemption as set out in detail below.

s. 479(1)

In considering if the company is to take advantage of these exemptions, the members and directors should also consider if an audit is beneficial or required for other reasons, such as providing peace of mind, to assist in obtaining financing, to meet banking terms or as a requirement of the Articles of Association or a shareholders' agreement.

13.2   Small companies – conditions for exemption from audit

A company is exempt from the requirements for the audit of its accounts in respect of a financial year if it qualifies as a small company. However, if the company is a member of a group, then further conditions in CA 2006, s. 479 apply (see **13.4**).

Whether a company qualifies as a small company is determined in accordance with CA 2006, s. 382(1)–(7), as set out in **Chapter 5**, and this should be the first step in determining if the company may not require audit.

Once it is established that the company is small, the company must also:

- not be excluded from small companies exemption (s. 478) (see **13.3**);
- if a member of a group, consider the group requirements (s. 478) (see **13.4**); and
- not have received notice requiring it to obtain an audit from 10% or more of members (s. 476) (see **13.6**).

The directors must also make the statements required by CA 2006, s. 475(2) and (3) before the signature on the balance sheet, as set out in **13.8**.

In addition, charitable companies have audit obligations under charity legislation, which in general set audit exemption at a much lower threshold. The sister volume to this publication, CCH *Preparing Charity Accounts*, deals with the disclosure and presentation requirements for a set of charity accounts.

13.3 Companies excluded from small companies' audit exemption

A non-group company is not entitled to the small companies audit exemption conferred by CA 2006, s. 477 if it was at any time within the financial year in question:

- a public company;
- a company that is an authorised insurance company, a banking company, an e-money issuer, a MiFID investment firm or a UCITS management company, or carries on insurance market activity; or
- a special register body as defined in s. 117(1) of the *Trade Union and Labour Relations (Consolidation) Act* 1992 (c. 52) or an employers' association as defined in s. 122 of that Act or Article 4 of the *Industrial Relations (Northern Ireland) Order* 1992 (SI 1992/807) (NI 5).

s. 478

13.4 Group companies – availability of small audit exemption

A company which in its own right meets the definition of a small company and is also a group company (being a parent company or a subsidiary undertaking) is only entitled to audit exemption if the following conditions are met:

(a) the group:

(i) qualifies as a small group (as determined in accordance with s. 383) in relation to that financial year; and

(ii) was not at any time in that year an ineligible group (as determined by s. 384(2) and (3)); or

s. 479(1)   (b) subsection (3) applies (dormant subsidiaries).

A dormant subsidiary undertaking being a group company and dormant during the financial year for the whole period it was a group company is also entitled to audit exemption. (This exemption applies to all sizes of groups with dormant subsidiaries.)

s. 479(3)

A group is ineligible if any of its members is:

(a) a traded company (this was changed from a public company by SI 2015/980, so only applies for accounting periods from 1 January 2016);

(b) a body corporate (other than a company) whose shares are admitted to trading on a regulated market in an EEA State;

(c) a person (other than a small company) who has permission under Pt. 4A of the *Financial Services and Markets Act* 2000 (c. 8) to carry on a regulated activity;

(ca) an e-money issuer;

(d) a small company that is an authorised insurance company, a banking company, a MiFID investment firm or a UCITS management company; or

(e) a person who carries on insurance market activity.

s. 384(2)

CA 2006, s. 479(4) defines a 'group' in relation to a group company as that company together with all its associated undertakings.

s. 479(4)

13.5   Subsidiaries of EEA companies – audit exemption

In accordance with CA 2006, s. 479A, a subsidiary company (irrespective of its size) is exempt from audit if it fulfils all of the following conditions:

(a) its parent undertaking is established under the law of an EEA state*;

(b) all members of the company must agree to the exemption in respect of the financial year in question;

(c) the parent gives a guarantee (under s. 479C) of all the outstanding liabilities to which the subsidiary is subject at the end of the financial year until they are satisfied in full;

(d) the company must be included in the consolidated accounts drawn up for that year or to an earlier date in that year by the parent undertaking in accordance with the provisions of Directive 2013/34/EU of the European Parliament and of the Council on the annual financial statements, consolidated statements and related reports of certain types of undertakings, or international accounting standards;

(e) the consolidated accounts drawn up by the parent must disclose the use of the audit exemption by the subsidiary by virtue of this section;

(f) the directors of the subsidiary must file the following documents at Companies House on or before the date that they file the subsidiary's accounts:

   (i) written notice of the agreement in (b);

   (ii) a written statement by the parent of the guarantee in (c); and

   (iii) a copy of the consolidated annual report and accounts referred to in (d) and the auditor's report on those accounts;

s. 479A(2)

(g) the company is not a traded company (as defined in s. 474(1));

(h) the company is not an authorised insurance company, a banking company, an e-money issuer, a MiFID investment firm or a UCITS management company, or carries on insurance market activity; and

(i) a special register body as defined in s. 117(1) of the *Trade Union and Labour Relations (Consolidation) Act* 1992 (c. 52) or an employers' association as defined in s. 122 of that Act or Article 4 of the *Industrial Relations (Northern Ireland) Order* 1992 (SI 1992/807) (NI 5).

s. 479B

* *A list of EEA states is available on the Registrar of Companies website at: www.gov.uk/eu-eea*

The directors of the subsidiary company must make the statements required by CA 2006, s. 475(2) and (3) before the signature on the balance sheet, as set out in **13.8**.

In making the decision as to whether the parent will provide the guarantee referred to in (c) above, the directors of the parent must consider if the guarantee provided exposes the parent to significant liabilities (actual and contingent).

If the company is a subsidiary of an entity which prepares a consolidated annual report and accounts in a language other than English, the group accounts will need to be translated into English and filed at Companies House together with form VT01 'Certified voluntary translation of an original document that is or has been delivered to the Registrar of Companies'.

Often, the purpose of the subsidiary structure is to limit the liability of the parent company. If the subsidiary has minority shareholders, or may be sold in the future, this may complicate matters further. In many cases, legal advice should be obtained before the parent enters into any such guarantee.

Furthermore, the parent should consider if there is any significant cost saving in taking advantage of the exemption as the figures included in the subsidiary company's accounts may have to be audited in any case as part of the group's audit.

13.6   Right to require an audit

s. 476(1)

The members of a company that would otherwise be entitled to exemption from audit (under CA 2006, s. 475(1)(a) (small or dormant companies)) may by notice require it to obtain an audit of its accounts for a financial year.

s. 476(2)

Any member or members holding not less than 10% in aggregate in the nominal value of the issued share capital of a company (or any class of it) or (if the company does not have share capital) not less than 10% in number of the members of the company may require an audit of the company's accounts.

s. 476(3)

To obtain an audit of the company's accounts, the member or members must deposit a notice in writing at the company's registered office during the financial year but not later than one month before the end of the year. The company is then not entitled to audit exemption for the year to which the notice relates.

There is no requirement for a company to advise members of their rights to require an audit (or the manner in which it may be exercised) nor, for example, of their rights to audit when the accounting year end is changed.

13.7   Audit or assurance reports on accounts of small companies

Many accounts of small companies may be prepared without any form of audit or assurance report being attached – simply because none is statutorily required. **Table 13.1** sets out the position.

Where a company is entitled to audit exemption, the directors may nevertheless wish (or be required by banking terms) to have the assurance of another type of report giving a lesser level of comfort over the financial statements.

The available report types are discussed in **Chapter 14**.

Table 13.1   Statutory audit reports for small companies and micro-entities

Type of accounts	*Type of assurance report*
Audit exemption – s. 477	
Small company accounts – audit exemption	No audit or other report required
Abridged accounts – audit exemption	No audit or other report required
Micro-entity accounts – audit exemption	No audit or other report required

---

Table 13.1   Statutory audit reports for small companies and micro-entities (cont'd)

Audit – s. 475

Small company accounts – audited *(if statutorily required)*	Auditor's report – s. 495
Small company accounts – audited *(at members' request – s. 476)*	Auditor's report – s. 495
Abridged accounts – audited	Auditor's report – s. 495
Micro-entity accounts – audited	Auditor's report – s. 495

(Note that for micro-entities, the list of matters on which the auditor must report by exception is amended to remove the matters that are not disclosed in micro-entity accounts, e.g. directors' remuneration. As mentioned in **9.1**, the micro-entity regime is not a fair presentation regime as covered by ISAs and so additional disclosures in the audit report may be required. Reference should be made to ISA 210 A.36 which is expected to be amended to refer to micro-entities and the issue with auditing them before summer 2016.)

13.8   Audit exemption – directors' statement

A company's annual accounts for a financial year must be audited unless the company is exempt from audit under CA 2006, s. 477 (small companies), 479A (subsidiary companies), 480 (dormant companies), or 482 (non-profit-making companies subject to public sector audit).   *s. 475*

The balance sheet of a small or subsidiary or dormant company taking advantage of the audit exemption must contain a statement by the directors to the effect that:

- the company is exempt from audit under CA 2006, s. 477 (small companies), 479A (subsidiary companies) or 480 (dormant companies);
- the members have not required the company to obtain an audit of its accounts for the year in question in accordance with CA 2006, s. 476; and
- the directors acknowledge their responsibilities for complying with the requirements of CA 2006 with respect to accounting records and the preparation of accounts.   *s. 475(2)–(3)*

The directors' statement required by CA 2006, s. 475 must appear on the balance sheet above the signature required by CA 2006, s. 414.   *s. 475(4)*

Where the directors of a company subject to the small companies regime deliver to the Registrar of Companies IAS accounts, or Companies Act accounts and do not deliver a copy of the company's profit and loss account or a copy of the directors' report, the copy of the balance sheet delivered to the Registrar of Companies must contain, in a prominent position, a statement that the company's annual accounts and reports have been delivered in accordance with the provisions applicable to companies subject to the small companies regime. See **Table 6.6** for a summary of statements required.   *s. 444(5)*

Examples of a form of directors' statement covering the above requirements are illustrated in **Example 13.1** the wording of which is derived from the example on the Companies House website.   *s. 475*

Example 13.1   Small company audit exemption directors' statements: balance sheet

For the financial year ended 31 December 2016, the company was entitled to exemption from audit under the *Companies Act* 2006, (s. 477 relating to small companies, s. 479A relating to subsidiary companies or s. 480 relating to dormant companies) and the members have not required the company to obtain an audit of its accounts for the year in question in accordance with s. 476. The directors acknowledge their responsibilities for complying with the requirements of the *Companies Act* 2006 with respect to accounting records and the preparation of accounts.

[Note 1]

The financial statements have been prepared in accordance with the special provisions relating to companies subject to the small companies regime within the *Companies Act* 2006, Pt. 15.

[Note 2]

and, if applicable

s. 444(5)

(These accounts have been delivered in accordance with the provisions applicable to companies subject to the small companies regime.)

Notes: (Words in italics are explanatory only)

The above statements are applicable as follows:

(1) applicable, where audit exemption applies, in:

    (a) small company (SI 2008/409) balance sheets (individual and group);

    (b) Sch. 1 (SI 2008/409) balance sheets;

(2) This statement applies to small companies that choose not to include a copy of the directors' report and/or a copy of the profit and loss account in the accounts filed with the Registrar of Companies. See also Table 6.6 which summarises statements required for different accounting options.

The responsibilities to keep adequate accounting records (under s. 386) and the requirements determining the contents of individual company accounts (under s. 394) are explained more fully in **Chapter 3** at **3.10** and **3.2** respectively. The obligation for directors of a company not to approve accounts unless they are satisfied that they give a true and fair view (of the company's assets, liabilities, financial position and profit or loss) is explained in **Chapter 3** at **3.3**. As previously mentioned, micro-entity accounts are deemed to give a true and fair view if they comply with the legal requirements regarding form and content.

Chapter 14   Example accounts

The example accounts set out in this chapter are entirely fictional.

14.1   About the example accounts

The example accounts do not represent a comprehensive checklist of the statutory disclosure requirements nor do they purport to be definitive or exhaustive. The intention is to illustrate the more common situations. Other presentations may be equally acceptable, provided that they adhere to the rules set out in CA 2006, supporting statutory regulations and relevant financial reporting and accounting standards.

14.1.1   Adapted accounts

As covered in **8.3.2** the provisions for adapted accounts allow both FRS 102 type terminology as well as alternative IFRS style presentation known as adpated accounts. The examples below are not adapted accounts, but if that is the desired route then cross refer to the requirements in **Table 8.4** in **Chapter 8**.

14.1.2   Abridged accounts

The accounts set out below in **14.2** for a small company are unabridged accounts, or 'full' statutory accounts. They are marked up, with grey tinted boxes around the relevant sections, to show which items could be omitted if the option to prepare abridged accounts were taken. Further information on abridged accounts is given in **Chapter 11**, which also clarifies that such accounts are not available for micro-entities adopting the micro-regime and must still give a true and fair view.

14.1.3   Filing requirements

With the abolition of abbreviated accounts, there is now no longer a specific set of accounts for filing, or as termed in the Act 'delivery to the Registrar'. Instead, the small company is able to take advantage of the filing exemptions and apply them to whichever set of accounts they have prepared, whether small company 'full', abridged, or micro-entity accounts. The effect of this is that there is no need to file the profit and loss account or the directors' report (which is not required to be prepared by a micro-entity in any case).

The example accounts for Simplifiedco Limited have guidance notes in italics, in grey tinted boxes to indicate when statements need not be filed. In respect of the notes, these are assumed to be a part of the relevant primary statement. Therefore, notes to the balance sheet, or other notes not directly connected to the profit and loss must be filed, whereas the profit and loss account and notes directly relating to the profit and loss account do not need to be filed (i.e. delivered to the registrar).

14.1.4   Audit and assurance reports

Depending on the circumstances, the accounts may contain:

- an appropriate auditor's report (where an audit is required or voluntarily completed);
- an assurance review report – an accountants' report covering both the proper compilation of the accounts and the directors' 'true and fair view' assertion;

- an agreed-upon procedures report – an accountants' report covering only some areas of the financial statements; or
- an accounts preparation/compilation report – an accountants' report on the proper compilation of the accounts.

These alternative reports are discussed in **Chapter 15**.

Where an audit is performed there are additional requirements regarding statements in the accounts, where the profit and loss account is not filed. Details of these are covered in **Chapter 6** and key requirements summarised in **Table 6.6**. An example statement is also included in square brackets within Simplifiedco below.

There are also additional statements required regarding audit exemption, where the company takes advantage of this. Again, these are dealt with in **Chapter 6** and summarised in **Table 6.6**.

14.1.5   Key to mark-up

In the example accounts, tinted or boxed items indicate the following:

- **grey tinted box** – text that may be omitted where the option to prepare abridged accounts is taken, subject to the accounts still presenting a true and fair view overall, together with required disclosure statements as listed in **Chapter 6**;
- **other boxed items** – text that is optional or may be omitted according to the circumstances;
- **italics with grey tint** – guidance or other instructions;
- **[square brackets]** – indicate optional text depending on the circumstances.

14.2   Accounts of Simplifiedco Limited – small company

The example accounts of Simplifiedco Limited illustrate the audited accounts of a small company (as defined in **Chapter 5**) producing accounts under the provisions of CA 2006 and SI 2008/409, Sch. 1 as amended by SI 2015/980, together with FRS 102, section 1A for a financial period beginning on or after 1 January 2016; the example year end is 31 December 2016. Full advantage is taken of the special provisions available to small companies.

(These model accounts would also be applicable to an entity choosing to early adopt both FRS 102, section 1A and the impact of the regulations in SI 2015/980 as they affect SI 2008/409. Early adoption is generally possible for periods commencing on or after 1 January 2015.)

In practice, a small company is entitled to exceed the basic minimum disclosure as is considered desirable or as required in order to give a 'true and fair' view.

Both the profit and loss account and the balance sheet are presented in Format 1 and although it is audit exempt its directors have decided to have an audit. The directors have taken advantage of the available exemptions in preparing the directors' report and exemption from preparing a strategic report.

Some companies also submit a detailed profit and loss account from their management information, but this is not required and is therefore not shown in the example.

Increasingly, accounts of small UK companies are being prepared in a foreign currency – principally in Euros (€) or US dollars ($). It is possible, under FRS 102, to present accounts in any currency – this being referred to as the presentation currency. However, the company must first determine its functional currency in accordance with the requirements of FRS 102. Essentially, the functional currency is the one in which the entity carries out mosts of its transactions or is mostly affected from an operational point of view. Presentational currency must be disclosed, usually by indicating a £ or € sign above the figures in the accounts. Translation of accounts into a presentational currency is outside the scope of this volume, but is covered in CCH's *Applying New UK GAAP* and on CCH Online.

14.2.1 Example Accounts for small company using FRS 102, section 1A

Model Company Accounts for companies preparing accounts in accordance with FRS 102, section 1A and the special provisions relating to companies subject to the small companies regime within Part 15 of the Companies Act 2006 and the small company regulations set out in SI 2008/409 as amended by SI 2015/980, and choosing to have an audit.

SIMPLIFIEDCO LIMITED
Company Information

Directors	A Smith
	B Smith
	A Jones
	B Jones
Secretary	A Smith
Company Number	9999999 (England and Wales)
Registered Office	123 High Street
	Reading
	Berkshire
	RG6 4PX
Auditors	Manley Tope & Co
	Accountants and Statutory Auditors
	45 High Street
	Clearford
	Surrey
	SU1 2TH

SIMPLIFIEDCO LIMITED
Contents

The following pages do not form part of the statutory accounts:

Trading profit and loss account and summaries   *(insert page numbers if included)*

SIMPLIFIEDCO LIMITED   Page 1

Directors' Report for the year ended 31 December 2016

The directors' report does not need to be filed.

The directors present their report and financial statements for the year ended 31 December 2016.

Statement of Directors' responsibilities

FRC Bulletin – 2010/02

The directors are responsible for preparing the Directors Report and the financial statements in accordance with applicable law and regulation.

Company law requires the directors to prepare financial statements for each financial year. Under that law, the directors have elected to prepare the financial statements in accordance with United Kingdom Generally Accepted Accounting Practice (United Kingdom Accounting Standards and applicable law). Under company law, the directors must not approve the financial statements unless they are satisfied that they give a true and fair view of the state of affairs of the company and of the profit or loss of the company for that period. In preparing these financial statements, the directors are required to:

- select suitable accounting policies and then apply them consistently;
- make judgements and estimates that are reasonable and prudent;
- prepare the financial statements on the going concern basis unless it is inappropriate to presume that the company will continue in business.

The directors are responsible for keeping adequate accounting records that disclose with reasonable accuracy at any time the financial position of the company and enable them to ensure that the financial statements comply with the *Companies Act* 2006. They are also responsible for safeguarding the assets of the company and hence for taking reasonable steps for the prevention and detection of fraud and other irregularities.

[where appropriate] The directors are responsible for the maintenance and integrity of the corporate and financial information included on the company's website. Legislation in the United Kingdom governing the preparation and dissemination of financial statements may differ from legislation in other jurisdictions.

Statement of disclosure of information to auditors

s. 418(2)

The directors of the company who held office at the date of approval of this directors report confirm that:

- so far as they are aware, there is no relevant audit information, (information needed by the company's auditors in connection with preparing their report), of which the company's auditors are unaware; and
- they have taken all the steps that they ought to have taken as directors in order to make themselves aware of any relevant audit information and to establish that the company's auditors are aware of that information.

s. 416(1)a   **Directors**

The directors who served during the year were:

A Smith
B Smith (appointed 1 September 2016)
A Jones
B Jones
F Jones (resigned 31 August 2016)

Auditors

The auditors, Manley Tope & Co, will be proposed for reappointed in accordance with s. 485 of the *Companies Act* 2006.

Or

The auditors, Manley Tope & Co are deemed to be reappointed under s. 487(2) of the *Companies Act* 2006.

Small company regime

s. 419(2)   This report has been prepared in accordance with the special provisions relating to companies subject to the small companies regime within Part 15 of the *Companies Act* 2006.

This report was approved by the board on 14 May 2017 and signed on its behalf.

A Smith

s. 419(1)   **A Smith**

Director

> *If the P/L is filed then the audit report must also be filed. If the P/L is not filed then, unless exemption from audit has been taken the balance sheet must include information about the audit report including details of any qualification or emphasis of matter, name of firm and senior statutory auditor.*

See Table 6.6, s. 444(5B)

INDEPENDENT AUDITOR'S REPORT TO THE MEMBERS OF SIMPLIFIEDCO LIMITED

FRC Bulletin 2010/01 and Bulletin 4 plus ISA 700 (UK and Ireland)

We have audited the financial statements of Simplifiedco Limited for the year ended 31 December 2016 on pages 5–10. The financial reporting framework that has been applied in their preparation is applicable law and United Kingdom Accounting Standards (United Kingdom Generally Accepted Accounting Practice), including FRS 102, section 1A 'The Financial Reporting Standard applicable in the UK and Republic of Ireland'.

This report is made solely to the company's members, as a body, in accordance with Chapter 3 of Part 16 of the *Companies Act* 2006. Our audit work has been undertaken so that we might state to the company's members those matters that we are required to state to them in an auditor's report and for no other purpose. To the fullest extent permitted by law, we do not accept or assume responsibility to anyone other than the company and the company's members as a body, for our audit work, or the opinions we have formed.

ICAEW TECH 01/03AAF

Respective responsibilities of directors and auditors

As explained more fully in the Directors' responsibilities statement set out on page 1, the directors are responsible for the preparation of the financial statements and for being satisfied that they give a true and fair view. Our responsibility is to audit and express an opinion on the financial statements in accordance with applicable law and International Standards on Auditing (UK and Ireland). Those standards require us to comply with the Auditing Practices Board Ethical Standards for Auditors [including Auditing Practices Board Ethical Standard – Provisions Available for Small Entities (Revised), in circumstances set out in note [x] to the financial statements].

Scope of the audit of the financial statements

A description of the scope of the audit of financial statements is provided on the Financial Reporting Council's website at *www.frc.org.uk/auditscopeukprivate*.

Opinion on financial statements

In our opinion the financial statements:

- give a true and fair view of the state of the company's affairs as at 31 December 2016 and of its profit for the year then ended;
- have been properly prepared in accordance with United Kingdom Generally Accepted Practice applicable to smaller entities; and
- have been prepared in accordance with the requirements of the *Companies Act* 2006.

s. 495(3)b

Opinion on other matter prescribed by the *Companies Act* 2006

In our opinion, based on the work undertaken in the course of the audit, the information given in the [Strategic Report and] Directors' Report for the financial year for which the financial statements are prepared is consistent with those financial statements and has been prepared in accordance with applicable legal requirements. No material misstatements in the [Strategic Report and] Directors' Report have been identified.

s. 496

s. 498   **Matters on which we are required to report by exception**

We have nothing to report in respect of the following matters where the *Companies Act* 2006 requires us to report to you if, in our opinion:

- adequate accounting records have not been kept, or returns adequate for our audit have not been received from branches not visited by us;
- the financial statements are not in agreement with the accounting records or returns;
- certain disclosures of directors' remuneration specified by law are not made;
- we have not received all the information and explanations we require for our audit; or
- the directors were not entitled to prepare the financial statements and the directors' report in accordance with the small companies regime.

Stuart Manley
(senior statutory auditor)
For and on behalf of Manley Tope & Co
Accountants and Statutory Auditors
45 High Street
Clearford
Surrey
SU1 2TH
Sunday, 14 May 2017

> *The profit and loss account does not need to be filed. If this exemption (or the exemption from filing the directors' report) is taken the balance sheet must contain a statement in a prominent position that the company's annual accounts and reports have been delivered in accordance with the provisions applicable to companies subject to the small companies' regime. See Table 6.6.*

s. 444(5)

SIMPLIFIEDCO LIMITED

PROFIT AND LOSS ACCOUNT

FOR THE YEAR ENDED 31 DECEMBER 2016

	Notes	2016 £	2015 £
Turnover		1,600,199	1,082,568
Cost of sales		(876,162)	(520,857)
Gross profit		724,037	561,711
Distribution costs		(130,926)	(123,350)
Administrative expenses		(465,329)	(334,223)
Other operating income		1,532	1,200
*		129,314	105,338
Interest receivable		1,706	1,858
Interest payable		(21,228)	(23,676)
Profit before tax	2	109,792	83,520
Taxation		(29,045)	(26,301)
Profit after taxation being profit for the financial year		80,747	57,219

> *If there were relevant transactions within other comprehensive income a small company is encouraged to include such a statement. This might be needed in order to give a true and fair view.*
>
> **Operating profit is not required to be disclosed, though may be included at this point if desired.*

The notes on pages 7–10 form part of these financial statements

	SIMPLIFIEDCO LIMITED					Page 6
BALANCE SHEET AT 31 DECEMBER 2016						
	Notes		2016		2015	
		£	£	£	£	
Fixed assets						
Tangible assets	4		224,757		181,069	
Current assets						
Stocks		11,826		19,856		
Debtors	5	150,835		73,020		
Cash at bank and in hand		27		60		
		162,688		92,936		
Creditors: amounts falling due within one year	6	(134,645)		(117,449)		
Net current assets (Liabilities)			28,043		(24,504)	
Total assets less current liabilities			252,800		156,565	
Creditors: amounts falling due after more than one year	7		(47,321)		(25,948)	
Provision for liabilities						
Deferred Taxation			(5,880)		(4,265)	
			199,599		126,352	
Capital and reserves						
Called up share capital			5,000		5,000	
Share premium account			12,500		12,500	
Profit and loss account			182,099		108,852	
Shareholders Funds			199,599		126,352	

s.414(1) and (2)
The financial statements, which have been prepared in accordance with the special provisions relating to companies subject to the small companies regime within Part 15 of the *Companies Act 2006*, were approved by the board of directors [on 14 May 2017] and signed on its behalf.

> *It is no longer required for a small company to indicate the date on which the accounts have been approved, although it might be helpful information and possibly required to give a true and fair view. We would therefore recommend retaining the date.*

s. 444(5B)

> *[The company's annual accounts and reports have been delivered in accordance with the provisions applicable to companies subject to the small companies' regime. The directors' report and profit and loss account have not therefore been filed. The audit report in respect of these accounts was unqualified with no emphasis of matter. The senior statutory auditor was Stuart Manley of Manley Tope and Co.]*

s. 444(2A)]

> *[All of the members have consented to the abridgement.]*

A Smith

s. 414(1) and (2)
A Smith (Director)

Company No. 9999999 (England and Wales)

The notes on pages 7–10 form part of these financial statements

SIMPLIFIEDCO LIMITED

NOTES TO THE FINANCIAL STATEMENTS FOR THE YEAR ENDED 31 DECEMBER 2016

1   ACCOUNTING POLICIES   *102.1AC.3–6*

1.1   Basis of preparation of financial statements

The financial statements have been prepared under the historical cost convention in accordance with the accounting policies set out below. These financial statements have been prepared in accordance with FRS 102, section 1A – The Financial Reporting Standard applicable in the UK and Republic of Ireland and the *Companies Act* 2006.

1.2   Revenue recognition

Revenue is measured at the fair value of the consideration received or receivable. Revenue is reduced for estimated customer returns, rebates and other similar allowances. Revenue from the sale of goods is recognised when goods are delivered and legal title has passed.

1.3   Tangible fixed assets

Tangible fixed assets held for the company's own use are stated at cost less accumulated depreciation and accumulated impairment losses. Depreciation is provided at rates calculated to write off the cost of fixed assets, less their estimated residual value, over their expected useful lives on a straight line basis at rates of 3–20% per annum.

Assets held under finance leases are depreciated in the same way as owned assets.

At each balance sheet date, the company reviews the carrying amount of its tangible fixed assets to determine whether there is any indication that any items have suffered an impairment loss. If any such indication exists, the recoverable amount of an asset is estimated in order to determine the extent of the impairment loss, if any. Where it is not possible to estimate the recoverable amount of the asset, the company estimates the recoverable amount of the cash-generating unit to which the asset belongs.

1.4   Leasing and hire purchase contracts

Assets obtained under hire purchase contracts and finance leases are capitalised as tangible fixed assets. Assets acquired under finance leases are depreciated over the shorter of the lease term and their useful lives. Assets acquired under hire purchase contracts are depreciated over their useful lives. Finance leases are those where substantially all of the benefits and risks of ownership are assumed by the company. Obligations under such agreements are included in creditors net of the finance charge allocated to future periods. The finance element of the rental payment is charged to the profit and loss account so as to produce a constant periodic rate of charge on the net obligation outstanding in each period.

Rentals applicable to operating leases where substantially all of the benefits and risks of ownership remain with the lessor are charged to profit and loss account on a straight line basis.

1.5   Stocks

Stocks are stated at the lower of cost and estimated selling price less costs to complete and sell (net realisable value). Costs, which comprise direct production costs, are based on the method most appropriate to the type of inventory class, but usually on a first-in-first-out basis. Overheads are charged to profit or loss as incurred. Net realisable value is based on the estimated selling price less any estimated completion or selling costs.

When stocks are sold, the carrying amount of those stocks is recognised as an expense in the period in which the related revenue is recognised. The amount of any write-down of stocks to net realisable value and all losses of stocks are recognised as an expense in the period in which the write-down or loss occurs. The amount of any reversal of any write-down of stocks is recognised as a reduction in the amount of stocks recognised as an expense in the period in which the reversal occurs.

1.6   Foreign currencies

Transactions in currencies, other than the functional currency of the company, are recorded at the rate of exchange on the date the transaction occurred. Monetary items denominated in other currencies are translated at the rate prevailing at the end of the reporting period. All differences are taken to the profit and loss account. Non-monetary items that are measured at historic cost in a foreign currency are not retranslated.

1.7   Taxation

Taxation represents the sum of tax currently payable and deferred tax.

The company's liability for current tax is calculated using tax rates that have been enacted or substantively enacted by the end of the reporting period.

Deferred tax is recognised on all timing differences between the carrying amounts of assets and liabilities in the financial statements and the corresponding tax bases used in the computation of taxable profit. The carrying amount of deferred tax assets is reviewed at the end of each reporting period and reduced to the extent that it is no longer probable that sufficient taxable profits will be available to allow all or part of the asset to be recovered.

Deferred tax assets and liabilities are measured at the tax rates that are expected to apply in the period in which the liability is settled or the asset realised, based on tax rates (and tax laws) that have been enacted or substantively enacted by the end of the reporting period.

1.8   Pensions

The company operates a defined contribution pension scheme, Simplifiedco Pension Scheme, and the pension charge represents the amounts payable by the company to the fund in respect of the year.

2   Profit before tax

Profit before tax is stated after charging:

	2016	2015
	£	£
Depreciation of tangible fixed assets	25,719	21,396
Auditors' remuneration	4,000	3,600
Bad debt written off	8,750	–

Sch. 1.19(3), 1.20(2)

SI 2008/489 4(1)

Sch. 1.61(2), 102.1AC.32

3   Employees

s. 411, 102.1AC.33

The average number of persons employed by the company (including directors) during the year was 23 (2015–21).

4   Tangible assets

Sch. 1.48, 102.1AC.12/13

	Land and buildings	Plant and machinery etc.	Total
	£	£	£
Cost or valuation			
At 1 January 2016	123,459	89,867	213,326
Additions	–	69,407	69,407
Disposals	–	(9,090)	(9,090)
At 31 December 2016	123,459	150,184	273,643
Depreciation			
At 1 January 2016	200	32,057	32,257
Relating to disposals	–	(9,090)	(9,090)
Charge for the year	2,069	23,650	25,719
At 31 December 2016	2,269	46,617	48,886
Net book value			
At 31 December 2016	121,190	103,567	224,757
At 31 December 2015	123,259	57,810	181,069

Page 9

Sch. 1, Section B formats

5   Debtors

	2016 £	2015 £
Due after more than one year		
Other debtors	5,000	
Due within one year		
Trade debtors	129,780	45,908
Other debtors	16,055	27,121
	150,835	73,029

Sch. 1, Section B formats

6   Creditors: amounts falling due within one year

	2016 £	2015 £
Bank loans and overdrafts (secured)	67,456	42,876
Net obligations under finance leases and hire purchase contracts (secured)	14,657	11,890
Trade creditors	23,870	32,105
Corporation tax	22,430	26,783
Other creditors	6,232	3,795
	134,645	117,449

Included within other creditors is an amount of £3,543 (2015 – £2,241) relating to social security and other taxes.

The bank loan is secured by a fixed and floating charge over the company's assets.

The finance leases are secured on the assets concerned.

For abridged accounts only the amount of creditors that are secured needs to be given, with the nature of the security and the assets secured. The total for the bank loans and overdraft and the finance leases could therefore be given with no split,

7   Creditors: amounts falling due after more than one year

	2016 £	2015 £
Preference shares	5,000	5,000
Bank Loan (secured)	30,000	15,000
Net obligations under finance leases and hire purchase contracts	12,321	5,948
	47,321	25,948

Sch. 1, 55(2), 102.1AC.28

For abridged accounts, only the amount of creditors that are secured needs to be given. The total for the bank loans and overdraft and the finance leases could therefore be given with no split.

Sch. 1.55(1),
102.1AC.27

Bank loans outstanding at the year end include instalments due after more than five years of £10,000 (2015 – £0). These loans are secured by a fixed and floating charge on the assets of the company.

Sch. 1.55(2)
102.1AC.28

The finance leases and hire purchase contracts are secured on the assets concerned.

Sch. 1.55(2)
102.1AC.28

The preference shares, which were issued at par, are redeemable between 31 December 2022 and 31 December 2023 at par at the option of the shareholder.

Sch. 1.55(1),
102.1AC.27

Preference shares amounts repayable in more than five years	5,000	5,000

8   Capital commitments

Sch. 1.57(1),
102.1AC.29

At 31 December 2016, the company had capital commitments contracted for but not provided for in these financial statements of £15,000 (2015 – £0).

9   Other commitments

Sch. 1.57(1),
102.1AC.29

At 31 December 2016, the company had total commitments under non-cancellable operating leases over the remaining life of those leases of £176,935 (2015 £77,890).

The split between capital and lease commitments is not strictly necessary, but may be easier to identify separately.

10   Pension commitments

Sch 1.57(3),
102.1AC.29

The company operates a defined contribution pension scheme, Simplifiedco Pension Scheme, for the directors and senior employees. The assets of the scheme are held separately from those of the company in an independently administered fund. At the balance sheet date, unpaid contributions of £1,205 (2015 – £954) were due to the fund. They are included in other creditors.

11   Loans to directors

Included within other debtors are the following loans to directors:

	at 1 Jan 2016	Amount Advanced	Amount Repaid	at 31 Dec 2016
A Director	800	1,400	400	1,800

s. 413,
102.1AC.36

The above loan is unsecured, interest free and repayable on demand.

12   Post balance sheet events

Sch. 1.64,
102.1AC.39

On 5 April 2017, the company acquired the goodwill and net assets of Italian Marketing Associates for £20,000 financed by a secured bank loan, repayable over five years.

13   General information

s. 396(A1)

Simplifiedco Limited is a private company limited by shares and incorporated in England. Its registered office is 123 High Street, Clearford, Surrey, SU1 2TH.

102.3.23

The financial statements are presented in Sterling, which is the functional currency of the company.

14.3 Unaudited accounts of Micro Company Limited under FRS 105

The example accounts illustrate the reduced requirements for accounts prepared by micro-entities using FRS 105 and complying with legislative requirements primarily in SI 2008/409 as amended by SI 2013/3008 and SI 2015/980.

14.3.1 Example micro-entity accounts using FRS 105

MICRO COMPANY LIMITED
COMPANY No. 4564567

Financial statements
for the year ended 31 December 2016

The example accounts have been prepared in accordance with FRS 105. The Financial Reporting Standard applicable to the Micro-entities Regime and Sch. 1, Pt. 1, Section C of the *Small Companies and Groups (Accounts and Directors Report) Regulations* 2008 (as amended by SI 2015/980).

The accounts have been treated as exempt from audit.

These accounts assume the company has no subsidiaries.

This page, inclusive of the company number, is optional.

If these accounts are filed at Companies House, then the Registrar's rules require that copy to include the company number on the balance sheet (or other document filed under *Companies Act* 2006 legislation).

Sch. 1.1(1A)

MICRO COMPANY LIMITED
Profit and loss account
For the year ended 31 December 2016

> *Formats for micro-entity accounts are given in Sch. 1, Section C*
> *The profit and loss accounts is not required to be filed.*

	2016	2015
	£	£
Turnover	160,020	108,257
Other income	171	186
Cost of raw materials and consumables	(15,321)	(10,123)
Staff costs	(90,665)	(57,363)
Depreciation and other amounts written off assets	(2,572)	(2,149)
Other charges	(40,654)	(30,456)
Profit or loss before taxation*	10,979	8,352
Tax	(2,904)	(2,630)
Profit or loss	8,075	5,722

> ** This line is optional because it is not required by the micro-entity regulations. The other lines are*
> *format headings in the regulations and cannot be changed.*

MICRO COMPANY LIMITED
Balance sheet
At 31 December 2016

Sch. 1.1(1A)

	2016	*2015*
	£	£
Fixed assets	22,476	18,107
Current assets	14,519	7,794
Prepayments and accrued income	1,750	1,500
Creditors: amounts falling due within one year	(13,465)	(11,745)
Net current assets (liabilities)	2,804	(2,451)
Total assets less current liabilities	25,280	15,656
Creditors: amounts falling due after more than one year	(4,732)	(2,595)
Provisions for liabilities	(588)	(426)
	19,960	12,635
Capital and reserves	19,960	12,635

[The following must be shown at the foot of the balance sheet rather than as part of separate notes to the accounts.]

(1) Accounting basis and standards
The financial statements have been prepared under the historical cost convention and in accordance with FRS 105 *The Financial Reporting Standard applicable to the Micro-entities Regime.**This note is optional because it is not required by FRS 105, but can be given as best practice.

(2) Directors' loans and guarantees
On 1 November 2016, the company made an interest free loan of £1,800 to one director. This loan is unsecured, interest free and repayable on demand.

s. 413

(3) Charges on assets
The company had bank loans and overdrafts totalling £9,746 (2015 – £5,788) and net obligations under finance leases and hire purchase contracts totalling £2,698 (2015 – £1,784) which are secured.
The bank loans are secured on a fixed and floating charge over the assets of the company and the finance leases and HP contracts are secured over the assets concerned.

Sch. 1.57(2)
SI 2008/409, reg. 5A

Sch. 1.57(2)

(4) Capital commitments
The company had capital commitments contracted but not provided for of £1,500 (2015 £nil).

Sch. 1.57(1)

(5) Contingent liabilities
The company had contingent liabilities in respect of foreign exchange contracts and bonds held by the company's bankers amounting to £2,176 (2015 – £1,547).

Sch. 1.57(1)

(6) Company Information
The company is registered in England and its registered number is 4564567. The company is a private company limited by shares. Its registered office is 45 High Street, Clearford, Surrey, SU1 2TH.

s. 396(A1)

MICRO COMPANY LIMITED
Balance sheet (cont'd)

The financial statements are prepared in accordance with the micro-entity provisions of the *Companies Act* 2006.

For the year ended 31 December 2016 the company was entitled to exemption from audit under *Companies Act* 2006, s. 477 relating to small companies and the members have not required the company to obtain an audit of its accounts for the year in question in accordance with s. 476 . The directors acknowledge their responsibilities for complying with the requirements of the *Companies Act* 2006 with respect to accounting records and the preparation of accounts.

The accounts were approved by the board of directors on [14 May 2017] and signed on its behalf by:

A Smith

A Smith

Company No 9999999

Note. In accordance with Companies Act 2006, s. 444(1)(a), only the balance sheet and footnotes from these accounts must be delivered to the registrar. The profit and loss account and the accountant's report are shown after the balance sheet in order to make it easier to remove them for filing accounts with the registrar.

It is no longer required for a small company to indicate the date on which the accounts have been approved.

Chartered Accountant's report to the board of directors on the preparation of the unaudited statutory accounts of Micro Company Limited for the year ended 31 December 2016

An accountants report is not required but commonly included. If included it should follow the format below, or as required by the relevant professional body.

In order to assist you to fulfil your duties under the *Companies Act* 2006, we have prepared for your approval the accounts of Micro Company Limited for the year ended 31 December 2016 as set out on pages 1–3 from the company's accounting records and from information and explanations you have given us.

As a practising member firm of the Institute of Chartered Accountants in England and Wales (ICAEW), we are subject to its ethical and other professional requirements which are detailed at icaew.com/membershandbook.

This report is made solely to the Board of Directors of Micro Company Limited, as a body, in accordance with the terms of our engagement letter dated .... Our work has been undertaken solely to prepare for your approval the accounts of Micro Company Limited and state those matters that we have agreed to state to the Board of Directors of Micro Company Limited, as a body, in this report in accordance with AAF 2/10 as detailed at www.icaew.com/compilation. To the fullest extent permitted by law, we do not accept or assume responsibility to anyone other than Micro Company Limited and its Board of Directors as a body for our work or for this report.*

It is your duty to ensure that Micro Company Limited has kept adequate accounting records and to prepare statutory accounts that give a true and fair view of the assets, liabilities, financial position and profit[/loss] of Micro Company Limited. You consider that Micro Company Limited is exempt from the statutory audit requirement for the year.*

We have not been instructed to carry out an audit or a review of the accounts of Micro Company Limited. For this reason, we have not verified the accuracy or completeness of the accounting records or information and explanations you have given to us and we do not, therefore, express any opinion on the statutory accounts.*

* These paragraphs are optional.

Stuart Manley

Stuart Manley
For and on behalf of Manley Tope & Co, Chartered Accountants
45 High Street
Clearford
Surrey
SU1 2TH

14 May 2017

14.4   Unaudited accounts of Dormant Small Company Limited

102.35.10(m)

The example dormant company accounts illustrate the unaudited accounts of a dormant small company, not applying the micro-entity regime. Dormant companies may take advantage of an exemption on transition to FRS 102 meaning that they do not need to change their accounting policies to comply with FRS 102 unless and until there are any new transactions or balances to report. It is assumed that the dormant company has taken advantage of this.

Dormant company definition – A dormant company is a company which (during any period) has no 'significant accounting transaction' and meets the criteria set out in **Chapter 10** at **10.3** and **10.4**.

s. 480

Unaudited dormant company accounts – These accounts illustrate the accounts of a company which has been dormant (within the meaning of CA 2006, s. 1169(1)) throughout the financial year and which is exempt from the provisions relating to the audit of accounts.

Filing exemptions are available to a dormant company as they are to other small companies, meaning that only the balance sheet and notes need to be filed. The profit and loss account and directors' report are not required to be filed, subject to certain statements being made. These statements are discussed in more detail in **Chapter 6** and summarised in **Table 6.6**.

Disclosure – The form and content of small dormant company accounts must have regard to SI 2008/409, Sch. 1 and 4 as amended (see **Appendix B**). The checklists given in **Appendix G** also cover disclosure requirements for dormant companies.

Registered number – In accordance with the Registrar's Rules 2009, **one** of the following documents **must** contain the name and registered number of the company: copy of Balance sheet, copy of the Profit and loss account, Directors' report, Directors' remuneration report and auditor's report (see **Chapter 16** for Registrar's Rules).

14.4.1   Example small dormant company accounts

DORMANT SMALL COMPANY LIMITED
ANNUAL REPORT AND UNAUDITED ACCOUNTS
YEAR ENDED 31 DECEMBER 2016

Registered number 017081896 England and Wales

Report of the directors

Not required to be filed.

The directors present their annual report with the unaudited accounts of the company for the year ended 31 December 2016. The company is dormant and has not traded during the year.

Julie Collins and William Gallagher were the directors of the company throughout the year.

In preparing this report, the directors have taken advantage of the small companies exemptions provided by CA 2006, s. 415A.

Signed on behalf of the board of directors by

W. Gallagher

William Gallagher

Director/Secretary Approved by the board: 9 April 2017

Profit and loss account for the year ended 31 December 2016

The company has not traded during the year or the preceding financial year. During these years, the company received no income and incurred no expenditure and therefore made neither profit nor loss.

FRS 102 transitional exemptions allow a dormant company to make no changes to its policies or accounts as a result of transition to FRS 102 until there is a change to the balances or there are any transactions. Small companies are not required to disclose that they have applied FRS 102 or to make disclosures regarding transition. It is permitted however to disclose both that the transitional exemption has been made use of if thought appropriate by the directors.

DORMANT SMALL COMPANY LIMITED
BALANCE SHEET – 31 DECEMBER 2016

	2016	2015
	£	£
Current assets		
Debtors		
Amounts owed by group undertakings		
(Ultimate parent company – Small Company Limited)	100	100
Total assets less current liabilities	£100	£100
Capital and reserves		
Called up share capital		
Allotted and fully paid 100 Ordinary shares of £1	100	100
Shareholders' funds	£100	£100

For the financial year ended 31 December 2016 the company was entitled to exemption from audit under CA 2006, s. 480 (as a dormant company) and no notice requiring an audit has been deposited under s. 476 [*member or members requesting an audit*].

The directors acknowledge their responsibilities for complying with the requirements of CA 2006 with respect to accounting records and the preparation of accounts.   *s. 475(3)*

[or (alternative): The directors acknowledge their responsibilities for ensuring that the company keeps accounting records which comply with s. 386 [of the Act] and for preparing accounts which give a true and fair view of the state of affairs of the company as at the end of the financial year and of its profit or loss for the financial year in accordance with the requirements of s. 394 and 395 and which otherwise comply with the requirements of the Companies Act 2006 relating to accounts, so far as applicable to the company.]

Signed on behalf of the board of directors by

W. Gallagher

William Gallagher

Director

Approved by the board: 9 April 2017

DORMANT SMALL COMPANY LIMITED
NOTES TO THE ACCOUNTS – 31 DECEMBER 2016

Note to the accounts

The company was dormant and has not traded during the year.

The Company is required to move to FRS 102 *The Financial Reporting Standard applicable in the UK and Republic of Ireland (2015)*. However, as a dormant company it has taken advantage of the exemption in FRS 102, paragraph 35.10(m) to not change any of its policies until such time as new transactions or changes in balance occur.

Note that the previous requirement to report whether the company had acted as agent was repealed in SI 2015/980.

Chapter 15   Small and micro company audit and assurance reports

15.1   Available report types

Some small companies are required by law to have an audit, for example, if they are part of a medium-sized group (and have not taken advantage of the subsidiary company audit exemption under s. 479A). Furthermore, some small companies may choose not to take advantage of the available small companies audit exemption and undergo a statutory audit in order to provide assurance to third parties such as lenders.

Note, however, that there are particular difficulties if a micro-entity decides to have an audit. As discussed in **7.2**, the micro-entity regime is not a fair presentation framework, as defined in ISAs (UK and Ireland) and therefore, it will be necessary to consider if the regime is appropriate for the entity and whether any audit report can avoid potential misunderstanding. ISA 210 is due to be updated to help deal with this situation by the summer of 2016. In addition, the ICAEW TECH 02/10 AAF and 03/10 AAF are expected to be updated in 2016 to help clarify the requirements when compilation reports are issued (see **15.9**).

If a company takes advantage of audit exemption in preparing its annual accounts, the directors of the company may nevertheless wish to have the comfort of some form of report from independent accountants. Any report attached to the accounts of the company where no statutory report is required should be addressed to the directors, since the accountants are engaged and instructed by the directors. A statutory audit report is addressed to the shareholders/members.

An audit provides the highest level of assurance available. If a lower level of assurance is required, the other options can provide varying levels of comfort over the accounts.

The available options are as follows, in decreasing order of assurance level provided:

- Audit report.
- Assurance review report – an accountants' report covering both the proper compilation of the accounts and the directors' 'true and fair view' assertion. These reports are discussed in **15.7** (and illustrated in **Example 15.4**).
- Agreed-upon procedures report – an accountants' report covering only some areas of the financial statements. These reports are discussed in **15.8**.
- Accounts preparation/compilation report – an accountants' report on the proper compilation of the accounts. Reports on accounts prepared for unaudited companies are discussed in **15.9** (and illustrated in **Example 15.5**).

15.2   Auditor's reports

This chapter comments on, and provides examples of, audit reports where a small company is subject to audit, either as required by statute or where the directors have requested a Companies Act audit. Audit reports must also be prepared having regard to International Standards on Auditing – ISAs (UK and Ireland).

No statutory report is required from an auditor where a small company is entitled to (and takes advantage of) one of the audit exemptions available (CA 2006, s. 477, 479A and 480); see **Chapter 13** and **Appendix D**.

Where an audit report is included, the directors are not required to make certain statements about their responsibilities on the face of the balance sheet. Instead, a more detailed statement of directors' responsibilities is required by the International Standards on Auditing and should appear either as a separate statement or as part of the directors' report. See **6.8.3**.

15.2.1   Audit – CA 2006, Pt. 16

Audit is covered in CA 2006, Pt. 16, which contains provisions (s. 475–539) concerning the requirement for audited accounts and the auditor's report.

15.2.2   Elements of an auditor's report

An auditor's report must include an introduction identifying the annual accounts and the financial reporting framework under which they are prepared, together with a description of the scope of the audit identifying the auditing standards adopted. In this year of change to FRS 102 or another new UK GAAP regime it will be helpful to ensure the description of the framework given in the audit report is specific. For example, state that it is FRS 102 *The Financial Reporting Standard applicable in the UK and Republic of Ireland (2015)* including the provisions in section 1A, rather than just UK Generally Accepted Accounting Practice.

In essence, under CA 2006, s. 495 and 496, the auditor is required to report his opinion on these elements.

(1)   *True and fair view* – whether the annual accounts show a 'true and fair view' (having regard to the directors' statutory duty under CA 2006, s. 393(1)).
(2)   *Relevant reporting framework* – whether the accounts have been prepared in accordance with the relevant financial reporting framework.
(3)   *Appropriate legislation* – whether the accounts have been prepared in accordance with CA 2006 (Pt. 15) or IAS (IAS Regulation Article 4), if applicable.
(4)   *Consistency of the Directors' Report and Strategic Report (if any)* – whether the information given in these reports is consistent with the accounts, prepared in accordance with the legal requirements and whether there are any identified misstatements.

s. 496

Note that SI 2015/980 amended s. 496 to include the requirement that the auditor state whether there are any misstatements in the strategic report or directors' report and whether the reports are prepared in accordance with the relevant legal requirements, rather than solely report on consistency. The auditor does this based on the work undertaken as part of the audit though. There is no additional requirement to search for misstatements outside of the scope of the audit.

s. 495

The auditor's report must be either 'unqualified or qualified' and contain reference to any emphasis of matter which the auditor may wish to include without qualifying the report.

15.2.3   Auditor's report – CA 2006, s. 495

The form of report to be adopted in Companies Act accounts is determined by CA 2006 and by the International Standards on Auditing as applicable within the UK. Following the adoption of International Standards on Auditing (ISAs), an auditor's report on accounts is required to follow ISA 700 (UK and Ireland) *The Auditor's Report on Financial Statements*. ISA 700 was revised in June 2013 and September 2014, but is likely to be subject to further revision in 2016, so it is always best to check the current version of the standard for details.

Example reports for the UK are included in FRC Bulletin 2010/02 (Revised), *Compendium of Illustrative Auditor's Reports on United Kingdom Private Sector Financial Statements for periods ended on or after 15 December 2010 (Revised)* with some of these updated further in FRC Bulletin 4 (Revised June 2015). As many parts of Bulletin 2010/02 are now out of date it is recommended that reference is made to Bulletin 4 and if needed further amendments based on that Bulletin are made to any examples from Bulletin 2010/02 that are required. The CCH Publication *The Audit Report Handbook* provides an updated version of the Bulletin examples. **Example 15.1** sets out a version updated with legislation to the time of writing in February 2016.

15.2.4 *Signature of auditor's report*

The auditor's report must state the name of the auditor and be signed and dated. However, where the auditor is a firm, the report delivered to the company's members must be signed by the 'senior statutory auditor' in his own name, for and on behalf of the auditor.

s. 504

Although the set of the accounts filed with the Registrar of Companies must contain the original signatures of the directors who have signed the accounts on behalf of the board of directors (where the paper accounts are being filed), a physical signature is not required on the auditor's report. In practice many auditors still prefer that the set submitted to the Registrar of Companies contains a signature. Where the auditor is a firm, the set filed with the Registrar of Companies can be signed in the name of the firm rather that in the name of the senior statutory auditor, although the name of the senior statutory auditor should be included.

The Registrar of Companies has requested that all signatures on the report and accounts should be in black ink, although in practice it has accepted ink that is suitably dark to allow the pages to be scanned legibly. However, most accounts are now filed electronically (75% in 2015) and so a signature is not included. Instead the Company Authentication Code acts as the equivalent of the director's signature and as explained the auditor does not need to sign the filed accounts.

15.3 ISA (UK and Ireland) 700 (Revised September 2014) The Independent Auditor's Report on Financial Statements

15.3.1 *ISAs (UK and Ireland) and the auditor's report*

The report of an auditor is required to follow ISA (UK and Ireland) 700 (Revised) *The Auditor's Report on Financial Statements*.

ISA (UK and Ireland) 700, although generally prescriptive as to the form and content of the auditor's report, does not preclude some flexibility when using the format and wording of the example reports prescribed by the Statement. The use of the term 'accounts', for example, in preference to 'financial statements' accords with CA 2006 and is essentially a question of personal choice, permissible provided the term is adequately defined.

From time to time, the APB[1] and latterly the FRC, have issued a Bulletin providing illustrative examples of auditor's reports. The FRC Bulletin 2010/02 (Revised), *Compendium of Illustrative Auditor's Reports on United Kingdom Private Sector Financial Statements for periods ended on or after 15 December 2010 (Revised)* is the most recent bulletin and was revised by the FRC in March 2012 and subsequently revised by FRC Bulletin 4 (April 2014 and June 2015). However, further legal changes continue not to be updated in a timely manner in such guidance, so checking of any amendments is needed.

ISA (UK and Ireland) 700 (Revised), *The Auditor's Report on Financial Statements*, facilitates, but does not mandate, a more concise auditor's report. This may be achieved by permitting the description of the scope of an audit and the auditor's reporting responsibilities to be made either within the body of the auditor's report (as was previously the norm) or by cross reference to the FRC's website (where a relevant statement of scope is maintained) or by cross reference to a 'Statement of the Scope of an Audit' that is included elsewhere within the Annual Report.

If it is decided to include the description of the scope of an audit within the auditor's report, Bulletin 4 suggests the description should be presented as follows:

[1] *Note that the APB was disbanded in July 2012. The function of the APB is now performed by the FRC's Audit and Assurance Council.*

> 'An audit involves obtaining evidence about the amounts and disclosures in the financial statements sufficient to give reasonable assurance that the financial statements are free from material misstatement, whether caused by fraud or error. This includes an assessment of: whether the accounting policies are appropriate to the [describe nature of entity] circumstances and have been consistently applied and adequately disclosed; the reasonableness of significant accounting estimates made by [describe those charged with governance]; and the overall presentation of the financial statements. In addition, we read all the financial and non-financial information in the [describe the annual report] to identify material inconsistencies with the audited financial statements and to identify any information that is apparently materially incorrect based on, or materially inconsistent with, the knowledge acquired by us in the course of performing the audit. If we become aware of any apparent material misstatements or inconsistencies we consider the implications for our report.'

If cross reference is made to the website, the relevant website address is www.frc.org.uk/auditscopeukprivate.

15.4   Example Auditor's Report on a small company

Example 15.1 is extracted from FRC Bulletin 2010/2 Revised (April 2014) (at Appendix 1, Example 1) and illustrates an 'unqualified' report with no 'emphasis of matter' paragraph for a small company where the audit is performed in accordance with International Standards on Auditing (UK and Ireland). The example has been updated for more recent changes in legislation and standards than are shown in the Bulletin. The example assumes:

- the company qualifies as a 'small company' and adopts FRS 102, including section 1A;
- the company does not prepare group financial statements;
- the company prepares a directors' report but no other 'surround information' (for example, strategic report, chairman's report, corporate governance statement or other financial commentary);
- the company adopts UK GAAP (not IAS); and
- the auditor does not take advantage of ES PASE (APB Ethical Standard – *Provisions Available for Small Entities (Revised)* (December 2010)) (except in circumstances where the report includes the text indicated by grey tinting).

Amendments in the example made (by the author), for completeness and illustrative purposes, are presented in **[bold text]**.

Example 15.1

INDEPENDENT AUDITOR'S REPORT TO THE MEMBERS *[Author's note (1)]* **OF [SMALL COMPANY LIMITED]**

We have audited the financial statements of **[Small Company Limited]** for the year ended **[31 December 2016]** which comprise the [specify the titles of the primary statements such as the Profit and Loss Account, the Balance Sheet, [the Cash Flow Statement, the Statement of Other Comprehensive Income, the Statement of Changes in Equity or give the page numbers] and the related notes. The financial reporting framework that has been applied in their preparation is applicable law and and United Kingdom Accounting Standards (United Kingdom Generally Accepted Accounting Practice), including FRS 102, section 1A '*The Financial Reporting Standard applicable in the UK and Republic of Ireland*'.

This report is made solely to the company's members, as a body, in accordance with Chapter 3 of Part 16 of the Companies Act 2006. Our audit work has been undertaken so that we might state to the company's members those matters that we are required to state to them in an auditor's report and for no other purpose. To the fullest extent permitted by law, we do not accept or assume responsibility to anyone other than the company and the company's members as a body, for our audit work, for this report, or for the opinions we have formed. [Author's note (2)]

Respective responsibilities of directors and auditor

As explained more fully in the Directors' Responsibilities Statement **[set out on page xx]**, the directors are responsible for the preparation of the financial statements and for being satisfied that they give a true and fair view. Our responsibility is to audit and express an opinion on the financial statements in accordance with applicable law and International Standards on Auditing (UK and Ireland). Those standards require us to comply with the Financial Reporting Council's Ethical Standards for Auditors [including 'Ethical Standard – Provisions Available for Small Entities (Revised)', in the circumstances set out in note [X] to the financial statements]. *[Author's note (3)]*

Scope of the audit of the financial statements

Either:

> A description of the scope of an audit of financial statements is [provided on the FRC's website at www.frc.org.uk/auditscopeukprivate] / [set out [on page X] of the Annual Report].

Or:

> An audit involves obtaining evidence about the amounts and disclosures in the financial statements sufficient to give reasonable assurance that the financial statements are free from material misstatement, whether caused by fraud or error. This includes an assessment of: whether the accounting policies are appropriate to the **company's** circumstances and have been consistently applied and adequately disclosed; the reasonableness of significant accounting estimates made by **the directors**; and the overall presentation of the financial statements. In addition, we read all the financial and non-financial information in the **directors' report** to identify material inconsistencies with the audited financial statements *and to identify any information that is apparently materially incorrect based on, or materially inconsistent with, the knowledge acquired by us in the course of performing the audit.* If we become aware of any apparent material misstatements or inconsistencies we consider the implications for our report.

[Author's note (4)]

Opinion on financial statements

In our opinion the financial statements:

- give a true and fair view of the state of the company's affairs as at **[31 December 2016]** and of its profit [loss] for the year then ended;
- have been properly prepared in accordance with United Kingdom Generally Accepted Accounting Practice applicable to smaller entities; and
- have been prepared in accordance with the requirements of the *Companies Act* 2006.

Opinion on other matter prescribed by the *Companies Act* 2006

In our opinion, based on the work undertaken in the course of the audit, the information given in the [Strategic Report and] Directors' Report for the financial year for which the financial statements are prepared is consistent with those financial statements and has been prepared in accordance with applicable legal requirements. No material misstatements in the [Strategic Report and] Directors' Report have been identified. *[Author's note (5)]*

Matters on which we are required to report by exception

We have nothing to report in respect of the following matters where the *Companies Act* 2006 requires us to report to you if, in our opinion:

- adequate accounting records have not been kept, or returns adequate for our audit have not been received from branches not visited by us;
- the financial statements are not in agreement with the accounting records and returns;
- certain disclosures of directors' remuneration specified by law are not made;

- we have not received all the information and explanations we require for our audit; or
- the directors were not entitled to (prepare the financial statements in accordance with the small companies regime) (and) (take advantage of the small companies' exemption in preparing the directors' report and take advantage of the small companies exemption from the requirement to prepare a strategic report).

Lucy Caldwell. *[Author's note (6)]*

....

Lucy Caldwell (Senior Statutory Auditor)
for and on behalf of TRUE & FAIRVIEW LLP, Statutory Auditor

17 Queens Place,
LONDON
23 April 2017

Author's notes and commentary to **Example 15.1**

(1) **Report to the members** – *The statutory auditor's report is made to the members of the company (CA 2006, s. 495). No statutory report is required where a small company is otherwise entitled to audit exemption (CA 2006, s. 477). A non-statutory audit report for an audit exempt company would be addressed to the directors of the company, in accordance with whose instructions the audit is conducted.*

(2) **Duty of care to third parties** – *the ICAEW recommends that auditors include additional wording in audit reports in order to clarify auditors' responsibilities to third parties – that is, other than to the members (or the directors, as the case may be) as a body. (Audit 1/03 – The Audit Report and The Auditors' Duty of Care to Third Parties.) (January 2003, most recent update January 2010.) A negligence case in 2015 confirmed that this disclaimer can be effective in limiting liability to third parties. See Barclays Bank plc v Grant Thornton UK LLP [2015].*

(3) **FRC Ethical Standard – Provisions Available for Small Entities (Revised)** *(ES PASE) – Paragraph 24 of ES PASE requires disclosure in the auditor's report where the audit firm has taken advantage of an exemption provided by ES PASE. The Appendix to ES PASE provides illustrative disclosures of relevant circumstances where the audit firm has taken advantage of an exemption (for example, where auditors have assisted in the preparation of accounts or provided tax advice). The words in square brackets in the above example should be deleted if the relief and exemptions provided by ES PASE are not utilised.*

[www.frc.org.uk/Our-Work/Codes-Standards/Audit-and-assurance/Standards-and-guidance/ Standards-and-guidance-for-auditors/Ethical-standards-for-auditors.aspx]

An example note illustrated within the FRC ES PASE Appendix provides that 'In common with many other businesses of our size and nature we use our auditors to prepare and submit returns to the tax authorities and assist with the preparation of the financial statements'.

(4) **Description of the scope of an audit of financial statements** – *ISA (UK and Ireland) 700 (Revised) requires that an auditor's report should either: cross refer to a Statement of the scope of an audit maintained on the FRC's website; or cross refer to such a scope statement that is included elsewhere within the Annual Report; or include a prescribed description of the scope of an audit.*

*The prescribed description of the scope of an audit (as illustrated in **Example 15.1**) is set out in ISA (UK and Ireland) 700 (Revised).*

(5) **Changes in the Act re narrative reporting** – *s. 496 of the Companies Act was updated by SI 2015/980. This added additional requirements for the auditor to consider whether the directors' report and any strategic report were not only consistent with the financial statements but also whether they were prepared according to the relevant requirements and whether there were any misstatements apparent from other audit work carried out. The requirement applies for accounting periods commencing on or after 1 January 2016.*

(6) **Signature and dating of auditor's report** – *CA 2006, s. 503 and ISA (UK and Ireland) 700 (Revised) The Auditor's Report on Financial Statements para. 23–26.*

15.5 Special Auditor's Report – abbreviated accounts

There is no longer any requirement for a special auditor's report on abbreviated accounts, as no such accounts exist since the implementation of SI 2015/980.

15.6 Filing exemptions

Where advantage is taken of s. 444 to not file the profit and loss account, it is necessary to provide information about any audit that has been conducted. **Chapter 6** sets out a summary of the requirements in **Table 6.6** and the details are set out below.

It is necessary to include the following information in the notes to the balance sheet (except for micro-entities):

s. 444(5B)

(a) state whether the auditors' report is qualified or unqualified;
(b) where the report was qualified disclose the basis of qualification, including whether any of the statements re adequate accounting records, etc. in s. 498 were made;
(c) where the report was unqualified include reference to any emphasis of matter items;
(d) state the name of the auditor and the name of the person who signed as senior statutory auditor; or
(e) if conditions in s. 506 exist (circumstances where names may be omitted) that a resolution has been passed and notified to the Secretary of State.

As small entities are generally audit exempt, the above statements are not required if the exemption has been taken advantage of. However, even if the company is audit exempt, if it decides to nonetheless have an audit, the above statements are required.

It should also be noted that if a small company chooses or is required to have an audit (e.g. because it is a member of a non-small group) then it would appear that the requirement to disclose auditor's remuneration still currently exists (the *Companies (Disclosure of Auditor Remuneration and Liability Limitation Agreements) Regulations* 2008 (SI 2008/480), reg. 4). It is expected that the requirement will be repealed by June 2016 when the amendments to enact the EU Audit Directive are made.

15.7 Assurance review reports

Guidance on the conduct of assurance reviews on accounts was published by the ICAEW in Technical Release (Audit and Assurance Faculty) TECH 09/13 AAF *Assurance Review Engagements on Historical Financial Statements*. The objectives of a review report for a small company would be to provide comfort to the directors and to enhance the credibility of the accounts of companies that are exempt from audit with third parties, including members and the Registrar of Companies.

The technical release states:

'Review engagements, like audit engagements, may help the accountant to report weaknesses and other issues that come to their attention to the directors. In other words, such engagements can generate much more value for the directors than just the assurance report itself. This represents a substantial degree of understanding of the client's circumstances. Further substantive testing is not required unless the chartered accountant has reason to be concerned about some aspect of the business. An assurance review engagement is therefore a flexible and proportionate service which can be adapted to suit different clients.'

TECH 09/13 AAF

The guidance is designed to assist with compliance with the International Standard for Review Engagements (ISRE) 2400 (Revised) issued by the IAASB which was revised in 2012 and came into effect for reviews of accounts for periods ending on or after 31 December 2013. It also provides example letters, statements and reports to support review engagements.

Further guidance can be found in the ICAEW's Assurance Sourcebook, published in July 2012.

Example 15.4 reproduces the example Assurance Review Report from TECH 09/13 AAF.

Example 15.4 Example Assurance Review ICAEW Technical Release (Audit and Assurance Faculty) – TECH 09/13 AAF (September 2013) Appendix 4: Illustrative Assurance Review Report

INDEPENDENT CHARTERED ACCOUNTANTS' REVIEW REPORT TO THE DIRECTORS OF XYZ LIMITED

We have reviewed the financial statements of XYZ Limited for the year ended [date], which comprise the [Profit and Loss Account, the Balance Sheet, the Cash Flow Statement, the Statement of Other *Comprehensive Income, the Statement of Changes in Equity*] and the related notes 1 to [X]. The financial reporting framework that has been applied in their preparation is applicable law and FRS 102 *The Financial Reporting Standard applicable in the UK and Republic of Ireland (2015) [including section 1A].*

This report is made solely to the Company's directors, as a body, in accordance with the terms of our engagement letter dated [date]. Our review has been undertaken so that we may state to the company's directors those matters that we have agreed to state to them in our engagement letter and for no other purpose. To the fullest extent permitted by law, we do not accept or assume responsibility to anyone other than the Company and the Company's directors as a body for our work, for this report or for the conclusions we have formed.

Directors' Responsibility for the Financial Statements

As explained more fully in the Directors' Responsibilities Statement [set out on pages ...], the directors are responsible for the preparation of the financial statements and for being satisfied that they give a true and fair view.

Accountants' Responsibility

Our responsibility is to express a conclusion based on our review of the financial statements. We conducted our review in accordance with International Standard on Review Engagements (ISRE) 2400 (Revised), Engagements to review historical financial statements and ICAEW Technical Release TECH 09/13 AAF Assurance review engagements on historical financial statements. ISRE 2400 also requires us to comply with the ICAEW Code of Ethics.

Scope of the Assurance Review

A review of financial statements in accordance with ISRE 2400 (Revised) is a limited assurance engagement. We have performed additional procedures to those required under a compilation engagement. These primarily consist of making enquiries of management and others within the entity, as appropriate, applying analytical procedures and evaluating the evidence obtained. The procedures performed in a review are substantially less than those performed in an audit conducted in accordance with International Standards on Auditing (UK and Ireland). Accordingly, we do not express an audit opinion on these financial statements.

Conclusion

Based on our review, nothing has come to our attention that causes us to believe that the financial statements have not been prepared:

- so as to give a true and fair view of the state of the company's affairs as at [date], and of its profit [loss] for the year then ended;
- in accordance with United Kingdom Generally Accepted Accounting Practice (applicable to Small Entities applying FRS 102 including section 1A); and
- in accordance with the requirements of the *Companies Act* 2006.

[Accountant's signature – name of individual or firm]

....

[Firm name]

Chartered Accountants

[Address]

[Date]

15.8   Agreed-upon procedures

The scope of an agreed-upon procedures engagement is formulated by discussion between the directors of the company and the chartered accountant performing the work.

The accountant prepares a report based on the results of the procedures performed on a factual basis and does not express any opinion or conclusion.

Examples might include:

- verification of existence and ownership of fixed assets;
- stock valuation review; or
- verification of controls being applied on purchase payments.

15.9   Compilation: reports on accounts prepared for unaudited companies – ICAEW Technical Release Audit 02/10

A Technical Release, issued by the Audit and Assurance Faculty of the Institute of Chartered Accountants in England and Wales in November 2010 (AAF 02/10 *Chartered Accountants' Reports on Compilation of Financial Statements of Incorporated Entities*), gives general guidance on the form and content of reports where accountants 'compile' (being the generally acknowledged term for 'prepare') accounts on behalf of client companies. At the time of writing it is understood that this guidance is being updated to take account of developments in new UK GAAP. Reference should be made to the most up to date version of the document.

The example accountants' report (a non-statutory (or contractual) report) contained in the Technical Release issued in November 2010 is reproduced in **Example 15.5**.

The example is essentially appropriate in circumstances where the directors wish the accountants to assist them in their meeting of the directors' statutory obligation under the Companies Act, to prepare annual accounts showing a true and fair view. Optional paragraphs (or text to be completed as appropriate) are indicated by [square brackets].

The use of the report remains voluntary – there is no requirement for companies to use professional accountants to help compile accounts or to obtain an accounts compilation report.

Where accounts are compiled by a professional accountant and an accountants' report is prepared on the lines of **Example 15.5**, the Technical Release AAF 02/10 stresses the importance of agreeing terms of engagement between the directors and the reporting accountants. The Technical Release provides example terms.

Example 15.5   Chartered Accountants' Report on the Compilation of Financial Statements of Incorporated Entities (AAF 02/10)

Chartered Accountant's/Accountants' report to the board of directors on the preparation of the unaudited statutory accounts of XYZ Limited for the year [/period] ended ...

In order to assist you to fulfil your duties under the *Companies Act* 2006, we have prepared for your approval the accounts of XYZ Limited for the year [/period] ended [date] [as set out on pages x–x/which comprise (insert statements)] from the company's accounting records and from information and explanations you have given us.

As a practising member [/member firm] of the Institute of Chartered Accountants in England and Wales (ICAEW), we are subject to its ethical and other professional requirements which are detailed at www.icaew.com/membershandbook.

[This report is made solely to the Board of Directors of XYZ Limited, as a body, in accordance with the terms of our engagement letter dated [date].] Our work has been undertaken [solely to prepare for your approval the accounts of XYZ Limited and state those matters that we have agreed to state to them/the Board of Directors of XYZ Limited, as a body, in this report] in accordance with AAF 2/10 as detailed at www.icaew.com/compilation. [To the fullest extent permitted by law, we do not accept or assume responsibility to anyone other than the XYZ Limited and its Board of Directors as a body for our work or for this report.]

[It is your duty to ensure that XYZ Limited has kept adequate accounting records and to prepare statutory accounts that give a true and fair view of the assets, liabilities, financial position and [profit/loss] of XYZ Limited. You consider that XYZ Limited is exempt from the statutory audit requirement for the year [/period].]

[We have not been instructed to carry out an audit or a review of the accounts of XYZ Limited. For this reason, we have not verified the accuracy or completeness of the accounting records or information and explanations you have given to us and we do not, therefore, express any opinion on the statutory accounts.]

[Explanatory paragraph: e.g. records destroyed by fire.] *Explanatory paragraph may be positioned in other places in the report depending on the nature of the matter described.*

Signature........................... *(The report is signed in the name of the professional accountant or, where appropriate, in the name of the accounting firm.)*

Typed name of professional accountant

Chartered Accountants

Address

Date ....

Optional paragraphs or choices in wording are included in square brackets above.

The first three optional paragraphs aim to assist the user in understanding the nature and extent of the work performed by the accountant and contain standard disclaimers.

The explanatory paragraph should be used in those (rare) situations where the accountant concludes that it remains appropriate for them to be associated with the accounts despite departure from an applicable accounting standard or the availability of only incomplete information (for example, when records have been lost in a fire). The explanatory paragraph serves to highlight disclosures relating to these issues.

Part IV   Filing accounts

Chapter 16 Accounts filing for small companies

16.1 Introduction

This book does not aim to cover the finer details of the filing requirements for the accounts of small companies but this chapter gives guidance on filing with both the Registrar of Companies and HMRC and explains some of the current filing methods which are introducing changes to the process which has existed for many years of paper filing of accounts with the Registrar and tax authorities.

In general, accounts of small companies need to be filed:

- with the Registrar of Companies within the filing deadline (see below); and
- with HMRC with the company's tax return (if the company is required to file a tax return) not more than 12 months following the end of the year to which they relate.

For a number of years now the Registrar of Companies has accepted electronic filing of some types of accounts. The number of accounts being submitted electronically is growing and by the end of 2015, 75% of accounts were filed electronically. This chapter sets out the various options for a company in relation to filing accounts electronically.

16.2 Filing deadlines

In general, private companies are required to file accounts with the Registrar of Companies within nine months from the end of the accounting period (accounting reference date or ARD).

When filing the company's first accounts, the deadline for delivery is 21 months after the date of incorporation. The deadline remains the same even if this company extends its first accounting period to the maximum of 18 months. It is calculated to the exact corresponding date in the 21st month following the incorporation. For example, a company incorporated on 29 January 2014 has until midnight on 29 October 2016 to submit its first accounts.

When the accounting period is extended, other than for the first accounts, the filing deadline remains as nine months after the end of the period. However, when a private company shortens the accounting period, the filing deadline for that period is the longer of the following:

- nine months after the new ARD; or
- three months after the date of the notice of the ARD change being delivered to the Registrar.

Companies submitting their accounts after the filing deadline has passed will incur a late filing penalty of at least £150. The penalty increases in line with the period of late submission. The maximum penalty for a private company which submits accounts six months after the normal filing deadline is £1,500. However, if the company files its accounts late two years in a row, the penalty in the second year is doubled. Further guidance from Companies House can be found on their website (see **Appendix H**).

16.3 Electronic tagging of accounts (iXBRL)

In March 2006, a review was carried out of HMRC's online services. One of the recommendations of the review, which was supported by the Government, was that HMRC and Companies House should work together to provide a joint filing facility. In support of these recommendations, Companies House has encouraged online filing wherever possible.

Inline Extensible Business Reporting Language (iXBRL) is an electronic format for embedding XBRL 'tags' into financial statements. XBRL itself is an open and global standard for exchanging business information.

The accounts tagged under iXBRL are still in a format which can be read 'manually' (as opposed to by a computer only): this is what the 'inline' refers to – the tags applied are hidden behind the scenes, in line with the normal text.

Embedding tags into an annual report and accounts document can be performed in a variety of ways:

- using an accounts preparation package which has the tagging facility built in;
- using tagging software to apply the tags to accounts created in a word-processed document; or
- engaging a third party tagging firm or accountant to create the iXBRL file from the word processed document file ('managed tagging').

HMRC maintain a list of approved providers of software and managed tagging providers at www.gov.uk/government/publications/corporation-tax-commercial-software-suppliers.

Taxonomies have been created for UK GAAP (both old and new) and IFRS which set out the available tags to be used in a set of financial statements. The FRC has taken over the function of dealing with UK GAAP taxonomies whilst the IASB look after the IFRS ones. Up until now charity accounts haven't had suitable 'tagging' terms within these taxonomies, but the FRC has recently issued a charities taxonomy and so Companies House expect soon to be able to offer an electronic filing option for charity accounts under new UK GAAP.

The FRC has issued a guide to taxonomies which can be found here www.frc.org.uk/Our-Work/ Publications/Accounting-and-Reporting-Policy/FRC-Taxonomies-Tagging-Guide.pdf as well as the taxonomies themselves. However, the latter are mostly only required for the software companies writing iXBRL compatible accounts production programmes.

16.4 Filing accounts with the Registrar of Companies

The Registrar of Companies is given authority under CA 2006 to make rules governing the filing of documents at Companies House. These 'Registrar's Rules' are secondary legislation, made under s. 1117 of the Act, and include the form, delivery and method of authentication for documents (including accounts) to be delivered to the Registrar.

The rules specify different filing requirements for hard copy and electronic filings. For example, although the Companies Act requirement for an original signature to be included on the accounts that are filed was repealed from 1 October 2009, signatures are still required by the Registrar's Rules to be included on balance sheets filed in paper form.

Furthermore, Companies House has reviewed its policy on filing documents with *original* signatures and has concluded that the Registrar of Companies will not reject documents 'simply because the signature does not appear to be original'.

A detailed list of the Registrar's Rules, including when amendments came into force, is available at www.gov.uk/government/publications/company-registrars-rules-and-powers.

The current version of these rules is GP 6 September 2014 which itself was updated in December 2014. The registrar encourages entities to use either software filing or WebFiling services. Software filing means using an external provider's software, such as CCH's Accounts Production, to create iXBRL versions of accounts for filing. WebFiling is Companies House's own service, designed for use by the smallest and simplest of entities who might not be expected to have access to specialist software.

Paper filing can be used optionally in all cases and in some cases it is the only way that certain sets of accounts can currently be filed, though Companies House are working hard to reduce situations when paper filing is needed.

From a practical point of view, Companies House report that there are fewer rejections of accounts when filed electronically (2.1% in 2015) compared to paper (12.8% in 2015) as the software checks a number of the elements prior to filing. This also results in fewer late filing penalties, as rejected accounts often cause deadlines to be missed.

Table 16.1   The Registrar's Rules

The Registrar's Rules consist of the following five volumes www.gov.uk/guidance/registrars-rules:

Registrar's (Electronic Form) Rules 2012 Volume 1 – Documents delivered in electronic form;

Registrar's Rules 2009 Volume 2 – Documents delivered in paper form;

Registrar's Rules 2009 Volume 3 – Documents (or parts thereof) delivered on a CD-ROM or DVD-ROM;

Registrar's Rules 2009 Volume 4 – Informal correction of a document delivered to the registrar;

Registrar's Rules 2009 Volume 5 – Authentication of a certificate sent by the Registrar by electronic means.

The website above also lists a table of changes to the filing requirements.

16.4.1   Filing accounts in paper form

Of particular relevance to the filing of accounts on paper at Companies House are the following rules relating to registered number, signatures and the form and content of documents.

Table 16.2   Filing accounts at Companies House

The Registrar's (requirements for paper documents) Rules 2009

Registered number

Paragraph 22(3) of Volume 2 of the amended Registrar's Rules 2009 lists the documents (delivered on paper) which must contain the name and registered number of the company to which the document relates (but only one of the documents filed must show this information):

- copy of balance sheet;
- (where applicable): copy of profit and loss account; copy of directors' report; or directors' remuneration report;
- copy of auditor's report.

The company name or registered number required as above must be in black typescript or handwritten in black ink in a 'prominent position' in the document filed; this does **not**, however, include, for example, the cover of an annual accounts package.

Be careful to ensure the name and number is exactly as stated on the Register as this is a common cause for rejection of accounts.

Signature – the following documents (filed in paper form) must be signed by a director:

- copy of balance sheet;
- annual accounts.

The signature must be applied to the document in a prominent position, **at the end of the balance sheet**.

Table 16.2   Filing accounts at Companies House (cont'd)

Form and content of documents:

Generally, paper documents sent to Companies House must state in a prominent position the registered name and number of the company. Paper documents must be:

- on A4 size, plain white paper with a matt finish *(note – Companies House does usually accept accounts on US letter sized paper and off-white paper as long as the document can be scanned legibly to A4)*;
- portrait orientation;
- **black**, clear and legible text, of uniform density; and
- clear and legible bold letters and numbers.

Documents should not have poor lettering or be photocopies, carbon copies, or produced from a dot matrix printer *(note – as this may cause problems scanning the documents)*.

16.4.1.1   Common reasons for accounts rejections at Companies House

Companies House regularly report, in webinars via the ICAEW for example, details of rejection reasons for accounts. The following are the main reasons in 2015 why paper accounts had been rejected:

- Made Up to Date is the same date as the last set of accounts;
- balance sheet signature is not present or as required;
- the Accounting Reference Date or Made Up to Date are incorrect or absent;
- the company number is invalid;
- not all relevant documents are filed.

For electronic accounts, only a very small percent (2.1% in 2015) are rejected and this is primarily due to the following reasons:

- Made Up to Date is a duplicate;
- the Accounting Reference Date or Made Up to Date are incorrect or absent;
- abbreviated or micro accounts submitted for a plc.

If such accounts are submitted close to the filing deadline and the corrected accounts cannot be returned before the filing deadline expires, an automatic late filing penalty will be issued.

16.4.2   Filing accounts in electronic form

There are four ways to file accounts electronically at Companies House.

- WebFiling;
- Filing of iXBRL accounts:
  - joint filing with HMRC;
  - electronic filing using enabled accounts production software;
  - electronic filing of iXBRL accounts using enabled company secretarial software or a third party web-based service.

16.4.2.1   WebFiling accounts

Companies House's WebFiling service allows the filing of a number of documents electronically, including (with some restrictions):

- dormant company accounts where they have never traded (DCA) AA02;
- audit exempt abbreviated accounts (facilities for the new abridged accounts will soon be added);

- audit exempt micro-entity accounts; and
- audit exempt full accounts.

Audited companies, community interest companies (CIC) and limited liability partnerships (LLP) cannot file annual accounts using the WebFiling service.

The Dormant Company Accounts (DCA) AA02 are online WebFilings where the information is completed on screen.

Audit Exempt Full Accounts (and the Joint Filing Accounts for joint filing with HMRC – see below) are downloadable templates that are filled in then uploaded to Companies House.

Electronic filing is particularly useful if accounts are filed near to the filing deadline when there is invariably a risk of incurring penalties for late filing in the event that Companies House does not receive the document in time. More information is available here: https://ewf.companieshouse.gov. uk/help/en/stdwf/faqHelp.html#companyAccounts.

Table 16.3 sets out the process for the filing of accounts at Companies House via the WebFiling service.

Table 16.3   WebFiling

Paragraph 6 of Volume 1 of the Registrar's (Electronic Form) Rules 2012, updated in 2015 require that: to deliver a document using WebFiling the presenter must:

(a) have access to the internet;
(b) have an email account;
(c) be a registered user of WebFiling (information about the registration process is available on the website); and
(d) subject to rule 6.(3), be in possession of the authentication code for the company (or other body) to which the document relates (unless it is an incorporation package).

Accounts delivered to the Registrar of Companies via WebFiling must be in the form of the template supplied for that purpose by the Registrar of Companies as part of the WebFiling facility.

Information must be input into the data input fields on the locally saved PDF copy of the template. The date input fields are specified here:

http://resources.companieshouse.gov.uk/about/policyDocuments/registrarsRules/volume1.pdf

Paragraph 9(3) of Volume 1 of the Registrar's (Electronic Form) Rules 2012

- WebFiled accounts must be, in form and substance, copies of the actual annual accounts in whole or part or dormant accounts prepared for the company, together with such additional information as may be required by the registrar.

To use WebFiling the company must first register for this service on the Companies House website: www.gov.uk/file-an-annual-return-with-companies-house.

WebFiling requires two codes for the submission of data for an individual company:

- a password to access the service (password is linked to the presenter's email address); and
- the Company's Authentication Code (CAC) which is the electronic equivalent of a company's officer's signature (CAC is linked to the company number).

The CAC must be requested via Companies House WebFiling page and it is sent by post to the company's registered office address.

Audit exempt full accounts filing via the WebFiling service uses a PDF template that registered users download and complete offline. A key feature of the template is that it contains in-built checks and help text which assists with avoiding the omission of key information and making calculation errors in the balance sheet and notes.

Once downloaded, the template prompts the user to make choices that define the content of the accounts. The accounts can then be completed offline over a period of time and saved drafts can then, for example, be e-mailed to colleagues or clients before submitting the final version to Companies House using the CAC. The completed template is then saved on the computer as a locked copy of the accounts filed with Companies House.

These accounts are delivered to Companies House by:

- selecting the 'submit' or 'send' button found at the end of the locally saved electronic copy of the template;
- supplying the company's registered number and CAC when prompted; and
- by supplying the presenter's email address when prompted.

The Dormant Company Accounts (DCA) AA02 cannot be downloaded and must be completed online while the user is logged onto the WebFiling service. It is important to remember that the presenter of a company's accounts must act under the specific authority of that company's directors in delivering the accounts to the Registrar.

A document delivered using WebFiling is considered as received when it is given an envelope number by the Registrar.

16.4.2.2   Joint Filing of accounts with HMRC

The joint filing service which submits iXBRL tagged accounts online to both HMRC and to Companies House can be accessed through the HMRC Online Services page:

https://www.gov.uk/file-an-annual-return-with-companies-house

A Government Gateway user ID and password is required to access HMRC Online Services and additionally the CAC must be entered into the template.

As with WebFiling, online joint iXBRL filing templates are designed primarily for small audit exempt companies with relatively straightforward financial information.

The intelligent PDF accounts template enables the accounts data to be entered offline and to be saved or printed during completion. It has built-in checks which ensure that the calculations are correct and it also takes into account different filing deadlines thereby enabling timely submissions to both HMRC and Companies House.

The user can select whether they wish to submit full or abbreviated accounts to Companies House (provision for abridged accounts is expected to be available soon). The submission is done directly from the template (not via WebFiling).

If abbreviated accounts are sent to Companies House, this data is extracted from the full accounts data and the full accounts data is held within the template awaiting submission to HMRC.

When HMRC filing is due the full accounts data can be filed; this can be done some time after filing accounts with Companies House.

16.4.2.3   Electronic filing of iXBRL accounts at Companies House

If the accounts production software being used produces UK GAAP accounts in iXBRL format, or the accounts are otherwise iXBRL tagged, then these can be filed directly with Companies House electronically.

The accounts can be filed either directly from the accounts production software (if the software includes this feature), or can be uploaded via an enabled company secretarial software package or third party web-based service.

Companies House maintains a list of suitable software packages at: www.gov.uk/company-filing-software/filing-annual-accounts-returns-and-tax-accounts.

The software filing service enables the submission of the following account types:

- abbreviated unaudited (abridged accounts will soon be available);
- full unaudited;
- full audited;
- dormant previously traded;
- dormant company accounts where they have never traded; and
- group.

To file accounts using software a company will need a Companies House online filing presenter account (applied for via the Companies House website).

16.5 Filing amended accounts

If it is found that a set of accounts submitted to Companies House is defective (i.e. contains errors or is not compliant with a requirement of the Companies Act), then the directors may submit amending financial statements to the Registrar of Companies. This may be because the company has realised that the accounts are defective or because the Registrar has written to the directors to request that they either give a satisfactory explanation for the accounts or prepare revised accounts.

The rules relating to revised accounts are set out in (CA 2006, Pt. 16, s. 454–459) and the *Companies (Revision of Defective Accounts and Reports) Regulations* 2008 (SI 2008/373):

Revised accounts sent to Companies House must be marked as 'amending'. It is recommended that the 'amending' is very clearly marked (to prevent rejection by Companies House for being made up to the same date as a set of accounts that has previously been filed). The highlighting should not obscure any part of the accounts, however, as they could then be rejected if they do not scan legibly.

The amending accounts must contain the following statements (in a prominent position):

- the revised accounts replace the original accounts for the financial year (specifying it);
- the revised accounts are now the statutory accounts for that year; and
- the revised accounts have been prepared as at the date of the original accounts, and not as at the date of the revision and accordingly do not deal with events between those dates.

The accounts must also contain details (in a prominent position) of:

- the way in which the original accounts did not comply with the requirements of CA 2006; and
- any significant amendments made as a result of correcting the defects.

SI 2008/373, Pt. 2, reg. 4

If the original accounts were audited, the amending accounts must contain an audit report on the revised accounts. This report differs from the original report and includes statements of whether:

- in the auditor's opinion, the revised accounts have been properly prepared in accordance with CA 2006;
- the revised accounts give a true and fair view of the individual balance sheet and profit and loss (consolidated in the case of group accounts), seen *as at the date the original accounts were approved*; and
- the original accounts failed to comply with the requirements of CA 2006 in the respects identified by the directors.

SI 2008/373, Pt. 2, reg. 7

SI 2008/373,
Pt. 2, reg. 5

Where a revised directors' report is prepared, the report must also state whether, in the auditor's opinion, the information given in that revised report is consistent with the accounts for the financial year.

SI 2008/373,
Pt. 2, reg. 8

If the previous set of accounts was not audited, but the revised set is found not to be exempt from audit, the company must also deliver an auditor's report to Companies House within 28 days after the date of revision of the accounts.

The original (defective) accounts will remain on the public record. Removing incorrect documents from the public record requires a court order (unless Companies House, in error, accepted an item which should have been rejected).

Companies House provides further guidance at: http://resources.companieshouse.gov.uk/ infoAndGuide/faq/amendingAccounts.shtml (Archived content).

16.6   Filing accounts with HMRC

A UK corporation tax return for a small limited company (preparing Companies Act or IAS individual accounts) includes form CT600, the accounts and the tax computation together with any accompanying information as required. This must be submitted to HMRC electronically. The accounts forming part of the return must be in iXBRL format. iXBRL tagging of UK statutory financial statements has been required for corporation tax purposes since 2011.

A dormant company will not have to deliver a return unless it is sent a statutory notice to do so. In most cases, if HMRC have been notified that a company is dormant, no notice to deliver a return will be issued.

Overseas companies resident in the UK must deliver the accounts required by a notice to deliver a return in iXBRL format. Also a company not resident in the UK, but carrying on a trade in the UK through a permanent establishment, branch or agency in the UK, must deliver any trading and profit and loss account and any balance sheet of the UK establishment, branch or agency required as part of its return in iXBRL format.

16.7   Planned changes in accounts filing

As part of the journey towards Companies House's aim of becoming a fully electronic registry, in 2010 Companies House announced that it expected all incorporations and filings of annual returns, accounts and the main company changes would be digital-only (electronic) by March 2013 for the standard company types.

Although mandatory electronic filing at Companies House has been put on hold until the government's moratorium on new regulation for small businesses has ended, the number of accounts being filed electronically has grown rapidly over the recent past.

The Companies House register is not yet fully electronic, but the vast majority (84.8% during 2015) of the documents submitted are being filed electronically.

There are many advantages in filing electronically, including the certainty that accounts have been accepted quickly, the inbuilt checks to prevent errors and the avoidance of delays or loss in the post. In addition, credit reference agencies use Companies House data and where it is available electronically the agencies can upload such information in their systems the day after it goes live on Companies House, allowing much more accurate and relevant data to be quickly available.

It can only be anticipated that this proportion will increase 'voluntarily' and will, indeed, become a requirement over the coming years. In the meantime, Companies House will be adding facilities for charities, LLPs and new UK GAAP accounts, including abridged accounts to be filed electronically.

Appendices

Appendix A   Guidelines and definitions

This appendix gives brief guidelines on statutory definitions, interpretation and analysis. Comment is not necessarily comprehensive but aims to cover those headings or terms that tend to present difficulty in practice for smaller companies. The text contains references to statute and accounting standards from where further guidance may be available.

Definitions are provided by accounting standards, as well as the legislation. Although the various Companies Acts have provided a measure of standardisation for company accounts (for example, in the form of prescriptive formats and codification of accounting rules and principles), legislation often only provides limited guidance in terms of definition or interpretation.

Most of the problems that arise in practice concern interpretation of statutory intent. Over the years, accounting standards have increasingly provided a measure of guidance and interpretation. Nevertheless, difficulties often concern topics such as: presentation, analysis of expenses, categorisation or composition of statutory headings, or simply accounts presentation.

Where there are no definitions or rules laid down by the Companies Act or provided by accounting standards (including IAS), it is necessary to:

* refer to definitions in accounting standards (note that definitions for FRS 102 are contained in the glossary at the end of the standard. Defined terms are in bold within the standard);
* determine a reasonable interpretation of the requirement;
* ensure the proposed interpretation is sensible and appropriate to the business; and
* adopt the interpretation consistently from year to year.

1   Accounts

Definitions of statutory terms concerning a company's accounts, prepared to show a 'true and fair view', are set out below.

1.1   Annual report

The directors of a company must prepare a directors' report and strategic report for each financial year of the company. For a financial year in which the company is a parent company (and the directors of the company prepare group accounts), the directors' report must be a consolidated report (a 'group directors' report') relating to the undertakings included in the consolidation.

For small companies, including micro-entities, an exemption is available from preparing a strategic report and for filing the directors' report with the Registrar of Companies. Additionally, micro-entities are exempt from the requirement to prepare a directors' report.

1.2   Annual accounts   s. 471

Individual accounts – the accounts of a company prepared by the directors, for each financial year: s. 394

* comprising a balance sheet (as at the last day of the year), a profit and loss account, and notes to the accounts;   s. 396
* showing a 'true and fair view'; and   s. 393
* complying with the provisions of CA 2006 and SI 2008/409, Sch. 1 (Small companies) (as to form, content and additional note information).   s. 396

155

s. 395
Individual accounts must be prepared in accordance with the appropriate framework and accordingly may be prepared:

- in accordance with CA 2006, s. 396 ('Companies Act individual accounts'); or
- in accordance with international accounting standards ('IAS individual accounts').

s. 404(1)
Group accounts – the accounts prepared, in addition to 'individual accounts', by the directors of a parent company:

- comprising consolidated accounts (consolidated balance sheet and consolidated profit and loss account of the parent and its 'subsidiary undertakings' and related notes); and
- showing a 'true and fair view' of the consolidated undertakings as a whole (so far as concerns members of the parent company).

s. 403
Group accounts must (with exceptions) be prepared either:

- in accordance with SI 2008/409, Sch. 6 (Small companies) or SI 2008/410, Sch. 6 (Large and medium-sized companies) ('Companies Act group accounts'); or
- in accordance with international accounting standards or if required by Article 4 of the IAS Regulation ('IAS group accounts').

Group accounts exemptions – the following exemptions from preparing group accounts are available:

- eligible small groups (CA 2006, s. 383) – see **Chapter 12**;
s. 400   - parent companies included in accounts of larger EEA group;
s. 401   - parent companies included in accounts of larger non-EEA group; and
s. 402   - if all subsidiary undertakings excluded from consolidation.

Entitlement to exemptions in all cases is determined upon conditions – see **Chapter 12**.

IAS accounts – accounts ('IAS individual accounts' or 'IAS group accounts') prepared in accordance with international accounting standards adopted by the EU (EC Regulation No. 1606/2002).

s. 471
Annual accounts of small companies – the individual or group accounts of small companies, as defined, prepared in accordance with the special provisions for small companies set out in CA 2006 and SI 2008/409, Sch. 1 and 6.

A company's 'annual accounts', in relation to a financial year, means the company's individual accounts for that year (CA 2006, s. 394) and any group accounts prepared by the company for that year (CA 2006, s. 398–399). CA 2006, s. 408 provides an option to omit an individual parent company's profit and loss account from annual accounts where the company prepares group accounts.

In the case of an unquoted company, its 'annual report and accounts' for a financial year are:

- its annual accounts;
- the directors' report (except for a micro-entity) which is not required to prepare one;
- the strategic report (though see exemptions for small entities in **Chapter 6**);
- any separate corporate governance statement; and
s. 446(1)   - the auditor's report on those accounts including the statement required in s. 496 regarding the
and (2)   directors'/strategic report and any corporate governance report.

s. 408
Individual profit and loss account of parent company – the profit and loss account of a parent company:

- prepared in addition to, but omitted from, 'group accounts'; and
- omitting the supplemental information required by CA 2006, s. 411 (information about employee numbers and costs).

156

The fact of omission and the amount of the parent company's profit or loss for the year must be disclosed in group accounts, and the individual profit and loss account of the parent company must still be approved by the board of directors (in accordance with CA 2006, s. 414(1)).

Notes to the accounts – notes forming part of the annual accounts (or annexed thereto), giving information required by any provision of CA 2006 or international accounting standards. *s. 472*

Income and expenditure account – the equivalent of a profit and loss account in the case of the undertaking not trading for profit. *s. 474(2)*

1.3 Statutory accounts

The accounts that must be prepared for members. These will be the annual accounts, together with the directors' report and also (if required) strategic report and auditor's report. *s. 444*

As explained in **Chapter 11** some companies can prepare abridged accounts, where they have the consent of all members. These abridged accounts would then form the basis of filing. Various exemptions for small companies permit either full or abridged accounts to be 'filleted' on filing, so that only the balance sheet and related notes for example are filed. See **Chapter 6**.

1.4 Abbreviated accounts

Abbreviated accounts have been abolished with effect from accounting periods commencing on or after 1 January 2016, or 1 January 2015 if the directors opt to apply the effect of SI 2015/980 early.

However, as mentioned above there are still filing exemptions allowing a 'filleted' version of accounts to be filed for small companies, omitting the profit and loss and directors' report. These are not separate sets of accounts for filing, as abbreviated accounts were, they are just the accounts the members receive (whether full, abridged, or micro-entity accounts) with sections omitted. See **Table 6.6** in **Chapter 6** for a summary of filing requirements.

2 Profit and loss account (or Income Statement/Statement of Comprehensive Income)

Profit and loss account Formats 1 and 3 headings include 'Cost of sales', 'Distribution costs' and 'Administrative expenses'. Allocation of costs and overheads often requires careful consideration, but, in practice, it has been found that expenses not conveniently or accurately falling under one of these statutory headings can be attributed to additional, more appropriate, headings. For example, a service or retail organisation may consider most of its overhead expenditure to be of a general nature rather than specifically 'distribution' or 'administrative'. Whilst the statutory format headings form the basic framework for the allocation of costs, the nature of the particular business will often suggest that a more informative (and, perhaps, more detailed) approach can be adopted.

2.1 Turnover/revenue

'The amounts derived from the provision of goods and services, after deduction of trade discounts, value added tax and any other taxes based on the amounts so derived.' *s. 474(1)*

Revenue (or turnover) is defined by FRS 102 as income that arises in the course of the ordinary activities of an entity. It can be referred to by a variety of names including sales, fees, interest, dividends, royalties and rent.

Commission or rental income, for example, where forming part of the principal activity of the company, would be included in turnover. The heading 'Turnover' could in such cases be amended

SI 2008/409,
Sch. 1.4(1)
to a more appropriate title (e.g. 'Commission income' or 'Income from investment properties') in view of the 'special nature of the company's business'.

FRS 102 provides guidance on the principles of revenue recognition and the treatment of turnover (see **7** (below)).

2.2   Costs in formats 1 and 3

Costs and overheads may be attributed to the headings 'Cost of sales', 'Distribution costs' and 'Administrative expenses'. There is no statutory interpretation of these items. Fair value adjustments through profit and loss, such as needed for investment properties and derivatives, will impact the relevant line item. For instance if a derivative relates to a cost of sales transaction, it would be logical to include the fair value movement in cost of sales. In some cases a separate line item may be needed to identify the nature of the item correctly. The Companies Act does not specify in which line item such fair value adjustments should be included.

2.3   Other operating income

'Other operating income' will include all other income not arising from turnover or the company's principal activities, except income dealt with elsewhere in the formats (e.g. dividends or interest, etc. receivable). It might include: commissions, rental income, profit on disposal of fixed assets or foreign currency trading gains.

2.4   Own work capitalised (Format 2)

The gross amount of items capitalised in the construction of a company's own tangible fixed assets, including direct labour, materials and overheads.

2.5   Other external charges (Format 2)

'Other external charges' may include other production-related costs, other costs related directly to generating turnover, or subcontractors' costs and costs of self-employed consultants.

2.6   Other operating charges (Format 2)

'Other operating charges' may include other overhead expenses (including audit and professional fees), other charges relating to ordinary activities or foreign currency trading losses.

In practice, the two headings 'Other external charges' and 'Other operating charges' have often been interpreted as alternatives. However defined, they should be used consistently.

2.7   Staff costs

The Companies Act 2006, s. 411(1) ('Information about employee numbers') applies to companies including those subject to the small companies regime apart from micro-entities (as amended by SI 2015/980). Non-small companies also need to provide information regarding staff costs.

'Staff costs' are wages and salaries, social security costs and other pension costs paid or payable to, or incurred by, the company on behalf of persons employed under contracts of service, i.e. employees of the company (including directors who are employees). This heading will not include subcontractors' costs or consultants, etc.

Social security costs: company (employers') contributions to any compulsory state, social security, National Insurance, or pension scheme, fund or arrangement.

Other pension costs: all other costs incurred by a company towards employee pensions (for example, company pension scheme).

The disclosure of the average number of employees within appropriate categories is to be determined by the directors 'having regard to the manner in which the company's activities are organised'. The number of employees included in this disclosure should be correlated with the amount disclosed for 'staff costs'.

2.8 Income from shares in group undertakings

Dividends received and receivable:

- parent company – from subsidiary undertakings;
- fellow subsidiary – from fellow group undertakings; and
- consolidated P&L account – from non-consolidated subsidiaries.

(In group accounts) the group's shares of earnings of non-consolidated (equity accounted) subsidiaries.

2.9 Income from participating interests

Individual company accounts – income (e.g. dividends received and receivable) from shares in associated companies, share of profits from partnerships, unincorporated associations.

Consolidated profit and loss account – group share of pre-tax profit (or loss) of associated companies.

2.10 Auditor's remuneration

Audit fee and related expenses charged in the accounts, including estimated money value of any benefits in kind, should be disclosed.

s. 494

The *Companies (Disclosure of Auditor Remuneration and Liability Limitation Agreements) Regulations* 2008 (SI 2008/409), reg. 4 as amended by SI 2011/2198 sets out the disclosure requirements concerning the remuneration of auditors of small and medium-sized companies.

A small or medium-sized company must disclose in a note to the annual accounts the amount of any remuneration receivable by the company's auditor for the auditing of those accounts. Where the remuneration includes benefits in kind, the nature and estimated money-value of those benefits must also be disclosed in a note.

SI 2008/489, reg. 4(1)–(2)

Separate disclosure is required for separate firms of auditors, for example where there is a change of auditor during the year. *(Note that these disclosure requirements are expected to be repealed for small companies by mid-June 2016, as part of the implementation of the EU Audit Directive.)*

SI 2008/489, reg. 4(3)

2.11 Interest payable and similar charges

The following might be included under this profit and loss account heading:

- Bank loan and overdraft interest, interest on other loans, interest on finance leases, hire-purchase interest, commitment fees, factoring charges, group interest (less interest capitalised).
- Dividends payable in respect of certain shares (for example, preference shares) treated as financial liabilities).
- Foreign currency losses arising from financing. (Gains of a similar nature may be included under 'Other interest receivable and similar income'.)

3   Abbreviations and Glossary

The following is a list of some of the most important abbreviations used throughout the text. In addition to this list, it should be remembered that definitions within FRS 102 are defined in the Glossary, which is Appendix 1 to the standard.

FRS 100 *Application of Financial Reporting Requirements (2015)*;

FRS 101 *Reduced disclosure framework – Disclosure exemptions from EU-adopted IFRS for qualifying entities (2015)*;

FRS 102 *The Financial Reporting Standard applicable in the UK and Republic of Ireland (2015)*; (References are supplied in the format 102.x.y, x being the section number and y being the paragraph number.)

FRS 102, section 1A – the section dealing with small company presentation and disclosure requirements;

FRS 103 *Insurance Contracts;*

FRS 104 *Interim Financial Reporting; and*

FRS 105 *The Financial Reporting Standard applicable to the Micro-entities Regime.*

FRSSE 2015 *Financial Reporting Standard for Smaller Entities (2015)*

SI 2015/980 *Companies, Partnerships and Groups (Accounts and Reports) Regulations* 2015

SI 2013/3008 *Small Companies (Micro-Entities' Accounts) Regulations* 2013

SI 2008/409 *Small Companies and Groups (Accounts and Directors' Report) Regulations* 2008

SI 2008/409, Sch. 1 (unless otherwise stated) with paragraph number stated after

SI 2008/409, Sch. 6 (unless otherwise stated) with paragraph number stated after

Abridged accounts – those prepared under the provisions in Sch. 1A

Filleted accounts – the accounts that are required to be filed with the registrar, so for small companies excluding the P/L and directors' report, but with certain additional statements required (see **Table 6.6**).

4   Alternative bases of accounting

The *Companies Act* 2006 permits two bases of accounting – historical cost accounting rules and alternative accounting rules. A company may choose whichever basis it wishes to follow and may use different bases within the same set of accounts; it is common practice, for example, to prepare accounts on a historical cost basis, but to revalue properties or investments. Note that micro-entities are not permitted to use the alternative accounting rules when preparing accounts under that regime.

Companies may, therefore, prepare accounts:

- on the pure historical cost convention;
- on the historical cost convention modified to include certain assets at valuation; or
- on the current cost convention.

Alternative methods of valuation permitted under the 'alternative accounting rules' and as set out in SI 2008/409 are illustrated in **Table A**.

Table A Alternative methods of valuation

Primary method of valuation	*Alternative method of valuation*	
Fixed assets	**('Alternative accounting rules')**	(Sch. 1.17–22)
Historical cost of purchase or production, less any provision for depreciation or diminution in value		
Intangible fixed assets, other than goodwill	Current cost	(Sch. 1.32(1))
Tangible fixed assets	Market value (as at the date of their last valuation)	
	or	
	Current cost	(Sch. 1.32(2))
Investments (fixed assets)	Market value (as at the date of their last valuation)	
	or	
	Directors' valuation (or any basis which the directors consider to be appropriate in the circumstances; the method of valuation and the reasons for adopting it must be disclosed)	(Sch. 1.32(3))
Current assets		
Primary method of valuation	**Alternative method of valuation**	
	('Alternative accounting rules')	
Cost (purchase price or production cost – other than distribution costs) or net realisable value, if lower		(Sch. 1.23–24)
Investments (current assets)	These were omitted by SI 2015/980. Previously current cost under Sch. 1.32(4)	
Stocks	These were omitted by SI 2015/980. Previously current cost under Sch. 1.32(5)	

4.1 Purchase price

This is the actual price paid adding any incidental expenses and subtracting any incidental reductions in the cost of acquisition.

SI 2008/409, Sch. 1.27

4.2 Production cost

The price of raw materials and consumables together with costs directly attributable to the production of the asset; a reasonable proportion of indirect costs (relating to the period of production); and interest on capital borrowed to finance the production of the asset (to the extent that it is accrued during the period of production).

SI 2008/409, Sch. 1.27

4.3 Revaluation reserve

This is the amount arising from a revaluation of fixed assets. The difference between the amount of any item determined according to one of the alternative accounting rules and the amount at which it would be determined on the historical cost accounting rules should be debited or credited, as applicable, to a 'revaluation reserve'. The amount of the revaluation reserve must be shown in the company's balance sheet under a separate sub-heading in the position given for the item

SI 2008/409, Sch. 1.35

Sch. 1.35(2)

'revaluation reserve' under 'Capital and reserves' in Format 1 or 2. (*This paragraph was amended by SI 2015/980 removing the option to call the revaluation reserve something different.*)

5   Groups – parent and subsidiary undertakings

The principal definitions for accounting purposes for a parent company and its subsidiaries, which cover 'undertakings' and not just 'bodies corporate', are set out below.

s. 474

A group comprises a parent undertaking and its subsidiary undertakings.

A company is a 'subsidiary' of another company, its 'holding company', if that other company:

- holds a majority of the voting rights in it; or
- is a member of it and has the right to appoint or remove a majority of its board of directors; or
- is a member of it and controls alone, pursuant to an agreement with other members, a majority of the voting rights in it; or

s. 1159(1)

- if it is a 'subsidiary' of a company that is itself a subsidiary of that other company.

A company is a 'wholly-owned subsidiary' of another company if it has no members except that other and that other's wholly-owned subsidiaries or persons acting on behalf of that other company or its wholly-owned subsidiaries.

s. 1159(2)

An undertaking is a 'parent undertaking' in relation to another undertaking ('a subsidiary undertaking') if:

- it holds a majority of the voting rights in the undertaking;
- it is a member of the undertaking and has the right to appoint or remove a majority of its board of directors;
- it has the right to exercise a dominant influence over the undertaking:
  - by virtue of provisions contained in the undertaking's articles;
  - by virtue of a control contract; or
- it is a member of the undertaking and controls alone, pursuant to an agreement with other shareholders or members, a majority of the voting rights in the undertaking.

s. 1162(2)

An undertaking is treated as a member of another undertaking:

- if any of its subsidiary undertakings is a member of that undertaking; or
- if any shares in that other undertaking are held by a person acting on behalf of the undertaking or any of its subsidiary undertakings.

s. 1162(3)

An undertaking is also a parent undertaking in relation to another undertaking (a subsidiary undertaking) if:

- it has the power to exercise, or actually exercises, a dominant influence or control over it; or
- it and the subsidiary undertaking are managed on a unified basis.

s. 1162(4)

s. 1161(1)

An 'undertaking' means:

- a body corporate or partnership; or
- an unincorporated association carrying on a trade or business, with or without a view to profit.

s. 1161(4)

'Fellow subsidiary undertakings' are undertakings which are subsidiary undertakings of the same parent undertaking but are not parent undertakings or subsidiary undertakings of each other.

s. 1161(5)

'Group undertaking' means an undertaking which is:

- a parent undertaking or subsidiary undertaking of that undertaking; or
- a subsidiary undertaking of any parent undertaking of that undertaking.

An interest in shares includes:

- an interest which is convertible into an interest in shares; and
- an option to acquire shares or any such interest.

SI 2008/409, Sch. 8(3)

An interest held on behalf of an undertaking shall be treated as held by it.

In the statutory balance sheet and profit and loss formats 'participating interest' does not include an interest in a group undertaking.

An 'associated undertaking' means an undertaking in which an undertaking, included in the consolidation, has a participating interest and over whose operating and financial policy it exercises a significant influence, and which is not:

- a subsidiary undertaking of the parent company; or
- a joint venture.

Where an undertaking holds 20% or more of the voting rights in another undertaking, it is presumed to exercise such 'significant influence' over it unless the contrary is shown.

SI 2008/409, Sch. 6.19

A *'joint venture'* may be dealt with in group accounts by the method of proportional consolidation. A 'joint venture' is an undertaking, which (not being a body corporate or subsidiary undertaking of the parent company) is managed jointly by two or more undertakings, one of which is included in a consolidation. Note however, that proportional consolidation is not permitted under FRS 102.

SI 2008/ 409, Sch. 6.18

References to 'shares' are references to:

- allotted shares (for an undertaking with a share capital);
- rights to share in the capital of the undertaking (for an undertaking with capital but no share capital); or
- interests:
  - conferring any right to share in the profits or liability to contribute to the losses of the undertaking; or
  - giving rise to an obligation to contribute to the debts or expenses of the undertaking in the event of a winding-up (undertaking without capital).

s. 1161(2)

6   Dividends

6.1   *Treatment of dividends*

The requirements for the disclosure of dividends in small company accounts were omitted with the application of SI 2015/980 to the Small Company Regulations (previously Sch. 1.43). FRS 102 in Appendix 1AD encourages the disclosure of dividends. Additionally, the payment of dividends could potentially be a related party transaction required to be disclosed, but for small companies only transactions not concluded under normal market conditions are disclosable.

Overall, therefore, consideration needs to be made as to whether disclosure of dividends is needed in order to give a true and fair view, as otherwise there are no specific disclosure requirements.

6.2   *Classification of preference dividends*

In FRS 102, as under previous GAAP, preference shares will often meet the definition of a liability and therefore the dividend becomes an expense, essentially interest, in the profit or loss.

Appendix B Small Companies and Groups (Accounts and Directors' Report) Regulations 2008 (SI 2008/409), as amended by SI 2015/980

Made on 19 February 2008 by the Secretary of State, in exercise of the powers conferred by s. 396(3), 404(3), 409(1)–(3), 412(1)–(3), 416(4), 444(3)(a) and (b), 677(3)(a), 712(2)(b)(i), 836(1) (b)(i) and 1292(1)(a) and (c) of the Companies Act 2006. Operative from 6 April 2008.

PART 1 – INTRODUCTION

Citation and interpretation

1(1) These Regulations may be cited as the Small Companies and Groups (Accounts and Directors' Report) Regulations 2008.

1(2) In these Regulations **'the 2006 Act'** means the Companies Act 2006.

Commencement and application

2(1) These Regulations come into force on 6th April 2008.

2(2) They apply in relation to financial years beginning on or after 6th April 2008.

2(3) They apply to companies which are subject to the small companies regime under Part 15 of the 2006 Act (see section 381 of that Act).

PART 2 – FORM AND CONTENT OF INDIVIDUAL ACCOUNTS

Companies Act individual accounts

3(1) Subject to the following provisions of this regulation and regulation 5A, Companies Act individual accounts under section 396 of the 2006 Act (Companies Act: individual accounts) must comply with the provisions of Schedule 1 to these Regulations as to the form and content of the balance sheet and profit and loss account, and additional information to be provided by way of notes to the accounts.

3(1A) Sections C (alternative accounting rules) and D (fair value accounting) in Part 2 of Schedule 1 to these Regulations do not apply to a company which qualifies as a micro-entity in relation to a financial year (see sections 384A and 384B of the 2006 Act) and whose accounts for that year are prepared in accordance with the exemption permitted by–

    (a) regulation 5A, or

    (b) paragraph 1(1A) of Section A in Part 1 of Schedule 1 to these Regulations.

3(2) [Omitted by SI 2015/980, reg. 14(2).]

3(3) Accounts are treated as having complied with any provision of Schedule 1 to these Regulations if they comply instead with the corresponding provision of Schedule 1 to the Large and Medium-Sized Companies and Groups (Accounts and Reports) Regulations 2008.

History – In reg. 3(1), 'Subject to the following provisions of this regulation and regulation 5A,' inserted; and reg. 3(1A) inserted by SI 2013/3008, reg. 9(1) and (2), with effect from 1 December 2013 in respect of (a) financial years ending on or after 30 September 2013; and (b) companies, which deliver the accounts required by s. 444 to the registrar on or after 1 December 2013.

Reg. 3(2) omitted by SI 2015/980, reg. 14(2), with effect in relation to–

    (a) financial years beginning on or after 1 January 2016, and

    (b) a financial year of a company beginning on or after 1 January 2015, but before 1 January 2016, if the directors of the company so decide.

Former reg. 3(2) read as follows:

    "**3(2)** The profit and loss account of a company that falls within section 408 of the 2006 Act (individual profit and loss account where group accounts prepared) need not contain the information specified in paragraphs 59 to 61 of Schedule 1 to these Regulations (information supplementing the profit and loss account)."

Information about related undertakings (Companies Act or IAS individual accounts)

4 [Omitted by SI 2015/980, reg. 14(3).]

History – Reg. 4 omitted by SI 2015/980, reg. 14(3), with effect in relation to–

(a) financial years beginning on or after 1 January 2016, and

(b) a financial year of a company beginning on or after 1 January 2015, but before 1 January 2016, if the directors of the company so decide.

Former reg. 4 read as follows:

"**4(1)** Subject to regulation 5A, Companies Act or IAS individual accounts must comply with the provisions of Schedule 2 to these Regulations as to information about related undertakings to be given in notes to the company's accounts.

4(2) Information otherwise required to be given by Schedule 2 to these Regulations need not be disclosed with respect to an undertaking that–

(a) is established under the law of a country outside the United Kingdom, or

(b) carries on business outside the United Kingdom, if the conditions specified in section 409(4) of the 2006 Act are met (see section 409(5) of the 2006 Act for disclosure required where advantage taken of this exemption).

This paragraph does not apply in relation to the information required by paragraphs 4 and 8 of Schedule 2 to these Regulations.

History – In reg. 4(1), 'Subject to regulation 5A,' inserted by SI 2013/3008, reg. 9(1) and (3), with effect from 1 December 2013 in respect of (a) financial years ending on or after 30 September 2013; and (b) companies, which deliver the accounts required by s. 444 to the registrar on or after 1 December 2013."

Information about directors' benefits: remuneration (Companies Act or IAS individual accounts)

5 [Omitted by SI 2015/980, reg. 14(4).]

History – Reg. 5 omitted by SI 2015/980, reg. 14(4), with effect in relation to–

(a) financial years beginning on or after 1 January 2016, and

(b) a financial year of a company beginning on or after 1 January 2015, but before 1 January 2016, if the directors of the company so decide.

Former reg. 5 read as follows:

"**5** Subject to regulation 5A, Companies Act or IAS individual accounts must comply with the provisions of Schedule 3 to these Regulations as to information about directors' remuneration to be given in notes to the company's accounts.

History – In reg. 5, 'Subject to regulation 5A,' inserted by SI 2013/3008, reg. 9(1) and (4), with effect from 1 December 2013 in respect of (a) financial years ending on or after 30 September 2013; and (b) companies, which deliver the accounts required by s. 444 to the registrar on or after 1 December 2013."

Companies Act individual accounts: micro-entities – notes to the accounts

5A Nothing in Schedule 1, 2 or 3 to these Regulations requires the Companies Act individual accounts of a company for a financial year in which the company qualifies as a micro-entity (see sections 384A and 384B of the 2006 Act) to contain any information by way of notes to the accounts, except that the company is required to disclose by way of notes to the accounts the information required by paragraph 57 in Part 3 of Schedule 1.

History – Reg. 5A inserted by SI 2013/3008, reg. 9(1) and (5), with effect from 1 December 2013 in respect of (a) financial years ending on or after 30 September 2013; and (b) companies, which deliver the accounts required by s. 444 to the registrar on or after 1 December 2013.

Accounts for delivery to Registrar of Companies (Companies Act individual accounts)

6 [Omitted by SI 2015/980, reg. 14(5).]

History – Reg. 6 omitted by SI 2015/980, reg. 14(5), with effect in relation to–

(a) financial years beginning on or after 1 January 2016, and

(b) a financial year of a company beginning on or after 1 January 2015, but before 1 January 2016, if the directors of the company so decide.

Former reg. 6 read as follows:

"**6(1)** Except where section 444(3B) of the 2006 Act applies, the directors of a company for which they are preparing Companies Act individual accounts may deliver to the registrar of companies under section 444 of the 2006 Act (filing obligations of companies subject to small companies regime) a copy of a balance sheet which complies with Schedule 4 to these Regulations rather than Schedule 1.

6(2) Companies Act individual accounts delivered to the registrar need not give the information required by–

    (a) paragraph 4 of Schedule 2 to these Regulations (shares of company held by subsidiary undertakings), or

    (b) Schedule 3 to these Regulations (directors' benefits).

History – In reg. 6(1), 'Except where section 444(3B) of the 2006 Act applies, the directors' substituted for 'The directors' by SI 2013/3008, reg. 9(1) and (6), with effect from 1 December 2013 in respect of (a) financial years ending on or after 30 September 2013; and (b) companies, which deliver the accounts required by s. 444 to the registrar on or after 1 December 2013."

PART 3 – DIRECTORS' REPORT

Directors' report

7   The report which the directors of a company are required to prepare under section 415 of the 2006 Act (duty to prepare directors' report) must disclose the matters specified in Schedule 5 to these Regulations.

PART 4 – FORM AND CONTENT OF GROUP ACCOUNTS

Companies Act group accounts

8(1)   Where the directors of a parent company which–

    (a) is subject to the small companies regime, and

    (b) has prepared Companies Act individual accounts in accordance with regulation 3, prepare Companies Act group accounts under section 398 of the 2006 Act (option to prepare group accounts), those accounts must comply with the provisions of Schedule 6 to these Regulations as to the form and content of the consolidated balance sheet and consolidated profit and loss account, and additional information to be provided by way of notes to the accounts.

8(2)   Accounts are treated as having complied with any provision of Schedule 6 if they comply instead with the corresponding provision of Schedule 6 to the Large and Medium-Sized Companies and Groups (Accounts and Reports) Regulations 2008.

History – In reg. 8, the words 'Part 1 of' omitted by SI 2015/980, reg. 15(2), with effect in relation to–

    (a) financial years beginning on or after 1 January 2016, and

    (b) a financial year of a company beginning on or after 1 January 2015, but before 1 January 2016, if the directors of the company so decide.

Information about directors' benefits: remuneration (Companies Act or IAS group accounts)

9   [Omitted by SI 2015/980, reg. 15(3).]

History – Reg. 9 omitted by SI 2015/980, reg. 15(3), with effect in relation to–

    (a) financial years beginning on or after 1 January 2016, and

    (b) a financial year of a company beginning on or after 1 January 2015, but before 1 January 2016, if the directors of the company so decide.

Former reg. 9 read as follows:

"**9** Companies Act or IAS group accounts must comply with the provisions of Schedule 3 to these Regulations as to information about directors' remuneration to be given in notes to the company's accounts."

Information about related undertakings (Companies Act or IAS group accounts)

10(1) Companies Act or IAS group accounts must comply with the provisions of Part 2 of Schedule 6 to these Regulations as to information about related undertakings to be given in notes to the company's accounts.

10(2) Information otherwise required to be given by Part 2 of Schedule 6 need not be disclosed with respect to an undertaking that–

    (a) is established under the law of a country outside the United Kingdom, or

    (b) carries on business outside the United Kingdom, if the conditions specified in section 409(4) of the 2006 Act are met (see section 409(5) of the 2006 Act for disclosure required where advantage taken of this exemption).

This paragraph does not apply in relation to the information required by paragraphs 26 and 35 of Schedule 6 to these Regulations.

Accounts for delivery to Registrar of Companies (Companies Act group accounts)

11 Companies Act group accounts delivered to the registrar of companies under section 444 of the 2006 Act need not give the information required by–

    (a) [omitted by SI 2015/980, reg. 15(4),]

    (b) paragraph 25 of Schedule 6 to these Regulations (shares of company held by subsidiary undertakings).

History – Reg. 11(a) omitted by SI 2015/980, reg. 15(4), with effect in relation to–

    (a) financial years beginning on or after 1 January 2016, and

    (b) a financial year of a company beginning on or after 1 January 2015, but before 1 January 2016, if the directors of the company so decide.

Former reg. 11(a) read as follows:

    "(a) Schedule 3 to these Regulations (directors' benefits), or"

PART 5 – INTERPRETATION

Definition of 'provisions'

12 Schedule 7 to these Regulations defines **'provisions'** for the purpose of these Regulations and for the purposes of–

    (a) section 677(3)(a) (Companies Act accounts: relevant provisions for purposes of financial assistance) in Part 18 of the 2006 Act,

    (b) section 712(2)(b)(i) (Companies Act accounts: relevant provisions to determine available profits for redemption or purchase by private company out of capital) in that Part,

    (c) section 836(1)(b)(i) (Companies Act accounts: relevant provisions for distribution purposes) in Part 23 of that Act, and

    (d) section 841(2)(a) (Companies Act accounts: provisions to be treated as realised losses) in that Part.

Notes – Para. (d) inserted by SI 2009/1581, reg. 11(1) and (2): 27 June 2009 applying in relation to financial years beginning on or after 6 April 2008 which have not ended before 27 June 2009.

General interpretation

13 Schedule 8 to these Regulations contains general definitions for the purposes of these Regulations.

SCHEDULE 1 – COMPANIES ACT INDIVIDUAL ACCOUNTS

Regulation 3(1)

Part 1 – General rules and formats

SECTION A GENERAL RULES

1(1) Subject to the following provisions of this Schedule–

(a) every balance sheet of a company must show the items listed in either of the balance sheet formats in Section B of this Part, and

(b) every profit and loss account must show the items listed in either of the profit and loss account formats in Section B.

1(1A) But, subject to the following provisions of this Schedule, in relation to a company which qualifies as a micro-entity in relation to a financial year (see sections 384A and 384B of the 2006 Act)–

(a) the only items which must be shown on the company's balance sheet for that year are those listed in either of the balance sheet formats in Section C of this Part, and

(b) the only items which must be shown on the company's profit and loss account for that year are those listed in the profit and loss account format in Section C.

1(2) References in this Schedule to the items listed in any of the formats in Section B and Section C are to those items read together with any of the notes following the formats which apply to those items.

1(3) Subject to paragraph 1A the items must be shown in the order and under the headings and sub-headings given in the particular format used, but–

(a) the notes to the formats may permit alternative positions for any particular items, and

(b) the heading or sub-heading for any item does not have to be distinguished by any letter or number assigned to that item in the format used.

History – In para. 1(1)(b), the word 'either' substituted for the words 'any one' by SI 2015/980, reg. 16(2)(a), with effect in relation to–

(a) financial years beginning on or after 1 January 2016, and

(b) a financial year of a company beginning on or after 1 January 2015, but before 1 January 2016, if the directors of the company so decide.

In para. 1(3), the words 'Subject to paragraph 1A' inserted by SI 2015/980, reg. 16(2)(b), with effect in relation to–

(a) financial years beginning on or after 1 January 2016, and

(b) a financial year of a company beginning on or after 1 January 2015, but before 1 January 2016, if the directors of the company so decide.

1A(1) Where appropriate to the circumstances of a company's business, the company's directors may, with reference to one of the formats in Section B, draw up an abridged balance sheet showing only those items in that format preceded by letters and roman numerals, provided that–

(a) in the case of format 1, note (5) of the notes to the formats is complied with,

(b) in the case of format 2, notes (5) and (10) of those notes are complied with, and

(c) all of the members of the company have consented to the drawing up of the abridged balance sheet.

1A(2) Where appropriate to the circumstances of a company's business, the company's directors may, with reference to one of the formats in Section B, draw up an abridged profit and loss account, combining under one item called 'Gross profit or loss'–

(a) items 1, 2, 3 and 6 in the case of format 1, and

(b) items 1 to 5 in the case of format 2

provided that, in either case, all of the members of the company have consented to the drawing up of the abridged profit and loss account.

1A(3)   Such consent as is referred to in sub-paragraphs (1) and (2) may only be given as regards the preparation of, as appropriate, the balance sheet or profit and loss account in respect of the preceding financial year.

1A(4)   Sub-paragraphs (1) and (2) do not apply in relation to the preparation of, as appropriate, a company's balance sheet or profit and loss account for a particular financial year if the company was a charity at any time within that year.

History – Para. 1A inserted by SI 2015/980, reg. 16(2)(c), with effect in relation to–

(a) financial years beginning on or after 1 January 2016, and

(b) a financial year of a company beginning on or after 1 January 2015, but before 1 January 2016, if the directors of the company so decide.

1B(1)   The company's directors may adapt one of the balance sheet formats in Section B so to distinguish between current and non-current items in a different way, provided that–

(a) the information given is at least equivalent to that which would have been required by the use of such format had it not been thus adapted, and

(b) the presentation of those items is in accordance with generally accepted accounting principles or practice.

1B(2)   The company's directors may, otherwise than pursuant to paragraph 1A(2), adapt one of the profit and loss account formats in Section B, provided that–

(a) the information given is at least equivalent to that which would have been required by the use of such format had it not been thus adapted, and

(b) the presentation is in accordance with generally accepted accounting principles or practice.

History – Para. 1B inserted by SI 2015/980, reg. 16(2)(c), with effect in relation to–

(a) financial years beginning on or after 1 January 2016, and

(b) a financial year of a company beginning on or after 1 January 2015, but before 1 January 2016, if the directors of the company so decide.

1C   So far as is practicable, the following provisions of Section A of this Part of this Schedule apply to the balance sheet or profit or loss account of a company notwithstanding any such abridgment or adaptation pursuant to paragraph 1A or 1B.

History – Para. 1C inserted by SI 2015/980, reg. 16(2)(c), with effect in relation to–

(a) financial years beginning on or after 1 January 2016, and

(b) a financial year of a company beginning on or after 1 January 2015, but before 1 January 2016, if the directors of the company so decide.

2(1)   Where in accordance with paragraph 1(1) a company's balance sheet or profit and loss account for any financial year has been prepared by reference to one of the formats in Section B, the company's directors must use the same format in preparing Companies Act individual accounts for subsequent financial years, unless in their opinion there are special reasons for a change.

2(2)   Particulars of any such change must be given in a note to the accounts in which the new format is first used, and the reasons for the change must be explained.

2A   Where in accordance with paragraph 1(1A) a company's balance sheet or profit and loss account for any financial year has been prepared by reference to one of the formats in Section C, the company's directors must use the same format in preparing Companies Act individual accounts for subsequent financial years, unless in their opinion there are special reasons for a change.

3(1)   Any item required to be shown in a company's balance sheet or profit and loss account may be shown in greater detail than required by the particular format used.

3(2)   The balance sheet or profit and loss account may include an item representing or covering the amount of any asset or liability, income or expenditure not otherwise covered by any of the items listed in the format used, save that none of the following may be treated as assets in any balance sheet–

(a) preliminary expenses,

(b) expenses of, and commission on, any issue of shares or debentures,

(c) costs of research.

4(1)   Where the special nature of the company's business requires it, the company's directors must adapt the arrangement, headings and sub-headings otherwise required in respect of items given an Arabic number in the balance sheet or profit and loss account format used.

4(2)   The directors may combine items to which Arabic numbers are given in any of the formats set out in Section B if–

(a) their individual amounts are not material to assessing the state of affairs or profit or loss of the company for the financial year in question, or

(b) the combination facilitates that assessment.

4(3)   Where sub-paragraph (2)(b) applies, the individual amounts of any items which have been combined must be disclosed in a note to the accounts.

5(1)   Subject to sub-paragraph (2), the directors must not include a heading or sub-heading corresponding to an item in the balance sheet or profit and loss account format used if there is no amount to be shown for that item for the financial year to which the balance sheet or profit and loss account relates.

5(2)   Where an amount can be shown for the item in question for the immediately preceding financial year that amount must be shown under the heading or sub-heading required by the format for that item.

6   Every profit and loss account other than one prepared by reference to the format in Section C must show the amount of a company's profit or loss before taxation.

History – In para. 6, the words 'on ordinary activities' omitted by SI 2015/980, reg. 16(2)(d), with effect in relation to–

(a) financial years beginning on or after 1 January 2016, and

(b) a financial year of a company beginning on or after 1 January 2015, but before 1 January 2016, if the directors of the company so decide.

7(1)   For every item shown in the balance sheet or profit and loss account the corresponding amount for the immediately preceding financial year must also be shown.

7(2)   Where that corresponding amount is not comparable with the amount to be shown for the item in question in respect of the financial year to which the balance sheet or profit and loss account relates, the former amount may be adjusted, and particulars of the non-comparability and of any adjustment must be disclosed in a note to the accounts.

8   Amounts in respect of items representing assets or income may not be set off against amounts in respect of items representing liabilities or expenditure (as the case may be), or vice versa.

9   The company's directors must, in determining how amounts are presented within items in the profit and loss account and balance sheet, have regard to the substance of the reported transaction or arrangement, in accordance with generally accepted accounting principles or practice.

History – The following amendments were made by SI 2013/3008, reg. 10(1) and (2), with effect from 1 December 2013 in respect of (a) financial years ending on or after 30 September 2013; and (b) companies, which deliver the accounts required by s. 444 to the registrar on or after 1 December 2013:

• Paragraph 1(1A) inserted.

• In para. 1(2), 'and Section C' inserted.

- In para. 2(1), 'paragraph 1(1)' substituted for 'paragraph 1'.
- Paragraph 2A inserted.
- In para. 6, 'other than one prepared by reference to the format in Section C' inserted.

9A Where an asset or liability relates to more than one item in the balance sheet, the relationship of such asset or liability to the relevant items must be disclosed either under those items or in the notes to the accounts.

History – Para. 9A inserted by SI 2015/980, reg. 16(2)(e), with effect in relation to–

(a) financial years beginning on or after 1 January 2016, and

(b) a financial year of a company beginning on or after 1 January 2015, but before 1 January 2016, if the directors of the company so decide.

SECTION B – THE REQUIRED FORMATS FOR THE ACCOUNTS OF COMPANIES OTHER THAN MICRO-ENTITIES

Balance sheet formats – Format 1

A. Called up share capital not paid *(1)*

B. Fixed assets

    I. Intangible assets

        1 Goodwill *(2)*

        2 Other intangible assets *(3)*

    II. Tangible assets

        1 Land and buildings

        2 Plant and machinery etc.

    III. Investments

        1 Shares in group undertakings and participating interests

        2 Loans to group undertakings and undertakings in which the company has a participating interest

        3 Other investments other than loans

        4 Other investments *(4)*

C. Current assets

    I. Stocks

        1 Stocks

        2 Payments on account

    II. Debtors *(5)*

        1 Trade debtors

        2 Amounts owed by group undertakings and undertakings in which the company has a participating interest

        3 Other debtors *(1)*

    III. Investments

        1 Shares in group undertakings

        2 Other investments *(4)*

    IV. Cash at bank and in hand

D. Prepayments and accrued income *(6)*

E. Creditors: amounts falling due within one year

    1 Bank loans and overdrafts

    2 Trade creditors

    3 Amounts owed to group undertakings and undertakings in which the company has a participating interest

    4 Other creditors *(7)*

F. Net current assets (liabilities) *(8)*

G. Total assets less current liabilities

H. Creditors: amounts falling due after more than one year

    1 Bank loans and overdrafts

    2 Trade creditors

    3 Amounts owed to group undertakings and undertakings in which the company has a participating interest

    4 Other creditors *(7)*

I. Provisions for liabilities

J. Accruals and deferred income *(7)*

K. Capital and reserves

    I. Called up share capital *(9)*

    II. Share premium account

    III. Revaluation reserve

    IV. Other reserves

    V. Profit and loss account

Balance sheet formats – Format 2

ASSETS

A. Called up share capital not paid *(1)*

B. Fixed assets

    I. Intangible assets

        1 Goodwill *(2)*

        2 Other intangible assets *(3)*

    II. Tangible assets

        1 Land and buildings

        2 Plant and machinery etc.

    III. Investments

        1 Shares in group undertakings and participating interests

        2 Loans to group undertakings and undertakings in which the company has a participating interest

       3   Other investments other than loans

       4   Other investments *(4)*

C.   Current assets

    I.   Stocks

       1   Stocks

       2   Payments on account

    II.   Debtors *(5)*

       1   Trade debtors

       2   Amounts owed by group undertakings and undertakings in which the company has a participating interest

       3   Other debtors *(1)*

    III. Investments

       1   Shares in group undertakings

       2   Other investments *(4)*

    IV. Cash at bank and in hand

D.   Prepayments and accrued income *(6)*

CAPITAL, RESERVES AND LIABILITIES

A.   Capital and reserves

    I.   Called up share capital *(9)*

    II.   Share premium account

    III. Revaluation reserve

    IV. Other reserves

    V.   Profit and loss account

B.   Provisions for liabilities

C.   Creditors *(10)*

       1   Bank loans and overdrafts

       2   Trade creditors

       3   Amounts owed to group undertakings and undertakings in which the company has a participating interest

       4   Other creditors *(7)*

D.   Accruals and deferred income *(7)*

Notes on the balance sheet formats

(1)   *Called up share capital not paid*
     (Formats 1 and 2, items A and C.II.3.)
     This item may either be shown at item A or included under item C.II.3 in Format 1 or 2.

(2)   *Goodwill*
     (Formats 1 and 2, item B.I.1.)
     Amounts representing goodwill must only be included to the extent that the goodwill was acquired for valuable consideration.

(3) *Other intangible assets*

(Formats 1 and 2, item B.I.2.)

Amounts in respect of concessions, patents, licences, trade marks and similar rights and assets must only be included in a company's balance sheet under this item if either–

(a) the assets were acquired for valuable consideration and are not required to be shown under goodwill, or

(b) the assets in question were created by the company itself.

(4) *Others: Other investments*

(Formats 1 and 2, items B.III.4 and C.III.2.)

Where amounts in respect of own shares held are included under either of these items, the nominal value of such shares must be shown separately.

(5) *Debtors*

(Formats 1 and 2, items C.II.1 to 3.)

The amount falling due after more than one year must be shown separately for each item included under debtors and, in the case of format 2, the aggregate amount falling due after more than one year must also be shown.

(6) *Prepayments and accrued income*

(Formats 1 and 2, item D.)

This item may alternatively be included under item C.II.3 in Format 1 or 2.

(7) *Other creditors*

(Format 1, items E.4, H.4 and J and Format 2, items C.4 and D.)

There must be shown separately–

(a) the amount of any convertible loans, and

(b) the amount for creditors in respect of taxation and social security.

Payments received on account of orders must be included in so far as they are not shown as deductions from stocks.

In Format 1, accruals and deferred income may be shown under item J or included under item E.4 or H.4, or both (as the case may require). In Format 2, accruals and deferred income may be shown under item D or within item C.4 under Liabilities.

(8) *Net current assets (liabilities)*

(Format 1, item F.)

In determining the amount to be shown under this item any prepayments and accrued income must be taken into account wherever shown.

(9) *Called up share capital*

(Format 1, item K.I and Format 2, Liabilities item A.I.)

The amount of allotted share capital and the amount of called up share capital which has been paid up must be shown separately.

(10) *Creditors*

(Format 2, Liabilities items C.1 to 4.)

Amounts falling due within one year and after one year must be shown separately for each of these items and for the aggregate of all of these items.

Profit and loss account formats – Format 1

(see note (14) below)

1 Turnover

2 Cost of sales *(11)*

3 Gross profit or loss

4 Distribution costs *(11)*

5 Administrative expenses *(11)*

6 Other operating income

7 Income from shares in group undertakings

8 Income from participating interests

9 Income from other fixed asset investments *(12)*

10 Other interest receivable and similar income *(12)*

11 Amounts written off investments

12 Interest payable and similar expenses *(13)*

13 Tax on profit or loss

14 Profit or loss after taxation

15 [Omitted]

16 [Omitted]

17 [Omitted]

18 [Omitted]

19 Other taxes not shown under the above items

20 Profit or loss for the financial year

Profit and loss account formats – Format 2

1 Turnover

2 Change in stocks of finished goods and in work in progress

3 Own work capitalised

4 Other operating income

5 (a) Raw materials and consumables

    (b) Other external charges

6 Staff costs

    (a) wages and salaries

    (b) social security costs

    (c) other pension costs

7 (a) Depreciation and other amounts written off tangible and intangible fixed assets

   (b) Amounts written off current assets, to the extent that they exceed write-offs which are normal in the undertaking concerned

8 Other operating expenses

9 Income from shares in group undertakings

10 Income from participating interests

11 Income from other fixed asset investments *(12)*

12 Other interest receivable and similar income *(12)*

13 Amounts written off investments

14 Interest payable and similar expenses *(13)*

15 Tax on profit or loss

16 Profit or loss after taxation

17 [Omitted]

18 [Omitted]

19 [Omitted]

20 [Omitted]

21 Other taxes not shown under the above items

22 Profit or loss for the financial year

Notes on the profit and loss account formats

(11) *Cost of sales: distribution costs: administrative expenses*

   (Format 1, items 2, 4 and 5.)

   These items must be stated after taking into account any necessary provisions for depreciation or diminution in value of assets.

(12) *Income from other fixed asset investments: other interest receivable and similar income*

   (Format 1, items 9 and 10; Format 2, items 11 and 12.)

   Income and interest derived from group undertakings must be shown separately from income and interest derived from other sources.

(13) *Interest payable and similar expenses*

   (Format 1, item 12; Format 2, item 14.)

   The amount payable to group undertakings must be shown separately.

History – New heading for section B substituted by SI 2013/3008, reg. 10(1) and (3), with effect from 1 December 2013 in respect of (a) financial years ending on or after 30 September 2013; and (b) companies, which deliver the accounts required by s. 444 to the registrar on or after 1 December 2013. Before substitution, the heading was 'SECTION B – THE REQUIRED FORMATS FOR ACCOUNTS'.

In section B, the following amendments were made by SI 2015/980, reg. 16(3), with effect in relation to–

   (a) financial years beginning on or after 1 January 2016, and

   (b) a financial year of a company beginning on or after 1 January 2015, but before 1 January 2016, if the directors of the company so decide:

      • the heading 'CAPITAL, RESERVES AND LIABILITIES' substituted for the word 'LIABILITIES'.

      • in note (5) of 'Notes on the balance sheet formats', the words 'and, in the case of format 2, the aggregate amount falling due after more than one year must also be shown' substituted for the words 'unless the aggregate amount of debtors falling due after more than one year is disclosed in the notes to the accounts'.

      • in note (10), the words 'unless the aggregate amount of creditors falling due within one year and the aggregate amount of creditors falling due after more than one year is disclosed in the notes to the accounts' omitted.

- in profit and loss account format 1–
    - at item 12, the word 'expenses' substitute for 'charges';
    - at item 13, the words 'on ordinary activities' omitted;
    - at item 14, the words 'on ordinary activities' omitted;
    - items 15–18 omitted.
- in profit and loss account format 2–
    - item 7(b) substituted;
    - at item 8, the word 'expenses' substitute for 'charges';
    - at item 14, the word 'expenses' substitute for 'charges';
    - at item 15, the words 'on ordinary activities' omitted;
    - at item 16, the words 'on ordinary activities' omitted;
    - items 17–20 omitted.
- profit and loss account format 3 omitted.
- profit and loss account format 4 omitted.
- in note (11) of 'Notes on the profit and loss account formats', the words 'and Format 3, items A 1, 2 and 3' omitted.
- in note (12), the words 'Format 3, items B 5 and 6 and Format 4, items B 7 and 8' omitted.
- in note (13) title, the word 'expenses' substitute for 'charges'; and the words 'Format 3, item A 5 and Format 4, item A 7' omitted.
- note (14) omitted.

SECTION C – THE REQUIRED FORMATS FOR THE ACCOUNTS OF MICRO-ENTITIES

Balance Sheet Formats

Format 1

(A)   Called up share capital not paid
(B)   Fixed assets
(C)   Current assets
(D)   Prepayments and accrued income
(E)   Creditors: amounts falling due within one year
(F)   Net current assets (liabilities)
(G)   Total assets less current liabilities
(H)   Creditors: amounts falling due after more than one year
(I)   Provisions for liabilities
(J)   Accruals and deferred income
(K)   Capital and reserves

Format 2

ASSETS

(A)   Called up share capital not paid
(B)   Fixed assets
(C)   Current Assets
(D)   Prepayments and accrued income

CAPITAL, RESERVES AND LIABILITIES

(A)   Capital and reserves
(B)   Provisions
(C)   Creditors (1)
(D)   Accruals and deferred income

Notes on the balance sheet formats

(1) *Creditors*

(Format 2, item C under Liabilities)

Aggregate amounts falling due within one year and after one year must be shown separately.

Profit and loss account format

(A)   Turnover

(B)   Other income

(C)   Cost of raw materials and consumables

(D)   Staff costs

(E)   Depreciation and other amounts written off assets

(F)   Other charges

(G)   Tax

(H)   Profit or loss

History – Section C inserted by SI 2013/3008, reg. 10(1) and (4), with effect from 1 December 2013 in respect of–

    (a) financial years ending on or after 30 September 2013; and

    (b) companies, which deliver the accounts required by s. 444 to the registrar on or after 1 December 2013.

In section C, the heading 'CAPITAL, RESERVES AND LIABILITIES' substituted for 'LIABILITIES' by SI 2015/980, reg. 16(4), with effect in relation to–

    (a) financial years beginning on or after 1 January 2016, and

    (b) a financial year of a company beginning on or after 1 January 2015, but before 1 January 2016, if the directors of the company so decide.

Part 2 – Accounting principles and rules

SECTION A – ACCOUNTING PRINCIPLES

Preliminary

10(1)   The amounts to be included in respect of all items shown in a company's accounts must be determined in accordance with the principles set out in this Section.

10(2)   But if it appears to the company's directors that there are special reasons for departing from any of those principles in preparing the company's accounts in respect of any financial year they may do so, in which case particulars of the departure, the reasons for it and its effect must be given in a note to the accounts.

Accounting principles

11   The company is presumed to be carrying on business as a going concern.

12   Accounting policies and measurement bases must be applied consistently within the same accounts and from one financial year to the next.

History – In para. 12, the words 'and measurement bases' inserted by SI 2015/980, reg. 17(2)(a), with effect in relation to–

    (a) financial years beginning on or after 1 January 2016, and

    (b) a financial year of a company beginning on or after 1 January 2015, but before 1 January 2016, if the directors of the company so decide.

13   The amount of any item must be determined on a prudent basis, and in particular–

(a)   only profits realised at the balance sheet date must be included in the profit and loss account,

(b)   all liabilities which have arisen in respect of the financial year to which the accounts relate or a previous financial year must be taken into account, including those which only become apparent between the balance sheet date and the date on which it is signed on behalf of the board of directors in accordance with section 414 of the 2006 Act (approval and signing of accounts) and

(c)   all provisions for diminution of value must be recognised, whether the result of the financial year is a profit or a loss.

History – Para. 13(c) (and the word 'and' preceding it) inserted; the word 'and' in para. (a) omitted by SI 2015/980, reg. 17(2) (b), with effect in relation to–

(a)   financial years beginning on or after 1 January 2016, and

(b)   a financial year of a company beginning on or after 1 January 2015, but before 1 January 2016, if the directors of the company so decide.

14   All income and charges relating to the financial year to which the accounts relate must be taken into account, without regard to the date of receipt or payment.

15   In determining the aggregate amount of any item, the amount of each individual asset or liability that falls to be taken into account must be determined separately.

15A   The opening balance sheet for each financial year shall correspond to the closing balance sheet for the preceding financial year.

History – Para. 15A inserted by SI 2015/980, reg. 17(2)(c), with effect in relation to–

(a)   financial years beginning on or after 1 January 2016, and

(b)   a financial year of a company beginning on or after 1 January 2015, but before 1 January 2016, if the directors of the company so decide.

SECTION B – HISTORICAL COST ACCOUNTING RULES

Preliminary

16   Subject to Sections C and D of this Part of this Schedule, the amounts to be included in respect of all items shown in a company's accounts must be determined in accordance with the rules set out in this Section.

Fixed assets

General rules

17(1)   The amount to be included in respect of any fixed asset must be its purchase price or production cost.

17(2)   This is subject to any provision for depreciation or diminution in value made in accordance with paragraphs 18 to 20.

Rules for depreciation and diminution in value

18   In the case of any fixed asset which has a limited useful economic life, the amount of–

(a)   its purchase price or production cost, or

(b)   where it is estimated that any such asset will have a residual value at the end of the period of its useful economic life, its purchase price or production cost less that estimated residual value, must be reduced by provisions for depreciation calculated to write off that amount systematically over the period of the asset's useful economic life.

19(1)   Where a fixed asset investment of a description falling to be included under item B.III of either of the balance sheet formats set out in Section B of Part 1 of this Schedule has diminished in value, provisions for diminution in value may be made in respect of it and the amount to be included in respect of it may be reduced accordingly.

19(2)   Provisions for diminution in value must be made in respect of any fixed asset which has diminished in value if the reduction in its value is expected to be permanent (whether its useful economic life is limited or not), and the amount to be included in respect of it must be reduced accordingly.

19(3)   Provisions made under sub-paragraph (1) or (2) must be charged to the profit and loss account and disclosed separately in a note to the accounts if not shown separately in the profit and loss account.

History – In para. 19(1), 'Section B of' inserted by SI 2013/3008, reg. 11(a), with effect from 1 December 2013 in respect of–

(a)   financial years ending on or after 30 September 2013; and

(b)   companies, which deliver the accounts required by s. 444 to the registrar on or after 1 December 2013.

Para. 19(3) substituted by SI 2015/980, reg. 17(3)(a), with effect in relation to–

(a)   financial years beginning on or after 1 January 2016, and

(b)   a financial year of a company beginning on or after 1 January 2015, but before 1 January 2016, if the directors of the company so decide.

Former para. 19(3) read as follows:

"**19(3)**   Any provisions made under sub-paragraph (1) or (2) which are not shown in the profit and loss account must be disclosed (either separately or in aggregate) in a note to the accounts."

20(1)   Where the reasons for which any provision was made in accordance with paragraph 19 have ceased to apply to any extent, that provision must be written back to the extent that it is no longer necessary.

20(1A)   But provision made in accordance with paragraph 19(2) in respect of goodwill must not be written back to any extent.

20(2)   Any amounts written back under sub-paragraph (1) must be recognised in the profit and loss account and disclosed separately in a note to the accounts if not shown separately in the profit and loss account.

History – Para. 20(1A) inserted by SI 2015/1672, reg. 3(2), with effect in relation to–

(a)   financial years beginning on or after 1 January 2016, and

(b)   a financial year of a company beginning on or after 1 January 2015 but before 1 January 2016, if the directors of the company have decided.

Para. 20(2) substituted by SI 2015/980, reg. 17(3)(b), with effect in relation to–

(a)   financial years beginning on or after 1 January 2016, and

(b)   a financial year of a company beginning on or after 1 January 2015, but before 1 January 2016, if the directors of the company so decide.

Former para. 20(2) read as follows:

"**20(2)**   Any amounts written back in accordance with sub-paragraph (1) which are not shown in the profit and loss account must be disclosed (either separately or in aggregate) in a note to the accounts."

Intangible Assets

21(1)   Where this is in accordance with generally accepted accounting principles or practice, development costs may be included in 'other intangible assets' under 'fixed assets' in the balance sheet formats set out in Section B of Part 1 of this Schedule.

21(2)   If any amount is included in a company's balance sheet in respect of development costs, the note on accounting policies (see paragraph 44 of this Schedule) must include the following information–

(a)   the period over which the amount of those costs originally capitalised is being or is to be written off, and

(b)   the reasons for capitalising the development costs in question.

History – Para. 21 and the heading preceding it substituted by SI 2015/980, reg. 17(3)(c), with effect in relation to–

(a) financial years beginning on or after 1 January 2016, and

(b) a financial year of a company beginning on or after 1 January 2015, but before 1 January 2016, if the directors of the company so decide.

Former para. 21 read as follows:

"Development costs

21(1) Development costs may only in special circumstances be included in 'other intangible assets' under 'fixed assets' in the balance sheet formats set out in Section B of Part 1 of this Schedule.

21(2) If any amount is included in a company's balance sheet in respect of development costs the following information must be given in a note to the accounts–

(a) the period over which the amount of those costs originally capitalised is being or is to be written off, and

(b) the reasons for capitalising the development costs in question.

History – Para. 21(1) substituted by SI 2013/3008, reg. 11(b), with effect from 1 December 2013 in respect of (a) financial years ending on or after 30 September 2013; and (b) companies, which deliver the accounts required by s. 444 to the registrar on or after 1 December 2013. Before substitution, the paragraph read:

"21(1) Notwithstanding that an item in respect of 'development costs' is included under 'fixed assets' in the balance sheet formats set out in Part 1 of this Schedule, an amount may only be included in a company's balance sheet in respect of development costs in special circumstances.""

22(1) Intangible assets must be written off over the useful economic life of the intangible asset.

22(2) Where in exceptional cases the useful life of intangible assets cannot be reliably estimated, such assets must be written off over a period chosen by the directors of the company.

22(3) The period referred to in sub-paragraph (2) must not exceed ten years.

22(4) There must be disclosed in a note to the accounts the period referred to in sub-paragraph (2) and the reasons for choosing that period.

History – Para. 22 substituted by SI 2015/980, reg. 17(3)(c), with effect in relation to–

(a) financial years beginning on or after 1 January 2016, and

(b) a financial year of a company beginning on or after 1 January 2015, but before 1 January 2016, if the directors of the company so decide.

Former para. 22 read as follows:

"22(1) The application of paragraphs 17 to 20 in relation to goodwill (in any case where goodwill is treated as an asset) is subject to the following.

22(2) Subject to sub-paragraph (3), the amount of the consideration for any goodwill acquired by a company must be reduced by provisions for depreciation calculated to write off that amount systematically over a period chosen by the directors of the company.

22(3) The period chosen must not exceed the useful economic life of the goodwill in question.

22(4) In any case where any goodwill acquired by a company is shown or included as an asset in the company's balance sheet there must be disclosed in a note to the accounts–

(a) the period chosen for writing off the consideration for that goodwill, and

(b) the reasons for choosing that period."

Current assets

23 Subject to paragraph 24, the amount to be included in respect of any current asset must be its purchase price or production cost.

24(1) If the net realisable value of any current asset is lower than its purchase price or production cost, the amount to be included in respect of that asset must be the net realisable value.

24(2) Where the reasons for which any provision for diminution in value was made in accordance with sub-paragraph (1) have ceased to apply to any extent, that provision must be written back to the extent that it is no longer necessary.

Miscellaneous and supplementary provisions

Excess of money owed over value received as an asset item

25(1) Where the amount repayable on any debt owed by a company is greater than the value of the consideration received in the transaction giving rise to the debt, the amount of the difference may be treated as an asset.

25(2) Where any such amount is so treated–

(a) it must be written off by reasonable amounts each year and must be completely written off before repayment of the debt, and

(b) if the current amount is not shown as a separate item in the company's balance sheet, it must be disclosed in a note to the accounts.

Assets included at a fixed amount

26(1) Subject to sub-paragraph (2), the following may be included at a fixed quantity and value in the balance sheet formats set out in Section B of Part 1 of this Schedule–

(a) assets which fall to be included amongst the fixed assets of a company under the item 'intangible assets', and

(b) raw materials and consumables within the item 'stocks'.

26(2) Sub-paragraph (1) applies to assets of a kind which are constantly being replaced where–

(a) their overall value is not material to assessing the company's state of affairs, and

(b) their quantity, value and composition are not subject to material variation.

History – Para. 26(1) substituted by SI 2013/3008, reg. 11(c), with effect from 1 December 2013 in respect of–

(a) financial years ending on or after 30 September 2013; and

(b) companies, which deliver the accounts required by s. 444 to the registrar on or after 1 December 2013. Before substitution, the paragraph read:

"**26(1)** Subject to sub-paragraph (2), assets which fall to be included–

(a) amongst the fixed assets of a company under the item 'tangible assets', or

(b) amongst the current assets of a company under the item 'raw materials and consumables', may be included at a fixed quantity and value."

Determination of purchase price or production cost

27(1) The purchase price of an asset is to be determined by adding to the actual price paid any expenses incidental to its acquisition and then subtracting any incidental reductions in the cost of acquisition.

27(2) The production cost of an asset is to be determined by adding to the purchase price of the raw materials and consumables used the amount of the costs incurred by the company which are directly attributable to the production of that asset.

27(3) In addition, there may be included in the production cost of an asset–

(a) a reasonable proportion of the costs incurred by the company which are only indirectly attributable to the production of that asset, but only to the extent that they relate to the period of production, and

(b) interest on capital borrowed to finance the production of that asset, to the extent that it accrues in respect of the period of production, provided, however, in a case within paragraph (b), that the inclusion of the interest in determining the cost of that asset and the amount of the interest so included is disclosed in a note to the accounts.

27(4)   In the case of current assets distribution costs may not be included in production costs.

History – In para. 27(1), the words 'and then subtracting any incidental reductions in the cost of acquisition' inserted by SI 2015/980, reg. 17(3)(d), with effect in relation to–

    (a) financial years beginning on or after 1 January 2016, and

    (b) a financial year of a company beginning on or after 1 January 2015, but before 1 January 2016, if the directors of the company so decide.

28(1)   The purchase price or production cost of–

    (a) any assets which, by virtue of regulation 3(1) and Section B of Part 1 of this Schedule, fall to be included under any item shown in a company's balance sheet under the general item 'stocks', and

    (b) any assets which are fungible assets (including investments), may be determined by the application of any of the methods mentioned in sub-paragraph (2) in relation to any such assets of the same class, provided that the method chosen is one which appears to the directors to be appropriate in the circumstances of the company.

28(2)   Those methods are–

    (a) the method known as 'first in, first out' (FIFO),

    (b) the method known as 'last in, first out' (LIFO),

    (c) a weighted average price, and

    (d) any other method reflecting generally accepted best practice.

28(3)   For the purposes of this paragraph, assets of any description must be regarded as fungible if assets of that description are substantially indistinguishable one from another.

History – In para. 28(1), ', by virtue of regulation 3(1) and Section B of Part 1 of this Schedule,' inserted by SI 2013/3008, reg. 11(d), with effect from 1 December 2013 in respect of–

    (a) financial years ending on or after 30 September 2013; and

    (b) companies, which deliver the accounts required by s. 444 to the registrar on or after 1 December 2013.

In para. 28(2)(d), the words 'reflecting generally accepted best practice' substituted for the words 'similar to any of the methods mentioned above' by SI 2015/980, reg. 17(3)(e), with effect in relation to–

    (a) financial years beginning on or after 1 January 2016, and

    (b) a financial year of a company beginning on or after 1 January 2015, but before 1 January 2016, if the directors of the company so decide.

Substitution of original stated amount where price or cost unknown

29(1)   This paragraph applies where–

    (a) there is no record of the purchase price or production cost of any asset of a company or of any price, expenses or costs relevant for determining its purchase price or production cost in accordance with paragraph 27, or

    (b) any such record cannot be obtained without unreasonable expense or delay.

29(2)   In such a case, the purchase price or production cost of the asset must be taken, for the purposes of paragraphs 17 to 24, to be the value ascribed to it in the earliest available record of its value made on or after its acquisition or production by the company.

Equity method in respect of participating interests

29A(1)   Participating interests may be accounted for using the equity method.

29A(2)   If participating interests are accounted for using the equity method–

    (a) the proportion of profit or loss attributable to a participating interest and recognised in the profit and loss account may be that proportion which corresponds to the amount of any dividends, and

(b) where the profit attributable to a participating interest and recognised in the profit and loss account exceeds the amount of any dividends, the difference must be placed in a reserve which cannot be distributed to shareholders.

29A(3)   The reference to **'dividends'** in sub-paragraph (2) includes dividends already paid and those whose payment can be claimed.

History – Para. 29A and the heading preceding it inserted by SI 2015/980, reg. 17(3)(f), with effect in relation to–

(a) financial years beginning on or after 1 January 2016, and

(b) a financial year of a company beginning on or after 1 January 2015, but before 1 January 2016, if the directors of the company so decide.

SECTION C – ALTERNATIVE ACCOUNTING RULES

Preliminary

30(1)   The rules set out in Section B are referred to below in this Schedule as the historical cost accounting rules.

30(2)   Those rules, with the omission of paragraphs 16, 22 and 26 to 29, are referred to below in this Part of this Schedule as the depreciation rules; and references below in this Schedule to the historical cost accounting rules do not include the depreciation rules as they apply by virtue of paragraph 33.

31   Subject to paragraphs 33 to 35, the amounts to be included in respect of assets of any description mentioned in paragraph 32 may be determined on any basis so mentioned.

Alternative accounting rules

32(1)   Intangible fixed assets, other than goodwill, may be included at their current cost.

32(2)   Tangible fixed assets may be included at a market value determined as at the date of their last valuation or at their current cost.

32(3)   Investments of any description falling to be included under item B III of either of the balance sheet formats set out Part 1 of this Schedule may be included either–

(a) at a market value determined as at the date of their last valuation, or

(b) at a value determined on any basis which appears to the directors to be appropriate in the circumstances of the company.

But in the latter case particulars of the method of valuation adopted and of the reasons for adopting it must be disclosed in a note to the accounts.

32(4)   [Omitted by SI 2015/980, reg. 17(4)(a).]

32(5)   [Omitted by SI 2015/980, reg. 17(4)(a).]

History – Para. 32(4) and (5) omitted by SI 2015/980, reg. 17(4)(a), with effect in relation to–

(a) financial years beginning on or after 1 January 2016, and

(b) a financial year of a company beginning on or after 1 January 2015, but before 1 January 2016, if the directors of the company so decide.

Former para. 32(4) and (5) read as follows:

"**32(4)**   Investments of any description falling to be included under item C III of either of the balance sheet formats set out in Part 1 of this Schedule may be included at their current cost.

32(5)   Stocks may be included at their current cost."

Application of the depreciation rules

33(1) Where the value of any asset of a company is determined on any basis mentioned in paragraph 32, that value must be, or (as the case may require) be the starting point for determining, the amount to be included in respect of that asset in the company's accounts, instead of its purchase price or production cost or any value previously so determined for that asset.

The depreciation rules apply accordingly in relation to any such asset with the substitution for any reference to its purchase price or production cost of a reference to the value most recently determined for that asset on any basis mentioned in paragraph 32.

33(2) The amount of any provision for depreciation required in the case of any fixed asset by paragraphs 18 to 20 as they apply by virtue of sub-paragraph (1) is referred to below in this paragraph as the adjusted amount, and the amount of any provision which would be required by any of those paragraphs in the case of that asset according to the historical cost accounting rules is referred to as the historical cost amount.

33(3) Where sub-paragraph (1) applies in the case of any fixed asset the amount of any provision for depreciation in respect of that asset–
- (a) included in any item shown in the profit and loss account in respect of amounts written off assets of the description in question, or
- (b) taken into account in stating any item so shown which is required by note (11) of the notes on the profit and loss account formats set out in Part 1 of this Schedule to be stated after taking into account any necessary provision for depreciation or diminution in value of assets included under it, may be the historical cost amount instead of the adjusted amount, provided that the amount of any difference between the two is shown separately in the profit and loss account or in a note to the accounts.

Additional information to be provided in case of departure from historical cost accounting rules

34(1) This paragraph applies where the amounts to be included in respect of assets covered by any items shown in a company's accounts have been determined on any basis mentioned in paragraph 32.

34(2) The items affected and the basis of valuation adopted in determining the amounts of the assets in question in the case of each such item must be disclosed in the note on accounting policies (see paragraph 44 of this Schedule).

34(3) In the case of each balance sheet item affected, the comparable amounts determined according to the historical cost accounting rules must be shown in a note to the accounts.

34(4) In sub-paragraph (3), references in relation to any item to the comparable amounts determined as there mentioned are references to–
- (a) the aggregate amount which would be required to be shown in respect of that item if the amounts to be included in respect of all the assets covered by that item were determined according to the historical cost accounting rules, and
- (b) the aggregate amount of the cumulative provisions for depreciation or diminution in value which would be permitted or required in determining those amounts according to those rules.

History – In para. 34(2), the words 'the note on accounting policies (see paragraph 44 of this Schedule)' substituted for the words 'a note to the accounts' by SI 2015/980, reg. 17(4)(b), with effect in relation to–
- (a) financial years beginning on or after 1 January 2016, and
- (b) a financial year of a company beginning on or after 1 January 2015, but before 1 January 2016, if the directors of the company so decide.

Para. 34(3) substituted by SI 2015/980, reg. 17(4)(c), with effect in relation to–

(a) financial years beginning on or after 1 January 2016, and

(b) a financial year of a company beginning on or after 1 January 2015, but before 1 January 2016, if the directors of the company so decide.

Former para. 34(3) read as follows:

"**34(3)** In the case of each balance sheet item affected (except stocks) either–

(a) the comparable amounts determined according to the historical cost accounting rules, or

(b) the differences between those amounts and the corresponding amounts actually shown in the balance sheet in respect of that item, must be shown separately in the balance sheet or in a note to the accounts."

Revaluation reserve

35(1)   With respect to any determination of the value of an asset of a company on any basis mentioned in paragraph 32, the amount of any profit or loss arising from that determination (after allowing, where appropriate, for any provisions for depreciation or diminution in value made otherwise than by reference to the value so determined and any adjustments of any such provisions made in the light of that determination) must be credited or (as the case may be) debited to a separate reserve ('the revaluation reserve').

35(2)   The amount of the revaluation reserve must be shown in the company's balance sheet under a separate sub-heading in the position given for the item 'revaluation reserve' under 'Capital and reserves' in Format 1 or 2 of the balance sheet formats set out in Part 1 of this Schedule.

35(3)   An amount may be transferred–

(a) from the revaluation reserve–

(i) to the profit and loss account, if the amount was previously charged to that account or represents realised profit, or

(ii) on capitalisation,

(b) to or from the revaluation reserve in respect of the taxation relating to any profit or loss credited or debited to the reserve.

The revaluation reserve must be reduced to the extent that the amounts transferred to it are no longer necessary for the purposes of the valuation method used.

35(4)   In sub-paragraph (3)(a)(ii) 'capitalisation', in relation to an amount standing to the credit of the revaluation reserve, means applying it in wholly or partly paying up unissued shares in the company to be allotted to members of the company as fully or partly paid shares.

35(5)   The revaluation reserve must not be reduced except as mentioned in this paragraph.

35(6)   The treatment for taxation purposes of amounts credited or debited to the revaluation reserve must be disclosed in a note to the accounts.

History – In para. 35(2), the words 'under "Capital and reserves"' inserted; and the words 'but need not be shown under that name' omitted by SI 2015/980, reg. 17(4)(d), with effect in relation to–

(a) financial years beginning on or after 1 January 2016, and

(b) a financial year of a company beginning on or after 1 January 2015, but before 1 January 2016, if the directors of the company so decide.

SECTION D – FAIR VALUE ACCOUNTING

Inclusion of financial instruments at fair value

36(1)   Subject to sub-paragraphs (2) to (5), financial instruments (including derivatives) may be included at fair value.

36(2)   Sub-paragraph (1) does not apply to financial instruments that constitute liabilities unless–

(a) they are held as part of a trading portfolio,

(b) they are derivatives, or

(c) they are financial instruments falling within sub-paragraph (4).

36(3)   Unless they are financial instruments falling within sub-paragraph (4), sub-paragraph (1) does not apply to–

(a) financial instruments (other than derivatives) held to maturity,

(b) loans and receivables originated by the company and not held for trading purposes,

(c) interests in subsidiary undertakings, associated undertakings and joint ventures,

(d) equity instruments issued by the company,

(e) contracts for contingent consideration in a business combination, or

(f) other financial instruments with such special characteristics that the instruments, according to generally accepted accounting principles or practice, should be accounted for differently from other financial instruments.

36(4)   Financial instruments which under international accounting standards may be included in accounts at fair value, may be so included, provided that the disclosures required by such accounting standards are made.

36(5)   If the fair value of a financial instrument cannot be determined reliably in accordance with paragraph 37, sub-paragraph (1) does not apply to that financial instrument.

36(6)   In this paragraph–

'associated undertaking' has the meaning given by paragraph 19 of Schedule 6 to these Regulations;

'joint venture' has the meaning given by paragraph 18 of that Schedule.

History – Para. 36(4) substituted by SI 2015/980, reg. 17(5)(a), with effect in relation to–

(a) financial years beginning on or after 1 January 2016, and

(b) a financial year of a company beginning on or after 1 January 2015, but before 1 January 2016, if the directors of the company so decide.

Former para. 36(4) read as follows:

"**36(4)**   Financial instruments that, under international accounting standards adopted by the European Commission on or before 5th September 2006 in accordance with the IAS Regulation, may be included in accounts at fair value, may be so included, provided that the disclosures required by such accounting standards are made."

Determination of fair value

37(1)   The fair value of a financial instrument is its value determined in accordance with this paragraph.

37(2)   If a reliable market can readily be identified for the financial instrument, its fair value is to be determined by reference to its market value.

37(3) If a reliable market cannot readily be identified for the financial instrument but can be identified for its components or for a similar instrument, its fair value is determined by reference to the market value of its components or of the similar instrument.

37(4) If neither sub-paragraph (2) nor (3) applies, the fair value of the financial instrument is a value resulting from generally accepted valuation models and techniques.

37(5) Any valuation models and techniques used for the purposes of sub-paragraph (4) must ensure a reasonable approximation of the market value.

Hedged items

38 A company may include any assets and liabilities, or identified portions of such assets or liabilities, that qualify as hedged items under a fair value hedge accounting system at the amount required under that system.

Other assets that may be included at fair value

39(1) This paragraph applies to–

   (a) stocks

   (b) investment property, and

   (c) living animals and plants.

39(2) Such stocks, investment property, and living animals and plants may be included at fair value, provided that, as the case maybe, all such stocks, investment property, and living animals and plants are so included where their fair value can reliably be determined.

39(3) In this paragraph, **'fair value'** means fair value determined in accordance with generally accepted accounting principles or practice.

History – Para. 39 substituted by SI 2015/980, reg. 17(5)(b), with effect in relation to–

   (a) financial years beginning on or after 1 January 2016, and

   (b) a financial year of a company beginning on or after 1 January 2015, but before 1 January 2016, if the directors of the company so decide.

Former para. 39 read as follows:

   "**39(1)** This paragraph applies to–

      (a) investment property, and

      (b) living animals and plants, that, under international accounting standards, may be included in accounts at fair value.

   39(2) Such investment property and such living animals and plants may be included at fair value, provided that all such investment property or, as the case may be, all such living animals and plants are so included where their fair value can reliably be determined.

   39(3) In this paragraph, **'fair value'** means fair value determined in accordance with relevant international accounting standards."

Accounting for changes in value

40(1) This paragraph applies where a financial instrument is valued in accordance with paragraph 36 or 38 or an asset is valued in accordance with paragraph 39.

40(2) Notwithstanding paragraph 13 in this Part of this Schedule, and subject to sub-paragraphs (3) and (4), a change in the value of the financial instrument or of the investment property or living animal or plant must be included in the profit and loss account.

40(3) Where–

   (a) the financial instrument accounted for is a hedging instrument under a hedge accounting system that allows some or all of the change in value not to be shown in the profit and loss account, or

(b) the change in value relates to an exchange difference arising on a monetary item that forms part of a company's net investment in a foreign entity, the amount of the change in value must be credited to or (as the case may be) debited from a separate reserve ('the fair value reserve').

40(4) Where the instrument accounted for–

(a) is an available for sale financial asset, and

(b) is not a derivative, the change in value may be credited to or (as the case may be) debited from the fair value reserve.

The fair value reserve

41(1) The fair value reserve must be adjusted to the extent that the amounts shown in it are no longer necessary for the purposes of paragraph 40(3) or (4).

41(2) [Omitted by SI 2015/980, reg. 17(5)(c).]

History – Para. 41(2) omitted by SI 2015/980, reg. 17(5)(c), with effect in relation to–

(a) financial years beginning on or after 1 January 2016, and

(b) a financial year of a company beginning on or after 1 January 2015, but before 1 January 2016, if the directors of the company so decide.

Former para. 41(2) read as follows:

"41(2) The treatment for taxation purposes of amounts credited or debited to the fair value reserve must be disclosed in a note to the accounts."

Part 3 – Notes to the accounts

Preliminary

42(1) Any information required in the case of a company by the following provisions of this Part of this Schedule must be given by way of a note to the accounts.

42(2) These notes must be presented in the order in which, where relevant, the items to which they relate are presented in the balance sheet and in the profit and loss account.

History – Para. 42 substituted by SI 2015/980, reg. 18(2), with effect in relation to–

(a) financial years beginning on or after 1 January 2016, and

(b) a financial year of a company beginning on or after 1 January 2015, but before 1 January 2016, if the directors of the company so decide.

Former para. 42 read as follows:

"42 Any information required in the case of any company by the following provisions of this Part of this Schedule must (if not given in the company's accounts) be given by way of a note to those accounts."

Reserves and dividends

43 [Omitted by SI 2015/980, reg. 18(3).]

History – Para. 43 omitted by SI 2015/980, reg. 18(3), with effect in relation to–

(a) financial years beginning on or after 1 January 2016, and

(b) a financial year of a company beginning on or after 1 January 2015, but before 1 January 2016, if the directors of the company so decide.

Former para. 43 read as follows:

"43 There must be stated–

(a) any amount set aside or proposed to be set aside to, or withdrawn or proposed to be withdrawn from, reserves,

(b) the aggregate amount of dividends paid in the financial year (other than those for which a liability existed at the immediately preceding balance sheet date),

(c) the aggregate amount of dividends that the company is liable to pay at the balance sheet date, and

(d)   the aggregate amount of dividends that are proposed before the date of approval of the accounts, and not otherwise disclosed under paragraph (b) or (c)."

Disclosure of accounting policies

44   The accounting policies adopted by the company in determining the amounts to be included in respect of items shown in the balance sheet and in determining the profit or loss of the company must be stated (including such policies with respect to the depreciation and diminution in value of assets).

Information supplementing the balance sheet

45   Paragraphs 48 to 57 require information which either supplements the information given with respect to any particular items shown in the balance sheet or is otherwise relevant to assessing the company's state of affairs in the light of the information so given.

History – In para. 45, '48 to 57' substituted for '46 to 58' by SI 2015/980, reg. 18(4), with effect in relation to–

(a)   financial years beginning on or after 1 January 2016, and

(b)   a financial year of a company beginning on or after 1 January 2015, but before 1 January 2016, if the directors of the company so decide.

Share capital

46   [Omitted by SI 2015/980, reg. 18(5).]

History – Para. 46 omitted by SI 2015/980, reg. 18(5), with effect in relation to–

(a)   financial years beginning on or after 1 January 2016, and

(b)   a financial year of a company beginning on or after 1 January 2015, but before 1 January 2016, if the directors of the company so decide.

Former para. 46 read as follows:

"**46(1)**   Where shares of more than one class have been allotted, the number and aggregate nominal value of shares of each class allotted must be given.

46(2)   In the case of any part of the allotted share capital that consists of redeemable shares, the following information must be given–

(a)   the earliest and latest dates on which the company has power to redeem those shares,

(b)   whether those shares must be redeemed in any event or are liable to be redeemed at the option of the company or of the shareholder, and

(c)   whether any (and, if so, what) premium is payable on redemption."

47   [Omitted by SI 2015/980, reg. 18(6).]

History – Para. 47 omitted by SI 2015/980, reg. 18(6), with effect in relation to–

(a)   financial years beginning on or after 1 January 2016, and

(b)   a financial year of a company beginning on or after 1 January 2015, but before 1 January 2016, if the directors of the company so decide.

Former para. 47 read as follows:

"**47**   If the company has allotted any shares during the financial year, the following information must be given–

(a)   the classes of shares allotted, and

(b)   as respects each class of shares, the number allotted, their aggregate nominal value, and the consideration received by the company for the allotment."

Fixed assets

48(1)   In respect of each item which is or would but for paragraph 4(2)(b) be shown under the general item 'fixed assets' in the company's balance sheet the following information must be given–

(a)   the appropriate amounts in respect of that item as at the date of the beginning of the financial year and as at the balance sheet date respectively,

(b)   the effect on any amount shown in the balance sheet in respect of that item of–

    (i)   any revision of the amount in respect of any assets included under that item made during that year on any basis mentioned in paragraph 32,

    (ii)   acquisitions during that year of any assets,

    (iii)   disposals during that year of any assets, and

    (iv)   any transfers of assets of the company to and from that item during that year.

48(2)   The reference in sub-paragraph (1)(a) to the appropriate amounts in respect of any item as at any date there mentioned is a reference to amounts representing the aggregate amounts determined, as at that date, in respect of assets falling to be included under that item on either of the following bases, that is to say–

    (a)   on the basis of purchase price or production cost (determined in accordance with paragraphs 27 and 28), or

    (b)   on any basis mentioned in paragraph 32, (leaving out of account in either case any provisions for depreciation or diminution in value).

48(3)   In respect of each item within sub-paragraph (1) there must also be stated–

    (a)   the cumulative amount of provisions for depreciation or diminution in value of assets included under that item as at each date mentioned in sub-paragraph (1)(a),

    (b)   the amount of any such provisions made in respect of the financial year,

    (c)   the amount of any adjustments made in respect of any such provisions during that year in consequence of the disposal of any assets, and

    (d)   the amount of any other adjustments made in respect of any such provisions during that year.

49   Where any fixed assets of the company (other than listed investments) are included under any item shown in the company's balance sheet at an amount determined on any basis mentioned in paragraph 32, the following information must be given–

    (a)   the years (so far as they are known to the directors) in which the assets were severally valued and the several values, and

    (b)   in the case of assets that have been valued during the financial year, the names of the persons who valued them or particulars of their qualifications for doing so and (whichever is stated) the bases of valuation used by them.

Investments

50   [Omitted by SI 2015/980, reg. 18(7).]

History – Para. 50 omitted by SI 2015/980, reg. 18(7), with effect in relation to–

    (a) financial years beginning on or after 1 January 2016, and

    (b) a financial year of a company beginning on or after 1 January 2015, but before 1 January 2016, if the directors of the company so decide.

Former para. 50 read as follows:

"**50(1)** In respect of the amount of each item which is or would but for paragraph 4(2)(b) be shown in the company's balance sheet under the general item 'investments' (whether as fixed assets or as current assets) there must be stated how much of that amount is ascribable to listed investments.

50(2) Where the amount of any listed investments is stated for any item in accordance with subparagraph (1), the following amounts must also be stated–

    (a) the aggregate market value of those investments where it differs from the amount so stated, and

    (b) both the market value and the stock exchange value of any investments of which the former value is, for the purposes of the accounts, taken as being higher than the latter."

Information about fair value of assets and liabilities

51(1)   This paragraph applies where financial instruments or other assets have been valued in accordance with, as appropriate, paragraph 36, 38 or 39.

51(2)   There must be stated–

  (a) the significant assumptions underlying the valuation models and techniques used to determine the fair values,

  (b) for each category of financial instrument or other asset, the fair value of the assets in that category and the changes in value–

     (i)   included directly in the profit and loss account, or

     (ii) credited to or (as the case may be) debited from the fair value reserve,in respect of those assets, and

  (c) for each class of derivatives, the extent and nature of the instruments, including significant terms and conditions that may affect the amount, timing and certainty of future cash flows.

51(3)   Where any amount is transferred to or from the fair value reserve during the financial year, there must be stated in tabular form–

  (a) the amount of the reserve as at the date of the beginning of the financial year and as at the balance sheet date respectively, and

  (b) the amount transferred to or from the reserve during that year.

History – Para. 51 substituted by SI 2015/980, reg. 18(8), with effect in relation to–

  (a) financial years beginning on or after 1 January 2016, and

  (b) a financial year of a company beginning on or after 1 January 2015, but before 1 January 2016, if the directors of the company so decide.

Former para. 51 read as follows:

"**51(1)**   This paragraph applies where financial instruments have been valued in accordance with paragraph 36 or 38.

51(2)   There must be stated–

  (a) the significant assumptions underlying the valuation models and techniques used where the fair value of the instruments has been determined in accordance with paragraph 37(4),

  (b) for each category of financial instrument, the fair value of the instruments in that category and the changes in value–

     (i)   included in the profit and loss account, or

     (ii) credited to or (as the case may be) debited from the fair value reserve, in respect of those instruments, and

  (c) for each class of derivatives, the extent and nature of the instruments, including significant terms and conditions that may affect the amount, timing and certainty of future cash flows.

51(3)   Where any amount is transferred to or from the fair value reserve during the financial year, there must be stated in tabular form–

  (a) the amount of the reserve as at the date of the beginning of the financial year and as at the balance sheet date respectively,

  (b) the amount transferred to or from the reserve during that year, and

  (c) the source and application respectively of the amounts so transferred."

52   [Omitted by SI 2015/980, reg. 18(9).]

History – Para. 52 omitted by SI 2015/980, reg. 18(9), with effect in relation to–

  (a) financial years beginning on or after 1 January 2016, and

  (b) a financial year of a company beginning on or after 1 January 2015, but before 1 January 2016, if the directors of the company so decide.

Former para. 52 read as follows:

"**52(1)**   This paragraph applies if–

  (a) the company has financial fixed assets that could be included at fair value by virtue of paragraph 36,

  (b) the amount at which those items are included under any item in the company's accounts is in excess of their fair value, and

  (c) the company has not made provision for diminution in value of those assets in accordance with paragraph 19(1) of this Schedule.

52(2)   There must be stated–

  (a) the amount at which either the individual assets or appropriate groupings of those individual assets are included in the company's accounts,

(b) the fair value of those assets or groupings, and

(c) the reasons for not making a provision for diminution in value of those assets, including the nature of the evidence that provides the basis for the belief that the amount at which they are stated in the accounts will be recovered."

Information where investment property and living animals and plants included at fair value

53 [Omitted by SI 2015/980, reg. 18(10).]

History – Para. 53 omitted by SI 2015/980, reg. 18(10), with effect in relation to–

(a) financial years beginning on or after 1 January 2016, and

(b) a financial year of a company beginning on or after 1 January 2015, but before 1 January 2016, if the directors of the company so decide.

Former para. 53 read as follows:

"**53(1)** This paragraph applies where the amounts to be included in a company's accounts in respect of investment property or living animals and plants have been determined in accordance with paragraph 39.

53(2) The balance sheet items affected and the basis of valuation adopted in determining the amounts of the assets in question in the case of each such item must be disclosed in a note to the accounts.

53(3) In the case of investment property, for each balance sheet item affected there must be shown, either separately in the balance sheet or in a note to the accounts–

(a) the comparable amounts determined according to the historical cost accounting rules, or

(b) the differences between those amounts and the corresponding amounts actually shown in the balance sheet in respect of that item.

53(4) In sub-paragraph (3), references in relation to any item to the comparable amounts determined in accordance with that sub-paragraph are to–

(a) the aggregate amount which would be required to be shown in respect of that item if the amounts to be included in respect of all the assets covered by that item were determined according to the historical cost accounting rules, and

(b) the aggregate amount of the cumulative provisions for depreciation or diminution in value which would be permitted or required in determining those amounts according to those rules."

Information about revalued fixed assets

54(1) This paragraph applies where fixed assets are measured at revalued amounts.

54(2) Where this paragraph applies, the following information must be given in tabular form–

(a) movements in the revaluation reserve in the financial year, with an explanation of the tax treatment of items therein, and

(b) the carrying amount in the balance sheet that would have been recognised had the fixed assets not been revalued.

History – Para. 54 and the heading preceding it substituted by SI 2015/980, reg. 18(11), with effect in relation to–

(a) financial years beginning on or after 1 January 2016, and

(b) a financial year of a company beginning on or after 1 January 2015, but before 1 January 2016, if the directors of the company so decide.

Former para. 54 read as follows:

"**Reserves and provisions**

54(1) This paragraph applies where any amount is transferred–

(a) to or from any reserves, or

(b) to any provisions for liabilities, or

(c) from any provision for liabilities otherwise than for the purpose for which the provision was established, and the reserves or provisions are or would but for paragraph 4(2)(b) be shown as separate items in the company's balance sheet.

54(2) The following information must be given in respect of the aggregate of reserves or provisions included in the same item–

(a) the amount of the reserves or provisions as at the date of the beginning of the financial year and as at the balance sheet date respectively,

(b) any amounts transferred to or from the reserves or provisions during that year, and

(c)   the source and application respectively of any amounts so transferred.

54(3)   Particulars must be given of each provision included in the item 'other provisions' in the company's balance sheet in any case where the amount of that provision is material."

Details of indebtedness

55(1)   For the aggregate of all items shown under 'creditors' in the company's balance sheet there must be stated the aggregate of the following amounts–

(a)   the amount of any debts included under 'creditors' which are payable or repayable otherwise than by instalments and fall due for payment or repayment after the end of the period of five years beginning with the day next following the end of the financial year, and

(b)   in the case of any debts so included which are payable or repayable by instalments, the amount of any instalments which fall due for payment after the end of that period.

55(2)   In respect of each item shown under 'creditors' in the company's balance sheet there must be stated the aggregate amount of any debts included under that item in respect of which any security has been given by the company with an indication of the nature and form of any such security.

55(3)   References above in this paragraph to an item shown under 'creditors' in the company's balance sheet include references, where amounts falling due to creditors within one year and after more than one year are distinguished in the balance sheet–

(a)   in a case within sub-paragraph (1), to an item shown under the latter of those categories,

(b)   in a case within sub-paragraph (2), to an item shown under either of those categories. References to items shown under 'creditors' include references to items which would but for paragraph 4(2)(b) be shown under that heading.

History – In para. 55(2), the words 'with an indication of the nature and form of any such security' inserted by SI 2015/980, reg. 18(12), with effect in relation to–

(a)   financial years beginning on or after 1 January 2016, and

(b)   a financial year of a company beginning on or after 1 January 2015, but before 1 January 2016, if the directors of the company so decide.

56   [Omitted by SI 2015/980, reg. 18(13).]

History – Para. 56 omitted by SI 2015/980, reg. 18(13), with effect in relation to–

(a)   financial years beginning on or after 1 January 2016, and

(b)   a financial year of a company beginning on or after 1 January 2015, but before 1 January 2016, if the directors of the company so decide.

Former para. 56 read as follows:

"56   If any fixed cumulative dividends on the company's shares are in arrear, there must be stated–

(a)   the amount of the arrears, and

(b)   the period for which the dividends or, if there is more than one class, each class of them are in arrear."

Guarantees and other financial commitments

57(1)   The total amount of any financial commitments, guarantees and contingencies that are not included in the balance sheet must be stated.

57(2)   An indication of the nature and form of any valuable security given by the company in respect of commitments, guarantees and contingencies within sub-paragraph (1) must be given.

57(3)   The total amount of any commitments within sub-paragraph (1) concerning pensions must be separately disclosed.

57(4)   The total amount of any commitments within sub-paragraph (1) which are undertaken on behalf of or for the benefit of–

(a) any parent undertaking, fellow subsidiary undertaking or any subsidiary undertaking of the company, or

(b) any undertaking in which the company has a participating interest

must be separately stated and those within paragraph (a) must also be stated separately from those within paragraph (b).

History – Para. 57 substituted by SI 2015/980, reg. 18(14), with effect in relation to–

(a) financial years beginning on or after 1 January 2016, and

(b) a financial year of a company beginning on or after 1 January 2015, but before 1 January 2016, if the directors of the company so decide.

Former para. 57 read as follows:

"**57(1)** Particulars must be given of any charge on the assets of the company to secure the liabilities of any other person, including, where practicable, the amount secured.

57(2) The following information must be given with respect to any other contingent liability not provided for–

(a) the amount or estimated amount of that liability,

(b) its legal nature, and

(c) whether any valuable security has been provided by the company in connection with that liability and if so, what.

57(3) There must be stated, where practicable, the aggregate amount or estimated amount of contracts for capital expenditure, so far as not provided for.

57(4) Particulars must be given of–

(a) any pension commitments included under any provision shown in the company's balance sheet, and

(b) any such commitments for which no provision has been made, and where any such commitment relates wholly or partly to pensions payable to past directors of the company separate particulars must be given of that commitment so far as it relates to such pensions.

57(5) Particulars must also be given of any other financial commitments that–

(a) have not been provided for, and

(b) are relevant to assessing the company's state of affairs.

57(6) Commitments within any of sub-paragraphs (1) to (5) which are undertaken on behalf of or for the benefit of–

(a) any parent undertaking or fellow subsidiary undertaking, or

(b) any subsidiary undertaking of the company, must be stated separately from the other commitments within that sub-paragraph, and commitments within paragraph

(a) must also be stated separately from those within paragraph (b)."

Miscellaneous matters

58 [Omitted by SI 2015/980, reg. 18(15).]

History – Para. 58 omitted by SI 2015/980, reg. 18(15), with effect in relation to–

(a) financial years beginning on or after 1 January 2016, and

(b) a financial year of a company beginning on or after 1 January 2015, but before 1 January 2016, if the directors of the company so decide.

Former para. 58 read as follows:

"**58** Particulars must be given of any case where the purchase price or production cost of any asset is for the first time determined under paragraph 29."

Information supplementing the profit and loss account

59 [Omitted by SI 2015/980, reg. 18(16).]

History – Para. 59 omitted by SI 2015/980, reg. 18(16), with effect in relation to–

(a) financial years beginning on or after 1 January 2016, and

(b) a financial year of a company beginning on or after 1 January 2015, but before 1 January 2016, if the directors of the company so decide.

Former para. 59 read as follows:

"**59** Paragraphs 60 and 61 require information which either supplements the information given with respect to any particular items shown in the profit and loss account or otherwise provides particulars of income or expenditure of the company or of circumstances affecting the items shown in the profit and loss account (see regulation 3(2) for exemption for companies falling within section 408 of the 2006 Act)."

Particulars of turnover

60 [Omitted by SI 2015/980, reg. 18(17).]

History – Para. 60 omitted by SI 2015/980, reg. 18(17), with effect in relation to–

    (a) financial years beginning on or after 1 January 2016, and

    (b) a financial year of a company beginning on or after 1 January 2015, but before 1 January 2016, if the directors of the company so decide.

Former para. 60 read as follows:

> **"60(1)** If the company has supplied geographical markets outside the United Kingdom during the financial year in question, there must be stated the percentage of its turnover that, in the opinion of the directors, is attributable to those markets.
>
> **60(2)** In analysing for the purposes of this paragraph the source of turnover, the directors of the company must have regard to the manner in which the company's activities are organised."

Miscellaneous matters

61(1) Where any amount relating to any preceding financial year is included in any item in the profit and loss account, the effect must be stated.

61(2) The amount and nature of any individual items of income or expenditure of exceptional size or incidence must be stated.

History – Para. 61(2) substituted for sub-para. (2) and (3) by SI 2015/980, reg. 18(18), with effect in relation to–

    (a) financial years beginning on or after 1 January 2016, and

    (b) a financial year of a company beginning on or after 1 January 2015, but before 1 January 2016, if the directors of the company so decide.

Sums denominated in foreign currencies

62 [Omitted by SI 2015/980, reg. 18(19).]

History – Para. 62 omitted by SI 2015/980, reg. 18(19), with effect in relation to–

    (a) financial years beginning on or after 1 January 2016, and

    (b) a financial year of a company beginning on or after 1 January 2015, but before 1 January 2016, if the directors of the company so decide.

Former para. 62 read as follows:

> **"62** Where sums originally denominated in foreign currencies have been brought into account under any items shown in the balance sheet or profit and loss account, the basis on which those sums have been translated into sterling (or the currency in which the accounts are drawn up) must be stated."

Dormant companies acting as agents

63 [Omitted by SI 2015/980, reg. 18(20).]

History – Para. 63 omitted by SI 2015/980, reg. 18(20), with effect in relation to–

    (a) financial years beginning on or after 1 January 2016, and

    (b) a financial year of a company beginning on or after 1 January 2015, but before 1 January 2016, if the directors of the company so decide.

Former para. 63 read as follows:

> **"63** Where the directors of a company take advantage of the exemption conferred by section 480 of the 2006 Act (dormant companies: exemption from audit), and the company has during the financial year in question acted as an agent for any person, the fact that it has so acted must be stated."

Post balance sheet events

64 The nature and financial effect of material events arising after the balance sheet date which are not reflected in the profit and loss account or balance sheet must be stated.

History – Para. 64 inserted by SI 2015/980, reg. 18(21), with effect in relation to–

    (a) financial years beginning on or after 1 January 2016, and

(b) a financial year of a company beginning on or after 1 January 2015, but before 1 January 2016, if the directors of the company so decide.

Parent undertaking information

65 Where the company is a subsidiary undertaking, the following information must be given in respect of the parent undertaking of the smallest group of undertakings for which group accounts are drawn up of which the company is a member–

    (a) the name of the parent undertaking which draws up the group accounts,

    (b) the address of the undertaking's registered office (whether in or outside the United Kingdom), or

    (c) if it is unincorporated, the address of its principal place of business.

History – Para. 65 inserted by SI 2015/980, reg. 18(21), with effect in relation to–

    (a) financial years beginning on or after 1 January 2016, and

    (b) a financial year of a company beginning on or after 1 January 2015, but before 1 January 2016, if the directors of the company so decide.

Related party transactions

66(1) Particulars may be given of transactions which the company has entered into with related parties, and must be given if such transactions are material and have not been concluded under normal market conditions with–

    (a) owners holding a participating interest in the company;

    (b) companies in which the company itself has a participating interest; and

    (c) the company's directors.

66(2) Particulars of the transactions required to be disclosed under sub-paragraph (1) must include–

    (a) the amount of such transactions,

    (b) the nature of the related party relationship, and

    (c) other information about the transactions necessary for an understanding of the financial position of the company.

66(3) Information about individual transactions may be aggregated according to their nature, except where separate information is necessary of an understanding of the effects of the related party transactions on the financial position of the company.

66(4) Particulars need not be given of transactions entered into between two or more members of a group, provided that any subsidiary undertaking which is a party to the transaction is wholly-owned by such a member.

66(5) In this paragraph, **'related party'** has the same meaning as in international accounting standards.

History – Para. 66 inserted by SI 2015/980, reg. 18(21), with effect in relation to–

    (a) financial years beginning on or after 1 January 2016, and

    (b) a financial year of a company beginning on or after 1 January 2015, but before 1 January 2016, if the directors of the company so decide.

SCHEDULE 2 – INFORMATION ABOUT RELATED UNDERTAKINGS WHERE COMPANY NOT PREPARING GROUP ACCOUNTS (COMPANIES ACT OR IAS INDIVIDUAL ACCOUNTS)

Regulation 4

History – Sch. 2 omitted by SI 2015/980, reg. 19, with effect in relation to–

(a) financial years beginning on or after 1 January 2016, and

(b) a financial year of a company beginning on or after 1 January 2015, but before 1 January 2016, if the directors of the company so decide.

Former Sch. 2 read as follows:

"SCHEDULE 2 – INFORMATION ABOUT RELATED UNDERTAKINGS
WHERE COMPANY NOT PREPARING GROUP ACCOUNTS
(COMPANIES ACT OR IAS INDIVIDUAL ACCOUNTS)

Regulation 4

Part 1 – Required disclosures

Subsidiary undertakings

1(1) The following information must be given where at the end of the financial year the company has subsidiary undertakings.

1(2) The name of each subsidiary undertaking must be stated.

1(3) There must be stated with respect to each subsidiary undertaking–

(a) if it is incorporated outside the United Kingdom, the country in which it is incorporated,

(b) if it is unincorporated, the address of its principal place of business.

Holdings in subsidiary undertakings

2(1) There must be stated in relation to shares of each class held by the company in a subsidiary undertaking–

(a) the identity of the class, and

(b) the proportion of the nominal value of the shares of that class represented by those shares.

2(2) The shares held by or on behalf of the company itself must be distinguished from those attributed to the company which are held by or on behalf of a subsidiary undertaking.

Financial information about subsidiary undertakings

3(1) There must be disclosed with respect to each subsidiary undertaking–

(a) the aggregate amount of its capital and reserves as at the end of its relevant financial year, and

(b) its profit or loss for that year.

3(2) That information need not be given if the company would (if it were not subject to the small companies regime) be exempt by virtue of section 400 or 401 of the 2006 Act (parent company included in accounts of larger group) from the requirement to prepare group accounts.

3(3) That information need not be given if the company's investment in the subsidiary undertaking is included in the company's accounts by way of the equity method of valuation.

3(4) That information need not be given if–

(a) the subsidiary undertaking is not required by any provision of the 2006 Act to deliver a copy of its balance sheet for its relevant financial year and does not otherwise publish that balance sheet in the United Kingdom or elsewhere, and

(b) the company's holding is less than 50% of the nominal value of the shares in the undertaking.

3(5) Information otherwise required by this paragraph need not be given if it is not material.

3(6)   For the purposes of this paragraph the **'relevant financial year'** of a subsidiary undertaking is–

    (a)   if its financial year ends with that of the company, that year, and

    (b)   if not, its financial year ending last before the end of the company's financial year.

Shares of company held by subsidiary undertakings

4(1)   The number, description and amount of the shares in the company held by or on behalf of its subsidiary undertakings must be disclosed.

4(2)   Sub-paragraph (1) does not apply in relation to shares in the case of which the subsidiary undertaking is concerned as personal representative or, subject as follows, as trustee.

4(3)   The exception for shares in relation to which the subsidiary undertaking is concerned as trustee does not apply if the company, or any subsidiary undertaking of the company, is beneficially interested under the trust, otherwise than by way of security only for the purposes of a transaction entered into by it in the ordinary course of a business which includes the lending of money.

4(4)   Part 2 of this Schedule has effect for the interpretation of the reference in sub-paragraph (3) to a beneficial interest under a trust.

Significant holdings in undertakings other than subsidiary undertakings

5(1)   The information required by paragraphs 6 and 7 must be given where at the end of the financial year the company has a significant holding in an undertaking which is not a subsidiary undertaking of the company.

5(2)   A holding is significant for this purpose if–

    (a)   it amounts to 20% or more of the nominal value of any class of shares in the undertaking, or

    (b)   the amount of the holding (as stated or included in the company's accounts) exceeds 20% of the amount (as so stated) of the company's assets.

6(1)   The name of the undertaking must be stated.

6(2)   There must be stated–

    (a)   if the undertaking is incorporated outside the United Kingdom, the country in which it is incorporated,

    (b)   if it is unincorporated, the address of its principal place of business.

6(3)   There must also be stated–

    (a)   the identity of each class of shares in the undertaking held by the company, and

    (b)   the proportion of the nominal value of the shares of that class represented by those shares.

7(1)   There must also be stated–

    (a)   the aggregate amount of the capital and reserves of the undertaking as at the end of its relevant financial year, and

    (b)   its profit or loss for that year.

7(2)   That information need not be given if–

    (a)   the company would (if it were not subject to the small companies regime) be exempt by virtue of section 400 or 401 of the 2006 Act (parent company included in accounts of larger group) from the requirement to prepare group accounts, and

    (b)   the investment of the company in all undertakings in which it has such a holding as is mentioned in sub-paragraph (1) is shown, in aggregate, in the notes to the accounts by way of the equity method of valuation.

7(3)   That information need not be given in respect of an undertaking if–

    (a)   the undertaking is not required by any provision of the 2006 Act to deliver to the registrar a copy of its balance sheet for its relevant financial year and does not otherwise publish that balance sheet in the United Kingdom or elsewhere, and

    (b)   the company's holding is less than 50% of the nominal value of the shares in the undertaking.

7(4)   Information otherwise required by this paragraph need not be given if it is not material.

7(5) For the purposes of this paragraph the 'relevant financial year' of an undertaking is–

   (a)   if its financial year ends with that of the company, that year, and

   (b)   if not, its financial year ending last before the end of the company's financial year.

Membership of certain undertakings

8(1) The information required by this paragraph must be given where at the end of the financial year the company is a member of a qualifying undertaking.

8(2) There must be stated–

   (a)   the name and legal form of the undertaking, and

   (b)   the address of the undertaking's registered office (whether in or outside the United (Kingdom) or, if it does not have such an office, its head office (whether in or outside the United Kingdom).

8(3) Where the undertaking is a qualifying partnership there must also be stated either–

   (a)   that a copy of the latest accounts of the undertaking has been or is to be appended to the copy of the company's accounts sent to the registrar under section 444 of the 2006 Act, or

   (b)   the name of at least one body corporate (which may be the company) in whose group accounts the undertaking has been or is to be dealt with on a consolidated basis.

8(4) Information otherwise required by sub-paragraph (2) need not be given if it is not material.

8(5) Information otherwise required by sub-paragraph (3)(b) need not be given if the notes to the company's accounts disclose that advantage has been taken of the exemption conferred by regulation 7 of the Partnerships (Accounts) Regulations 2008.

8(6) In sub-paragraph (1) **'member'**, in relation to a qualifying undertaking which is a qualifying partnership, has the same meaning as in the Partnerships (Accounts) Regulations 2008.

8(7) In this paragraph–

'dealt with on a consolidated basis' and **'qualifying partnership'** have the same meanings as in the Partnerships (Accounts) Regulations 2008;

'qualifying undertaking' means–

   (a)   a qualifying partnership, or

   (b)   an unlimited company each of whose members is–

      (i)   a limited company,

      (ii)   another unlimited company each of whose members is a limited company,

      (iii)   a Scottish partnership which is not a limited partnership, each of whose members is a limited company, or

      (iv)   a Scottish partnership which is a limited partnership, each of whose general partners is a limited company.

8(8) In sub-paragraph (7) the references to a limited company, another unlimited company, a Scottish partnership which is not a limited partnership or a Scottish partnership which is a limited partnership include a comparable undertaking incorporated in or formed under the law of a country or territory outside the United Kingdom.

8(9) In sub-paragraph (7) **'general partner'** means–

   (a)   in relation to a Scottish partnership which is a limited partnership, a person who is a general partner within the meaning of the Limited Partnerships Act 1907, and

   (b)   in relation to an undertaking incorporated in or formed under the law of any country or territory outside the United Kingdom and which is comparable to a Scottish partnership which is a limited partnership, a person comparable to such a general partner.

8(10) In sub-paragraphs (7), (8) and (9) **'limited partnership'** means a partnership registered under the Limited Partnerships Act 1907.

History – In para. 8(5), 'Partnerships (Accounts) Regulations 2008' substituted for 'Partnerships and Unlimited Companies (Accounts) Regulations 1993' by SI 2008/569, reg. 17(1)(a), with effect from 6 April 2008.

Para. 8(6) substituted and 8(7)–(10) inserted by SI 2013/2005, reg. 5, with effect from 1 September 2013 applying in relation to a financial year of a company beginning on or after 1 October 2013. The version of para. 8 applying to financial years beginning before 1 October 2013 read as follows:

"**8(1)**   The information required by this paragraph must be given where at the end of the financial year the company is a member of a qualifying undertaking.

8(2)   There must be stated–

    (a)   the name and legal form of the undertaking, and

    (b)   the address of the undertaking's registered office (whether in or outside the United (Kingdom) or, if it does not have such an office, its head office (whether in or outside the United Kingdom).

8(3)   Where the undertaking is a qualifying partnership there must also be stated either–

    (a)   that a copy of the latest accounts of the undertaking has been or is to be appended to the copy of the company's accounts sent to the registrar under section 444 of the 2006 Act, or

    (b)   the name of at least one body corporate (which may be the company) in whose group accounts the undertaking has been or is to be dealt with on a consolidated basis.

8(4)   Information otherwise required by sub-paragraph (2) need not be given if it is not material.

8(5)   Information otherwise required by sub-paragraph (3)(b) need not be given if the notes to the company's accounts disclose that advantage has been taken of the exemption conferred by regulation 7 of the Partnerships (Accounts) Regulations 2008.

8(6)   In this paragraph–

    'dealt with on a consolidated basis', **'member'** and **'qualifying partnership'** have the same meanings as in the Partnerships (Accounts) Regulations 2008;

    'qualifying undertaking' means–

    (a)   a qualifying partnership, or

    (b)   an unlimited company each of whose members is–

        (i)   a limited company,

        (ii)   another unlimited company each of whose members is a limited company, or

        (iii)   a Scottish partnership each of whose members is a limited company, and references in this paragraph to a limited company, another unlimited company or a Scottish partnership include a comparable undertaking incorporated in or formed under the law of a country or territory outside the United Kingdom."

Parent undertaking drawing up accounts for larger group

9(1)   Where the company is a subsidiary undertaking, the following information must be given with respect to the parent undertaking of–

    (a)   the largest group of undertakings for which group accounts are drawn up and of which the company is a member, and

    (b)   the smallest such group of undertakings.

9(2)   The name of the parent undertaking must be stated.

9(3)   There must be stated–

    (a)   if the undertaking is incorporated outside the United Kingdom, the country in which it is incorporated,

    (b)   if it is unincorporated, the address of its principal place of business.

9(4)   If copies of the group accounts referred to in sub-paragraph (1) are available to the public, there must also be stated the addresses from which copies of the accounts can be obtained.

Identification of ultimate parent company

10(1)   Where the company is a subsidiary undertaking, the following information must be given with respect to the company (if any) regarded by the directors as being the company's ultimate parent company.

10(2)   The name of that company must be stated.

10(3)   If that company is incorporated outside the United Kingdom, the country in which it is incorporated must be stated (if known to the directors).

10(4)   In this paragraph 'company' includes any body corporate.

Construction of references to shares held by company

11(1)   References in this Part of this Schedule to shares held by a company are to be construed as follows.

11(2)   For the purposes of paragraphs 2 and 3 (information about subsidiary undertakings)–

   (a)   there must be attributed to the company any shares held by a subsidiary undertaking, or by a person acting on behalf of the company or a subsidiary undertaking; but

   (b)   there must be treated as not held by the company any shares held on behalf of a person other than the company or a subsidiary undertaking.

11(3)   For the purposes of paragraphs 5 to 7 (information about undertakings other than subsidiary undertakings)–

   (a)   there must be attributed to the company shares held on its behalf by any person; but

   (b)   there must be treated as not held by a company shares held on behalf of a person other than the company.

11(4)   For the purposes of any of those provisions, shares held by way of security must be treated as held by the person providing the security–

   (a)   where apart from the right to exercise them for the purpose of preserving the value of the security, or of realising it, the rights attached to the shares are exercisable only in accordance with his instructions, and

   (b)   where the shares are held in connection with the granting of loans as part of normal business activities and apart from the right to exercise them for the purpose of preserving the value of the security, or of realising it, the rights attached to the shares are exercisable only in his interests.

Part 2 – Interpretation of references to 'beneficial interest'

Introduction

12(1)   References in this Schedule to a beneficial interest are to be interpreted in accordance with the following provisions.

12(2)   This Part of this Schedule applies in relation to debentures as it applies in relation to shares.

Residual interests under pension and employees' share schemes

13(1)   Where shares in an undertaking are held on trust for the purposes of a pension scheme or an employees' share scheme, there must be disregarded any residual interest of the undertaking or any of its subsidiary undertakings (the 'residual beneficiary') that has not vested in possession.

13(2)   A 'residual interest' means a right to receive any of the trust property in the event of–

   (a)   all the liabilities arising under the scheme having been satisfied or provided for, or

   (b)   the residual beneficiary ceasing to participate in the scheme, or

   (c)   the trust property at any time exceeding what is necessary for satisfying the liabilities arising or expected to arise under the scheme.

13(3)   In sub-paragraph (2)–

   (a)   references to a right include a right dependent on the exercise of a discretion vested by the scheme in the trustee or any other person, and

   (b)   references to liabilities arising under a scheme include liabilities that have resulted or may result from the exercise of any such discretion.

13(4)   For the purposes of this paragraph a residual interest vests in possession–

   (a)   in a case within sub-paragraph (2)(a), on the occurrence of the event there mentioned, whether or not the amount of the property receivable pursuant to the right mentioned in that sub-paragraph is then ascertained,

   (b)   in a case within sub-paragraph (2)(b) or (c), when the residual beneficiary becomes entitled to require the trustee to transfer to it any of the property receivable pursuant to that right.

Employer's charges and other rights of recovery

14(1)   Where shares in an undertaking are held on trust there must be disregarded–

(a)   if the trust is for the purposes of a pension scheme, any such rights as are mentioned in sub-paragraph (2),

(b)   if the trust is for the purposes of an employees' share scheme, any such rights as are mentioned in paragraph

(a)   of that sub-paragraph, being rights of the undertaking or any of its subsidiary undertakings.

14(2)   The rights referred to are–

(a)   any charge or lien on, or set-off against, any benefit or other right or interest under the scheme for the purpose of enabling the employer or former employer of a member of the scheme to obtain the discharge of a monetary obligation due to him from the member,

(b)   any right to receive from the trustee of the scheme, or as trustee of the scheme to retain, an amount that can be recovered or retained under section 61 of the Pension Schemes Act 1993 or section 57 of the Pension Schemes (Northern Ireland) Act 1993 (deduction of contributions equivalent premium from refund of scheme contributions) or otherwise, as reimbursement or partial reimbursement for any contributions equivalent premium paid in connection with the scheme under Chapter 3 of Part 3 of that Act.

Trustee's right to expenses, remuneration, indemnity etc.

15(1)   Where an undertaking is a trustee, there must be disregarded any rights which the undertaking has in its capacity as trustee.

15(2)   This includes in particular–

(a)   any right to recover its expenses or be remunerated out of the trust property, and

(b)   any right to be indemnified out of that property for any liability incurred by reason of any act or omission of the undertaking in the performance of its duties as trustee.

Meaning of 'pension scheme'

16(1)   In this Part of this Schedule 'pension scheme' means any scheme for the provision of benefits consisting of or including relevant benefits for or in respect of employees or former employees.

16(2)   For this purpose 'relevant benefits' means any pension, lump sum, gratuity or other like benefit given or to be given on retirement or on death or in anticipation of retirement or, in connection with past service, after retirement or death.

Application of provisions to directors

17   In paragraphs 14(2) and 16, 'employee' and 'employer' are to be read as if a director of an undertaking were employed by it."

SCHEDULE 3 – INFORMATION ABOUT DIRECTORS' BENEFITS: REMUNERATION (COMPANIES ACT OR IAS ACCOUNTS)

Regulations 5 and 9

History – Sch. 3 omitted by SI 2015/980, reg. 20, with effect in relation to–

    (a)   financial years beginning on or after 1 January 2016, and

    (b)   a financial year of a company beginning on or after 1 January 2015, but before 1 January 2016, if the directors of the company so decide.

Former Sch. 3 read as follows:

"SCHEDULE 3 – INFORMATION ABOUT DIRECTORS' BENEFITS: REMUNERATION
(COMPANIES ACT OR IAS ACCOUNTS)

Regulations 5 and 9

Part 1 – Information required to be disclosed

Total amount of directors' remuneration etc.

    1(1)   There must be shown the overall total of the following amounts–

       (a)   the amount of remuneration paid to or receivable by directors in respect of qualifying services;

       (b)   the amount of money paid to or receivable by directors, and the net value of assets (other than money, share options or shares) received or receivable by directors, under long term incentive schemes in respect of qualifying services; and

       (c)   the value of any company contributions–

          (i)   paid, or treated as paid, to a pension scheme in respect of directors' qualifying services, and

          (ii)   by reference to which the rate or amount of any money purchase benefits that may become payable will be calculated.

    1(2)   There must be shown the number of directors (if any) to whom retirement benefits are accruing in respect of qualifying services–

       (a)   under money purchase schemes, and

       (b)   under defined benefit schemes.

Compensation to directors for loss of office

    2(1)   There must be shown the aggregate amount of any payments made to directors or past directors for loss of office.

    2(2)   **'Payment for loss of office'** has the same meaning as in section 215 of the 2006 Act.

Sums paid to third parties in respect of directors' services

    3(1)   There must be shown the aggregate amount of any consideration paid to or receivable by third parties for making available the services of any person–

       (a)   as a director of the company, or

       (b)   while director of the company–

          (i)   as director of any of its subsidiary undertakings, or

          (ii)   otherwise in connection with the management of the affairs of the company or any of its subsidiary undertakings.

    3(2)   In sub-paragraph (1)–

       (a)   the reference to consideration includes benefits otherwise than in cash, and

       (b)   in relation to such consideration the reference to its amount is to the estimated money value of the benefit.

The nature of any such consideration must be disclosed.

3(3) For the purposes of this paragraph a **'third party'** means a person other than–

    (a)   the director himself or a person connected with him or body corporate controlled by him, or

    (b)   the company or any of its subsidiary undertakings.

Part 2 – Supplementary provisions

General nature of obligations

4(1) This Schedule requires information to be given only so far as it is contained in the company's books and papers or the company has the right to obtain it from the persons concerned.

4(2) For the purposes of this Schedule any information is treated as shown if it is capable of being readily ascertained from other information which is shown.

Provisions as to amounts to be shown

5(1) The following provisions apply with respect to the amounts to be shown under this Schedule.

5(2) The amount in each case includes all relevant sums, whether paid by or receivable from the company, any of the company's subsidiary undertakings or any other person.

5(3) References to amounts paid to or receivable by a person include amounts paid to or receivable by a person connected with him or a body corporate controlled by him (but not so as to require an amount to be counted twice).

5(4) Except as otherwise provided, the amounts to be shown for any financial year are–

    (a)   the sums receivable in respect of that year (whenever paid) or,

    (b)   in the case of sums not receivable in respect of a period, the sums paid during that year.

5(5) Sums paid by way of expenses allowance that are charged to United Kingdom income tax after the end of the relevant financial year must be shown in a note to the first accounts in which it is practicable to show them and must be distinguished from the amounts to be shown apart from this provision.

5(6) Where it is necessary to do so for the purpose of making any distinction required in complying with this Schedule, the directors may apportion payments between the matters in respect of which they have been paid or are receivable in such manner as they think appropriate.

Exclusion of sums liable to be accounted for to company etc.

6(1) The amounts to be shown under this Schedule do not include any sums that are to be accounted for–

    (a)   to the company or any of its subsidiary undertakings, or

    (b)   by virtue of sections 219 and 222(3) of the 2006 Act (payments in connection with share transfers: duty to account), to persons who sold their shares as a result of the offer made.

6(2) Where–

    (a)   any such sums are not shown in a note to the accounts for the relevant financial year on the ground that the person receiving them is liable to account for them, and

    (b)   the liability is afterwards wholly or partly released or is not enforced within a period of two years, those sums, to the extent to which the liability is released or not enforced, must be shown in a note to the first accounts in which it is practicable to show them and must be distinguished from the amounts to be shown apart from this provision.

Meaning of 'remuneration'

7(1) In this Schedule **'remuneration'** of a director includes–

    (a)   salary, fees and bonuses, sums paid by way of expenses allowance (so far as they are chargeable to United Kingdom income tax), and

    (b)   subject to sub-paragraph (2), the estimated money value of any other benefits received by him otherwise than in cash.

7(2)   The expression does not include–

    (a)   the value of any share options granted to a director or the amount of any gains made on the exercise of any such options,

    (b)   any company contributions paid, or treated as paid, in respect of him under any pension scheme or any benefits to which he is entitled under any such scheme, or

    (c)   any money or other assets paid to or received or receivable by him under any long term incentive scheme.

Meaning of 'long term incentive scheme'

8(1)   In this Schedule **'long term incentive scheme'** means an agreement or arrangement–

    (a)   under which money or other assets may become receivable by a director, and

    (b)   which includes one or more qualifying conditions with respect to service or performance which cannot be fulfilled within a single financial year.

8(2)   For this purpose the following must be disregarded–

    (a)   bonuses the amount of which falls to be determined by reference to service or performance within a single financial year;

    (b)   compensation for loss of office, payments for breach of contract and other termination payments; and

    (c)   retirement benefits.

Meaning of 'shares' and 'share option' and related expressions

9   In this Schedule–

    (a)   **'shares'** means shares (whether allotted or not) in the company, or any undertaking which is a group undertaking in relation to the company, and includes a share warrant as defined by section 779(1) of the 2006 Act; and

    (b)   **'share option'** means a right to acquire shares.

Meaning of 'pension scheme' and related expressions

10(1)   In this Schedule–

'pension scheme' means a retirement benefits scheme as defined by section 611 of the Income and Corporation Taxes Act 1988; and **'retirement benefits'** has the meaning given by section 612(1) of that Act.

10(2)   In this Schedule, **'company contributions'**, in relation to a pension scheme and a director, means any payments (including insurance premiums) made, or treated as made, to the scheme in respect of the director by a person other than the director.

10(3)   In this Schedule, in relation to a director–

'defined benefits' means retirement benefits payable under a pension scheme that are not money purchase benefits;

'defined benefit scheme' means a pension scheme that is not a money purchase scheme; 'money purchase benefits' means retirement benefits payable under a pension scheme the rate or amount of which is calculated by reference to payments made, or treated as made, by the director or by any other person in respect of the director and which are not average salary benefits; and 'money purchase scheme' means a pension scheme under which all of the benefits that may become payable to or in respect of the director are money purchase benefits.

10(4)   Where a pension scheme provides for any benefits that may become payable to or in respect of any director to be whichever are the greater of–

    (a)   money purchase benefits as determined by or under the scheme; and

    (b)   defined benefits as so determined, the company may assume for the purposes of this paragraph that those benefits will be money purchase benefits, or defined benefits, according to whichever appears more likely at the end of the financial year.

10(5)   For the purpose of determining whether a pension scheme is a money purchase or defined benefit scheme, any death in service benefits provided for by the scheme are to be disregarded.

References to subsidiary undertakings

11(1) Any reference in this Schedule to a subsidiary undertaking of the company, in relation to a person who is or was, while a director of the company, a director also, by virtue of the company's nomination (direct or indirect) of any other undertaking, includes that undertaking, whether or not it is or was in fact a subsidiary undertaking of the company.

11(2) Any reference to a subsidiary undertaking of the company–

    (a) for the purposes of paragraph 1 (remuneration etc.) is to an undertaking which is a subsidiary undertaking at the time the services were rendered, and

    (b) for the purposes of paragraph 2 (compensation for loss of office) is to a subsidiary undertaking immediately before the loss of office as director.

Other minor definitions

12(1) In this Schedule–

'net value', in relation to any assets received or receivable by a director, means value after deducting any money paid or other value given by the director in respect of those assets;

'qualifying services', in relation to any person, means his services as a director of the company, and his services while director of the company–

    (a) as director of any of its subsidiary undertakings; or

    (b) otherwise in connection with the management of the affairs of the company or any of its subsidiary undertakings.

12(2) For the purposes of this Schedule, remuneration paid or receivable or share options granted in respect of a person's accepting office as a director are treated as emoluments paid or receivable or share options granted in respect of his services as a director."

SCHEDULE 4 – COMPANIES ACT ABBREVIATED ACCOUNTS FOR DELIVERY TO REGISTRAR OF COMPANIES

Regulation 6(1)

History – Sch. 4 omitted by SI 2015/980, reg. 21, with effect in relation to–

    (a)   financial years beginning on or after 1 January 2016, and

    (b)   a financial year of a company beginning on or after 1 January 2015, but before 1 January 2016, if the directors of the company so decide.

Former Sch. 4 read as follows:

"SCHEDULE 4 – COMPANIES ACT ABBREVIATED ACCOUNTS FOR DELIVERY TO REGISTRAR OF COMPANIES

Regulation 6(1)

Part 1 – The required balance sheet formats

1(1)   A company may deliver to the registrar a copy of the balance sheet showing the items listed in either of the balance sheet formats set out below, in the order and under the headings and sub-headings given in the format adopted, but in other respects corresponding to the full balance sheet.

1(2)   The copy balance sheet must contain in a prominent position a statement that it has been prepared in accordance with the provisions applicable to companies subject to the small companies regime.

Balance sheet formats – Format 1

A.   Called up share capital not paid

B.   Fixed assets

    I.   Intangible assets

    II.   Tangible assets

    III.   Investments

C.   Current assets

    I.   Stocks

    II.   Debtors *(1)*

    III.   Investments

    IV.   Cash at bank and in hand

D.   Prepayments and accrued income

E.   Creditors: amounts falling due within one year

F.   Net current assets (liabilities)

G.   Total assets less current liabilities

H.   Creditors: amounts falling due after more than one year

I.   Provisions for liabilities

J.   Accruals and deferred income

K.   Capital and reserves

    I.   Called up share capital

    II.   Share premium account

    III.   Revaluation reserve

    IV.   Other reserves

    V.   Profit and loss account

Balance sheet formats – Format 2

ASSETS

A. Called up share capital not paid

B. Fixed assets

  I. Intangible assets

  II. Tangible assets

  III. Investments

C. Current assets

  I. Stocks

  II. Debtors *(1)*

  III. Investments

  IV. Cash at bank and in hand

  D. Prepayments and accrued income

LIABILITIES

A. Capital and reserves

  I. Called up share capital

  II. Share premium account

  III. Revaluation reserve

  IV. Other reserves

  V. Profit and loss account

B. Provisions for liabilities

C. Creditors *(2)*

D. Accruals and deferred income

Notes on the balance sheet formats

(1) *Debtors*
(Formats 1 and 2, items C.II.)

  The aggregate amount of debtors falling due after more than one year must be shown separately, unless it is disclosed in the notes to the accounts.

(2) *Creditors*
(Format 2, Liabilities item C.)

  The aggregate amount of creditors falling due within one year and of creditors falling due after more than one year must be shown separately, unless it is disclosed in the notes to the accounts.

Part 2 – Notes to the accounts

Preliminary

  2 Any information required in the case of any company by the following provisions of this Part of this Schedule must (if not given in the company's accounts) be given by way of a note to those accounts.

Disclosure of accounting policies

3   The accounting policies adopted by the company in determining the amounts to be included in respect of items shown in the balance sheet and in determining the profit or loss of the company must be stated (including such policies with respect to the depreciation and diminution in value of assets).

INFORMATION SUPPLEMENTING THE BALANCE SHEET

Share capital and debentures

4(1)   Where shares of more than one class have been allotted, the number and aggregate nominal value of shares of each class allotted must be given.

4(2)   In the case of any part of the allotted share capital that consists of redeemable shares, the following information must be given–

    (a)   the earliest and latest dates on which the company has power to redeem those shares,

    (b)   whether those shares must be redeemed in any event or are liable to be redeemed at the option of the company or of the shareholder, and

    (c)   whether any (and, if so, what) premium is payable on redemption.

5   If the company has allotted any shares during the financial year, the following information must be given–

    (a)   the classes of shares allotted, and

    (b)   as respects each class of shares, the number allotted, their aggregate nominal value, and the consideration received by the company for the allotment.

Fixed assets

6(1)   In respect of each item to which a letter or Roman number is assigned under the general item 'fixed assets' in the company's balance sheet the following information must be given–

    (a)   the appropriate amounts in respect of that item as at the date of the beginning of the financial year and as at the balance sheet date respectively,

    (b)   the effect on any amount shown in the balance sheet in respect of that item of–

        (i)   any revision of the amount in respect of any assets included under that item made during that year on any basis mentioned in paragraph 32 of Schedule 1 to these Regulations,

        (ii)   acquisitions during that year of any assets,

        (iii)   disposals during that year of any assets, and

        (iv)   any transfers of assets of the company to and from that item during that year.

6(2)   The reference in sub-paragraph (1)(a) to the appropriate amounts in respect of any item as at any date there mentioned is a reference to amounts representing the aggregate amounts determined, as at that date, in respect of assets falling to be included under that item on either of the following bases, that is to say–

    (a)   on the basis of purchase price or production cost (determined in accordance with paragraphs 27 and 28 of Schedule 1 to these Regulations), or

    (b)   on any basis mentioned in paragraph 32 of that Schedule, (leaving out of account in either case any provisions for depreciation or diminution in value).

6(3)   In respect of each item within sub-paragraph (1) there must also be stated–

    (a)   the cumulative amount of provisions for depreciation or diminution in value of assets included under that item as at each date mentioned in sub-paragraph (1)(a),

    (b)   the amount of any such provisions made in respect of the financial year,

    (c)   the amount of any adjustments made in respect of any such provisions during that year in consequence of the disposal of any assets, and

    (d)   the amount of any other adjustments made in respect of any such provisions during that year.

Financial fixed assets

7(1) This paragraph applies if–

(a) the company has financial fixed assets that could be included at fair value by virtue of paragraph 36 of Schedule 1 to these Regulations,

(b) the amount at which those items are included under any item in the company's accounts is in excess of their fair value, and

(c) the company has not made provision for diminution in value of those assets in accordance with paragraph 19(1) of that Schedule.

7(2) There must be stated–

(a) the amount at which either the individual assets or appropriate groupings of those individual assets are included in the company's accounts,

(b) the fair value of those assets or groupings, and

(c) the reasons for not making a provision for diminution in value of those assets, including the nature of the evidence that provides the basis for the belief that the amount at which they are stated in the accounts will be recovered.

Details of indebtedness

8(1) For the aggregate of all items shown under 'creditors' in the company's balance sheet there must be stated the aggregate of the following amounts–

(a) the amount of any debts included under 'creditors' which are payable or repayable otherwise than by instalments and fall due for payment or repayment after the end of the period of five years beginning with the day next following the end of the financial year, and

(b) in the case of any debts so included which are payable or repayable by instalments, the amount of any instalments which fall due for payment after the end of that period.

8(2) In respect of each item shown under 'creditors' in the company's balance sheet there must be stated the aggregate amount of any debts included under that item in respect of which any security has been given by the company.

Sums denominated in foreign currencies

9 Where sums originally denominated in foreign currencies have been brought into account under any items shown in the balance sheet or profit and loss account, the basis on which those sums have been translated into sterling (or the currency in which the accounts are drawn up) must be stated.

Dormant companies acting as agents

10 Where the directors of a company take advantage of the exemption conferred by section 480 of the 2006 Act (dormant companies: exemption from audit), and the company has during the financial year in question acted as an agent for any person, the fact that it has so acted must be stated."

SCHEDULE 5 – MATTERS TO BE DEALT WITH IN DIRECTORS' REPORT

Introduction

1 In addition to the information required by section 416 of the 2006 Act, the directors' report must contain the following information.

Political donations and expenditure

2(1) If–

    (a) the company (not being the wholly-owned subsidiary of a company incorporated in the United Kingdom) has in the financial year–

        (i) made any political donation to any political party or other political organisation,

        (ii) made any political donation to any independent election candidate, or

        (iii) incurred any political expenditure, and

    (b) the amount of the donation or expenditure, or (as the case may be) the aggregate amount of all donations and expenditure falling within paragraph (a), exceeded £2000, the directors' report for the year must contain the following particulars.

2(2) Those particulars are–

    (a) as respects donations falling within sub-paragraph (1)(a)(i) or

        (ii) –

        (i) the name of each political party, other political organisation or independent election candidate to whom any such donation has been made, and

        (ii) the total amount given to that party, organisation or candidate by way of such donations in the financial year; and

    (b) as respects expenditure falling within sub-paragraph (1)(a)(iii), the total amount incurred by way of such expenditure in the financial year.

2(3) If–

    (a) at the end of the financial year the company has subsidiaries which have, in that year, made any donations or incurred any such expenditure as is mentioned in sub-paragraph (1)(a), and

    (b) it is not itself the wholly-owned subsidiary of a company incorporated in the United Kingdom, the directors' report for the year is not, by virtue of sub-paragraph (1), required to contain the particulars specified in sub-paragraph (2).

But, if the total amount of any such donations or expenditure (or both) made or incurred in that year by the company and the subsidiaries between them exceeds £2000, the directors' report for the year must contain those particulars in relation to each body by whom any such donation or expenditure has been made or incurred.

2(4) Any expression used in this paragraph which is also used in Part 14 of the 2006 Act (control of political donations and expenditure) has the same meaning as in that Part.

3(1) If the company (not being the wholly-owned subsidiary of a company incorporated in the United Kingdom) has in the financial year made any contribution to a non-EU political party, the directors' report for the year must contain–

    (a) a statement of the amount of the contribution, or

    (b) (if it has made two or more such contributions in the year) a statement of the total amount of the contributions.

3(2) If—

    (a) at the end of the financial year the company has subsidiaries which have, in that year, made any such contributions as are mentioned in sub-paragraph (1), and

    (b) it is not itself the wholly-owned subsidiary of a company incorporated in the United Kingdom, the directors' report for the year is not, by virtue of sub-paragraph (1), required to contain any such statement as is there mentioned, but it must instead contain a statement of the total amount of the contributions made in the year by the company and the subsidiaries between them.

3(3) In this paragraph, **'contribution'**, in relation to an organisation, means—

    (a) any gift of money to the organisation (whether made directly or indirectly);

    (b) any subscription or other fee paid for affiliation to, or membership of, the organisation; or

    (c) any money spent (otherwise than by the organisation or a person acting on its behalf) in paying any expenses incurred directly or indirectly by the organisation.

3(4) In this paragraph, **'non-EU political party'** means any political party which carries on, or proposes to carry on, its activities wholly outside the member States.

Charitable donations

4 [Repealed.]

History – Para. 4 repealed by SI 2013/1970, reg. 8(1) and (2), with effect from 1 October 2013 in respect of financial years ending on or after 30 September 2013. Prior to repeal, para. 4 read as follows:

"**4(1)** If—

    (a) the company (not being the wholly-owned subsidiary of a company incorporated in the United Kingdom) has in the financial year given money for charitable purposes, and

    (b) the money given exceeded £2000 in amount, the directors' report for the year must contain, in the case of each of the purposes for which money has been given, a statement of the amount of money given for that purpose.

4(2) If—

    (a) at the end of the financial year the company has subsidiaries which have, in that year, given money for charitable purposes, and

    (b) it is not itself the wholly owned subsidiary of a company incorporated in the United Kingdom, sub-paragraph (1) does not apply to the company. But, if the amount given in that year for charitable purposes by the company and the subsidiaries between them exceeds £2000, the directors' report for the year must contain, in the case of each of the purposes for which money has been given by the company and the subsidiaries between them, a statement of the amount of money given for that purpose.

4(3) Money given for charitable purposes to a person who, when it was given, was ordinarily resident outside the United Kingdom is to be left out of account for the purposes of this paragraph.

4(4) For the purposes of this paragraph, **'charitable purposes'** means purposes which are exclusively charitable, and as respects Scotland a purpose is charitable if it is listed in section 7(2) of the Charities and Trustee Investment (Scotland) Act 2005."

Disclosure concerning employment etc. of disabled persons

5(1) This paragraph applies to the directors' report where the average number of persons employed by the company in each week during the financial year exceeded 250.

5(2) That average number is the quotient derived by dividing, by the number of weeks in the financial year, the number derived by ascertaining, in relation to each of those weeks, the number of persons who, under contracts of service, were employed in the week (whether throughout it or not) by the company, and adding up the numbers ascertained.

5(3) The directors' report must in that case contain a statement describing such policy as the company has applied during the financial year—

    (a) for giving full and fair consideration to applications for employment by the company made by disabled persons, having regard to their particular aptitudes and abilities,

   (b) for continuing the employment of, and for arranging appropriate training for, employees of the company who have become disabled persons during the period when they were employed by the company, and

   (c) otherwise for the training, career development and promotion of disabled persons employed by the company.

5(4) In this paragraph–

   (a) **'employment'** means employment other than employment to work wholly or mainly outside the United Kingdom, and 'employed' and 'employee' are to be construed accordingly; and

   (b) **'disabled person'** means the same as in the *Disability Discrimination Act* 1995.

Disclosure required by company acquiring its own shares etc.

6 [Repealed.]

History – Para. 6 repealed by SI 2013/1970, reg. 8(1) and (3), with effect from 1 October 2013 in respect of financial years ending on or after 30 September 2013. Prior to repeal, para. 6 read as follows:

"**6(1)** This paragraph applies where shares in a company–

   (a) are purchased by the company or are acquired by it by forfeiture or surrender in lieu of forfeiture, or in pursuance of any of the following provisions (acquisition of own shares by company limited by shares)–

      (i)   section 143(3) of the Companies Act 1985,

      (ii) Article 153(3) of the Companies (Northern Ireland) Order 1986, or

      (iii) section 659 of the 2006 Act, or

   (b) are acquired by another person in circumstances where paragraph (c) or (d) of any of the following provisions applies (acquisition by company's nominee, or by another with company financial assistance, the company having a beneficial interest)–

      (i)   section 146(1) of the Companies Act 1985,

      (ii) Article 156(1) of the Companies (Northern Ireland) Order 1986, or

      (iii) section 662(1) of the 2006 Act, or

   (c) are made subject to a lien or other charge taken (whether expressly or otherwise) by the company and permitted by any of the following provisions (exceptions from general rule against a company having a lien or charge on its own shares)–

      (i)   section 150(2) or (4) of the Companies Act 1985,

      (ii) Article 160(2) or (4) of the Companies (Northern Ireland) Order 1986, or

      (iii) section 670(2) or (4) of the 2006 Act.

6(2) The directors' report for a financial year must state–

   (a) the number and nominal value of the shares so purchased, the aggregate amount of the consideration paid by the company for such shares and the reasons for their purchase;

   (b) the number and nominal value of the shares so acquired by the company, acquired by another person in such circumstances and so charged respectively during the financial year;

   (c) the maximum number and nominal value of shares which, having been so acquired by the company, acquired by another person in such circumstances or so charged (whether or not during that year) are held at any time by the company or that other person during that year;

   (d) the number and nominal value of the shares so acquired by the company, acquired by another person in such circumstances or so charged (whether or not during that year) which are disposed of by the company or that other person or cancelled by the company during that year;

   (e) where the number and nominal value of the shares of any particular description are stated in pursuance of any of the preceding sub-paragraphs, the percentage of the called-up share capital which shares of that description represent;

   (f) where any of the shares have been so charged the amount of the charge in each case; and

   (g) where any of the shares have been disposed of by the company or the person who acquired them in such circumstances for money or money's worth the amount or value of the consideration in each case."

SCHEDULE 6 – GROUP ACCOUNTS

Regulations 8(1) and 10

Part 1 – Form and content of Companies Act group accounts

General rules

1(1) Subject to the following provisions of this Schedule, group accounts must comply so far as practicable with the provisions of Schedule 1 to these Regulations (Companies Act individual accounts) as if the undertakings included in the consolidation ('the group') were a single company.

1(1A) Paragraph 1A of Schedule 1 to these Regulations does not apply to group accounts.

1(2) For item B.III in each balance sheet format set out in Section B of Part 1 of that Schedule substitute–

"B.

III. Investments

1 Shares in group undertakings

2 Interests in associated undertakings

3 Other participating interests

4 Loans to group undertakings and undertakings in which a participating interest is held

5 Other investments other than loans

6 Others"

1(3) In the profit and loss account formats in Section B of Part 1 of that Schedule replace the items headed 'Income from participating interests', that is–

(a) in Format 1, item 8, and

(b) in Format 2, item 10,

(c) omitted,

(d) omitted.

History – In para. 1(1), the words 'the following provisions of this Schedule' substituted for the words 'sub-paragraphs (1) and (2)' by SI 2015/980, reg. 22(2), with effect in relation to–

(a) financial years beginning on or after 1 January 2016, and

(b) a financial year of a company beginning on or after 1 January 2015, but before 1 January 2016, if the directors of the company so decide.

Para. 1(1A) inserted by SI 2015/980, reg. 22(3), with effect in relation to–

(a) financial years beginning on or after 1 January 2016, and

(b) a financial year of a company beginning on or after 1 January 2015, but before 1 January 2016, if the directors of the company so decide.

In para. 1(2), 'Section B of Part 1 of' inserted and in para. 1(3), 'in Section B of Part 1 of that Schedule' inserted by SI 2013/3008, reg. 12(a), with effect from 1 December 2013 in respect of (a) financial years ending on or after 30 September 2013; and (b) companies, which deliver the accounts required by s. 444 to the registrar on or after 1 December 2013.

Para. 1(3)(c) and (d) omitted; and the word 'and' in para. (a) inserted by SI 2015/980, reg. 22(4), with effect in relation to–

(a) financial years beginning on or after 1 January 2016, and

(b) a financial year of a company beginning on or after 1 January 2015, but before 1 January 2016, if the directors of the company so decide.

2(1) The consolidated balance sheet and profit and loss account must incorporate in full the information contained in the individual accounts of the undertakings included in the consolidation, subject to the adjustments authorised or required by the following provisions of this Schedule and to such other adjustments (if any) as may be appropriate in accordance with generally accepted accounting principles or practice.

2(1A) Group accounts must be drawn up as at the same date as the accounts of the parent company.

2(2) If the financial year of a subsidiary undertaking included in the consolidation does not end with that of the parent company, the group accounts must be made up–

  (a) from the accounts of the subsidiary undertaking for its financial year last ending before the end of the parent company's financial year, provided that year ended no more than three months before that of the parent company, or

  (b) from interim accounts prepared by the subsidiary undertaking as at the end of the parent company's financial year.

History – Para. 2(1A) inserted by SI 2015/980, reg. 22(5), with effect in relation to–

  (a) financial years beginning on or after 1 January 2016, and

  (b) a financial year of a company beginning on or after 1 January 2015, but before 1 January 2016, if the directors of the company so decide.

3(1) Where assets and liabilities to be included in the group accounts have been valued or otherwise determined by undertakings according to accounting rules differing from those used for the group accounts, the values or amounts must be adjusted so as to accord with the rules used for the group accounts.

3(2) If it appears to the directors of the parent company that there are special reasons for departing from sub-paragraph (1) they may do so, but particulars of any such departure, the reasons for it and its effect must be given in a note to the accounts.

3(3) The adjustments referred to in this paragraph need not be made if they are not material for the purpose of giving a true and fair view.

4 Any differences of accounting rules as between a parent company's individual accounts for a financial year and its group accounts must be disclosed in a note to the latter accounts and the reasons for the difference given.

5 Amounts that in the particular context of any provision of this Schedule are not material may be disregarded for the purposes of that provision.

Elimination of group transactions

6(1) Debts and claims between undertakings included in the consolidation, and income and expenditure relating to transactions between such undertakings, must be eliminated in preparing the group accounts.

6(2) Where profits and losses resulting from transactions between undertakings included in the consolidation are included in the book value of assets, they must be eliminated in preparing group accounts.

6(3) The elimination required by sub-paragraph (2) may be effected in proportion to the group's interest in the shares of the undertakings.

6(4) Sub-paragraphs (1) and (2) need not be complied with if the amounts concerned are not material for the purpose of giving a true and fair view.

Acquisition and merger accounting

7(1) The following provisions apply where an undertaking becomes a subsidiary undertaking of the parent company.

7(2) That event is referred to in those provisions as an 'acquisition', and references to the 'undertaking acquired' are to be construed accordingly.

8 An acquisition must be accounted for by the acquisition method of accounting unless the conditions for accounting for it as a merger are met and the merger method of accounting is adopted.

9(1) The acquisition method of accounting is as follows.

9(2) The identifiable assets and liabilities of the undertaking acquired must be included in the consolidated balance sheet at their fair values as at the date of acquisition.

9(3) The income and expenditure of the undertaking acquired must be brought into the group accounts only as from the date of the acquisition.

9(4) There must be set off against the acquisition cost of the interest in the shares of the undertaking held by the parent company and its subsidiary undertakings the interest of the parent company and its subsidiary undertakings in the adjusted capital and reserves of the undertaking acquired.

9(5) The resulting amount if positive must be treated as goodwill, and if negative as a negative consolidation difference.

9(6) Negative goodwill may be transferred to the consolidated profit and loss account where such a treatment is in accordance with the principles and rules of Part 2 of Schedule 1 to these Regulations.

History – Para. 9(6) inserted by SI 2015/980, reg. 22(6), with effect in relation to–

  (a) financial years beginning on or after 1 January 2016, and

  (b) a financial year of a company beginning on or after 1 January 2015, but before 1 January 2016, if the directors of the company so decide.

10 The conditions for accounting for an acquisition as a merger are–

  (a) that the undertaking whose shares are acquired is ultimately controlled by the same party both before and after the acquisition,

  (b) that the control referred to in paragraph (a) is not transitory, and

  (c) that adoption of the merger method accords with generally accepted accounting principles or practice.

History – Para. 10 substituted by SI 2015/980, reg. 22(7), with effect in relation to–

  (a) financial years beginning on or after 1 January 2016, and

  (b) a financial year of a company beginning on or after 1 January 2015, but before 1 January 2016, if the directors of the company so decide.

Former para. 10 read as follows:

"**10(1)** The conditions for accounting for an acquisition as a merger are–

  (a) that at least 90% of the nominal value of the relevant shares in the undertaking acquired (excluding any shares in the undertaking held as treasury shares) is held by or on behalf of the parent company and its subsidiary undertakings,

  (b) that the proportion referred to in paragraph–

    (i) was attained pursuant to an arrangement providing for the issue of equity shares by the parent company or one or more of its subsidiary undertakings,

  (c) that the fair value of any consideration other than the issue of equity shares given pursuant to the arrangement by the parent company and its subsidiary undertakings did not exceed 10% of the nominal value of the equity shares issued, and

(d) that adoption of the merger method of accounting accords with generally accepted accounting principles or practice.

10(2) The reference in sub-paragraph (1)(a) to the 'relevant shares' in an undertaking acquired is to those carrying unrestricted rights to participate both in distributions and in the assets of the undertaking upon liquidation."

11(1) The merger method of accounting is as follows.

11(2) The assets and liabilities of the undertaking acquired must be brought into the group accounts at the figures at which they stand in the undertaking's accounts, subject to any adjustment authorised or required by this Schedule.

11(3) The income and expenditure of the undertaking acquired must be included in the group accounts for the entire financial year, including the period before the acquisition.

11(4) The group accounts must show corresponding amounts relating to the previous financial year as if the undertaking acquired had been included in the consolidation throughout that year.

11(5) There must be set off against the aggregate of–

(a) the appropriate amount in respect of qualifying shares issued by the parent company or its subsidiary undertakings in consideration for the acquisition of shares in the undertaking acquired, and

(b) the fair value of any other consideration for the acquisition of shares in the undertaking acquired, determined as at the date when those shares were acquired,

the nominal value of the issued share capital of the undertaking acquired held by the parent company and its subsidiary undertakings.

11(6) The resulting amount must be shown as an adjustment to the consolidated reserves.

11(7) In sub-paragraph (5)(a) **'qualifying shares'** means–

(a) shares in relation to which any of the following provisions applies (merger relief), and in respect of which the appropriate amount is the nominal value–
(i) section 131 of the Companies Act 1985,
(ii) Article 141 of the Companies (Northern Ireland) Order 1986, or
(iii) section 612 of the 2006 Act, or

(b) shares in relation to which any of the following provisions applies (group reconstruction relief), and in respect of which the appropriate amount is the nominal value together with any minimum premium value within the meaning of that section–
(i) section 132 of the Companies Act 1985,
(ii) Article 142 of the Companies (Northern Ireland) Order 1986, or
(iii) section 611 of the 2006 Act.

12(1) Where a group is acquired, paragraphs 9 to 11 apply with the following adaptations.

12(2) References to shares of the undertaking acquired are to be construed as references to shares of the parent undertaking of the group.

12(3) Other references to the undertaking acquired are to be construed as references to the group; and references to the assets and liabilities, income and expenditure and capital and reserves of the undertaking acquired must be construed as references to the assets and liabilities, income and expenditure and capital and reserves of the group after making the set-offs and other adjustments required by this Schedule in the case of group accounts.

13(1) The following information with respect to acquisitions taking place in the financial year must be given in a note to the accounts.

13(2) There must be stated–

(a) the name of the undertaking acquired or, where a group was acquired, the name of the parent undertaking of that group, and

(b) whether the acquisition has been accounted for by the acquisition or the merger method of accounting; and in relation to an acquisition which significantly affects the figures shown in the group accounts, the following further information must be given.

13(3) The composition and fair value of the consideration for the acquisition given by the parent company and its subsidiary undertakings must be stated.

13(4) Where the acquisition method of accounting has been adopted, the book values immediately prior to the acquisition, and the fair values at the date of acquisition, of each class of assets and liabilities of the undertaking or group acquired must be stated in tabular form, including a statement of the amount of any goodwill or negative consolidation difference arising on the acquisition, together with an explanation of any significant adjustments made.

13(5) In ascertaining for the purposes of sub-paragraph (4) the profit or loss of a group, the book values and fair values of assets and liabilities of a group or the amount of the assets and liabilities of a group, the set-offs and other adjustments required by this Schedule in the case of group accounts must be made.

14(1) There must also be stated in a note to the accounts the cumulative amount of goodwill resulting from acquisitions in that and earlier financial years which has been written off otherwise than in the consolidated profit and loss account for that or any earlier financial year.

14(2) That figure must be shown net of any goodwill attributable to subsidiary undertakings or businesses disposed of prior to the balance sheet date.

15 Where during the financial year there has been a disposal of an undertaking or group which significantly affects the figure shown in the group accounts, there must be stated in a note to the accounts–

(a) the name of that undertaking or, as the case may be, of the parent undertaking of that group, and

(b) the extent to which the profit or loss shown in the group accounts is attributable to profit or loss of that undertaking or group.

16 The information required by paragraph 13, 14 or 15 need not be disclosed with respect to an undertaking which–

(a) is established under the law of a country outside the United Kingdom, or

(b) carries on business outside the United Kingdom,

if in the opinion of the directors of the parent company the disclosure would be seriously prejudicial to the business of that undertaking or to the business of the parent company or any of its subsidiary undertakings and the Secretary of State agrees that the information should not be disclosed.

16A Where an acquisition has taken place in the financial year and the merger method of accounting has been adopted, the notes to the accounts must also disclose–

(a) the address of the registered office of the undertaking acquired (whether in or outside the United Kingdom),

(b) the name of the party referred to in paragraph 10(a),

(c) the address of the registered office of that party (whether in or outside the United Kingdom), and

(d) the information referred to in paragraph 11(6).

History – Para. 16A inserted by SI 2015/980, reg. 22(8), with effect in relation to–

(a) financial years beginning on or after 1 January 2016, and

(b) a financial year of a company beginning on or after 1 January 2015, but before 1 January 2016, if the directors of the company so decide.

Non-controlling interests

17(1)   The formats set out in Section B of Part 1 of Schedule 1 to these Regulations have effect in relation to group accounts with the following additions.

17(2)   In the Balance Sheet Formats there must be shown, as a separate item and under the heading 'non-controlling interests', the amount of capital and reserves attributable to shares in subsidiary undertakings included in the consolidation held by or on behalf of persons other than the parent company and its subsidiary undertakings.

17(3)   In the Profit and Loss Account Formats there must be shown, as a separate item and under the heading 'non-controlling interests', the amount of any profit or loss attributable to shares in subsidiary undertakings included in the consolidation held by or on behalf of persons other than the parent company and its subsidiary undertakings.

17(4)   For the purposes of paragraph (4) of Schedule 1 (power to adapt or combine items)–

(a)   the additional item required by sub-paragraph (2) above is treated as one to which a letter is assigned, and

(b)   the additional item required by sub-paragraph (3) above is treated as one to which an Arabic number is assigned.

History – Para. 17 and the heading preceding it substituted by SI 2015/980, reg. 22(9), with effect in relation to–

(a)   financial years beginning on or after 1 January 2016, and

(b)   a financial year of a company beginning on or after 1 January 2015, but before 1 January 2016, if the directors of the company so decide.

Former para. 17 read as follows:

"Minority interests

17(1)   The formats set out in Section B of Part 1 of Schedule 1 to these Regulations have effect in relation to group accounts with the following additions.

17(2)   In the Balance Sheet Formats there must be shown, as a separate item and under an appropriate heading, the amount of capital and reserves attributable to shares in subsidiary undertakings included in the consolidation held by or on behalf of persons other than the parent company and its subsidiary undertakings.

17(3)   In the Profit and Loss Account Formats there must be shown, as a separate item and under an appropriate heading–

(a)   the amount of any profit or loss on ordinary activities, and

(b)   the amount of any profit or loss on extraordinary activities, attributable to shares in subsidiary undertakings included in the consolidation held by or on behalf of persons other than the parent company and its subsidiary undertakings.

17(4)   For the purposes of paragraph 4 of Schedule 1 (power to adapt or combine items)–

(a)   the additional item required by sub-paragraph (2) is treated as one to which a letter is assigned, and

(b)   the additional items required by sub-paragraph (3)(a) and

(c)   are treated as ones to which an Arabic number is assigned.

History – In para. 17(1), 'Section B of Part 1 of' inserted by SI 2013/3008, reg. 12(b), with effect from 1 December 2013 in respect of (a) financial years ending on or after 30 September 2013; and (b) companies, which deliver the accounts required by section 444 to the registrar on or after 1 December 2013."

Joint ventures

18(1)   Where an undertaking included in the consolidation manages another undertaking jointly with one or more undertakings not included in the consolidation, that other undertaking ('the joint venture') may, if it is not–

(a)   a body corporate, or

(b)   a subsidiary undertaking of the parent company, be dealt with in the group accounts by the method of proportional consolidation.

18(2)   The provisions of this Schedule relating to the preparation of consolidated accounts and sections 402 and 405 of the 2006 Act apply, with any necessary modifications, to proportional consolidation under this paragraph.

18(3) In addition to the disclosure of the average number of employees employed during the financial year (see section 411(7) of the 2006 Act), there must be a separate disclosure in the notes to the accounts of the average number of employees employed by undertakings that are proportionately consolidated.

History – In para. 18(2), the words 'and sections 402 and 405 of the 2006 Act' inserted by SI 2015/980, reg. 22(10), with effect in relation to–

(a) financial years beginning on or after 1 January 2016, and

(b) a financial year of a company beginning on or after 1 January 2015, but before 1 January 2016, if the directors of the company so decide.

Para. 18(3) inserted by SI 2015/980, reg. 22(11), with effect in relation to–

(a) financial years beginning on or after 1 January 2016, and

(b) a financial year of a company beginning on or after 1 January 2015, but before 1 January 2016, if the directors of the company so decide.

Associated undertakings

19(1) An **'associated undertaking'** means an undertaking in which an undertaking included in the consolidation has a participating interest and over whose operating and financial policy it exercises a significant influence, and which is not–

(a) a subsidiary undertaking of the parent company, or

(b) a joint venture dealt with in accordance with paragraph 18.

19(2) Where an undertaking holds 20% or more of the voting rights in another undertaking, it is presumed to exercise such an influence over it unless the contrary is shown.

19(3) The voting rights in an undertaking means the rights conferred on shareholders in respect of their shares or, in the case of an undertaking not having a share capital, on members, to vote at general meetings of the undertaking on all, or substantially all, matters.

19(4) The provisions of paragraphs 5 to 11 of Schedule 7 to the 2006 Act (parent and subsidiary undertakings: rights to be taken into account and attribution of rights) apply in determining for the purposes of this paragraph whether an undertaking holds 20% or more of the voting rights in another undertaking.

20(1) The interest of an undertaking in an associated undertaking, and the amount of profit or loss attributable to such an interest, must be shown by the equity method of accounting (including dealing with any goodwill arising in accordance with paragraphs 17 to 20 and 22 of Schedule 1 to these Regulations).

20(2) Where the associated undertaking is itself a parent undertaking, the net assets and profits or losses to be taken into account are those of the parent and its subsidiary undertakings (after making any consolidation adjustments).

20(3) The equity method of accounting need not be applied if the amounts in question are not material for the purpose of giving a true and fair view.

Deferred tax balances

20A Deferred tax balances must be recognised on consolidation where it is probable that a charge to tax will arise within the foreseeable future for one of the undertakings included in the consolidation.

History – Para. 20A and the heading preceding it inserted by SI 2015/980, reg. 22(12), with effect in relation to–

(a) financial years beginning on or after 1 January 2016, and

(b) a financial year of a company beginning on or after 1 January 2015, but before 1 January 2016, if the directors of the company so decide.

Related party transactions

20B   Paragraph 66 of Schedule 1 to these Regulations applies to transactions which the parent company, or other undertakings included in the consolidation, have entered into with related parties, unless they are intra-group transactions.

History – Para. 20B and the heading preceding it inserted by SI 2015/980, reg. 22(12), with effect in relation to–

 (a) financial years beginning on or after 1 January 2016, and

 (b) a financial year of a company beginning on or after 1 January 2015, but before 1 January 2016, if the directors of the company so decide.

Part 2 – Information about related undertakings where company preparing group accounts (Companies Act or IAS group accounts)

Introduction and interpretation

21   In this Part of this Schedule **'the group'** means the group consisting of the parent company and its subsidiary undertakings.

Subsidiary undertakings

22(1)   The following information must be given with respect to the undertakings that are subsidiary undertakings of the parent company at the end of the financial year.

22(2)   The name of each undertaking must be stated.

22(3)   There must be stated–

 (a) the address of the undertaking's registered office (whether in or outside the United Kingdom),

 (b) if it is unincorporated, the address of its principal place of business.

22(4)   It must also be stated whether the subsidiary undertaking is included in the consolidation and, if it is not, the reasons for excluding it from consolidation must be given.

22(5)   It must be stated with respect to each subsidiary undertaking by virtue of which of the conditions specified in section 1162(2) or (4) of the 2006 Act it is a subsidiary undertaking of its immediate parent undertaking.

That information need not be given if the relevant condition is that specified in subsection (2) (a) of that section (holding of a majority of the voting rights) and the immediate parent undertaking holds the same proportion of the shares in the undertaking as it holds voting rights.

History – Para. 22(3)(a) substituted by SI 2015/980, reg. 23(2), with effect in relation to–

 (a) financial years beginning on or after 1 January 2016, and

 (b) a financial year of a company beginning on or after 1 January 2015, but before 1 January 2016, if the directors of the company so decide.

Holdings in subsidiary undertakings

23(1)   The following information must be given with respect to the shares of a subsidiary undertaking held–

 (a) by the parent company, and

 (b) by the group, and the information under paragraphs (a) and (b) must (if different) be shown separately.

23(2)   There must be stated–

(a)   the identity of each class of shares held, and

(b)   the proportion of the nominal value of the shares of that class represented by those shares.

Financial information about subsidiary undertakings not included in the consolidation

24(1)   There must be shown with respect to each subsidiary undertaking not included in the consolidation–

(a)   the aggregate amount of its capital and reserves as at the end of its relevant financial year, and

(b)   its profit or loss for that year.

24(2)   That information need not be given if the group's investment in the undertaking is included in the accounts by way of the equity method of valuation or if–

(a)   the undertaking is not required by any provision of the 2006 Act to deliver a copy of its balance sheet for its relevant financial year and does not otherwise publish that balance sheet in the United Kingdom or elsewhere, and

(b)   the holding of the group is less than 50% of the nominal value of the shares in the undertaking.

24(3)   Information otherwise required by this paragraph need not be given if it is not material.

24(4)   For the purposes of this paragraph the **'relevant financial year'** of a subsidiary undertaking is–

(a)   if its financial year ends with that of the company, that year, and

(b)   if not, its financial year ending last before the end of the company's financial year.

Shares of company held by subsidiary undertakings

25(1)   The number, description and amount of the shares in the company held by or on behalf of its subsidiary undertakings must be disclosed.

25(2)   Sub-paragraph (1) does not apply in relation to shares in the case of which the subsidiary undertaking is concerned as personal representative or, subject as follows, as trustee.

25(3)   The exception for shares in relation to which the subsidiary undertaking is concerned as trustee does not apply if the company or any of its subsidiary undertakings is beneficially interested under the trust, otherwise than by way of security only for the purposes of a transaction entered into by it in the ordinary course of a business which includes the lending of money.

25(4)   Part 2 of Schedule 2 to these Regulations has effect for the interpretation of the reference in sub-paragraph (3) to a beneficial interest under a trust.

Joint ventures

26(1)   The following information must be given where an undertaking is dealt with in the consolidated accounts by the method of proportional consolidation in accordance with paragraph 18 of this Schedule (joint ventures)–

(a)   the name of the undertaking,

(b)   the address of the undertaking's registered office (whether in or outside the United Kingdom),

(c) the factors on which joint management of the undertaking is based, and

(d) the proportion of the capital of the undertaking held by or on behalf of undertakings included in the consolidation.

26(2)   Where the financial year of the undertaking did not end with that of the company, there must be stated the date on which a financial year of the undertaking last ended before that date.

History – Para. 26(1)(b) substituted by SI 2015/980, reg. 23(3), with effect in relation to–

(a) financial years beginning on or after 1 January 2016, and

(b) a financial year of a company beginning on or after 1 January 2015, but before 1 January 2016, if the directors of the company so decide.

In para. 26(1)(d), the words 'or on behalf of' inserted by SI 2015/980, reg. 23(4), with effect in relation to–

(a) financial years beginning on or after 1 January 2016, and

(b) a financial year of a company beginning on or after 1 January 2015, but before 1 January 2016, if the directors of the company so decide.

Associated undertakings

27(1)   The following information must be given where an undertaking included in the consolidation has an interest in an associated undertaking.

27(2)   The name of the associated undertaking must be stated.

27(3)   There must be stated–

(a) the address of the undertaking's registered office (whether in or outside the United Kingdom),

(b) if it is unincorporated, the address of its principal place of business.

27(4)   The following information must be given with respect to the shares of the undertaking held–

(a) by the parent company, and

(b) by the group, and the information under paragraphs (a) and (b) must be shown separately.

27(5)   There must be stated–

(a) the identity of each class of shares held, and

(b) the proportion of the nominal value of the shares of that class represented by those shares.

27(6)   In this paragraph **'associated undertaking'** has the meaning given by paragraph 19 of this Schedule; and the information required by this paragraph must be given notwithstanding that paragraph 20(3) of this Schedule (materiality) applies in relation to the accounts themselves.

History – Para. 27(3)(a) substituted by SI 2015/980, reg. 23(5), with effect in relation to–

(a) financial years beginning on or after 1 January 2016, and

(b) a financial year of a company beginning on or after 1 January 2015, but before 1 January 2016, if the directors of the company so decide.

Other significant holdings of parent company or group

28(1)   The information required by paragraphs 29 and 30 must be given where at the end of the financial year the parent company has a significant holding in an undertaking which is not one of its subsidiary undertakings and does not fall within paragraph 26 (joint ventures) or paragraph 27 (associated undertakings).

28(2) A holding is significant for this purpose if–

  (a) it amounts to 20% or more of the nominal value of any class of shares in the undertaking, or

  (b) the amount of the holding (as stated or included in the company's individual accounts) exceeds 20% of the amount of its assets (as so stated).

29(1) The name of the undertaking must be stated.

29(2) There must be stated–

  (a) the address of the undertaking's registered office (whether in or outside the United Kingdom),

  (b) if it is unincorporated, the address of its principal place of business.

29(3) The following information must be given with respect to the shares of the undertaking held by the parent company.

29(4) There must be stated–

  (a) the identity of each class of shares held, and

  (b) the proportion of the nominal value of the shares of that class represented by those shares.

History – Para. 29(2)(a) substituted by SI 2015/980, reg. 23(6), with effect in relation to–

  (a) financial years beginning on or after 1 January 2016, and

  (b) a financial year of a company beginning on or after 1 January 2015, but before 1 January 2016, if the directors of the company so decide.

30(1) There must also be stated–

  (a) the aggregate amount of the capital and reserves of the undertaking as at the end of its relevant financial year, and

  (b) its profit or loss for that year.

30(2) That information need not be given in respect of an undertaking if–

  (a) the undertaking is not required by any provision of the 2006 Act to deliver a copy of its balance sheet for its relevant financial year and does not otherwise publish that balance sheet in the United Kingdom or elsewhere, and

  (b) the company's holding is less than 50% of the nominal value of the shares in the undertaking.

30(3) Information otherwise required by this paragraph need not be given if it is not material.

30(4) For the purposes of this paragraph the 'relevant financial year' of an undertaking is–

  (a) if its financial year ends with that of the company, that year, and

  (b) if not, its financial year ending last before the end of the company's financial year.

31(1) The information required by paragraphs 32 and 33 must be given where at the end of the financial year the group has a significant holding in an undertaking which is not a subsidiary undertaking of the parent company and does not fall within paragraph 26 (joint ventures) or paragraph 27 (associated undertakings).

31(2) A holding is significant for this purpose if–

  (a) it amounts to 20% or more of the nominal value of any class of shares in the undertaking, or

  (b) the amount of the holding (as stated or included in the group accounts) exceeds 20% of the amount of the group's assets (as so stated).

32(1)   The name of the undertaking must be stated.

32(2)   There must be stated–

(a) the address of the undertaking's registered office (whether in or outside the United Kingdom),

(b) if it is unincorporated, the address of its principal place of business.

32(3)   The following information must be given with respect to the shares of the undertaking held by the group.

32(4)   There must be stated–

(a) the identity of each class of shares held, and

(b) the proportion of the nominal value of the shares of that class represented by those shares.

History – Para. 32(2)(a) substituted by SI 2015/980, reg. 23(7), with effect in relation to–

(a) financial years beginning on or after 1 January 2016, and

(b) a financial year of a company beginning on or after 1 January 2015, but before 1 January 2016, if the directors of the company so decide.

33(1)   There must also be stated–

(a) the aggregate amount of the capital and reserves of the undertaking as at the end of its relevant financial year, and

(b) its profit or loss for that year.

33(2)   That information need not be given if–

(a) the undertaking is not required by any provision of the 2006 Act to deliver a copy of its balance sheet for its relevant financial year and does not otherwise publish that balance sheet in the United Kingdom or elsewhere, and

(b) the holding of the group is less than 50% of the nominal value of the shares in the undertaking.

33(3)   Information otherwise required by this paragraph need not be given if it is not material.

33(4)   For the purposes of this paragraph the **'relevant financial year'** of an outside undertaking is–

(a) if its financial year ends with that of the parent company, that year, and

(b) if not, its financial year ending last before the end of the parent company's financial year.

PARENT COMPANY'S OR GROUP'S MEMBERSHIP OF CERTAIN UNDERTAKINGS

34(1)   The information required by this paragraph must be given where at the end of the financial year the parent company or group is a member of a qualifying undertaking.

34(2)   There must be stated–

(a) the name and legal form of the undertaking, and

(b) the address of the undertaking's registered office (whether in or outside the United (Kingdom) or, if it does not have such an office, its head office (whether in or outside the United Kingdom).

34(3)   Where the undertaking is a qualifying partnership there must also be stated either–

(a) that a copy of the latest accounts of the undertaking has been or is to be appended to the copy of the company's accounts sent to the registrar under section 444 of the 2006 Act, or

(b) the name of at least one body corporate (which may be the company) in whose group accounts the undertaking has been or is to be dealt with on a consolidated basis.

34(4) Information otherwise required by sub-paragraph (2) need not be given if it is not material.

34(5) Information otherwise required by sub-paragraph (3)(b) need not be given if the notes to the company's accounts disclose that advantage has been taken of the exemption conferred by regulation 7 of the Partnerships (Accounts) Regulations 2008.

34(6) In sub-paragraph (1) **'member'**, in relation to a qualifying undertaking which is a qualifying partnership, has the same meaning as in the Partnerships (Accounts) Regulations 2008.

34(7) In this paragraph–

'dealt with on a consolidated basis' and **'qualifying partnership'** have the same meanings as in the Partnerships (Accounts) Regulations 2008;

'qualifying undertaking' means–

(a) a qualifying partnership, or

(b) an unlimited company each of whose members is–

    (i) a limited company,

    (ii) another unlimited company each of whose members is a limited company,

    (iii) a Scottish partnership which is not a limited partnership, each of whose members is a limited company, or

    (iv) a Scottish partnership which is a limited partnership, each of whose general partners is a limited company.

34(8) In sub-paragraph (7) the references to a limited company, another unlimited company, a Scottish partnership which is not a limited partnership or a Scottish partnership which is a limited partnership include a comparable undertaking incorporated in or formed under the law of a country or territory outside the United Kingdom.

34(9) In sub-paragraph (7) **'general partner'** means–

(a) in relation to a Scottish partnership which is a limited partnership, a person who is a general partner within the meaning of the Limited Partnerships Act 1907, and

(b) in relation to an undertaking incorporated in or formed under the law of any country or territory outside the United Kingdom and which is comparable to a Scottish partnership which is a limited partnership, a person comparable to such a general partner.

34(10) In sub-paragraphs (7), (8) and (9) **'limited partnership'** means a partnership registered under the Limited Partnerships Act 1907.

History – In para. 34(5), 'Partnerships (Accounts) Regulations 2008' substituted for 'Partnerships and Unlimited Companies (Accounts) Regulations 1993' by SI 2008/569, reg. 17(1)(b), with effect from 6 April 2008.

Para. 34(6) substituted and 34(7)–(10) inserted by SI 2013/2005, reg. 5, with effect from 1 September 2013 applying in relation to a financial year of a company beginning on or after 1 October 2013. The version of para. 34 applying to financial years beginning before 1 October 2013 read as follows:

"34(1) The information required by this paragraph must be given where at the end of the financial year the parent company or group is a member of a qualifying undertaking.

34(2) There must be stated–

(a) the name and legal form of the undertaking, and

(b) the address of the undertaking's registered office (whether in or outside the United (Kingdom) or, if it does not have such an office, its head office (whether in or outside the United Kingdom).

34(3) Where the undertaking is a qualifying partnership there must also be stated either–

(a) that a copy of the latest accounts of the undertaking has been or is to be appended to the copy of the company's accounts sent to the registrar under section 444 of the 2006 Act, or

(b) the name of at least one body corporate (which may be the company) in whose group accounts the undertaking has been or is to be dealt with on a consolidated basis.

34(4)   Information otherwise required by sub-paragraph (2) need not be given if it is not material.

34(5)   Information otherwise required by sub-paragraph (3)(b) need not be given if the notes to the company's accounts disclose that advantage has been taken of the exemption conferred by regulation 7 of the Partnerships (Accounts) Regulations 2008.

34(6)   In this paragraph–

'dealt with on a consolidated basis', **'member'** and **'qualifying partnership'** have the same meanings as in the Partnerships (Accounts) Regulations 2008;

'qualifying undertaking' means–

    (a)   a qualifying partnership, or

    (b)   an unlimited company each of whose members is–

        (i)   a limited company,

        (ii)   another unlimited company each of whose members is a limited company, or

        (iii)   a Scottish partnership each of whose members is a limited company, and references in this paragraph to a limited company, another unlimited company or a Scottish partnership include a comparable undertaking incorporated in or formed under the law of a country or territory outside the United Kingdom."

Parent undertaking drawing up accounts for larger group

35(1)   Where the parent company is itself a subsidiary undertaking, the following information must be given with respect to that parent undertaking of the company which heads–

    (a)   the largest group of undertakings for which group accounts are drawn up and of which that company is a member, and

    (b)   the smallest such group of undertakings.

35(2)   The name of the parent undertaking must be stated.

35(3)   There must be stated–

    (a)   if the undertaking is incorporated outside the United Kingdom, the country in which it is incorporated,

    (b)   if it is unincorporated, the address of its principal place of business.

35(4)   If copies of the group accounts referred to in sub-paragraph (1) are available to the public, there must also be stated the addresses from which copies of the accounts can be obtained.

Identification of ultimate parent company

36(1)   Where the parent company is itself a subsidiary undertaking, the following information must be given with respect to the company (if any) regarded by the directors as being that company's ultimate parent company.

36(2)   The name of that company must be stated.

36(3)   If that company is incorporated outside the United Kingdom, the country in which it is incorporated must be stated (if known to the directors).

36(4)   In this paragraph **'company'** includes any body corporate.

Construction of references to shares held by parent company or group

37(1)   References in this Part of this Schedule to shares held by the parent company or the group are to be construed as follows.

37(2) For the purposes of paragraphs 23, 27(4) and (5) and 28 to 30 (information about holdings in subsidiary and other undertakings)–

(a) there must be attributed to the parent company shares held on its behalf by any person; but

(b) there must be treated as not held by the parent company shares held on behalf of a person other than the company.

37(3) References to shares held by the group are to any shares held by or on behalf of the parent company or any of its subsidiary undertakings; but any shares held on behalf of a person other than the parent company or any of its subsidiary undertakings are not to be treated as held by the group.

37(4) Shares held by way of security must be treated as held by the person providing the security–

(a) where apart from the right to exercise them for the purpose of preserving the value of the security, or of realising it, the rights attached to the shares are exercisable only in accordance with his instructions, and

(b) where the shares are held in connection with the granting of loans as part of normal business activities and apart from the right to exercise them for the purpose of preserving the value of the security, or of realising it, the rights attached to the shares are exercisable only in his interests.

SCHEDULE 7 – INTERPRETATION OF TERM PROVISIONS

Regulation 12

Part 1 – Meaning for purposes of these regulations

Definition of 'provisions'

1(1) In these Regulations, references to provisions for depreciation or diminution in value of assets are to any amount written off by way of providing for depreciation or diminution in value of assets.

1(2) Any reference in the profit and loss account formats set out in Part 1 of Schedule 1 to these Regulations to the depreciation of, or amounts written off, assets of any description is to any provision for depreciation or diminution in value of assets of that description.

2 References in these Regulations to provisions for liabilities are to any amount retained as reasonably necessary for the purpose of providing for any liability the nature of which is clearly defined and which is either likely to be incurred, or certain to be incurred but uncertain as to amount or as to the date on which it will arise.

2A At the balance sheet date, a provision must represent the best estimate of the expenses likely to be incurred or, in the case of a liability, of the amount required to meet that liability.

History – Para. 2A inserted by SI 2015/980, reg. 24, with effect in relation to–

(a) financial years beginning on or after 1 January 2016, and

(b) a financial year of a company beginning on or after 1 January 2015, but before 1 January 2016, if the directors of the company so decide.

2B Provisions must not be used to adjust the values of assets.

History – Para. 2B inserted by SI 2015/980, reg. 24, with effect in relation to–

(a) financial years beginning on or after 1 January 2016, and

(b) a financial year of a company beginning on or after 1 January 2015, but before 1 January 2016, if the directors of the company so decide.

Part 2 – Meaning for purposes of Parts 18 and 23 of the 2006 Act

Financial assistance for purchase of own shares

3 The specified provisions for the purposes of section 677(3)(a) of the 2006 Act (Companies Act accounts: relevant provisions for purposes of financial assistance) are provisions for liabilities within paragraph 2 of this Schedule.

Redemption or purchase by private company out of capital

4 The specified provisions for the purposes of section 712(2)(b)(i) of the 2006 Act (Companies Act accounts: relevant provisions to determine available profits for redemption or purchase out of capital) are provisions of any of the kinds mentioned in paragraphs 1 and 2 of this Schedule.

Justification of distribution by references to accounts

5 The specified provisions for the purposes of section 836(1)(b)(i) of the 2006 Act (Companies Act accounts: relevant provisions for distribution purposes) are provisions of any of the kinds mentioned in paragraphs 1 and 2 of this Schedule.

Realised losses

6   The specified provisions for the purposes of section 841(2)(a) of the 2006 Act (Companies Act accounts: treatment of provisions as realised losses) are provisions of any of the kinds mentioned in paragraphs 1 and 2 of this Schedule.

Notes – Para. 6 inserted by SI 2009/1581 reg 11(1) and (3): 27 June 2009 applying in relation to financial years beginning on or after 6 April 2008 which have not ended before 27 June 2009

SCHEDULE 8 – GENERAL INTERPRETATION

Financial instruments

1 References to **'derivatives'** include commodity-based contracts that give either contracting party the right to settle in cash or in some other financial instrument, except where such contracts–

 (a) were entered into for the purpose of, and continue to meet, the company's expected purchase, sale or usage requirements,

 (b) were designated for such purpose at their inception, and

 (c) are expected to be settled by delivery of the commodity.

2(1) The expressions listed in sub-paragraph (2) have the same meaning as they have in Directive 2013/34/EU of the European Parliament and of the Council of 26 June 2013 on the annual financial statements etc of certain types of undertakings.

2(2) Those expressions are 'available for sale financial asset', 'business combination', 'commodity-based contracts', 'derivative', 'equity instrument', 'exchange difference', 'fair value hedge accounting system', 'financial fixed asset', 'financial instrument', 'foreign entity', 'hedge accounting', 'hedge accounting system', 'hedged items', 'hedging instrument', 'held for trading purposes', 'held to maturity', 'monetary item', 'receivables', 'reliable market' and 'trading portfolio'.

History – Para. 2(1) substituted by SI 2015/980, reg. 25(2), with effect in relation to–

 (a) financial years beginning on or after 1 January 2016, and

 (b) a financial year of a company beginning on or after 1 January 2015, but before 1 January 2016, if the directors of the company so decide.

Former para. 2(1) read as follows:

 "**2(1)** The expressions listed in sub-paragraph (2) have the same meaning as they have in Council Directive 78/660/EEC on the annual accounts of certain types of companies."

Fixed and current assets

3 **'Fixed assets'** means assets of a company which are intended for use on a continuing basis in the company's activities, and **'current assets'** means assets not intended for such use.

Historical cost accounting rules

4 References to the historical cost accounting rules are to be read in accordance with paragraph 30 of Schedule 1 to these Regulations.

Listed investments

5(1) **'Listed investment'** means an investment as respects which there has been granted a listing on–

 (a) a recognised investment exchange other than an overseas investment exchange, or

 (b) a stock exchange of repute outside the United Kingdom.

5(2) **'Recognised investment exchange'** and **'overseas investment exchange'** have the meaning given in Part 18 of the Financial Services and Markets Act 2000.

Loans

6 A loan is treated as falling due for repayment, and an instalment of a loan is treated as falling due for payment, on the earliest date on which the lender could require repayment or (as the case may be) payment, if he exercised all options and rights available to him.

Materiality

7   Amounts which in the particular context of any provision of Schedule 1 to these Regulations are not material may be disregarded for the purposes of that provision.

Participating interests

8(1)   A **'participating interest'** means an interest held by an undertaking in the shares of another undertaking which it holds on a long-term basis for the purpose of securing a contribution to its activities by the exercise of control or influence arising from or related to that interest.

8(2)   A holding of 20% or more of the shares of the undertaking is to be presumed to be a participating interest unless the contrary is shown.

8(3)   The reference in sub-paragraph (1) to an interest in shares includes–

(a)   an interest which is convertible into an interest in shares, and

(b)   an option to acquire shares or any such interest, and an interest or option falls within paragraph (a) or (b) notwithstanding that the shares to which it relates are, until the conversion or the exercise of the option, unissued.

8(4)   For the purposes of this paragraph an interest held on behalf of an undertaking is to be treated as held by it.

8(5)   In the balance sheet and profit and loss formats set out in Section B of Part 1 of Schedule 1 to these Regulations, **'participating interest'** does not include an interest in a group undertaking.

8(6)   For the purpose of this paragraph as it applies in relation to the expression 'participating interest'–

(a)   in those formats as they apply in relation to group accounts, and

(b)   in paragraph 19 of Schedule 6 (group accounts: undertakings to be accounted for as associated undertakings), the references in sub-paragraphs (1) to (4) to the interest held by, and the purposes and activities of, the undertaking concerned are to be construed as references to the interest held by, and the purposes and activities of, the group (within the meaning of paragraph 1 of that Schedule).

History – In para. 8(5), 'Section B of' inserted by SI 2013/3008, reg. 13(1) and (2), with effect from 1 December 2013 in respect of–

(a)   financial years ending on or after 30 September 2013; and

(b)   companies, which deliver the accounts required by s. 444 to the registrar on or after 1 December 2013.

In para. 8(5), the words 'and Part 1 of Schedule 4' omitted by SI 2015/980, reg. 25(3), with effect in relation to–

(a)   financial years beginning on or after 1 January 2016, and

(b)   a financial year of a company beginning on or after 1 January 2015, but before 1 January 2016, if the directors of the company so decide.

Purchase price

9   **'Purchase price'**, in relation to an asset of a company or any raw materials or consumables used in the production of such an asset, includes any consideration (whether in cash or otherwise) given by the company in respect of that asset or those materials or consumables, as the case may be.

Realised profits and losses

10   **'Realised profits'** and **'realised losses'** have the same meaning as in section 853(4) and (5) of the 2006 Act.

Staff costs

11(1) **'Social security costs'** means any contributions by the company to any state social security or pension scheme, fund or arrangement.

11(2) **'Pension costs'** includes–

    (a) any costs incurred by the company in respect of any pension scheme established for the purpose of providing pensions for persons currently or formerly employed by the company,

    (b) any sums set aside for the future payment of pensions directly by the company to current or former employees, and

    (c) any pensions paid directly to such persons without having first been set aside.

11(3) Any amount stated in respect of the item 'social security costs' or in respect of the item 'wages and salaries' in the profit and loss account Format 2 in Section B of Part 1 of Schedule 1 must be determined by reference to payments made or costs incurred in respect of all persons employed by the company during the financial year under contracts of service.

History – In para. 11(3), 'the profit and loss account Formats 2 and 4 in Section B of Part 1 of Schedule 1' substituted for 'the company's profit and loss account' by SI 2013/3008, reg. 13(1) and (3), with effect from 1 December 2013 in respect of–

    (a) financial years ending on or after 30 September 2013; and

    (b) companies, which deliver the accounts required by s. 444 to the registrar on or after 1 December 2013.

In para. 11(3), the words 'Format 2' substituted for the words 'Formats 2 and 4' by SI 2015/980, reg. 25(4), with effect in relation to–

    (a) financial years beginning on or after 1 January 2016, and

    (b) a financial year of a company beginning on or after 1 January 2015, but before 1 January 2016, if the directors of the company so decide.

Appendix B1　Exemptions from group accounts

Extracts from CA 2006

Exemption for company included in EEA group accounts of larger group

s. 400

400(1)　A company is exempt from the requirement to prepare group accounts if it is itself a subsidiary undertaking and its immediate parent undertaking is established under the law of an EEA State, in the following cases:

  (a)　where the company is a wholly-owned subsidiary of that parent undertaking;

  (b)　where that parent undertaking holds 90% or more of the allotted shares in the company and the remaining shareholders have approved the exemption;

  (c)　where that parent undertaking holds more than 50% (but less than 90%) of the allotted shares in the company and notice requesting the preparation of group accounts has not been served on the company by the shareholders holding in aggregate at least 5% of the allotted shares in the company.

Such notice must be served at least six months before the end of the financial year to which it relates.

400(2)　Exemption is conditional upon compliance with all of the following conditions:

  (a)　the company must be included in consolidated accounts for a larger group drawn up to the same date, or to an earlier date in the same financial year, by a parent undertaking established under the law of an EEA State;

  (b)　those accounts must be drawn up and audited, and that parent undertaking's annual report must be drawn up, according to that law:

    (i)　in accordance with the provisions of Directive 2013/34/EU of the European Parliament and of the Council on the annual financial statements, consolidated financial statements and related reports of certain types of undertakings; or

    (ii)　in accordance with international accounting standards;

  (c)　the company must disclose in the notes to its individual accounts that it is exempt from the obligation to prepare and deliver group accounts;

  (d)　the company must state in its individual accounts the name of the parent undertaking that draws up the group accounts referred to above and:

    (i)　the address of the undertaking's registered office (whether in or outside the United Kingdom); or

    (ii)　if it is unincorporated, the address of its principal place of business;

  (e)　the company must deliver to the registrar, within the period for filing its accounts and reports for the financial year in question, copies of:

    (i)　those group accounts; and

    (ii)　the parent undertaking's annual report, together with the auditor's report on them;

  (f)　any requirement of Part 35 of this Act as to the delivery to the registrar of a certified translation into English must be met in relation to any document comprised in the accounts and reports delivered in accordance with paragraph (e).

400(3)   For the purposes of subsection (1)(b) and (c) shares held by a wholly-owned subsidiary of the parent undertaking, or held on behalf of the parent undertaking or a wholly-owned subsidiary, shall be attributed to the parent undertaking.

400(4)   The exemption does not apply to a company which is a traded company.

400(5)   Shares held by directors of a company for the purpose of complying with any share qualification requirement shall be disregarded in determining for the purposes of this section whether the company is a wholly-owned subsidiary.

400(6)   [Omitted by SI 2015/980, reg. 5(7)(e).]

s. 401   ### Exemption for company included in non-EEA group accounts of larger group

401(1)   A company is exempt from the requirement to prepare group accounts if it is itself a subsidiary undertaking and its parent undertaking is not established under the law of an EEA State, in the following cases:

(a)   where the company is a wholly-owned subsidiary of that parent undertaking;

(b)   where that parent undertaking holds 90% or more of the allotted shares in the company and the remaining shareholders have approved the exemption; or

(c)   where that parent undertaking holds more than 50% (but less than 90%) of the allotted shares in the company and notice requesting the preparation of group accounts has not been served on the company by the shareholders holding in aggregate at least 5% of the allotted shares in the company.

Such notice must be served at least six months before the end of the financial year to which it relates.

401(2)   Exemption is conditional upon compliance with all of the following conditions:

(a)   the company and all of its subsidiary undertakings must be included in consolidated accounts for a larger group drawn up to the same date, or to an earlier date in the same financial year, by a parent undertaking;

(b)   those accounts and, where appropriate, the group's annual report, must be drawn up:
   (i)   in accordance with the provisions of Directive 2013/34/EU of the European Parliament and of the Council of 26 June 2013 on the annual financial statements, consolidated financial statements and related reports of certain types of undertakings;
   (ii)   in a manner equivalent to consolidated accounts and consolidated reports so drawn up;
   (iii)   in accordance with international accounting standards adopted pursuant to the IAS Regulation; or
   (iv)   in accordance with accounting standards which are equivalent to such international accounting standards, as determined pursuant to Commission Regulation (EC) No. 1569/2007(6) of 21 December 2007 establishing a mechanism for the determination of equivalence of accounting standards applied by third country issuers of securities pursuant to Directives 2003/71/EC and 2004/109/EC of the European Parliament and of the Council;

(c)   the group accounts must be audited by one or more persons authorised to audit accounts under the law under which the parent undertaking which draws them up is established;

(d)   the company must disclose in its individual accounts that it is exempt from the obligation to prepare and deliver group accounts;

(e)   the company must state in its individual accounts the name of the parent undertaking which draws up the group accounts referred to above and:

> (i)   the address of the undertaking's registered office (whether in or outside the United Kingdom); or
>
> (ii) if it is unincorporated, the address of its principal place of business;

(f)   the company must deliver to the registrar, within the period for filing its accounts and reports for the financial year in question, copies of:

> (i)   the group accounts; and
>
> (ii) where appropriate, the consolidated annual report, together with the auditor's report on them;

(g)   any requirement of Part 35 of this Act as to the delivery to the registrar of a certified translation into English must be met in relation to any document comprised in the accounts and reports delivered in accordance with paragraph (f).

401(3)   For the purposes of subsection (1)(b) and (c), shares held by a wholly-owned subsidiary of the parent undertaking, or held on behalf of the parent undertaking or a wholly-owned subsidiary, are attributed to the parent undertaking.

401(4)   The exemption does not apply to a company which is a traded company.

401(5)   Shares held by directors of a company for the purpose of complying with any share qualification requirement shall be disregarded in determining for the purposes of this section whether the company is a wholly-owned subsidiary.

401(6)   [Omitted by SI 2015/980, reg. 5(8)(f).]

Exemption if no subsidiary undertakings need be included in the consolidation   *s. 402*

402   A parent company is exempt from the requirement to prepare group accounts if under section 405 all of its subsidiary undertakings could be excluded from consolidation in Companies Act group accounts.

Appendix C   Small company accounts exemptions decision chart

The decision chart below is designed to help determine which accounts are appropriate or available in different circumstances. Options for accounts include using, subject to meeting the relevant criteria, the micro-entity regime, the small company regime, including FRS 102, section 1A and the abridged accounts options. The chart also sets out the alternatives for companies not following the regime for small companies and where guidance can be found.

Accounting periods beginning on or after 1 January 2016 (or optionally from 1 January 2015)

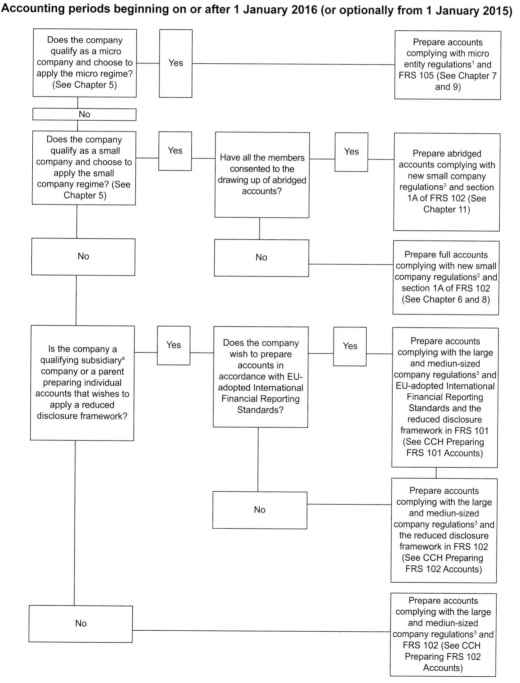

> [1] Micro entity regulations are set out in the *Small Companies and Groups (Accounts and Directors' Report) Regulations* 2008 (SI 2008/409), as amended by the *Small Companies (Micro-Entities' Accounts) Regulations* 2013 (SI 2013/3008) and by the *Companies, Partnerships and Groups (Accounts and Reports) Regulations* 2015 (SI 2015/980).
>
> [2] New small company regulations are set out in the *Companies, Partnerships and Groups (Accounts and Reports) Regulations* 2015 (SI 2015/980) which updated SI 2008/409.
>
> [3] Large and medium-sized company regulations are set out in *Large and Medium-sized Companies and Groups (Accounts and Directors' Report) Regulations* 2008 (SI 2008/410) as amended by the *Companies, Partnerships and Groups (Accounts and Reports) Regulations* 2015 (SI 2015/980).
>
> [4] A qualifying subsidiary is a member of a group where the parent of that group prepares publicly available consolidated financial statements which are intended to give a true and fair view (of the assets, liabilities, financial position and profit or loss) and that member is included in the consolidation. A charity may not be a qualifying entity.

Notes on eligibility

'Eligible company?'

s. 384

s. 384(2)

s. 384(1)

The following companies are not eligible and are not therefore entitled to prepare small company accounts (or therefore micro-entity accounts), irrespective of size:

- public companies;
- members of 'ineligible' (see below) groups;
- a company carrying on an insurance market activity; and
- a company that is an authorised insurance company, a banking company, an e-money issuer, a MiFID investment firm or a UCITS management company (see **5.1**, **Chapter 5**).

A group is 'ineligible' if any of its members is a traded company; a body corporate (other than a company (i.e. other than a company as defined by CA 2006)) whose shares are admitted to trading on a regulated market in an EEA State; a person (other than a small company) who has permission under FSMA 2000, Pt. 4 to carry on a regulated activity; a small company that is an authorised insurance company, a banking company, an e-money issuer, an MiFID investment firm or a UCITS management company; or a person who carries on insurance market activity (CA 2006, s. 384(2)).

s. 384(3)

A company is a 'small company' for this purpose of ineligibility if it qualified as small in relation to its last financial year ending on or before the end of the financial year to which the accounts relate.

As explained in **Chapter 5**, a company only falls out of the small regime after failing to meet for criteria for two consecutive years. Therefore, even if the thresholds are not met in the current year, if they were met in the prior year the company continues to be treated as small, for example.

Further details regarding qualifying for the different regimes are set out in **Chapter 5**.

Appendix D   Small and subsidiary company audit exemptions decision chart

The decision chart below is designed to determine whether a company qualifies in any particular year to exemption from audit.

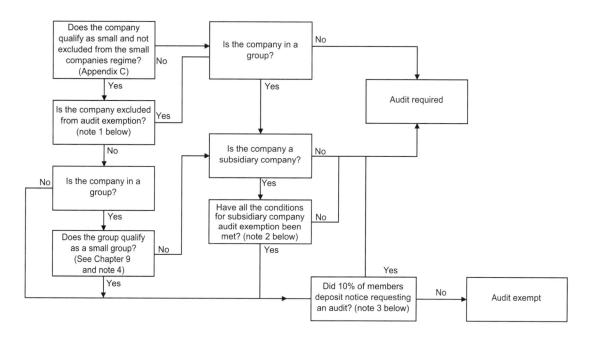

Note 1 – companies excluded from audit exemption

A company is not entitled to the small companies audit exemption conferred by CA 2006, s. 477 if it was at any time within the financial year in question:

- a public company;
- a company that is an authorised insurance company, a banking company, an e-money issuer, a MiFID investment firm or a UCITS management company, or carries on insurance market activity; or
- a special register body as defined in s. 117(1) of the *Trade Union and Labour Relations (Consolidation) Act* 1992 (c. 52) or an employers' association as defined in s. 122 of that Act or Article 4 of the *Industrial Relations (Northern Ireland) Order* 1992 (SI 1992/807 (NI 5)).   *s. 478*

Note that the first two bullet points above would also exclude the company from the small companies regime and thus render it ineligible for the small companies audit exemption on that basis as well.

Note 2 – Subsidiaries of EEA companies – audit exemption

In accordance with CA 2006, s. 479A, a subsidiary company (irrespective of its size) is exempt from audit if it fulfils all of the following conditions:

(a)   its parent undertaking is established under the law of an EEA state[1];
(b)   all members of the company must agree to the exemption in respect of the financial year in question;

(c)   the parent gives a guarantee (under s. 479C) of all the outstanding liabilities to which the subsidiary is subject at the end of the financial year until they are satisfied in full;

(d)   the company must be included in the consolidated accounts drawn up for that year or to an earlier date in that year by the parent undertaking in accordance with the provisions of Directive 2013/34/EU of the European Parliament and of the Council on the annual financial statements, consolidated statements and related reports of certain types of undertakings, or international accounting standards;

(e)   the consolidated accounts drawn up by the parent must disclose the use of the audit exemption by the subsidiary by virtue of this section;

(f)   the directors of the subsidiary must file the following documents at Companies House on or before the date that they file the subsidiary's accounts:

  (i)   written notice of the agreement in (b);

  (ii)   a written statement by the parent of the guarantee in (c);

  (iii)   a copy of the consolidated annual report and accounts referred to in (d) and the auditor's
s. 479A(2)   report on those accounts;

(g)   the company is not a traded company (as defined in s. 474(1)).

(h)   the company is not an authorised insurance company, a banking company, an e-money issuer, a MiFID investment firm or a UCITS management company, or carries on insurance market activity; or

(i)   a special register body as defined in s. 117(1) of the *Trade Union and Labour Relations (Consolidation) Act* 1992 (c. 52) or an employers' association as defined in s. 122 of that Act
s. 479B   or Article 4 of the *Industrial Relations (Northern Ireland) Order* 1992 (SI 1992/807) (NI 5).

The directors of the subsidiary company must make the statements required by CA 2006, s. 475(2) and (3) before the signature on the balance sheet, as set out in **13.8**.

See **13.5** for further details .

Note 3 – Right of members to request an audit

If shareholders holding 10% or more of the company's issued share capital deposit a notice in writing at the company's registered office during the financial year but not later than one month before the end of the year, the company is then not entitled to audit exemption for the year to which
s. 476   the notice relates. See **13.6**.

Note 4 – Group company eligibility for small audit exemption

A company which in its own right meets the definition of a small company and is also a group company (being a parent company or a subsidiary undertaking) is only entitled to audit exemption if the following conditions are met:

(a)   the group:

  (i)   qualifies as a small group (as determined in accordance with s. 383) in relation to that financial year; and

  (ii)   was not at any time in that year an ineligible group (as determined by s. 384(2) and (3); or

s. 479(1)   (b)   subsection (3) applies (dormant subsidiaries).

A dormant subsidiary undertaking being a group company and dormant during the financial year for the whole period it was a group company is also entitled to audit exemption. (This exemption
s. 479(3)   applies to dormant subsidiaries of any size.)

A group is ineligible if any of its members is:

(a)   a traded company (this was changed from a public company by SI 2015/980);
(b)   a body corporate (other than a company) whose shares are admitted to trading on a regulated market in an EEA state;
(c)   a person (other than a small company) who has permission under the *Financial Services and Markets Act* 2000, Pt. 4A (c. 8) to carry on a regulated activity;
(ca) an e-money issuer;
(d)   a small company that is an authorised insurance company, a banking company, a MiFID investment firm or a UCITS management company; or   *s. 384(2)*
(e)   a person who carries on insurance market activity.

CA 2006, s. 479(4) defines a 'group' in relation to a group company as that company together with all its associated undertakings.   *s. 479(4)*

Appendix E Small Company Accounts Checklist – FRS 102 with Section 1A

Small Company Checklist FRS 102 with Section 1A

*This checklist is for a small company preparing accounts in accordance with the reduced disclosure requirements of **FRS 102, section 1A for small companies**. It does not include the disclosure requirements for a small LLP. There is a separate checklist in Appendix G for abridged small company accounts.*

Disclosures shown by this checklist should be marked with a 'Y' to indicate Yes correct disclosure, a 'N' for No incorrect disclosure and 'NA' for Not Applicable.

The references to legislation and financial reporting standards shown in this checklist are as follows:

s = Companies Act 2006 section number.
R-C = Accounts Regulations for Companies in SI 2008/409, Small Companies and Groups (Accounts and Directors' Report) Regulations 2008 as amended by SI 2015/980, The Companies, Partnerships and Groups (Accounts and Reports) Regulations 2015.
FRS 102 = FRS 102 The Financial Reporting Standard applicable in the UK and the Republic of Ireland inclusive of July 2015 amendments for small entities.

FRS 102.1A.17 states that a small entity is not required to comply with a number of the disclosure requirements in full FRS 102; as a result, these are not included in this checklist. The paragraph goes on to state that because those disclosures are usually considered relevant to giving a true and fair view, a small entity is encouraged to consider providing any disclosures that are relevant to material transactions, other events or conditions of the small entity.

Reference to FRS 102 can be made if it is believed that further disclosures are required in order to meet the requirement to give a true and fair view.

The main checklist is for a stand alone company with unaudited accounts.

Appendices are included as follows, which should only be completed as appropriate:

Appendix 1 *Audited accounts.*
Appendix 2 *Assurance review report.*
Appendix 3 *Parent company not preparing group accounts.*
Appendix 4 *Political donations.*

The checklist includes the format 1 Balance Sheet and the format 1 Profit and Loss Account for a small company preparing full accounts in accordance with Sch. 1, Section B of the Small Company Accounts Regulations.

*Information on format 2 profit and loss account and balance sheets can be found in **Chapter 6**.*

SMALL COMPANY ACCOUNTS – MAIN CHECKLIST

Client		Year-end	
		Reference	*Y, N, N/A*
1	**DIRECTORS' REPORT**		
1.01	The directors' report for a financial year must state the names of the persons who, at any time during the financial year, were directors of the company.	s. 416(1)a	
1.02	If the company employs more than an average monthly number of 250 UK employees, give a statement describing the policy during the year in respect of disabled persons regarding consideration to applications for employment, continuing their employment and their training, career development and promotion.	R-C Sch. 5.5(3)	
1.03	If the company has made any political donations, complete **Appendix 4**.		
1.04	A statement must be made where a qualifying third party indemnity provision is, at the time the report is approved, or was, at any time during the financial year, in force for the benefit of one or more directors of the company or of an associated company.	s. 236(1)	
1.05	If advantage is taken of any of the exemptions to the directors' report available to small companies, then the report must contain a statement that it is prepared in accordance with the small companies regime in a prominent position above the signature.	s. 419(2)	
1.06	The name of the director or secretary who has signed the directors' report on behalf of the board of directors to indicate their approval of the report.	s. 419(1)	
2	**AUDITOR'S AND ACCOUNTANT'S REPORTS**		
	Auditor's reports		
2.01	If an audit report is to be given, complete **Appendix 1**.		
	Assurance review report		
2.02	If an assurance review report is to be given, complete **Appendix 2**.		
	Accountant's reports on the compilation of financial statements		
	*For **ICAEW** firms, the provisions of AAF 02/10 as set out in 2.03 and 2.04 below are not a requirement. However, they are best practice and hence have been included in this checklist.* *For **ACCA** firms, the wording of question 2.13 is based on AAF 02/10 issued by the ICAEW, which itself is based on the CCAB compilation report issued in November 2010. The equivalent guidance for ACCA members is Technical Factsheet 163: Audit Exempt Companies – ACCA Accounts Preparation Report.* *The requirements are very similar, except Factsheet 163 refers to the ACCA rather than the ICAEW, the ACCA ethical guidelines and other professional requirements website at http://www.accaglobal.com/gb/en/member/professional-standards/rules-standards.html and the final paragraph states the firm has not been instructed to carry out an audit or a review of the accounts.*		

2.03	Does the accountant's report on the financial statements of the company include:	AAF 02/10	
	(a) a title identifying the persons to whom the report is addressed (usually the Board of Directors) and including the words 'Chartered Accountant's / Accountants' Report to ....';		
	(b) a statement that, in order to assist the directors to fulfil their duties under the *Companies Act* 2006, the accountants have prepared for the directors' approval the financial statements which comprise [either: state the primary financial statements such as the Profit and Loss Account, the Balance Sheet, the Cash Flow Statement, the Statement of Total Recognised Gains and Losses and the related notes] [or: as set out on pages x-x] from the company's accounting records and information and explanations supplied by the client;		
	(c) a statement that the accountant is a practising member/member firm of the Institute of Chartered Accountants in England and Wales and is subject to its ethical and other professional requirements which are detailed at icaew.com/members handbook;		
	(d) *Optional paragraph.* A statement that the report is made to the Company's Board of Directors as a body in accordance with the terms of engagement. An explanation as to the work carried out being in accordance with the requirements of ICAEW guidance and the purpose of the work and that, to the fullest extent permitted by law, no responsibility will be accepted for the work or the report to anyone other than the Company and the Company's Board of Directors, as a body;		
	(e) *Optional paragraph.* A statement that the directors have acknowledged their duty to ensure that the company has kept adequate accounting records and to prepare statutory accounts that give a true and fair view of the assets, liabilities, financial position and profit or loss of the company and that they consider that the company is exempt from the statutory audit requirement for the year;		
	(f) *Optional paragraph.* A statement that the accountants have not been instructed to carry out an audit or a review of the accounts of the company and that for this reason, they have not verified the accuracy or completeness of the accounting records or information and explanations given to them and they do not, therefore, express any opinion on the statutory accounts;		
	(g) the name and signature of the accountant and any appropriate designation (but not 'Registered Auditor'/'Statutory Auditor'); and		
	(h) the date of the report.		
2.04	Do the financial statements contain a reference to the fact that they are unaudited either on the front cover or on each page of the financial statements?	AAF 02/10	

3	**FINANCIAL STATEMENTS PRESENTATION**		
	Compliance with FRS 102		
3.01	The accounts must disclose any additional information that is necessary to show a true and fair view.	s. 396(4), FRS 102-1A.6	
3.02	Present a complete set of financial statements including all of the following: (a) a statement of financial position as at the reporting date; (b) an income statement for the reporting period; and (c) notes.	FRS 102-1A.8	
3.03	When an entity departs from a requirement of FRS 102 in accordance with paragraph 3.4, or from a requirement of applicable legislation, it shall disclose the following: (a) that management has concluded that the financial statements give a true and fair view of the entity's financial position, financial performance and, when required to be presented, cash flows; (b) that it has complied with FRS 102 or applicable legislation, except that it has departed from a particular requirement of this FRS or applicable legislation to the extent necessary to give a true and fair view; (c) the nature and effect of the departure; (d) the treatment that FRS 102 or applicable legislation would require; (e) the reason why that treatment would be so misleading in the circumstances that it would conflict with the objective of financial statements set out in FRS 102, section 2; and (f) the treatment adopted.	s. 396(5), FRS 102-3.5	
3.04	When an entity has departed from a requirement of FRS 102 or applicable legislation in a prior period, and that departure affects the amounts recognised in the financial statements for the current period, it shall disclose: (a) the nature of the departure; (b) the treatment that FRS 102 or applicable legislation would require; (c) the reason why that treatment would be so misleading in the circumstances that it would conflict with the objective of financial statements set out in FRS 102, section 2; and (d) the treatment adopted.	FRS 102-3.6	
3.05	If it appears to the small entity that there are special reasons for departing from any of the principles set out in company law in preparing the small entity's financial statements in respect of any reporting period, it may do so, in which disclose in the notes to the financial statements particulars of the departure, the reasons for it, and its effects.	R-C Sch. 1.10(2), FRS 102-1AC.10	
	Frequency of reporting		
3.06	When the end of the reporting period changes and the annual financial statements are presented for a period longer or shorter than one year, disclose the following:	FRS 102-3.10	

	(a) that fact;		
	(b) the reason for using a longer or shorter period; and		
	(c) the fact that comparative amounts presented in the financial statements (including the related notes) are not entirely comparable.		
	Consistency of presentation		
3.07	When comparative amounts are reclassified, disclose the following: (a) the nature of the reclassification; (b) the amount of each item or class of items that is reclassified; and (c) the reason for the reclassification.	R-C Sch. 1.7(2), FRS 102-3.12	
3.08	If it is impracticable to reclassify comparative amounts, disclose why reclassification was not practicable.	FRS 102-3.13	
	Comparative information		
3.09	Present comparative information in respect of the preceding period: (a) for all amounts presented in the current period's financial statements unless specifically exempted; and (b) for narrative and descriptive information when it is relevant to an understanding of the current period's financial statements.	R-C Sch. 1.7(1), FRS 102-3.14	
	Materiality and aggregation		
3.10	Present separately: (a) each material class of similar items; and (b) items of a dissimilar nature or function unless they are immaterial.	FRS 102-3.15	
	Identification of the financial statements		
3.11	Display the following information prominently, and repeat it when necessary for an understanding of the information presented: (a) the name of the reporting entity; (b) any change in its name since the end of the preceding reporting period; (c) whether the financial statements cover the individual entity or a group of entities; (d) the date of the end of the reporting period and the period covered by the financial statements; (e) the presentation currency, as defined in FRS 102, section 30; and (f) the level of rounding, if any, used in presenting amounts in the financial statements.	FRS 102-3.23	
3.12	Disclose the following in the notes: (a) the legal form of the entity; (b) its country of incorporation; (c) the address of its registered office (or principal place of business, if different from the registered office);	FRS 102-3.24(a)	
	Formats		
3.13	Disclose in the notes to the accounts the directors' reasons for any change from one format to another.	R-C Sch. 1.2(2)	

4	**STATEMENT OF FINANCIAL POSITION**		
4.01	Present a statement of financial position in accordance with the requirements for a balance sheet set out in Sch. 1 to the Small Companies Accounts Regulations using either Format 1 (see below) or Format 2 (see Sch. 1, Section B to the Regulations)	R-C Sch. 1, Section B FRS 102-1A.12	
	Balance sheet – Format 1 – Full accounts		
	A. Called-up share capital not paid		
	B. Fixed assets		
	I. Intangible assets		
	1 Goodwill		
	2 Other intangible assets		
	II. Tangible assets		
	1 Land and buildings		
	2 Plant and machinery, etc.		
	III. Investments		
	1 Shares in group undertakings and participating interests		
	2 Loans to group undertakings and undertakings in which the company has a participating interest		
	3 Other investments other than loans		
	4 Other investments		
	C. Current assets		
	I. Stocks		
	1 Stocks		
	2 Payments on account		
	II. Debtors		
	1 Trade debtors		
	2 Amounts owed by group undertakings and undertakings in which the company has a participating interest		
	3 Other debtors		
	III. Investments		
	1 Shares in group undertakings		
	2 Other investments		
	IV. Cash at bank and in hand		
	D. Prepayments and accrued income		
	E. Creditors: amounts falling due within one year		
	1 Bank loans and overdrafts		
	2 Trade creditors		
	3 Amounts owed to group undertakings and undertakings in which the company has a participating interest		
	Taxation and social security		
	4 Other creditors		
	F. Net current assets (liabilities)		
	G. Total assets less current liabilities		

	H. Creditors: amounts falling due after more than one year		
	1 Bank loans and overdrafts		
	2 Trade creditors		
	3 Amounts owed to group undertakings and undertakings in which the company has a participating interest		
	Taxation and social security		
	4 Other creditors		
	I. Provisions for liabilities		
	J. Accruals and deferred income		
	K. Capital and reserves		
	I. Called-up share capital		
	II. Share premium account		
	III. Revaluation reserve		
	IV. Other reserves		
	V. Profit and loss account		
5	**STATEMENT OF COMPREHENSIVE INCOME**		
5.01	Present the profit or loss for the period in an income statement in accordance with the requirements for a profit and loss account set out in Sch. 1 to the Small Companies Accounts Regulations using either Format 1 (see below) or Format 2.	R-C Sch. 1, Section B FRS 102-1A.14	
	Profit and loss account – Format 1 – Full accounts		
	1 Turnover		
	2 Cost of sales		
	3 Gross profit or loss		
	4 Distribution costs		
	5 Administrative expenses		
	6 Other operating income		
	7 Income from shares in group undertakings		
	8 Income from participating interests		
	9 Income from other fixed asset investments		
	10 Other interest receivable and similar income		
	11 Amounts written off investments		
	12 Interest payable and similar expenses		
	13 Tax on profit or loss		
	14 Profit or loss after taxation		
	15 Other taxes not shown under the above items		
	16 Profit or loss for the financial year		
5.02	Show the amount of a company's profit or loss before taxation.	R-C Sch. 1.6	
5.03	Where any amount relating to any previous financial year is included in any item in the profit and loss account, state the effect.	R-C Sch. 1.61(1)	

6	**NOTES TO THE FINANCIAL STATEMENTS**		
6.01	Present sufficient information to meet the requirement for the financial statements to meet the requirements to give a true and fair view of the assets, liabilities, financial position and profit or loss for the reporting period.	FRS 102-1A.16	
6.02	Disclose any provision for permanent diminution in value of fixed assets (including fixed asset investments) if not shown separately in the profit and loss account and, if appropriate, the amount of any provision written back.	R-C Sch. 1.19(3), 1.20(2)	
6.03	Disclose the amount and nature of any individual items of income or expenses of exceptional size or incidence.	R-C Sch. 1.61(2), FRS 102-1AC.32	
6.04	Disclose the average number of persons employed by the small entity in the reporting period.	s. 411, FRS 102-1AC.33	
6.05	Disclose the interest payable and similar expenses on loans from group undertakings.	R-C Sch. 1.9(13)	
7	**ACCOUNTING POLICIES**		
7.01	Disclose the accounting policies adopted by the small entity in determining the amounts to be included in respect of items shown in the statement of financial position and in determining the profit or loss of the small entity (including such policies with respect to the depreciation and impairment of assets).	R-C Sch. 1.44, FRS 102-1AC.3	
7.02	If any amount is included in a small entity's statement of financial position in respect of development costs, disclose in the note on accounting policies the following information: (a) the period over which the amount of those costs originally capitalised is being or is to be written off; and (b) the reasons for capitalising the development costs in question.	R-C Sch. 1.21(2), FRS 102-1AC.4	
7.03	Where development costs are shown or included as an asset in the small entity's financial statements and the amount is not treated as a realised loss because there are special circumstances justifying this, disclose in a note to the financial statements the reasons for showing development costs as an asset and that it is not a realised loss.	s. 844, FRS 102-1AC.5	
7.04	Where in exceptional cases the useful life of intangible assets cannot be reliably estimated, disclose in a note to the financial statements the period over which those intangible assets are being written off and the reasons for choosing that period.	R-C Sch. 1.22(4), FRS 102-1AC.6	
	Changes in presentation and accounting policies and corrections of prior period errors		
7.05	Where there is a change in the presentation of a small entity's statement of financial position or income statement, disclose and explain, in a note to the financial statements in which the new presentation is first used, particulars of any such change, and the reasons for the change.	R-C Sch. 1.2(2), FRS 102-1AC.7	
7.06	Where the corresponding amount for the immediately preceding financial year is not comparable with the amount to be shown for the item in question in respect of the reporting period, and the corresponding amount is adjusted, disclose in a note to the financial statements the particulars of the non-comparability and of any adjustment.	R-C Sch. 1.7(2), FRS 102-1AC.8	

7.07	Where any amount relating to a preceding reporting period is included in any item in the income statement, disclose the effect.	R-C Sch. 1.61(1), FRS 102-1AC.9	
8	**FINANCIAL INSTRUMENTS**		
8.01	Disclose the following for each item in fixed asset investments shown separately either in the statement of financial position, or in the notes:		
	(a) the aggregate amount (on the basis of cost or revaluation): (i) at the beginning of the period; and (ii) at the end of the period.	R-C Sch. 1.48(1) & (2), FRS 102-1AC.12(a)	
	(b) the effect of the following during the period: (i) any revaluation; (ii) acquisitions; (iii) disposals; and (iv) any transfers.	R-C Sch. 1.48(1) & (2), FRS 102-1AC.12(b)	
8.02	Disclose the following for each item in fixed asset investments shown separately either in the statement of financial position, or in the notes:	R-C Sch. 1.48(3), FRS 102-1AC.13(a)	
	(a) the cumulative amount of provisions for depreciation and impairment of assets: (i) at the beginning of the period; and (ii) at the end of the period.		
	(b) provision for depreciation and impairment during the period;		
	(c) adjustments to provisions during the period arising from disposals; and		
	(d) other adjustments to provisions during the period.		
8.03	If items of fixed asset investments are stated at revalued amounts:	R-C Sch. 1.34, FRS 102-1AC.14,16	
	(a) state which items;		
	(b) state in the accounting policies the basis of valuation; and		
	(c) state the comparable amounts of cost and accumulated depreciation on the historical cost basis.		
8.04	For revalued fixed asset investments, other than listed investments, show:	R-C Sch. 1.49, FRS 102-1AC.15	
	(a) the year in which they were revalued;		
	(b) the amount of each valuation; and		
	(c) if valued during the year, the names or qualifications of the valuers and the basis of valuation.		
8.05	Where fixed asset investments are measured at revalued amount, disclose the following in tabular form:	R-C Sch. 1.54(2), FRS 102-1AC.17	
	(a) movements in the revaluation reserve in the reporting period, with an explanation of the tax treatment of items therein; and		
	(b) the carrying amount in the statement of financial position that would have been recognised had the fixed asset investments not been revalued.		

8.06	Where fixed asset investments are measured at revalued amount, disclose the treatment for taxation purposes of amounts credited or debited to the revaluation reserve in a note to the financial statements.	R-C Sch. 1.35(6), FRS 102-1AC.18	
8.07	Disclose provisions for impairment of fixed asset investments in a note to the financial statements if not shown separately in the income statement.	R-C Sch. 1.19(3), FRS 102-1AC.20	
8.08	Disclose, either separately or in aggregate, provisions for impairment of fixed asset investments that are reversed because the reasons for which they were made cease to apply, in a note to the financial statements if not shown separately in the income statement.	R-C Sch. 1.20(2), FRS 102-1AC.21	
8.09	Where fixed asset investments are included at a valuation which is not market value (e.g. Directors' valuation), state the method used and the reason for adopting it.	R-C Sch. 1.32(3)	
8.10	Where financial instruments have been measured at fair value through the profit and loss, disclose: (a) the significant assumptions underlying the valuation models and techniques used to determine the fair values; (b) for each category of financial instrument, the fair value of the assets in that category and the change in value: (i) included directly in the income statement; or (ii) credited to or debited from the fair value reserve.	R-C Sch. 1.51(2)(a), (b), FRS 102-1AC.22	
8.11	Where financial instruments have been measured at fair value through the profit and loss , disclose for each class of derivatives, the extent and nature of the instruments, including significant terms and conditions that may affect the amount, timing and certainty of future cash flows.	R-C Sch. 1.51(2)(c) FRS 102-1AC.23	
8.12	Where any amount is transferred to or from the fair value reserve during the reporting period, disclose in tabular form: (a) the amount of the reserve at the beginning and end of the period; and (b) the amount transferred to or from the reserve during the period.	R-C Sch. 1.51(3), FRS 102-1AC.24	
8.13	Disclose in a note to the financial statements the treatment for taxation purposes of amounts credited or debited to the fair value reserve.	R-C Sch. 1.41(2), FRS 102-1AC.25	
8.14	Give disclosures required by international accounting standards (see section 11 in checklist 4) in respect of financial instruments which are included, in the permitted circumstances, in the accounts at fair value under international accounting standards.	R-C Sch. 1.36(4), FRS 102-1AC.26	
8.15	Disclose for each category of debtor any amounts falling due after one year.	R-C Sch. 1.9(5)	
8.16	Where the amount repayable on any debt owed by the company exceeds the value of the consideration originally received, and the surplus is treated as an asset, it should be subject to annual amortisation, and fully written off before repayment of the debt. If the current amount is not shown separately in the balance sheet, disclose the assets in a note.	R-C Sch. 1.25	

8.17	Disclose the aggregate for all items under creditors of: (a) the total amount falling due after five years and not repayable by instalments; (b) for any amounts payable by instalments, the total amount of those instalments which are payable after five years; and (c) in respect of each item shown under 'creditors' in the balance sheet for which security has been given, disclose: (i) the aggregate amount of any debts included; and (ii) an indication of the nature and form of security.	R-C Sch. 1.55(1) & (2), FRS 102-1AC.27, 28	
8.18	The amount of any convertible debts, including debenture loans, must be shown separately from other debts or debentures.	R-C Sch. 1.9(7)(a)	
9	**INVENTORIES**		
9.01	Not used		
10	**INVESTMENT PROPERTY**		
10.01	Disclose the following for investment property:		
	(a) the aggregate amount (on the basis of cost or revaluation): (i) at the beginning of the period; and (ii) at the end of the period.	R-C Sch. 1.48(1), (2), FRS 102-1AC.12(a)	
	(b) the effect of the following during the period: (i) any revaluation; (ii) acquisitions; (iii) disposals; and (iv) any transfers.	R-C Sch. 1.48(1), (2), FRS 102-1AC.12(b)	
10.02	Disclose the following for investment property: (a) the cumulative amount of provisions for depreciation and impairment of assets: (i) at the beginning of the period; and (ii) at the end of the period; (b) provision for depreciation and impairment during the period; (c) adjustments to provisions during the period arising from disposals; and (d) other adjustments to provisions during the period.	R-C Sch. 1.48(3), FRS 102-1AC.13(a)	
10.03	Disclose the aggregate amount of any finance cost capitalised and included in the production cost of any asset.	R-C Sch. 1.27(3)(b), FRS 102-1AC.19	
10.04	Disclose provisions for impairment of property, plant and equipment in a note to the financial statements if not shown separately in the income statement.	R-C Sch. 1.19(3), FRS 102-1AC.20	
10.05	Disclose, either separately or in aggregate, provisions for impairment of investment property that are reversed because the reasons for which they were made cease to apply, in a note to the financial statements if not shown separately in the income statement.	R-C Sch. 1.20(2), FRS 102-1AC.21	

11	**PROPERTY, PLANT AND EQUIPMENT**		
11.01	Disclose the following for each class of tangible fixed assets shown separately either in the statement of financial position, or in the notes:		

	(a) the aggregate amount (on the basis of cost or revaluation):
	     (i) at the beginning of the period; and
	     (ii) at the end of the period.
		R-C Sch. 1.48(1), (2), FRS 102-1AC.12(a)	

	(b) the effect of the following during the period:
	     (i) any revaluation;
	     (ii) acquisitions;
	     (iii) disposals; and
	     (iv) any transfers.
		R-C Sch. 1.48(1), (2), FRS 102-1AC.12(b)	

11.02	Disclose the following for each class of tangible fixed assets shown separately either in the statement of financial position, or in the notes:	R-C Sch. 1.48(3), FRS 102-1AC.13(a)	

	(a) the cumulative amount of provisions for depreciation and impairment of assets:
	     (i) at the beginning of the period; and
	     (ii) at the end of the period;		

	(b) provision for depreciation and impairment during the period;		
	(c) adjustments to provisions during the period arising from disposals; and		
	(d) other adjustments to provisions during the period.		
11.03	If items of property, plant and equipment are stated at revalued amounts:	R-C Sch. 1.34, FRS 102-1AC.14,16	
	(a) state which items;		
	(b) state in the accounting policies the basis of valuation; and		
	(c) state the comparable amounts of cost and accumulated depreciation on the historical cost basis.		
11.04	For revalued property, plant and equipment show: (a) the year in which they were revalued; (b) the amount of each valuation; and (c) if valued during the year, the names or qualifications of the valuers and the basis of valuation.	R-C Sch. 1.49, FRS 102-1AC.15	
11.05	Where property, plant and equipment is measured at revalued amount, disclose the following in tabular form:	R-C Sch. 1.54(2), FRS 102-1AC.17	
	(a) movements in the revaluation reserve in the reporting period, with an explanation of the tax treatment of items therein; and		
	(b) the carrying amount in the statement of financial position that would have been recognised had the property, plant and equipment not been revalued.		
11.06	Where property, plant and equipment is measured at revalued amount, disclose the treatment for taxation purposes of amounts credited or debited to the revaluation reserve in a note to the financial statements.	R-C Sch. 1.35(6), FRS 102-1AC.18	
11.07	Disclose the aggregate amount of any finance cost capitalised and included in the production cost of any asset.	R-C Sch. 1.27(3)(b), FRS 102-1AC.19	

11.08	Disclose provisions for impairment of property, plant and equipment in a note to the financial statements if not shown separately in the income statement.	R-C Sch. 1.19(3), FRS 102-1AC.20	
11.09	Disclose, either separately or in aggregate, provisions for impairment of property, plant and equipment that are reversed because the reasons for which they were made cease to apply, in a note to the financial statements if not shown separately in the income statement.	R-C Sch. 1.20(2), FRS 102-1AC.21	
12	**INTANGIBLE ASSETS**		
12.01	Disclose the following for each class of intangible fixed assets shown separately either in the statement of financial position, or in the notes: (a) the aggregate amount (on the basis of cost or revaluation): (i) at the beginning of the period; and (ii) at the end of the period. (b) the effect of the following during the period: (i) any revaluation; (ii) acquisitions; (iii) disposals; and (iv) any transfers.	R-C Sch. 1.48(1) & (2), FRS 102-1AC.12(a) R-C Sch. 1.48(1), (2), FRS 102-1AC.12(b)	
12.02	Disclose the following for each class of intangible fixed assets shown separately either in the statement of financial position, or in the notes: (a) the cumulative amount of provisions for depreciation and impairment of assets: (i) at the beginning of the period; and (ii) at the end of the period; (b) provision for depreciation and impairment during the period; (c) adjustments to provisions during the period arising from disposals; and (d) other adjustments to provisions during the period.	R-C Sch. 1.48(3), FRS 102-1AC.13(a)	
12.03	If intangible assets are stated at revalued amounts: (a) state which items; (b) state in the accounting policies the basis of valuation; and (c) state the comparable amounts of cost and accumulated depreciation on the historical cost basis.	R-C Sch. 1.34, FRS 102-1AC.14,16	
12.04	For revalued intangible assets show: (a) the year in which they were revalued; (b) the amount of each valuation; and (c) if valued during the year, the names or qualifications of the valuers and the basis of valuation.	R-C Sch. 1.49, FRS 102-1AC.15	
12.05	Where intangible assets are measured at revalued amount, disclose the following in tabular form: (a) movements in the revaluation reserve in the reporting period, with an explanation of the tax treatment of items therein; and (b) the carrying amount in the statement of financial position that would have been recognised had the property, plant and equipment not been revalued.	R-C Sch. 1.54(2), FRS 102-1AC.17	

12.06	Where intangible assets are measured at revalued amount, disclose the treatment for taxation purposes of amounts credited or debited to the revaluation reserve in a note to the financial statements.	R-C Sch. 1.35(6), FRS 102-1AC.18	
12.07	Disclose the aggregate amount of any finance cost capitalised and included in the production cost of any asset.	R-C Sch. 1.27(3)(b), FRS 102-1AC.19	
12.08	Disclose provisions for impairment of intangible assets in a note to the financial statements if not shown separately in the income statement.	R-C Sch. 1.19(3), FRS 102-1AC.20	
12.09	Disclose, either separately or in aggregate, provisions for impairment of intangible assets that are reversed because the reasons for which they were made cease to apply, in a note to the financial statements if not shown separately in the income statement.	R-C Sch. 1.20(2), FRS 102-1AC.21	
12.10	For development costs state: (a) the period of write off; and (b) the reason for capitalising.	R-C Sch. 1.21(2)	
12.11	Where the useful economic life of an intangible asset cannot be reliably estimated and it is being written off over a period not exceeding 10 years, disclose: (a) the period chosen; and (b) the reason for choosing that period.	R-C Sch. 1.22(4)	
13	**CONTINGENCIES AND COMMITMENTS**		
13.01	Disclose the total amount of each of the following that are not included in the balance sheet: (a) financial commitments; (b) guarantees; (c) contingencies.	R-C Sch. 1.57(1), FRS 102-1AC.29	
	[Guidance] *FRS 102-1AC.29 indicates that such commitments can arise in a variety of situations, including in relation to group entities, investments, property, plant and equipment, leases and pension obligations.*		
13.02	Give an indication of the nature and form of any variable security given by the company for each class of the following: (a) financial commitments; (b) guarantees; (c) contingencies.	R-C Sch. 1.57(2), FRS 102-1AC.30	
	[Guidance] *FRS 102-1AC.30 indicates that paragraphs 11.46 basic financial instruments, 13.22 inventories, 16.10 investment property, 17.32 property, plant and equipment and 18.28 intangible assets, address similar requirements.*		
13.03	Disclose the total amount of any commitments included in 13.01 above concerning pensions.	R-C Sch. 1.57(3), FRS 102-1AC.29	

13.04	Disclose separately the total amount of any commitments included in 13.01 above which are undertaken on behalf of or for the benefit of: (a) any parent, fellow subsidiary or any subsidiary of the small entity; or (b) any undertaking in which the small entity has a participating interest.	R-C Sch. 1.57(4), FRS 102-1AC.29	
13.05	Disclose the risks or benefits arising from arrangements that the small entity is, or has been a party to during the reporting period, and which are not reflected in the statement of financial position; disclosure should be to the extent necessary to enable the financial position of the small entity to be assessed.	s. 410A(2)(a), FRS 102-1AC.31	
	[Guidance] *FRS 102-1AC.31 states that examples of off-balance sheet arrangements include risk and benefit-sharing arrangements or obligations arising from a contract such as debt factoring, combined sale and repurchase arrangements, consignment stock arrangements, take or pay arrangements, securitisation arranged through separate entities, pledged assets, operating lease arrangements, outsourcing and the like. In many cases, the disclosures about financial commitments and contingencies required by 13.01, 13.02, 13.03 and 13.04 above will also address such arrangements.*		
14	**RELATED PARTY DISCLOSURES**		
14.01	Where the small entity is a subsidiary, disclose the following information in respect of the parent of the smallest group for which consolidated financial statements are drawn up of which the small entity is a member: (a) the name of the parent which draws up the consolidated financial statements; (b) the address of the parent's registered office (whether in or outside the UK); or (c) if it is unincorporated, the address of its principal place of business.	R-C Sch. 1.65, FRS 102-1AC.34	
14.02	Disclose particulars of material transactions the small entity has entered into that have not been concluded under normal market conditions with: (a) owners holding a participating interest in the small entity; (b) companies in which the small entity itself has a participating interest; and (c) the small entity's directors [or members of its governing body].	R-C Sch. 1.66, FRS 102-1AC.35	

14.03	In particular disclose: (a) the amount of such transactions; (b) the nature of the related party relationship; and (c) other information about the transactions necessary for an understanding of the financial position of the small entity.	R-C Sch. 1.66, FRS 102-1AC.35	
	[Guidance] *Information about individual transactions may be aggregated according to their nature, except where separate information is necessary for an understanding of the effects of the related party transactions on the financial position of the small entity.* *Particulars need not be given of transactions entered into between two or more members of a group, provided that any subsidiary which is a party to the transaction is wholly-owned by such a member.*		
14.04	Disclose in the notes to the financial statements the following details of advances and credits granted by the small entity to its directors and guarantees of any kind entered into by the small entity on behalf of its directors: (a) its amount; (b) an indication of the interest rate; (c) its main conditions; (d) any amounts repaid; (e) any amounts written off; (f) any amounts waived; (g) the total of 'a'; (h) the total of 'd'; (i) the total of 'e'; (j) the total of 'f'.	s. 413, FRS 102-1AC.36	
14.05	Disclose the following details of any guarantees granted on behalf of a director: (a) its main terms; (b) the amount of the maximum liability that may be incurred by the small entity; (c) any amount paid and any liability incurred by the small entity for the purpose of fulfilling the guarantee (including any loss incurred by reason of enforcement of the guarantee); (d) the total of 'b'; (e) the total of 'c'.	s. 413, FRS 102-1AC.36	
15	**OTHER**		
15.01	Disclose in the financial statements: (a) the part of the UK in which the small entity is registered; (b) the small entity's registered number; (c) whether small entity is limited by shares or by guarantee; (d) the address of the small entity's registered office; and (e) where appropriate, the fact that the entity is being wound up.	s. 396, FRS 102-1AC.37	

15.02	Disclose in a note to the financial statements the individual amounts where items to which Arabic numbers are given in any of the formats have been combined, unless they are not material.	R-C Sch. 1.4(3), FRS 102-1AC.38	
15.03	Disclose the nature and financial effect of material events arising after the reporting date which are not reflected in the income statement or statement of financial position.	R-C Sch. 1.64, FRS 102-1AC.39	
15.04	If the accounts are prepared in accordance with the small companies regime, then the balance sheet must contain, above the signature of the directors, a statement that the accounts have been prepared in accordance with the provisions applicable to companies subject to the small companies regime.	s. 414(3)	
15.05	If the company is taking advantage of the exemption from an audit available under s. 477 (small companies) or s. 480 (dormant companies), the balance sheet must contain a statement by the directors, above the director's signature to the effect that, for the year in question:		
	(a) the company was entitled to exemption from audit under s. 477 (or s. 480 as appropriate);	s. 475(2)	
	(b) the members have not required the company to obtain an audit of its accounts for the year in accordance with s. 476; and	s. 475(3)(a)	
	(c) the directors acknowledge their responsibilities for complying with the requirements of the *Companies Act* 2006 with respect to accounting records and the preparation of accounts.	s. 475(3)(b)	
	[Guidance] *The requirements for accounting records and preparation of accounts are set out in s. 386 and s. 393–414 respectively. However, there is no requirement to elaborate on these requirements or refer to the section numbers in the balance sheet statement.* *The wording in (a) to (c) above follows the Companies House suggested wording.*		
15.06	The registered number of the company must be shown in a prominent position on the balance sheet or one of the other documents required to be filed under the Companies Act.	s. 1068(3)(c)	
15.07	An entity shall disclose on the balance sheet:	s. 414(1) & (2)	
	(b) the name of the director who signed on behalf of the board; and		
	(c) if a copy of the accounts is sent to Companies House, that copy must include the signature of that director.		
15.08	If the company is a parent company **not** preparing group accounts, complete **Appendix 3**.		
15.09	If the company is a parent company voluntarily preparing group accounts, reference should be made to CCH Preparing FRS 102 Accounts.		

SMALL COMPANY ACCOUNTS CHECKLIST – APPENDIX 1

A1   Appendix 1

Audited accounts

	Directors' report	*Reference*	*Y, N, N/A*

A1.01	Where accounts require an audit, include a statement of directors' responsibilities either as part of the directors' report or as a separate statement. This statement should include the following points:
	
	(a) that the directors are responsible for preparing the Directors' Report and the financial statements in accordance with applicable law and regulations and in accordance with United Kingdom Generally Accepted Accounting Practice;
	
	(b) that company law requires the directors must not approve the financial statements unless they are satisfied that they give a true and fair view of the state of affairs of the company and of the profit or loss of the company for that period;
	
	(c) that in preparing the financial statements the directors are required to:
	
	   (i) select suitable accounting policies and then apply them consistently;
	
	   (ii) make judgements and accounting estimates that are reasonable and prudent;
	
	   (iii) state whether applicable accounting standards have been followed, subject to any material departures disclosed and explained in the financial statements; and
	
	   (iv) prepare the financial statements on the going concern basis unless it is inappropriate to presume that the company will continue in business.
	
	(d) that the directors are responsible for keeping adequate accounting records that are sufficient to show and explain the company's transactions and disclose with reasonable accuracy at any time the financial position of the company and that enable them to ensure that the financial statements comply with the Companies Act;
	
	(e) that the directors are responsible for safeguarding the assets of the company and hence for taking reasonable steps for the prevention and detection of fraud and other irregularities; and
	
	(f) that, where appropriate, the directors are responsible for the maintenance and integrity of the corporate and financial information included on the company's website. It is important to bear in mind that legislation in the United Kingdom governing the preparation and dissemination of financial statements may differ from legislation in other jurisdictions.
		FRC Bulletin-2010/2	

	[Guidance] *The requirements of Bulletin 2010/2 (Revised March 2012) are persuasive rather than prescriptive; however they do represent best practice, hence they are included in this checklist.*		

A1.02	Where accounts require an audit, the directors' report must contain a statement to the effect that, in the case of each of the persons who are directors at the time when the report is approved, the following applies:	s. 418(2)	
	(a) so far as each director is aware, there is no relevant audit information (information needed by the company's auditors in connection with preparing their report) of which the company's auditors are unaware; and		
	(b) each director has taken all the steps that he ought to have taken as a director in order to make himself aware of any relevant audit information and to establish that the company's auditors are aware of that information.		
	Auditor's report		
A1.03	An ISA style report in accordance with Bulletin 2010/2 (Revised March 2012).	FRC Bulletin-2010/2	
A1.04	The term 'Independent Auditor' should be used in the title of the auditors' report.	FRC Bulletin-2010/2	
A1.05	The auditor's report should include an explanation of the respective responsibilities of directors and auditor.	ISA 700-15, FRC Bulletin-2010/2	
A1.06	The scope paragraph of the auditor's report shall, either:	s. 495(2)b ISA 700-16, FRC Bulletin-2010/2	
	(a) Cross refer to a 'Statement of the Scope of an Audit' that is maintained on the FRC's website; or		
	(b) Cross refer to a 'Statement of the Scope of an Audit' that is included elsewhere within the Annual Report; or		
	(c) Include the description of the scope of an audit included in Bulletin 2010/2 (Revised March 2012), as amended by FRC Bulletin 4 (April 2014).		
A1.07	Detailed contents of the audit report		
	The auditor's report must:		
	(a) have an appropriate title;	ISA 700-12	
	(b) be appropriately addressed;	ISA 700-13	
	(c) identify the financial statements of the entity that have been audited, including the date of, and period covered by, the financial statements and include an introduction identifying the financial reporting framework that has been applied in their preparation;	s. 495(2)(a) ISA 700-14	
	(d) include a statement that those charged with governance are responsible for the preparation of the financial statements and a statement that the responsibility of the auditor is to audit and express an opinion on the financial statements in accordance with applicable legal requirements and International Standards on Auditing (UK and Ireland);	ISA 700-15	
	(e) state that those Standards on Auditing require the auditor to comply with the APB's Ethical Standards for Auditors;	ISA 700-15	
	(f) state clearly whether in the auditor's opinion the annual accounts have been properly prepared in accordance with the requirements of this Act;	s. 495(3)(c) ISA 700-17	
	(g) state in particular whether the annual accounts give a true and fair view, in accordance with the relevant financial reporting framework:	ISA 700-18	
	(i) in the case of an individual balance sheet, of the state of affairs of the company as at the end of the financial year;	s. 495(3)(a)(i)	
	(ii) in the case of an individual profit and loss account, of the profit or loss of the company for the financial year;	s. 495(3)(a)(ii)	

	(iii)	in the case of group accounts, of the state of affairs as at the end of the financial year and of the profit or loss for the financial year, of the undertakings included in the consolidation as a whole, so far as concerns members of the company;	s. 495(3)(a)(iii)
	(iv)	have been properly prepared in accordance with the relevant financial reporting framework;	s. 495(3)(b)
(h)		state whether, in his opinion, based on the work undertaken in the course of the audit:	
	(i)	the information given in the strategic report (if any) and the directors' report is consistent with the financial statements; and	s. 496(a)(i)
	(ii)	any such strategic report and the directors' report have been prepared in accordance with applicable legal requirements;	s. 496(a)(ii)
(i)		state whether, in the light of the knowledge and understanding of the company and its environment obtained in the course of the audit, he has identified material misstatements in the strategic report (if any) and the directors' report;	s. 496(b)
(j)		if applicable, give an indication of the nature of each of the misstatements referred to in (i) above.	s. 496(c)
(k)		be either unqualified or qualified;	s. 495(4)(a)
(l)		include a reference to any matters to which the auditor wishes to draw attention by way of emphasis without qualifying the report;	s. 495(4)(b)
(m)		when an auditor is engaged to issue an opinion on the compliance of the financial statements with an additional financial reporting framework the second opinion shall be clearly separated from the first opinion on the financial statements, by use of an appropriate heading;	ISA 700-19
(n)		when the auditor addresses other reporting responsibilities within the auditor's report on the financial statements, the opinion arising from such other responsibilities shall be set out in a separate section of the auditor's report following the opinion[s] on the financial statements;	ISA 700-21
(o)		if the auditor is required to report on certain matters by exception the auditor shall describe its responsibilities under the heading 'Matters on which we are required to report by exception' and incorporate a suitable conclusion in respect of such matters;	ISA 700-22
(p)		the date of an auditor's report on a reporting entity's financial statements shall be the date on which the auditor signed the report expressing an opinion on those financial statements;	ISA 700-23
(q)		the auditor shall not sign, and hence date, the report earlier than the date on which all other information contained in a report of which the audited financial statements form a part have been approved by those charged with governance and the auditor has considered all necessary available evidence;	ISA 700-24
(r)		the report shall name the location of the office where the auditor is based; and	ISA 700-25
(s)		the auditor's report shall state the name of the auditor and be signed and dated.	ISA 700-26

A1.08	The auditor must state in his report if in his opinion:		
	(a) adequate accounting records have not been kept by the company;	s. 498(2)(a)	
	(b) proper returns adequate for their audit have not been received from branches not visited by him;	s. 498(2)(a)	
	(c) the company's accounts are not in agreement with the accounting records and returns;	s. 498(2)(b)	
	(d) all the information and explanations necessary for the purposes of his audit have not been obtained;	s. 498(3)	
	(e) the directors have prepared the accounts in accordance with the small companies regime when not eligible;	s. 498(4), 498(5)(a)	
	(f) the directors have taken advantage of small companies exemption in preparing the directors' report when not eligible; and	s. 498(5)(b)	
	(g) the directors have taken advantage of small companies exemption from the requirement to prepare a strategic report when not eligible.	s. 498(5)(b)	
A1.09	If the disclosure requirements concerning directors' emoluments are not complied with in the annual accounts, the auditor must give the required particulars in his report, so far as he is reasonably able to do so.	s. 498(4)	
A1.10	If the audit report is qualified and the company proposes to make a distribution, the auditor must state whether, in his opinion, the matter in respect of which his report is qualified is material for determining whether the distribution would contravene the Companies Act provisions. This may form part of the normal audit report, or be submitted subsequently in writing.	s. 837(4)(a)	
A1.11	Include the Bannerman wording as recommended by ICAEW Technical Release Audit 1/03.		
A1.12	For the name of auditor, state:		
	(a) where the auditor is not an individual, the name of the senior statutory auditor;	s. 503(3), 505(1)(a)	
	[Guidance] *Client's copy of accounts* *The signed copy of the report issued to the client must be signed personally by the senior statutory auditor in their own name for and on behalf of the firm.*		
	(b) where the auditor is not an individual, the name of the audit firm; and	s. 505(1)(a)	
	[Guidance] *Companies House copy of accounts* *The copy of the report delivered to Companies House need not be signed (by the senior statutory auditor or the audit firm). Signed copies of the report for other purposes may be signed in the name of the firm by any RI.*		
	(c) that the firm are Statutory Auditors.	s. 505	
A1.13	When the prior year's financial statements are not audited, the incoming auditor should state in the auditor's report that the corresponding figures are unaudited.	ISA 700-19	

	Notes to the financial statements		
A1.14	Disclose the following in respect of auditors remuneration: (a) the amount of any remuneration receivable by the company's auditor for the auditing of the accounts; (b) the nature of any benefits in kind; (c) the estimated monetary value of any benefits in kind; and (d) where more than one person has been appointed as a company's auditor during the period: separate disclosure in respect of the remuneration for each such person.	SI 2008/489-4(1)	
A1.15	Where a company does not disclose information concerning auditor's remuneration because that information is required to be disclosed in the group accounts on a consolidated basis: give a statement to that effect.	SI 2008/489-6(3)	
A1.16	A company, which has entered into a liability limitation agreement with its auditor, must disclose: (a) its principal terms; (b) the date of the resolution approving the agreement; and (c) in the case of a private company, the date of the resolution waiving the need for such approval.	SI 2008/489-8	
	[Guidance] *The accounts in which disclosure is required are those for the financial year to which the agreement relates unless the agreement was entered into too late for it to be reasonably practical for the disclosure to be made, in which case disclosure should be made in the company's next following annual accounts.*		

SMALL COMPANY ACCOUNTS CHECKLIST – APPENDIX 2

A2   Appendix 2

Assurance review report

		Reference	Y, N, N/A
A2.01	Is the report consistent with that in TECH 09/13 Assurance review engagements on historical financial statements in respect of the following: (a) Title; (b) Introductory paragraphs; (c) Directors' responsibility; (d) Accountants' responsibility; (e) Scope of the assurance review; (f) Conclusion.	TECH 09/13	

SMALL COMPANY ACCOUNTS CHECKLIST – APPENDIX 3

A3   Appendix 3

Parent company not preparing group accounts

		Reference	Y, N, N/A
A3.01	Where the company is exempt from the requirement to prepare group accounts because it is itself a subsidiary undertaking, the company must: (a) disclose in the notes to its individual accounts that it is exempt from the obligation to prepare and deliver group accounts; and (b) state in its individual accounts: (i) the name of the parent undertaking which draws up group accounts; and (ii) the address of the undertaking's registered office (whether in or outside the United Kingdom), or if it is unincorporated, the address of its principal place of business.	s. 400(1),(2), s. 401(1),(2)	
	[Guidance] *Basis of intermediate company exemption* *This exemption is only available if:* *(a) the immediate parent undertaking is established under the law of an EEA state;* *(b) the company is a wholly owned subsidiary, or the company is a 90% or more subsidiary and the remaining shareholders have approved the exemption, or the company is a more than 50% but less than 90% subsidiary and notice requesting the preparation of group accounts has not been served on the company by the shareholders holding in aggregate at least 5% of the company's shares;* *(c) the company is included in consolidated accounts for a larger group which are drawn up to the same date, or an earlier date in the same financial year, by apparent undertaking established under the law of an EEA State and in accordance with the provisions of Directive 2013/34/EU of the European Parliament and of the Council on the annual financial statements, consolidated financial statements and related reports of certain types of undertakings, or in accordance with international accounting standards;* *(d) the consolidated accounts are audited; and* *(e) a copy of the consolidated accounts and audit report are filed at Companies House with a certified translation if not in English.*		
A3.02	Where advantage is taken of the exemption to restrict information relating to certain foreign undertakings (with the agreement of the Secretary of State), state that fact in a note to the accounts.	s. 409(5)	
A3.03	State the number, description and amount of any shares in the company which are held by subsidiary undertakings, with the exception of certain trustee holdings (see the Act for details).	R-C Sch. 2.4(1)	

A3.04	Show the amounts of any guarantees and financial commitments, analysing between any amounts relating to parent or fellow subsidiary undertakings, and any amounts relating to subsidiary undertakings of the company itself, and include:	R-C Sch. 1.57(6)	
	(a) particulars of any charge on the assets and, where practicable, the amount secured;		
	(b) the nature, security and estimated amount of any unprovided contingent liability;		
	(c) capital expenditure contracted for but not provided for;		
	(d) particulars of any pension commitment (specifying whether provided for or not, and showing separately amounts relating wholly or partly to past directors); and		
	(e) particulars of any other financial commitments which have not been provided for and are relevant to assessing the company's state of affairs.		

SMALL COMPANY ACCOUNTS CHECKLIST – APPENDIX 4

A4   Appendix 4

		Reference	Y, N, N/A
Political donations			
A4.01	Where the company is not itself the wholly owned subsidiary of a UK incorporated company and has made any donation to any EU political party, other EU political organisation or independent election candidate, or incurred any political expenditure, and it does not have subsidiaries which have made such contributions, and the amount of the donation or expenditure, or the aggregate amount of all such donations, exceeds £2,000 disclose: (a) the name of each EU political party, other EU political organisation or independent election candidate to whom any such donation has been made; (b) the total amount given to that party, organisation or candidate by way of such donations in the financial year; and (c) the total amount of political expenditure incurred within the financial year.	R-C Sch. 5.2(2)	
A4.02	Where the company is not itself the wholly owned subsidiary of a UK incorporated company and any of the company's subsidiaries have made any donation to any EU political party, other EU political organisation or independent election candidate, or incurred any political expenditure, and the total amount of any such donations or expenditure (or both) made or incurred in that year by the company and the subsidiaries between them exceeds £2,000, the company must disclose in respect of it and its subsidiaries: (a) the name of each EU political party, other EU political organisation or independent election candidate to whom any such donation has been made; (b) the total amount given to that party, organisation or candidate by way of such donations in the financial year; and (c) the total amount of political expenditure incurred within the financial year.	R-C Sch. 5.2(3)	
A4.03	Where the company is not itself the wholly owned subsidiary of a UK incorporated company and the company has made any contribution to a non-EU political party, and it does not have any subsidiaries which have made such contributions, disclose: (a) a statement of the amount of the contribution; or (b) where the company has made two or more such contributions in the year, a statement of the total amount of the contributions.	R-C Sch. 5.3(1)	
	[Guidance] *Definition of Contribution & Non-EU political party* *Contribution, in relation to an organisation, means:* *(a) any gift of money to the organisation (whether made directly or indirectly);* *(b) any subscription or other fee paid for affiliation to, or membership of, the organisation; or* *(c) any money spent (otherwise than by the organisation or a person acting on its behalf) in paying any expenses incurred directly or indirectly by the organisation.*		

			273
	Non-EU political party means any political party which carries on, or proposes to carry on, its activities wholly outside the EU member states. *(SI 2008/410-L Sch. 7.4(3) & (4))*		
A4.04	Where any of the company's subsidiaries have made any contribution to a non-EU political party, disclose the total amount of the contributions made in the year by the company and the subsidiaries between them.	R-C Sch. 5.3(2)	

Appendix F   Micro-entities accounts checklist

The table below contains an accounts disclosure checklist for micro-entities based on FRS 105 to be applied for accounting periods commencing on or after 1 January 2016, or from 1 January 2015 should the directors wish to adopt the requirements early.

The Micro-Entities' Accounts Regulations are effective in respect of financial years ended on or after 30 September 2013, and FRS 105 is effective for accounting periods commencing on or after 1 January 2016 (although early adoption is permitted).

The checklist assumes that the company meets the definition of a micro-entity (**Chapter 5**) and that the directors wish to take full advantage of the exemptions available. It also assumes that the accounts are unaudited due to the available audit exemption being taken.

Legislation sources are references to section numbers in the *Companies Act* 2006 and to schedule numbers in *Small Companies and Groups (Accounts and Directors' Report) Regulations* 2008 (SI 2008/409), both as amended by *Small Companies (Micro-Entities' Accounts) Regulations* 2013 (SI 2013/3008) and by *Companies, Partnerships and Groups (Accounts and Reports) Regulations* 2015 (SI 2015/980). FRS 105 Source references refer to the Financial Reporting Standard applicable to the Micro-Entities Regime.

The checklist provides only a summary of the requirements. It is recommend that reference is also made to both example accounts (see **Chapter 14**) and to underlying legislation and standards.

MICRO-ENTITY ACCOUNTS CHECKLIST			
Client		**Year-end**	
		Reference	*Y, N, N/A*
1	**General**		
1.01	The accounts must state: (a) the part of the United Kingdom in which the company is registered; (b) the company's registered number; (c) whether the company is a public or private company and whether it is limited by shares or guarantee; (d) the address of the company's registered office; (e) where appropriate, the fact that the company is being wound up; (f) the name of the company and any change in its name since the end of the preceding reporting period; (g) the date of the end of the reporting period and the period covered by the financial statements; (h) the presentation currency; and (i) the level of rounding, if any, used in presenting amounts in the financial statements.	s. 396(A1) FRS 105-3.13	
2	**Formats**		

2.01	Prepare accounts in accordance with the prescribed format headings as set out below:
	(a) **Balance sheet format 1.**
	   Called up share capital not paid;
	   Fixed assets;
	   Current assets;
		Sch. 1, Section C, FRS 105-4.3, 5.3	

	Prepayments and accrued income; Creditors: amounts falling due within one year; Net current assets/(liabilities); Total assets less current liabilities; Creditors: amounts falling due after more than one year; Provisions for liabilities; Accruals and deferred income; Capital and reserves. (b) **Profit and loss account.** Turnover; Other income; Cost of raw materials and consumables; Staff costs; Depreciation and other amounts written off assets; Other charges; Tax; Profit or loss.		
2.02	In respect of every item shown in the company's financial statements the corresponding amount for the accounting period immediately preceding that to which the financial statements relate shall also be shown.	Sch. 1.7(1), FRS 105-3.7	
2.03	Where a corresponding amount is not comparable with the amount to be shown for the item in question in respect of the accounting period to which the balance sheet or profit and loss account relate: (a) the former amount shall be adjusted; and (b) particulars of the adjustment and the reasons for it shall be disclosed in a note to the financial statements.	Sch. 1.7(2), FRS 105-3.6	
3	**Directors' report**		
	There is no requirement for a company qualifying as a micro-entity to prepare a Directors' report and therefore a disclosure checklist is not included in this product. If a Directors' report is prepared then the checklist for small companies (checklist 3) should be used for guidance.	s. 415(1)(A)	
4	**Accountant's reports**		
	Accountant's reports on the compilation of financial statements		
	*For **ICAEW** firms, the provisions of AAF 02/10 as set out in 4.01 and 4.02 below are not a requirement. However, they are best practice and hence have been included in this checklist.* *For **ACCA** firms, the wording of question 4.01 is based on AAF 02/10 issued by the ICAEW, which itself is based on the CCAB compilation report issued in November 2010. The equivalent guidance for ACCA members is Technical Factsheet 163: Audit Exempt Companies – ACCA Accounts Preparation Report. The requirements are very similar, except Factsheet 163 refers to the ACCA rather than the ICAEW, the ACCA ethical guidelines and other professional requirements website at www.accaglobal.com/gb/en/member/ professional-standards/rules-standards.html and the final paragraph states the firm has not been instructed to carry out an audit or a review of the accounts.*		
4.01	Does the accountant's report on the financial statements of the company include: (a) a title identifying the persons to whom the report is addressed (usually the Board of Directors) and including the words 'Chartered Accountant's/Accountants' Report to .... ;	AAF 02/10	

	(b) a statement that, in order to assist the directors to fulfil their duties under the *Companies Act* 2006, the accountants have prepared for the directors' approval the financial statements which comprise [*either*: state the primary financial statements such as the Profit and Loss Account, the Balance Sheet, the Cash Flow Statement, the Statement of Total Recognised Gains and Losses and the related notes] [*or*: as set out on pages x-x] from the company's accounting records and information and explanations supplied by the client;		
	(c) a statement that the accountant is a practising member/ member firm of the Institute of Chartered Accountants in England and Wales and is subject to its ethical and other professional requirements which are detailed at icaew.com/ membershandbook;		
	(d) *Optional paragraph*. A statement that the report is made to the Company's Board of Directors as a body in accordance with the terms of engagement. An explanation as to the work carried out being in accordance with the requirements of ICAEW guidance and the purpose of the work and that, to the fullest extent permitted by law, no responsibility will be accepted for the work or the report to anyone other than the Company and the Company's Board of Directors, as a body;		
	(e) *Optional paragraph*. A statement that the directors have acknowledged their duty to ensure that the company has kept adequate accounting records and to prepare statutory accounts that give a true and fair view of the assets, liabilities, financial position and profit or loss of the company and that they consider that the company is exempt from the statutory audit requirement for the year;		
	(f) *Optional paragraph*. A statement that the accountants have not been instructed to carry out an audit or a review of the accounts of the company and that for this reason, they have not verified the accuracy or completeness of the accounting records or information and explanations given to them and they do not, therefore, express any opinion on the statutory accounts;		
	(g) the name and signature of the accountant and any appropriate designation (but not 'Registered Auditor'/'Statutory Auditor'); and		
	(h) the date of the report.		
4.02	Do the financial statements contain a reference to the fact that they are unaudited either on the front cover or on each page of the financial statements?	AAF 02/10	
5	**Directors' advances, credits and guarantees**		
5.01	Disclose details, at the foot of the balance sheet, of:	s. 472(1A),	
	(a) for each advance or credit granted by the company to a director disclose: (i) its amount; (ii) an indication of the interest rate; (iii) its main conditions; (iv) any amounts repaid; (v) any amounts written off; and (vi) any amounts waived.	s. 413(1)(a), s. 413(3), FRS 105-6A.1	
	(b) also disclose in the notes: (i) the total of amounts stated in (a)(i); (iii) the total of amounts stated in (a)(iv); (iv) the total of amounts stated in (a)(v); and (v) the total of amounts stated in (a)(vi);	s. 413(5) FRS 105-6A.1	

	(c) guarantees of any kind entered into by the company on behalf of its directors, must be shown in the notes to its individual accounts. For each guarantee disclose:
	    (i) its main terms;
	    (ii) the amount of the maximum liability that may be incurred by the company (or its subsidiary); and
	    (iii) any amount paid and any liability incurred by the company (or its subsidiary) for the purpose of fulfilling the guarantee (including any loss incurred by reason of enforcement of the guarantee); and
		s. 413(1)(b),
		s. 413(4),
		FRS 105-6A.1	

	(d) also disclose in the notes:
	    (i) the total of amounts stated in (c)(ii); and
	    (ii) the total of amounts stated in (c)(iii).
		s. 413(5),
		FRS 105-6A.1	

	Note 1. The disclosure required re (a) and (c) is in respect of each advance or credit granted or guarantee. There is limited guidance where there are numerous transactions with a director during the year in the form of a director's current account. Where disclosure of such information is given in an aggregated or summarised form, this fact will need to be disclosed. *Note 2. S. 413 does not require disclosure of the name of the director to whom an advance is made or credit granted.*		
6	**Other disclosures**		
6.01	Disclose, at the foot of the balance sheet, the total amount of each of the following that are not included in the balance sheet: (a) financial commitments; (b) guarantees; and (c) contingencies.	Sch. 1.57(1), FRS 105-6A.2, 9.28, 11.9, 12.28, 13.17, 14.3, 15.17, 15.33, 16.19, 23.22, 27.5	
6.02	Disclose, at the foot of the balance sheet, an indication of the nature and form of any variable security given by the company for each class of the following: (a) financial commitments; (b) guarantees; and (c) contingencies.	Sch. 1.57(2), FRS 105-6A.3, 9.29, 10.22, 12.29, 13.18, 27.6	
6.03	Disclose, at the foot of the balance sheet, the total amount of any financial commitments included above concerning pensions, in particular, when a micro company participates in a defined benefit multi-employer plan, include a description of the extent to which it can be liable to the plan for other entities' obligations under the terms and conditions of the multi-employer plan.	Sch. 1.57(3), FRS 105-6A.2, 23.22	
6.04	Disclose separately, at the foot of the balance sheet, the total amount of any financial commitments included above which are undertaken on behalf of or for the benefit of: (a) any parent undertaking, fellow subsidiary undertaking or any subsidiary undertaking of the company, or (b) any undertaking in which the company has a participating interest.	Sch. 1.57(4), FRS 105-6A.2	
6.05	An entity shall disclose on the balance sheet: (a) the date when the financial statements were approved by the board of directors; and (b) the name of the director who signed on behalf of the board and, if a copy of the accounts is sent to Companies House, that copy must include the signature of that director.	s. 414(1) & (2)	
6.06	The balance sheet must contain, in a prominent position above the signature of the directors, a statement that the financial statements are prepared in accordance with the micro-entity provisions of the *Companies Act* 2006.	s. 414(3), FRS 105-3.14	

6.07	If the company is taking advantage of the exemption from an audit available under s. 477 (small companies) or s. 480 (dormant companies), the balance sheet must contain a statement by the directors, above the director's signature to the effect that, for the year in question:		
	(a) the company was entitled to exemption from audit under s. 477 (or s. 480 as appropriate);	s. 475(2)	
	(b) the members have not required the company to obtain an audit of its accounts for the year in accordance with s. 476; and	s. 475(3)(a)	
	(c) the directors acknowledge their responsibilities for complying with the requirements of the *Companies Act* 2006 with respect to accounting records and the preparation of accounts.	s. 475(3)(b)	
	Note. The requirements for accounting records and preparation of accounts are set out in s. 386 and s. 393–414 respectively. However, there is no requirement to elaborate on these requirements or refer to the section numbers in the balance sheet statement.		
	The wording in (a) to (c) above follows the Companies House suggested wording.		
6.08	If the company includes additional information in the notes to the financial statements to the micro-entity minimum accounting items, include the disclosure required by the Small Entities of FRS 102, section 1A (see checklist 3) that relates to that information.	FRS 105-1.3 & 6.1	

Appendix G   Small company abridged accounts checklist

The option to prepare abridged accounts is available to small companies, if they have the consent of all of their members. Such abridged accounts are not available to micro-entities (though, they would hardly be necessary given the very limited disclosure requirements in micro-entity accounts – see **Chapter 7**). The checklist does not cover LLPs as at the time of writing legislation has yet to be passed to update the LLP Regulations enabling the use of abridged accounts.

The references to legislation shown in this checklist are as follows:

s – *Companies Act* 2006 section number.

R-C – Accounts Regulations for Companies in the *Small Companies and Groups (Accounts and Directors' Report) Regulations* 2008 (SI 2008/409) as amended by the *Companies, Partnerships and Groups (Accounts and Reports) Regulations* 2015 (SI 2015/980).

FRS 102 – FRS 102 The Financial Reporting Standard applicable in the UK and the Republic of Ireland inclusive of July 2015 amendments for small entities.

Appendices are included as follows, which should only be completed as appropriate:

Appendix 1   Audited accounts.

Appendix 2   Assurance review report.

Appendix 3   Parent company not preparing group accounts.

Appendix 4   Political donations.

The checklist includes the format 1 Abridged Balance Sheet and the format 1 Abridged Profit and Loss Account for a small company preparing abridged accounts in accordance with paragraph 1(A) of the Small Company Accounts Regulations on condition that all of the members of the company have consented to the drawing up of the abridged balance sheet and abridged profit and loss account.

Details of the format 2 Abridged Balance Sheet and the format 2 Abridged Profit and Loss Account can be found in **Chapter 11**.

Checklist for small company abridged accounts

ABRIDGED ACCOUNTS – MAIN CHECKLIST

Client		Year-end	
		Reference	Y, N, N/A
1	**DIRECTORS' REPORT**		
1.01	The directors' report for a financial year must state the names of the persons who, at any time during the financial year, were directors of the company.	s. 416(1)(a)	
1.02	If the company employs more than an average monthly number of 250 UK employees, give a statement describing the policy during the year in respect of disabled persons regarding consideration to applications for employment, continuing their employment and their training, career development and promotion.	R-C Sch. 5.5(3)	
1.03	If the company has made any political donations, complete **Appendix 4**.		
1.04	A statement must be made where a qualifying third party indemnity provision is, at the time the report is approved, or was, at any time during the financial year, in force for the benefit of one or more directors of the company or of an associated company.	s. 236(1)	
1.05	If advantage is taken of any of the exemptions to the directors' report available to small companies, then the report must contain a statement that it is prepared in accordance with the small companies regime in a prominent position above the signature.	s. 419(2)	
1.06	The name of the director or secretary who has signed the directors' report on behalf of the board of directors to indicate their approval of the report.	s. 419(1)	
2	**AUDITOR'S AND ACCOUNTANT'S REPORTS**		
	Auditor's reports		
2.01	If an audit report is to be given, complete **Appendix 1**.		
	Assurance review report		
2.02	If an assurance review report is to be given, complete **Appendix 2**. **Accountant's reports on the compilation of financial statements** *For **ICAEW** firms, the provisions of AAF 02/10 as set out in 2.03 and 2.04 below are not a requirement. However, they are best practice and hence have been included in this checklist.* *For **ACCA** firms, the wording of question 2.13 is based on AAF 02/10 issued by the ICAEW, which itself is based on the CCAB compilation report issued in November 2010. The equivalent guidance for ACCA members is Technical Factsheet 163: Audit Exempt Companies – ACCA Accounts Preparation Report. The requirements are very similar, except <u>Factsheet 163</u> refers to the ACCA rather than the ICAEW, the ACCA ethical guidelines and other professional requirements website at www.accaglobal.com/gb/en/member/ professional-standards/rules-standards.html and the final paragraph states the firm has not been instructed to carry out an audit or a review of the accounts.*		
2.03	Does the accountant's report on the financial statements of the company include: (a) a title identifying the persons to whom the report is addressed (usually the Board of Directors) and including the words 'Chartered Accountant's/Accountants' Report to ....';	AAF 02/10	

	(b) a statement that, in order to assist the directors to fulfil their duties under the Companies Act 2006, the accountants have prepared for the directors' approval the financial statements which comprise [*either*: state the primary financial statements such as the Profit and Loss Account, the Balance Sheet, the Cash Flow Statement, the Statement of Total Recognised Gains and Losses and the related notes] [*or*: as set out on pages x-x] from the company's accounting records and information and explanations supplied by the client;		
	(c) a statement that the accountant is a practising member/ member firm of the Institute of Chartered Accountants in England and Wales and is subject to its ethical and other professional requirements which are detailed at icaew.com/members handbook;		
	(d) *Optional paragraph.* A statement that the report is made to the Company's Board of Directors as a body in accordance with the terms of engagement. An explanation as to the work carried out being in accordance with the requirements of ICAEW guidance and the purpose of the work and that, to the fullest extent permitted by law, no responsibility will be accepted for the work or the report to anyone other than the Company and the Company's Board of Directors, as a body;		
	(e) *Optional paragraph.* A statement that the directors have acknowledged their duty to ensure that the company has kept adequate accounting records and to prepare statutory accounts that give a true and fair view of the assets, liabilities, financial position and profit or loss of the company and that they consider that the company is exempt from the statutory audit requirement for the year;		
	(f) *Optional paragraph.* A statement that the accountants have not been instructed to carry out an audit or a review of the accounts of the company and that for this reason, they have not verified the accuracy or completeness of the accounting records or information and explanations given to them and they do not, therefore, express any opinion on the statutory accounts;		
	(g) the name and signature of the accountant and any appropriate designation (but not 'Registered Auditor'/'Statutory Auditor'); and		
	(h) the date of the report.		
2.04	Do the financial statements contain a reference to the fact that they are unaudited either on the front cover or on each page of the financial statements?	AAF 02/10	
3	**FINANCIAL STATEMENTS PRESENTATION**		
	Compliance with FRS 102		
3.01	The accounts must disclose any additional information that is necessary to show a true and fair view.	s. 396(4), FRS 102-1A.6	
3.02	Present a complete set of financial statements including all of the following:	FRS 102-1A.8	
	(a) a statement of financial position as at the reporting date;		
	(b) an income statement for the reporting period; and		
	(c) notes.		
3.03	When an entity departs from a requirement of FRS 102 in accordance with paragraph 3.4, or from a requirement of applicable legislation, it shall disclose the following:	s. 396(5), FRS 102-3.5	
	(a) that management has concluded that the financial statements give a true and fair view of the entity's financial position, financial performance and, when required to be presented, cash flows;		

	(b) that it has complied with FRS 102 or applicable legislation, except that it has departed from a particular requirement of this FRS or applicable legislation to the extent necessary to give a true and fair view;		
	(c) the nature and effect of the departure;		
	(d) the treatment that FRS 102 or applicable legislation would require;		
	(e) the reason why that treatment would be so misleading in the circumstances that it would conflict with the objective of financial statements set out in FRS 102, section 2; and		
	(f) the treatment adopted.		
3.04	When an entity has departed from a requirement of FRS 102 or applicable legislation in a prior period, and that departure affects the amounts recognised in the financial statements for the current period, it shall disclose: (a) the nature of the departure; (b) the treatment that FRS 102 or applicable legislation would require; (c) the reason why that treatment would be so misleading in the circumstances that it would conflict with the objective of financial statements set out in FRS 102, section 2; and (d) the treatment adopted.	FRS 102-3.6	
3.05	If it appears to the small entity that there are special reasons for departing from any of the principles set out in company law in preparing the small entity's financial statements in respect of any reporting period, it may do so, in which disclose in the notes to the financial statements particulars of the departure, the reasons for it, and its effects.	S-C 1.10(2), FRS 102-1AC.10	
	Frequency of reporting		
3.06	When the end of the reporting period changes and the annual financial statements are presented for a period longer or shorter than one year, disclose the following: (a) that fact; (b) the reason for using a longer or shorter period; and (c) the fact that comparative amounts presented in the financial statements (including the related notes) are not entirely comparable.	FRS 102-3.10	
	Consistency of presentation		
3.07	When comparative amounts are reclassified, disclose the following: (a) the nature of the reclassification; (b) the amount of each item or class of items that is reclassified; and (c) the reason for the reclassification.	R-C Sch. 1.7(2), FRS 102-3.12	
3.08	If it is impracticable to reclassify comparative amounts, disclose why reclassification was not practicable.	FRS 102-3.13	
	Comparative information		
3.09	Present comparative information in respect of the preceding period: (a) for all amounts presented in the current period's financial statements unless specifically exempted; and (b) for narrative and descriptive information when it is relevant to an understanding of the current period's financial statements.	R-C Sch. 1.7(1), FRS 102-3.14	

	Materiality and aggregation		
3.10	Present separately: (a) each material class of similar items; and (b) items of a dissimilar nature or function unless they are immaterial.	FRS 102-3.15	
	Identification of the financial statements		
3.11	Display the following information prominently, and repeat it when necessary for an understanding of the information presented: (a) the name of the reporting entity; (b) any change in its name since the end of the preceding reporting period; (c) whether the financial statements cover the individual entity or a group of entities; (d) the date of the end of the reporting period and the period covered by the financial statements; (e) the presentation currency, as defined in FRS 102, section 30; and (f) the level of rounding, if any, used in presenting amounts in the financial statements.	FRS 102-3.23	
3.12	Disclose the following in the notes: (a) the legal form of the entity; (b) its country of incorporation; (c) the address of its registered office (or principal place of business, if different from the registered office).	FRS 102-3.24(a)	
	Formats		
3.13	Disclose in the notes to the accounts the directors' reasons for any change from one format to another.	R-C Sch. 1.2(2)	
4	**STATEMENT OF FINANCIAL POSITION**		

4.01	Present a statement of financial position in accordance with the requirements for a balance sheet set out in Sch. 1 to the Small Companies Accounts Regulations showing at least those items in the chosen format; either Format 1 (see below) or Format 2 (see **Chapter 11**).
	
	 Balance sheet – Format 1 – Abridged accounts
	
	 A Called-up share capital not paid
	
	 B Fixed assets
	    I Intangible assets
	    II Tangible assets
	    III Investments
	
	 C Current assets
	    I Stocks
	    II Debtors
	    III Investments
	    IV Cash at bank and in hand
	
	 D Prepayments and accrued income
	
	 E Creditors: amounts falling due within one year
	
	 F Net current assets (liabilities)
	
	 G Total assets less current liabilities
	
	 H Creditors: amounts falling due after more than one year
		R-C Sch. 1.1A(1), FRS 102-1A.12	

	I **Provisions for liabilities**		
	J **Accruals and deferred income**		
	K **Capital and reserves**		
	I Called-up share capital		
	II Share premium account		
	III Revaluation reserve		
	IV Other reserves		
	V Profit and loss account		
5	**STATEMENT OF COMPREHENSIVE INCOME**		
5.01	Present the profit or loss for the period in an income statement in accordance with the requirements for a profit and loss account set out in Sch. 1 to the Small Companies Accounts Regulations showing at least those items in the chosen format; either Format 1 (see below) or Format 2 (see **Chapter 11**).	R-C Sch. 1.1A(2), FRS 102-1A.14	
	Profit and loss account – Format 1 – Abridged accounts		
	3 Gross profit or loss		
	4 Distribution costs		
	5 Administrative expenses		
	7 Income from shares in group undertakings		
	8 Income from participating interests		
	9 Income from other fixed asset investments		
	10 Other interest receivable and similar income		
	11 Amounts written off investments		
	12 Interest payable and similar expenses		
	13 Tax on profit or loss		
	14 Profit or loss after taxation		
	15 Other taxes not shown under the above items		
	16 Profit or loss for the financial year		
5.02	Show the amount of a company's profit or loss before taxation.	R-C Sch. 1.6	
5.03	Where any amount relating to any previous financial year is included in any item in the profit and loss account, state the effect.	R-C Sch. 1.61(1)	
6	**NOTES TO THE FINANCIAL STATEMENTS**		
6.01	Present sufficient information to meet the requirement for the financial statements to meet the requirements to give a true and fair view of the assets, liabilities, financial position and profit or loss for the reporting period.	FRS 102-1A.16	
6.02	Disclose any provision for permanent diminution in value of fixed assets (including fixed asset investments) if not shown separately in the profit and loss account and, if appropriate, the amount of any provision written back.	R-C Sch. 1.19(3), 1.20(2)	
6.03	Disclose the amount and nature of any individual items of income or expenses of exceptional size or incidence.	R-C Sch. 1.61(2), FRS 102-1AC.32	
6.04	Disclose the average number of persons employed by the small entity in the reporting period.	s. 411 FRS 102-1AC.33	
6.05	Disclose the interest payable and similar expenses on loans from group undertakings.	R-C Sch. 1.9(13)	

7	**ACCOUNTING POLICIES**		
7.01	Disclose the accounting policies adopted by the small entity in determining the amounts to be included in respect of items shown in the statement of financial position and in determining the profit or loss of the small entity (including such policies with respect to the depreciation and impairment of assets).	S-C 1.44, FRS 102-1AC.3	
7.02	If any amount is included in a small entity's statement of financial position in respect of development costs, disclose in the note on accounting policies the following information: (a) the period over which the amount of those costs originally capitalised is being or is to be written off; and (b) the reasons for capitalising the development costs in question.	S-C 1.21(2), FRS 102-1AC.4	
7.03	Where development costs are shown or included as an asset in the small entity's financial statements and the amount is not treated as a realised loss because there are special circumstances justifying this, disclose in a note to the financial statements the reasons for showing development costs as an asset and that it is not a realised loss.	s. 844, FRS 102-1AC.5	
7.04	Where in exceptional cases the useful life of intangible assets cannot be reliably estimated, disclose in a note to the financial statements the period over which those intangible assets are being written off and the reasons for choosing that period.	S-C 1.22(4), FRS 102-1AC.6	
	Changes in presentation and accounting policies and corrections of prior period errors		
7.05	Where there is a change in the presentation of a small entity's statement of financial position or income statement, disclose and explain, in a note to the financial statements in which the new presentation is first used, particulars of any such change, and the reasons for the change.	S-C 1.2(2), FRS 102-1AC.7	
7.06	Where the corresponding amount for the immediately preceding financial year is not comparable with the amount to be shown for the item in question in respect of the reporting period, and the corresponding amount is adjusted, disclose in a note to the financial statements the particulars of the non-comparability and of any adjustment.	S-C 1.7(2), FRS 102-1AC.8	
7.07	Where any amount relating to a preceding reporting period is included in any item in the income statement, disclose the effect.	S-C 1.61(1), FRS 102-1AC.9	
8	**FINANCIAL INSTRUMENTS**		

8.01	Disclose the following for the total of fixed asset investments:
	
	(a) the aggregate amount (on the basis of cost or revaluation):
	
	    (i) at the beginning of the period; and
	    (ii) at the end of the period;
		R-C Sch. 1.48(1) & (2), FRS 102-1AC.12(a)	

	(b) the effect of the following during the period:
	
	    (i) any revaluation;
	    (ii) acquisitions; and
	    (iii) disposals.
		R-C Sch. 1.48(1) & (2), FRS 102-1AC.12(b)	

8.02	Disclose the following for the total of fixed asset investments:
	
	(a) the cumulative amount of provisions for depreciation and impairment of assets:
	
	   (i) at the beginning of the period; and
	   (ii) at the end of the period;
	
	(b) provision for depreciation and impairment during the period;
	(c) adjustments to provisions during the period arising from disposals; and
	(d) other adjustments to provisions during the period.
		R-C Sch. 1.48(3), FRS 102-1AC.13(a)	

8.03	If items of fixed asset investments are stated at revalued amounts: (a) state which items; (b) state in the accounting policies the basis of valuation; and (c) state the comparable amounts of cost and accumulated depreciation on the historical cost basis.	R-C Sch. 1.34, FRS 102-1AC.14,16	
8.04	For revalued fixed asset investments, other than listed investments, show: (a) the year in which they were revalued; (b) the amount of each valuation; and (c) if valued during the year, the names or qualifications of the valuers and the basis of valuation.	R-C Sch. 1.49, FRS 102-1AC.15	
8.05	Where fixed asset investments are measured at revalued amount, disclose the following in tabular form: (a) movements in the revaluation reserve in the reporting period, with an explanation of the tax treatment of items therein; and (b) the carrying amount in the statement of financial position that would have been recognised had the property, plant and equipment not been revalued.	R-C Sch. 1.54(2), FRS 102-1AC.17	
8.06	Where fixed asset investments are measured at revalued amount, disclose the treatment for taxation purposes of amounts credited or debited to the revaluation reserve in a note to the financial statements.	R-C Sch. 1.35(6), FRS 102-1AC.18	
8.07	Disclose provisions for impairment of fixed asset investments in a note to the financial statements if not shown separately in the income statement.	R-C Sch. 1.19(3), FRS 102-1AC.20	
8.08	Disclose in aggregate, provisions for impairment of fixed asset investments that are reversed because the reasons for which they were made cease to apply, in a note to the financial statements if not shown separately in the income statement.	R-C Sch. 1.20(2), FRS 102-1AC.21	
8.09	Where fixed asset investments are included at a valuation which is not market value (e.g. directors' valuation), state the method used and the reason for adopting it.	R-C Sch. 1.32(3)	

8.10	Where financial instruments have been measured at fair value through the profit and loss, disclose:
	
	(a) the significant assumptions underlying the valuation models and techniques used to determine the fair values;
	(b) for each category of financial instrument, the fair value of the assets in that category and the change in value:
	
	   (i) included directly in the income statement; or
	   (ii) credited to or debited from the fair value reserve.
		R-C Sch. 1.51(2) (a), (b), FRS 102-1AC.22	

8.11	Where financial instruments have been measured at fair value through the profit and loss, disclose for each class of derivatives, the extent and nature of the instruments, including significant terms and conditions that may affect the amount, timing and certainty of future cash flows.	R-C Sch. 1.51(2)(c), FRS 102-1AC.23	
8.12	Where any amount is transferred to or from the fair value reserve during the reporting period, disclose in tabular form: (a) the amount of the reserve at the beginning and end of the period; and (b) the amount transferred to or from the reserve during the period.	R-C Sch. 1.51(3), FRS 102-1AC.24	
8.13	Disclose in a note to the financial statements the treatment for taxation purposes of amounts credited or debited to the fair value reserve.	R-C Sch. 1.41(2), FRS 102-1AC.25	
8.14	Give disclosures required by international accounting standards (see section 11 in checklist 4) in respect of financial instruments which are included, in the permitted circumstances, in the accounts at fair value under international accounting standards.	R-C Sch. 1.36(4), FRS 102-1AC.26	
8.15	Disclose for each category of debtor any amounts falling due after one year.	R-C Sch. 1.9(5)	
8.16	Where the amount repayable on any debt owed by the company exceeds the value of the consideration originally received, and the surplus is treated as an asset, it should be subject to annual amortisation, and fully written off before repayment of the debt. If the current amount is not shown separately in the balance sheet, disclose the assets in a note.	R-C Sch. 1.25	

8.17	Disclose the aggregate for all items under creditors of:
	
	(a) the total amount falling due after five years and not repayable by instalments;
	(b) for any amounts payable by instalments, the total amount of those instalments which are payable after five years; and
	(c) in respect of each item shown under 'creditors' in the balance sheet for which security has been given, disclose:
	
	   (i) the aggregate amount of any debts included; and
	   (ii) an indication of the nature and form of security.
		R-C Sch. 1.55(1) & (2), FRS 102-1AC.27, 28	

8.18	The amount of any convertible debts, including debenture loans, must be shown separately from other debts or debentures.	R-C Sch. 1.9(7)(a)	
9	**INVENTORIES**		
	Not used		
10	**INVESTMENT PROPERTY**		
	Not relevant to abridged accounts		
11	**PROPERTY, PLANT AND EQUIPMENT**		

11.01	Disclose the following for the total of tangible fixed assets, including investment property:
	
	(a) the aggregate amount (on the basis of cost or revaluation):
	
	   (i) at the beginning of the period; and
	   (ii) at the end of the period.
	
	(b) the effect of the following during the period:
	
	   (i) any revaluation;
	   (ii) acquisitions; and
	   (iii) disposals.
		R-C Sch. 1.48(1), (2), FRS 102-1AC.12(a)
		
		R-C Sch. 1.48(1), (2), FRS 102-1AC.12(b)	

11.02	Disclose the following for the total of tangible fixed assets:
	
	(a) the cumulative amount of provisions for depreciation and impairment of assets:
	
	   (i) at the beginning of the period; and
	   (ii) at the end of the period;
	
	(b) provision for depreciation and impairment during the period;
	(c) adjustments to provisions during the period arising from disposals; and
	(d) other adjustments to provisions during the period.
		R-C Sch. 1.48(3), FRS 102-1AC.13(a)	

11.03	If items of property, plant and equipment are stated at revalued amounts: (a) state which items; (b) state in the accounting policies the basis of valuation; and (c) state the comparable amounts of cost and accumulated depreciation on the historical cost basis.	R-C Sch. 1.34, FRS 102-1AC. 14,16	
11.04	For revalued property, plant and equipment show: (a) the year in which they were revalued; (b) the amount of each valuation; and (c) if valued during the year, the names or qualifications of the valuers and the basis of valuation.	R-C Sch. 1.49, FRS 102-1AC.15	
11.05	Where property, plant and equipment is measured at revalued amount, disclose the following in tabular form: (a) movements in the revaluation reserve in the reporting period, with an explanation of the tax treatment of items therein; and (b) the carrying amount in the statement of financial position that would have been recognised had the property, plant and equipment not been revalued.	R-C Sch. 1.54(2), FRS 102-1AC.17	
11.06	Where property, plant and equipment is measured at revalued amount, disclose the treatment for taxation purposes of amounts credited or debited to the revaluation reserve in a note to the financial statements.	R-C Sch. 1.35(6), FRS 102-1AC.18	
11.07	Disclose the aggregate amount of any finance cost capitalised and included in the production cost of any asset.	R-C Sch. 1.27(3)(b), FRS 102-1AC.19	
11.08	Disclose provisions for impairment of property, plant and equipment in a note to the financial statements if not shown separately in the income statement.	R-C Sch. 1.19(3), FRS 102-1AC.20	
11.09	Disclose, either separately or in aggregate, provisions for impairment of property, plant and equipment that are reversed because the reasons for which they were made cease to apply, in a note to the financial statements if not shown separately in the income statement.	R-C Sch. 1.20(2), FRS 102-1AC.21	
12	**INTANGIBLE ASSETS**		

12.01	Disclose the following for the total of intangible fixed assets:
	
	(a) the aggregate amount (on the basis of cost or revaluation):
	
	   (i) at the beginning of the period; and
	   (ii) at the end of the period;
	
	(b) the effect of the following during the period:
	
	   (i) any revaluation;
	   (ii) acquisitions; and
	   (iii) disposals.
		R-C Sch. 1.48(1) & (2), FRS 102-1AC.12(a)
		
		R-C Sch. 1.48(1), (2), FRS 102-1AC.12(b)	

12.02	Disclose the following for the total of intangible fixed assets:
	
	(a) the cumulative amount of provisions for depreciation and impairment of assets:
	
	   (i) at the beginning of the period; and
	   (ii) at the end of the period;
	
	(b) provision for depreciation and impairment during the period;
	(c) adjustments to provisions during the period arising from disposals; and
	(d) other adjustments to provisions during the period.
		R-C Sch. 1.48(3), FRS 102-1AC.13(a)	

12.03	If intangible assets are stated at revalued amounts: (a) state which items; (b) state in the accounting policies the basis of valuation; and (c) state the comparable amounts of cost and accumulated depreciation on the historical cost basis.	R-C Sch. 1.34, FRS 102-1AC.14,16	
12.04	For revalued intangible assets show: (a) the year in which they were revalued; (b) the amount of each valuation; and (c) if valued during the year, the names or qualifications of the valuers and the basis of valuation.	R-C Sch. 1.49, FRS 102-1AC.15	
12.05	Where intangible assets are measured at revalued amount, disclose the following in tabular form: (a) movements in the revaluation reserve in the reporting period, with an explanation of the tax treatment of items therein; and (b) the carrying amount in the statement of financial position that would have been recognised had the property, plant and equipment not been revalued.	R-C Sch. 1.54(2), FRS 102-1AC.17	
12.06	Where intangible assets are measured at revalued amount, disclose the treatment for taxation purposes of amounts credited or debited to the revaluation reserve in a note to the financial statements.	R-C Sch. 1.35(6), FRS 102-1AC.18	
12.07	Disclose the aggregate amount of any finance cost capitalised and included in the production cost of any asset.	R-C Sch. 1.27(3)(b), FRS 102-1AC.19	
12.08	Disclose provisions for impairment of intangible assets in a note to the financial statements if not shown separately in the income statement.	R-C Sch. 1.19(3), FRS 102-1AC.20	
12.09	Disclose, either separately or in aggregate, provisions for impairment of intangible assets that are reversed because the reasons for which they were made cease to apply, in a note to the financial statements if not shown separately in the income statement.	R-C Sch. 1.20(2), FRS 102-1AC.21	
12.10	For development costs state: (a) the period of write off; and (b) the reason for capitalising.	R-C Sch. 1.21(2)	
12.11	Where the useful economic life of an intangible asset cannot be reliably estimated and it is being written off over a period not exceeding ten years, disclose: (a) the period chosen; and (b) the reason for choosing that period.	R-C Sch. 1.22(4)	

13	**PROVISIONS AND CONTINGENCIES**		
13.01	Disclose the total amount of each of the following that are not included in the balance sheet: (a) financial commitments; (b) guarantees; and (c) contingencies. *[Guidance]* *FRS 102-1AC.29 indicates that such commitments can arise in a variety of situations, including in relation to group entities, investments, property, plant and equipment, leases and pension obligations.*	R-C Sch. 1.57(1), FRS 102-1AC.29	
13.02	Give an indication of the nature and form of any variable security given by the company for each class of the following: (a) financial commitments; (b) guarantees; and (c) contingencies.	R-C Sch. 1.57(2), FRS 102-1AC.30	
	[Guidance] *FRS 102-1AC.30 indicates that paragraphs 11.46 basic financial instruments, 13.22 inventories, 16.10 investment property, 17.32 property, plant and equipment and 18.28 intangible assets, address similar requirements.*		
13.03	Disclose the total amount of any commitments included in 13.01 above concerning pensions.	R-C Sch. 1.57(3), FRS 102-1AC.29	
13.04	Disclose separately the total amount of any commitments included in 13.01 above which are undertaken on behalf of or for the benefit of: (a) any parent, fellow subsidiary or any subsidiary of the small entity; or (b) any undertaking in which the small entity has a participating interest.	R-C Sch. 1.57(4), FRS 102-1AC.29	
13.05	Disclose the risks or benefits arising from arrangements that the small entity is, or has been a party to during the reporting period, and which are not reflected in the statement of financial position; disclosure should be to the extent necessary to enable the financial position of the small entity to be assessed. *[Guidance]* *FRS 102-1AC.31 states that examples of off-balance sheet arrangements include risk and benefit-sharing arrangements or obligations arising from a contract such as debt factoring, combined sale and repurchase arrangements, consignment stock arrangements, take or pay arrangements, securitisation arranged through separate entities, pledged assets, operating lease arrangements, outsourcing and the like. In many cases the disclosures about financial commitments and contingencies required by 13.01, 13.02, 13.03 and 13.04 above will also address such arrangements.*	s. 410A(2)(a), FRS 102-1AC.31	
14	**RELATED PARTY DISCLOSURES**		
14.01	Where the small entity is a subsidiary, disclose the following information in respect of the parent of the smallest group for which consolidated financial statements are drawn up of which the small entity is a member: (a) the name of the parent which draws up the consolidated financial statements; (b) the address of the parent's registered office (whether in or outside the UK); or (c) if it is unincorporated, the address of its principal place of business.	R-C Sch. 1.65, FRS 102-1AC.34	

14.02	Disclose particulars of material transactions the small entity has entered into that have not been concluded under normal market conditions with: (a) owners holding a participating interest in the small entity; (b) companies in which the small entity itself has a participating interest; and (c) the small entity's directors [or members of its governing body].	R-C Sch. 1.66, FRS 102-1AC.35	
14.03	In particular disclose: (a) the amount of such transactions; (b) the nature of the related party relationship; and (c) other information about the transactions necessary for an understanding of the financial position of the small entity. *[Guidance]* *Information about individual transactions may be aggregated according to their nature, except where separate information is necessary for an understanding of the effects of the related party transactions on the financial position of the small entity.* *Particulars need not be given of transactions entered into between two or more members of a group, provided that any subsidiary which is a party to the transaction is wholly-owned by such a member.*		
14.04	Disclose in the notes to the financial statements the following details of advances and credits granted by the small entity to its directors and guarantees of any kind entered into by the small entity on behalf of its directors: (a) its amount; (b) an indication of the interest rate; (c) its main conditions; (d) any amounts repaid; (e) any amounts written off; (f) any amounts repaid; (g) the total of 'a'; (h) the total of 'd'; (i) the total of 'e'; (j) the total of 'f'.	s. 413, FRS 102-1AC.36	
14.05	Disclose the following details of any guarantees granted on behalf of a director: (a) its main terms; (b) the amount of the maximum liability that may be incurred by the small entity; (c) any amount paid and any liability incurred by the small entity for the purpose of fulfilling the guarantee (including any loss incurred by reason of enforcement of the guarantee); (d) the total of 'b'; (e) the total of 'c'.	s. 413 FRS 102-1AC.36	
15	**OTHER**		
15.01	Disclose in the financial statements: (a) the part of the UK in which the small entity is registered; (b) the small entity's registered number; (c) whether the small entity is a public or a private company and whether the small entity is limited by shares or by guarantee; (d) the address of the small entity's registered office; and (e) where appropriate, the fact that the entity is being wound up.	s. 396, FRS 102-1AC.37	
15.02	Disclose in a note to the financial statements the individual amounts where items to which Arabic numbers are given in any of the formats have been combined, unless they are not material.	R-C Sch. 1.4(3), FRS 102-1AC.38	

15.03	Disclose the nature and financial effect of material events arising after the reporting date which are not reflected in the income statement or statement of financial position.	R-C Sch. 1.64, FRS 102-1AC.39	
15.04	If the accounts are prepared in accordance with the small companies regime, then the balance sheet must contain, above the signature of the directors, a statement that the accounts have been prepared in accordance with the provisions applicable to companies subject to the small companies regime.	s. 414(3)	
15.05	If the company is taking advantage of the exemption from an audit available under s. 477 (small companies) or s. 480 (dormant companies), the balance sheet must contain a statement by the directors, above the director's signature to the effect that, for the year in question:		
	(a) the company was entitled to exemption from audit under s. 477 (or s. 480 as appropriate);	s. 475(2)	
	(b) the members have not required the company to obtain an audit of its accounts for the year in accordance with s. 476; and	s. 475(3)(a)	
	(c) the directors acknowledge their responsibilities for complying with the requirements of the *Companies Act* 2006 with respect to accounting records and the preparation of accounts.	s. 475(3)(b)	
	[Guidance] *The requirements for accounting records and preparation of accounts are set out in s. 386 and s. 393–414 respectively. However, there is no requirement to elaborate on these requirements or refer to the section numbers in the balance sheet statement.* *The wording in (a) to (c) above follows the Companies House suggested wording.*		
15.06	The registered number of the company must be shown in a prominent position on the balance sheet or one of the other documents required to be filed under the Companies Act.	s. 1068(3)(c)	
15.07	An entity shall disclose on the balance sheet:	s. 414(1)&(2)	
	(a) the name of the director/designated member who signed on behalf of the board/members; and		
	(b) if a copy of the accounts is sent to Companies House, that copy must include the signature of that director/designated member.		
15.08	If the company is a parent company **not** preparing group accounts, complete **Appendix 3**.		
15.09	If the company is a parent company voluntarily preparing group accounts, reference should be made to CCH Preparing FRS 102 Accounts.		
15.10	Include a statement that the members have consented to the preparation of abridged accounts (or deliver a separate statement to the Registrar to this effect).	s. 444(2A)	

ABRIDGED ACCOUNTS CHECKLIST – APPENDIX 1

A1   Appendix 1

Audited accounts

	Directors' report	*Reference*	*Y, N, N/A*

A1.01	Where accounts require an audit, include a statement of directors' responsibilities either as part of the directors' report or as a separate statement. This statement should include the following points:
	
	(a) that the directors are responsible for preparing the Directors' Report and the financial statements in accordance with applicable law and regulations and in accordance with United Kingdom Generally Accepted Accounting Practice;
	
	(b) that company law requires the directors must not approve the financial statements unless they are satisfied that they give a true and fair view of the state of affairs of the company and of the profit or loss of the company for that period;
	
	(c) that in preparing the financial statements the directors are required to:
	
	   (i) select suitable accounting policies and then apply them consistently;
	
	   (ii) make judgements and accounting estimates that are reasonable and prudent;
	
	   (iii) state whether applicable accounting standard shave been followed, subject to any material departures disclosed and explained in the financial statements; and
	
	   (iv) prepare the financial statements on the going concern basis unless it is inappropriate to presume that the company will continue in business;
	
	(d) that the directors are responsible for keeping adequate accounting records that are sufficient to show and explain the company's transactions and disclose with reasonable accuracy at any time the financial position of the company and that enable them to ensure that the financial statements comply with the Companies Act;
	
	(e) that the directors are responsible for safeguarding the assets of the company and hence for taking reasonable steps for the prevention and detection of fraud and other irregularities; and
	
	(f) that, where appropriate, the directors are responsible for the maintenance and integrity of the corporate and financial information included on the company's website. It is important to bear in mind that legislation in the United Kingdom governing the preparation and dissemination of financial statements may differ from legislation in other jurisdictions.
	
	[Guidance]
	The requirements of Bulletin 2010/2 (Revised March 2012) are persuasive rather than prescriptive; however they do represent best practice, hence they are included in this checklist.
		FRC Bulletin-2010/2	

A1.02	Where accounts require an audit, the directors' report must contain a statement to the effect that, in the case of each of the persons who are directors at the time when the report is approved, the following applies:	s. 418(2)	
	(a) so far as each director is aware, there is no relevant audit information (information needed by the company's auditors in connection with preparing their report) of which the company's auditors are unaware; and		
	(b) each director has taken all the steps that he ought to have taken as a director in order to make himself aware of any relevant audit information and to establish that the company's auditors are aware of that information.		
	Auditor's report		
A1.03	An ISA style report in accordance with Bulletin 2010/2 (Revised March 2012).	FRC Bulletin-2010/2	
A1.04	The term 'Independent Auditor' should be used in the title of the auditors' report.	FRC Bulletin-2010/2	
A1.05	The auditor's report should include an explanation of the respective responsibilities of directors and auditor.	ISA 700-15, FRC Bulletin-2010/2	
A1.06	The scope paragraph of the auditor's report shall, either:	s. 495(2)(b), ISA 700-16, FRC Bulletin-2010/2	
	(a) Cross refer to a 'Statement of the Scope of an Audit' that is maintained on the FRC's website; or		
	(b) Cross refer to a 'Statement of the Scope of an Audit' that is included elsewhere within the Annual Report; or		
	(c) Include the description of the scope of an audit included in Bulletin 2010/2 (Revised March 2012), as amended by FRC Bulletin 4 (April 2014).		
A1.07	Detailed contents of the audit report The auditor's report must:		
	(a) have an appropriate title;	ISA 700-12	
	(b) be appropriately addressed;	ISA 700-13	
	(c) identify the financial statements of the entity that have been audited, including the date of, and period covered by, the financial statements and include an introduction identifying the financial reporting framework that has been applied in their preparation;	s. 495(2)(a), ISA 700-14	
	(d) include a statement that those charged with governance are responsible for the preparation of the financial statements and a statement that the responsibility of the auditor is to audit and express an opinion on the financial statements in accordance with applicable legal requirements and International Standards on Auditing (UK and Ireland);	ISA 700-15	
	(e) state that those Standards on Auditing require the auditor to comply with the APB's Ethical Standards for Auditors;	ISA 700-15	
	(f) state clearly whether in the auditor's opinion the annual accounts have been properly prepared in accordance with the requirements of this Act;	s. 495(3)(c), ISA 700-17	
	(g) state in particular whether the annual accounts give a true and fair view, in accordance with the relevant financial reporting framework:	ISA 700-18	
	(i) in the case of an individual balance sheet, of the state of affairs of the company as at the end of the financial year;	s. 495(3)(a)(i)	
	(ii) in the case of an individual profit and loss account, of the profit or loss of the company for the financial year;	s. 495(3)(a)(ii)	

	(iii)	in the case of group accounts, of the state of affairs as at the end of the financial year and of the profit or loss for the financial year, of the undertakings included in the consolidation as a whole, so far as concerns members of the company; and	s. 495(3)(a)(iii)	
	(iv)	have been properly prepared in accordance with the relevant financial reporting framework;	s. 495(3)(b)	
(h)	state whether, in his opinion, based on the work undertaken in the course of the audit:		
	(i)	the information given in the strategic report (if any) and the directors' report is consistent with the financial statements; and	s. 496(a)(i)	
	(ii)	any such strategic report and the directors' report have been prepared in accordance with applicable legal requirements;	s. 496(a)(ii)	
(i)	state whether, in the light of the knowledge and understanding of the company and its environment obtained in the course of the audit, he has identified material misstatements in the strategic report (if any) and the directors' report;		s. 496(b)	
(j)	if applicable, give an indication of the nature of each of the misstatements referred to in (I) above;		s. 496(c)	
(k)	be either unqualified or qualified;		s. 495(4)(a)	
(l)	include a reference to any matters to which the auditor wishes to draw attention by way of emphasis without qualifying the report;		s. 495(4)(b)	
(m)	when an auditor is engaged to issue an opinion on the compliance of the financial statements with an additional financial reporting framework the second opinion shall be clearly separated from the first opinion on the financial statements, by use of an appropriate heading;		ISA 700-19	
(n)	when the auditor addresses other reporting responsibilities within the auditor's report on the financial statements, the opinion arising from such other responsibilities shall be set out in a separate section of the auditor's report following the opinion[s] on the financial statements;		ISA 700-21	
(o)	if the auditor is required to report on certain matters by exception the auditor shall describe its responsibilities under the heading 'Matters on which we are required to report by exception' and incorporate a suitable conclusion in respect of such matters;		ISA 700-22	
(p)	the date of an auditor's report on a reporting entity's financial statements shall be the date on which the auditor signed the report expressing an opinion on those financial statements;		ISA 700-23	
(q)	the auditor shall not sign, and hence date, the report earlier than the date on which all other information contained in a report of which the audited financial statements form a part have been approved by those charged with governance and the auditor has considered all necessary available evidence;		ISA 700-24	
(r)	the report shall name the location of the office where the auditor is based; and		ISA 700-25	
(s)	the auditor's report shall state the name of the auditor and be signed and dated.		ISA 700-26	

A1.08	The auditor must state in his report if in his opinion:		
	(a) adequate accounting records have not been kept by the company;	s. 498(2)(a)	
	(b) proper returns adequate for their audit have not been received from branches not visited by him;	s. 498(2)(a)	
	(c) the company's accounts are not in agreement with the accounting records and returns;	s. 498(2)(b)	
	(d) all the information and explanations necessary for the purposes of his audit have not been obtained;	s. 498(3)	
	(e) the directors have prepared the accounts in accordance with the small companies regime when not eligible;	s. 498(4) s. 498(5)(a)	
	(f) the directors have taken advantage of small companies exemption in preparing the directors' report when not eligible; and	s. 498(5)(b)	
	(g) the directors have taken advantage of small companies exemption from the requirement to prepare a strategic report when not eligible.	s. 498(5)(b)	
A1.09	If the disclosure requirements concerning directors' emoluments are not complied with in the annual accounts, the auditor must give the required particulars in his report, so far as he is reasonably able to do so.	s. 498(4)	
A1.10	If the audit report is qualified and the company proposes to make a distribution, the auditor must state whether, in his opinion, the matter in respect of which his report is qualified is material for determining whether the distribution would contravene the Companies Act provisions. This may form part of the normal audit report, or be submitted subsequently in writing.	s. 837(4)(a)	
A1.11	Include the Bannerman wording as recommended by ICAEW Technical Release Audit 1/03.		
A1.12	For the name of auditor, state:		
	(a) where the auditor is not an individual, the name of the senior statutory auditor;	s. 503(3), 505(1)(a)	
	[Guidance] *Client's copy of accounts* *The signed copy of the report issued to the client must be signed personally by the senior statutory auditor in their own name for and on behalf of the firm.*		
	(b) where the auditor is not an individual, the name of the audit firm; and	s. 505(1)(a)	
	[Guidance] *Companies House copy of accounts* *The copy of the report delivered to Companies House need not be signed (by the senior statutory auditor or the audit firm). Signed copies of the report for other purposes may be signed in the name of the firm by any RI.*		
	(c) that the firm are Statutory Auditors.	s. 505	
A1.13	When the prior year's financial statements are not audited, the incoming auditor should state in the auditor's report that the corresponding figures are unaudited.	ISA 700-19	
	Notes to the financial statements		
A1.14	Disclose the following in respect of auditors remuneration:	SI 2008/489-4(1)	
	(a) the amount of any remuneration receivable by the company's auditor for the auditing of the accounts;		

	(b) the nature of any benefits in kind; (c) the estimated monetary value of any benefits in kind; and (d) where more than one person has been appointed as a company's auditor during the period: separate disclosure in respect of the remuneration for each such person. *[Guidance]* *Disclosure requirements for auditor's remuneration in small company accounts is expected to be repealed in June 2016 when the audit directive changes are implemented.*		
A1.15	Where a company does not disclose information concerning auditor's remuneration because that information is required to be disclosed in the group accounts on a consolidated basis: give a statement to that effect.	SI 2008/489-6(3)	
A1.16	A company, which has entered into a liability limitation agreement with its auditor, must disclose: (a) its principal terms; (b) the date of the resolution approving the agreement; and (c) in the case of a private company, the date of the resolution waiving the need for such approval. *[Guidance]* *The accounts in which disclosure is required are those for the financial year to which the agreement relates unless the agreement was entered into too late for it to be reasonably practical for the disclosure to be made, in which case disclosure should be made in the company's next following annual accounts.*	SI 2008/489-8	

ABRIDGED ACCOUNTS CHECKLIST – APPENDIX 2

A2   Appendix 2

Assurance review report

		Reference	Y, N, N/A
A2.01	Is the report consistent with that in TECH 09/13 Assurance review engagements on historical financial statements in respect of the following: (a) Title; (b) Introductory paragraphs; (c) Directors' responsibility; (d) Accountants' responsibility; (e) Scope of the assurance review; (f) Conclusion.	TECH 09/13	

ABRIDGED ACCOUNTS CHECKLIST – APPENDIX 3

A3   Appendix 3

Parent company not preparing group accounts

		Reference	*Y, N, N/A*

A3.01	Where the company is exempt from the requirement to prepare group accounts because it is itself a subsidiary undertaking, the company must:
	
	(a) disclose in the notes to its individual accounts that it is exempt from the obligation to prepare and deliver group accounts; and
	
	(b) state in its individual accounts:
	
	   (i) the name of the parent undertaking which draws up group accounts; and
	
	   (ii) the address of the undertaking's registered office (whether in or outside the United Kingdom), or if it is unincorporated, the address of its principal place of business.
	
	[Guidance]
	This exemption is only available if:
	(a) the immediate parent undertaking is established under the law of an EEA state;
	(b) the company is a wholly owned subsidiary, or the company is a 90% or more subsidiary and the remaining shareholders have approved the exemption, or the company is a more than 50% but less than 90% subsidiary and notice requesting the preparation of group accounts has not been served on the company by the shareholders holding in aggregate at least 5% of the company's shares;
	(c) the company is included in consolidated accounts for a larger group which are drawn up to the same date, or an earlier date in the same financial year, by apparent undertaking established under the law of an EEA State and in accordance with the provisions of Directive 2013/34/EU of the European Parliament and of the Council on the annual financial statements, consolidated financial statements and related reports of certain types of undertakings, or in accordance with international accounting standards;
	(d) the consolidated accounts are audited; and
	(e) a copy of the consolidated accounts and audit report are filed at Companies House with a certified translation if not in English.
		s. 400(1), (2),
		s. 401(1), (2)	

A3.02	Where advantage is taken of the exemption to restrict information relating to certain foreign undertakings (with the agreement of the Secretary of State), state that fact in a note to the accounts.	s. 409(5)	
A3.03	State the number, description and amount of any shares in the company which are held by subsidiary undertakings, with the exception of certain trustee holdings (see the Act for details).	S-C Sch. 2.4(1)	

A3.04	Show the amounts of any guarantees and financial commitments, analysing between any amounts relating to parent or fellow subsidiary undertakings, and any amounts relating to subsidiary undertakings of the company itself, and include:	S-C Sch. 1.57(6)	
	(a) particulars of any charge on the assets and, where practicable, the amount secured;		
	(b) the nature, security and estimated amount of any unprovided contingent liability;		
	(c) capital expenditure contracted for but not provided for;		
	(d) particulars of any pension commitment (specifying whether provided for or not, and showing separately amounts relating wholly or partly to past directors); and		
	(e) particulars of any other financial commitments which have not been provided for and are relevant to assessing the company's state of affairs.		

ABRIDGED ACCOUNTS CHECKLIST – APPENDIX 4

A4   Appendix 4

Political donations

		Reference	Y, N, N/A
A4.01	Where the company is not itself the wholly owned subsidiary of a UK incorporated company and has made any donation to any EU political party, other EU political organisation or independent election candidate, or incurred any political expenditure, and it does not have subsidiaries which have made such contributions, and the amount of the donation or expenditure, or the aggregate amount of all such donations, exceeds £2,000 disclose: (a) the name of each EU political party, other EU political organisation or independent election candidate to whom any such donation has been made; (b) the total amount given to that party, organisation or candidate by way of such donations in the financial year; and (c) the total amount of political expenditure incurred within the financial year.	R-C Sch. 5.2(2)	
A4.02	Where the company is not itself the wholly owned subsidiary of a UK incorporated company and any of the company's subsidiaries have made any donation to any EU political party, other EU political organisation or independent election candidate, or incurred any political expenditure, and the total amount of any such donations or expenditure (or both) made or incurred in that year by the company and the subsidiaries between them exceeds £2,000, the company must disclose in respect of it and its subsidiaries: (a) the name of each EU political party, other EU political organisation or independent election candidate to whom any such donation has been made; (b) the total amount given to that party, organisation or candidate by way of such donations in the financial year; and (c) the total amount of political expenditure incurred within the financial year.	R-C Sch. 5.2(3)	
A4.03	Where the company is not itself the wholly owned subsidiary of a UK incorporated company and the company has made any contribution to a non-EU political party, and it does not have any subsidiaries which have made such contributions, disclose: (a) a statement of the amount of the contribution; or (b) where the company has made two or more such contributions in the year, a statement of the total amount of the contributions.	R-C Sch. 5.3(1)	

	[Guidance] *Contribution, in relation to an organisation, means:* *(a) any gift of money to the organisation (whether made directly or indirectly);* *(b) any subscription or other fee paid for affiliation to, or membership of, the organisation; or* *(c) any money spent (otherwise than by the organisation or a person acting on its behalf) in paying any expenses incurred directly or indirectly by the organisation.* *Non-EU political party means any political party which carries on, or proposes to carry on, its activities wholly outside the EU member States.* *(SI 2008/410-L, Sch. 7.4(3) & (4))*		
A4.04	Where any of the company's subsidiaries have made any contribution to a non-EU political party, disclose the total amount of the contributions made in the year by the company and the subsidiaries between them.	R-C Sch. 5.3(2)	

Appendix H   Selected reading and reference material

This appendix provides a selection of the websites and literature to which this book might form a companion.

Wolters Kluwer online resources and Accounting and Auditing Standards

CCH daily including Accountancy Live	www.cchdaily.co.uk
Navigate GAAP	Your comprehensive easy-to-search New UK GAAP online resource
CCH Online	The professional online library for tax, audit, accounting and finance
Accounting Standards 2016–17	Wolters Kluwer (UK) Ltd
Auditing Standards 2016–17	Wolters Kluwer (UK) Ltd

Checklists and other useful publications

Company Accounts Disclosure Checklist and the Interactive Companies Accounts Disclosure Checklist	SWAT UK Ltd	Wolters Kluwer (UK) Ltd
New UK GAAP: An at a glance comparison	Helen Lloyd	Wolters Kluwer (UK) Ltd
Appying New UK GAAP (focus on FRS 102)	Various technical writers	Wolters Kluwer (UK) Ltd
Preparing FRS 102 Accounts (focus on medium-sized and large entities)	James Lole	Wolters Kluwer (UK) Ltd
Preparing FRS 101 Accounts	Helen Lloyd	Wolters Kluwer (UK) Ltd
Deloitte UK GAAP Commentary	Deloitte LLP	Wolters Kluwer (UK) Ltd
The Audit Report Handbook	David Duvall	Wolters Kluwer (UK) Ltd

Useful websites

Financial Reporting Council	www.frc.org.uk
International Accounting Standard Board	www.ifrs.org
International Auditing and Assurance Standards Board	www.ifac.org/auditing-assurance
The International Federation of Accountants	www.ifac.org

Federation of European Accountants (Fédération des Experts-comptables Européens)	www.fee.be
Department for Business, Innovation and Skills (BIS)	www.gov.uk/government/organisations/ department-for-business-innovation-skills
Companies House	www.gov.uk/government/organisations/ companies-house
UK legislation and statutory instruments	www.legislation.gov.uk
European legislation	www.eur-lex.europa.eu
Institute of Chartered Accountants in England and Wales	www.icaew.com
Institute of Chartered Accountants of Scotland	www.icas.org.uk

FRC guidance

Compendium of Illustrative Auditor's Reports on United Kingdom Public Sector Financial Statements for periods ended on or after 15 December 2010 (Revised)	APB Bulletin 2010/2 (Revised March 2012 and updated by Bulletin 4 below)
Recent Developments in Company Law, The Listing Rules and Auditing Standards that affect United Kingdom Auditor's Reports	Financial Reporting Council Bulletin 4 (June 2015)

Companies House – useful pages for filing

Filing an annual return	www.gov.uk/file-an-annual-return-with-companieshouse
Guidance on annual requirements for a company including accounts and audit	www.gov.uk/government/publications/life-of-acompany-annual-requirements
HMRC and Companies House compatible iXBRL software	www.gov.uk/company-filing-software
How to obtain an authentication code for companies wishing to file online	www.gov.uk/guidance/company-authenticationcodes-for-online-filing
Future legislative changes affecting the information at Companies House	www.gov.uk/government/news/the-small-businessenterprise-and-employment-bill-is-coming

Index

307